PROFESSIONAL
MICROSOFT® SEARCH

G000112132

PROFESSIONAL

Microsoft® Search

PROFESSIONAL

Microsoft® Search

FAST SEARCH, SHAREPOINT® SEARCH, AND SEARCH SERVER

Mark Bennett, Jeff Fried, Miles Kehoe,
and Natalya Voskresenskaya

Wiley Publishing, Inc.

Professional Microsoft® Search: FAST Search, SharePoint® Search, and Search Server

Published by
Wiley Publishing, Inc.
10475 Crosspoint Boulevard
Indianapolis, IN 46256
www.wiley.com

Copyright © 2010 by Wiley Publishing, Inc., Indianapolis, Indiana

Published simultaneously in Canada

ISBN: 978-0-470-58466-8

Manufactured in the United States of America

10 9 8 7 6 5 4 3 2 1

For general information on our other products and services please contact our Customer Care Department within the United States at (877) 762-2974, outside the United States at (317) 572-3993 or fax (317) 572-4002.

Wiley also publishes its books in a variety of electronic formats. Some content that appears in print may not be available in electronic books.

Library of Congress Control Number: 2010932420

I'd like to thank Mom and Dad for buying the Apple][that started me on this path so many years ago. Spending that money was a leap of faith, and filled up an otherwise very boring summer.

—MARK

This book would not have been possible without the support of my wonderful wife Evie, who put up with a lot and kept encouraging me anyway.

—JEFF

Thanks to my friends who put up with "the book" as an excuse for my not being available; and to all those teachers and editors who have corrected my writing for so long that it sometimes approaches readable.

—MILES

Special thanks to Michael and Ivan for just being there, family and friends for not giving up on me during "another chapter" time, and thanks to Harry for pulling the weight of the world during this time.

—NATALYA

ABOUT THE AUTHORS

MARK BENNETT is the cofounder, CTO, and Senior Technical Analyst of New Idea Engineering, Inc., a Silicon Valley consultancy specializing in the business and technology of search. He speaks at industry trade shows about the current and future trends in search technology, writes for several online sites, and is active in the Open Source software community. He also cofounded and was CTO of Searchbutton, Inc., one of the earliest companies offering hosted search solutions during the dot-com boom. He has also worked on patent applications at several companies and has consulted on intellectual property cases. He was the founder of the "Stanford Quantum Groupies" online physics group, and participates in various technical and social causes. Prior to NIE and Searchbutton, Mr. Bennett served as technical support manager at Verity, Inc., where he produced the company's first Customer Care CD. His experience also includes engineering and database development positions at Access Technology and Portsmouth Naval Shipyard. Mark grew up in Somersworth, NH.

JEFF FRIED began writing software at the tender age of 13 and has been hooked ever since. He has worked extensively with Enterprise Search, including roles as SVP, Products for the semantic search startup LingoMotors and VP, Advanced Solutions for FAST Search and Transfer. FAST's acquisition landed him at Microsoft, where he is a senior technical product manager specializing in strategic applications of search technology. Jeff has also served as CTO for Empirix (test and management software), as founder and CTO of Teloquent (call center software), and on several industry boards and standards groups. Jeff is a frequent speaker and writer in the industry, holds 15 patents, has authored more than 50 technical papers, and has led the creation of pioneering offerings in next generation search engines, networks, and contact centers. He is also a co-author of the Wrox book *Professional SharePoint 2010 Development*. Jeff is an amateur musician and lives with his lovely wife and three delicious children in Newton, Massachusetts.

MILES KEHOE has worked in the business of Enterprise Search for more than 20 years since he moved from technical positions at HP in 1989 and started working at Verity and later at Fulcrum Technologies. He cofounded New Idea Engineering Inc. in 1996 when it was clear that poor implementation was the biggest problem companies faced in getting Enterprise Search right. He cofounded SearchButton, Inc. in 1998 when software as a service — and what we now know as cloud-based solutions — could help companies have great site search in hours rather than months. Since 2001, New Idea Engineering has focused on both the business and the technology of search. Miles has written a number of books, authored a monthly column in *HP Professional* magazine, speaks at industry trade shows, and authors a number of search-related blogs. His focus now as a senior business analyst is to help organizations realize that search is a business problem as much as a technical problem. He is a private pilot and soccer fan, and lives in Cupertino, California.

NATALYA VOSKRESENSKAYA has been working in the field of Information Technology for over 10 years, with experience in design, architecture, development, and deployment of Web-based applications. Since early 2000, her main area of concentration had been the development of portal solutions. Natalya delivers enterprise portal applications and business solutions, as well as portal systems architecture, design, implementation, and best practices guidance. She has been involved in SharePoint Technologies since the 2003 version. An avid blogger at `http://spforsquirrels. blogspot.com/` and writer, Natalya strives to share her passion for SharePoint and its community, and often speaks at SharePoint community events and conferences. Besides SharePoint, Natalya's interest had been captured by another enterprise-level search technology, FAST. To her joy, these technologies have been combined to compliment each other's functionality. In 2009, Natalya co-founded Arcovis LLC, a business solutions consulting company focused on high quality SharePoint delivery. She was awarded the prestigious Microsoft Most Valuable Professional award for the first time in 2008.

ABOUT THE TECHNICAL EDITORS

CARL GRIMM heads enterprise strategy at New Idea Engineering where he focuses on best-of-breed, novel, and emerging technologies related to information retrieval. His interests include the application of machine learning and collaborative filtering as an alternative to term frequency-inverse document frequency–based relevancy systems. Prior to NIE, Carl specialized in user experience design as the Creative Director of Interactive Media at Firebelly. He has also held senior management positions in the Enterprise Search and financial services sector. A graduate of Miami University, Carl holds his Bachelors of Science in Business Administration.

JOHN T. KANE is currently working with Microsoft's NextGen and Incubation team and as a Search Consultant on a search-related project. He has over 20 years in Information Technology, working at everything from Fortune 100 corporations to small startup companies with emerging technologies. He has a passion for structured (SQL Server and relational databases), unstructured (FAST ESP and search engines), and social media (social search and collaboration) technologies and believes that unifying these diverse disciplines will provide businesses and customers with the best of these worlds, such as described in this book. John's work has included technical sales, premier support, requirement analysis, architectural design, and the implementation search technologies in various roles, including Search Architect. John blogs on search and social media technologies (`http://www. EnterpriseSearch.NET`) and can be found on Twitter (`http://twitter.com/enterprisesrch`).

JASON NOBLE serves as Neudesic's General Manager of Product Development with over 15 years of experience in building complex, mission-critical applications. Jason has extensive knowledge in advanced enterprise applications, specializing in web, database, and portal application development using Microsoft SharePoint Server. Jason is currently focused on social technologies and their adoption within the enterprise and is overseeing the development of Pulse, an enterprise social application that helps enterprises embrace this new form of communication.

CREDITS

ACQUISITIONS EDITOR
Paul Reese

PROJECT EDITOR
Sydney Jones Argenta

TECHNICAL EDITORS
Carl Grimm
John T. Kane
Jason Noble

PRODUCTION EDITOR
Eric Charbonneau

COPY EDITOR
Foxxe Editorial

EDITORIAL DIRECTOR
Robyn B. Siesky

EDITORIAL MANAGER
Mary Beth Wakefield

ASSOCIATE DIRECTOR OF MARKETING
David Mayhew

PRODUCTION MANAGER
Tim Tate

VICE PRESIDENT AND EXECUTIVE GROUP PUBLISHER
Richard Swadley

VICE PRESIDENT AND EXECUTIVE PUBLISHER
Barry Pruett

ASSOCIATE PUBLISHER
Jim Minatel

PROJECT COORDINATOR, COVER
Lynsey Stanford

PROOFREADER
Jen Larsen, Word One

INDEXER
Johnna VanHoose Dinse

COVER DESIGNER
Michael E. Trent

COVER IMAGE
© istockphoto.com/
Niklas Johansson

ACKNOWLEDGMENTS

THIS BOOK IS A COLLECTIVE contribution of four authors, all with busy day jobs, and has been supported by many wonderful people. The authors are all grateful to Wrox editors Paul Reese and Sydney Jones Argenta for taking on this book and working through countless details with us. We'd also like to thank those in the Microsoft Enterprise Search Group who provided encouragement and support, notably Jared Spataro, Richard Riley, Larry Kaye, Steve Peshka, Keller Smith, and Brian Barry. Special thanks go to John Kane and Carl Grimm for their technical reviews and valuable input.

CONTENTS

PART III: IMPLEMENTING SEARCH WITH ESP

CHAPTER 7: INTRODUCTION TO FAST ESP   197

PART IV: ENTERPRISE SEARCH 2.0

INTRODUCTION

AS THE EXPONENTIAL GROWTH of information continues both on the Internet and in private data stores, companies can find themselves drowning in their own data. They turn to Enterprise Search for the answer.

Enterprise Search provides the capability to find information across an organization. It is rooted in information retrieval, a deep discipline that focuses on developing frameworks to represent information, inquiries, and their relationships. Enterprise Search is now a technology that is pervasive, growing rapidly, and strategic to most organizations. Yet it is not widely understood in any depth, and the complex inner workings of search are mysterious to most, perhaps because it looks so simple on the outside.

The Enterprise Search industry has changed dramatically over the last two years, most notably with Microsoft's acquisition of FAST Search and Transfer in 2008. Microsoft has now introduced new Enterprise Search products based on FAST and updated existing ones. The result is a set of products that accommodates pretty much any Enterprise Search need, although the lineup can be confusing at times. All of these products are brand-new in 2010. They are the first search products from Microsoft that provide the scalability and capability to power all the search needs in an enterprise — internal and customer-facing search — for large and small corporations worldwide.

Professional Microsoft Search sheds light on search in the enterprise with a focus on Microsoft Search technology. It covers the full breadth of technologies from Search Server and SharePoint Server, to the new products based on FAST technology. It is intended for a range of folks, from the business manager budgeting for a new search project to the IT administrator tasked with deploying and administering these new search products, to the developer writing search applications. For all of these roles, understanding the new Microsoft search technology and how to work with it is essential for solving the information access issues they face.

Microsoft's acquisition of FAST, paired with its own previously existing search technology, now gives Microsoft a full range of search engine offerings. It offers free search, mobile search, departmental search, and high-end search that scales to handle terabytes of data and offers virtually every advanced search feature on the market today. However, with more advanced technology and product choices, Microsoft's customers and partners are now faced with more complexity in the selection, design, and implementation of search. Which product is best for a particular set of requirements? Which advanced features would work best to search a specific data set? How will all this technology integrate into the existing security and SharePoint infrastructure? How can Microsoft partners come up to speed quickly on the FAST Search for Internet Business product — including Linux-based offerings? These are the types of issues this book addresses.

MICROSOFT SEARCH HAS CHANGED

If you are familiar with Microsoft search already, you will find yourself in a new world. Microsoft has now introduced high-end search technology, and has improved its entry-level and infrastructure search offerings significantly.

A previous Wrox book entitled *Professional Microsoft Search: SharePoint 2007 and Search Server 2008* was published in 2008, as Microsoft introduced its entry-level, free, downloadable search offering. (That book is still a good introduction to search, by the way.)

Our book has a deceptively similar title, but it covers two different types of FAST high-end search technology as well as much more sophisticated versions of SharePoint search and Search Server. These have advanced features including guided navigation, entity extraction, and advanced linguistics. Their architecture is more scalable and modular, allowing for full fault tolerance and extreme scale. The FAST technology in particular provides the flexibility for extensive customization.

WHO THIS BOOK IS FOR

This book is meant for IT and software development professionals as well as for business management, content owners, and marketing staff involved with Enterprise Search. We span many topics in this book to cover the breadth of planning, deploying, administering, and developing on all the Microsoft Enterprise Search technologies.

Search touches many areas of an organization and interacts with a myriad of other systems, so there are a wide range of readers that can benefit from this book. We expect the core readership for this book to be those tasked with implementing and managing Enterprise Search — programmers developing search-driven applications as well as architects, managers, planners, and IT professionals responsible for planning, deployment, and operations. IT and development engineers and managers in companies that use SharePoint heavily will benefit from reading this book, even if they are not deeply involved with Enterprise Search. Conversely, those focused on providing great Internet experiences independent of SharePoint will find a lot of useful content.

For content owners and line-of-business managers, we discuss how companies are organizing for search success, and how to create a business plan for search that can be valuable for any organization considering implementing and managing Enterprise Search acquisition.

This book is structured in such a way that you can read it from end to end. However, we have organized the book into four parts in order to serve the breadth of readership. Depending on your interests you might read some parts deeply and skim others.

For example, business managers might wish to focus on Part I, "Introduction," skim Parts II and III, which have more focus on how to deploy and develop, and read Part IV, "Enterprise Search 2.0 — New Directions in Enterprise Search," to understand the current and future state of hot topics in search. These sections give an overview of what you should expect in any Enterprise Search platform, regardless of the vendor.

Technical staff experienced with SharePoint and search might read Parts I and IV and skim Part III, but focus most heavily on Part II, "Implementing Search." Those planning on deploying standalone high-end search or extending existing FAST ESP deployments might read Parts I and IV and skim Part II, but focus most heavily on Part IV, "Implementing Search with ESP."

Within Parts II, III, and IV, the developer materials will be important for the administrator to understand, since developers and administrators have to work together to make search work. On the flip side, the administrator material will be important for developers to understand the architecture and administration of search because, without this knowledge, writing to the APIs will be more difficult. Most readers will benefit from reading all the chapters in this book.

WHAT THIS BOOK COVERS

With such a wide audience and range of different technologies, it is challenging to provide comprehensive material even in a full-length book. Luckily there is material available from other sources — a handful of other books about aspects of Enterprise Search as well as training and documentation available from Microsoft and its partners. The appendix at the end of this book provides a resource center for this material.

This book concentrates on material that is generally not found anywhere else. This book is entirely about the latest versions of Microsoft Enterprise Search technology, introduced in 2010. We don't cover previous versions (except briefly where it is crucial to understanding what is new in 2010). We do cover topics found in product documentation or evaluation guides, but our focus is on what you need to know. We don't cover search technology from other vendors (except at a very high level in the FAQ section of Chapter 1 and the "Choosing a Search Platform" section of Chapter 2, where it is important for IT professionals and business managers to understand more than Microsoft technologies).

We do provide material that we think is unique and useful. For example, Chapter 2 has material about the Search Center of Excellence (SCOE) because those that view search technology as strategic will benefit from this practice. Chapter 3 is the only place that covers the entire Microsoft Enterprise Search product portfolio that we know of. Chapter 8 pays attention to multi-node configurations for standalone FAST technology because it is essential for deployment and not found elsewhere. Chapter 10 and Chapter 11 provide both a general perspective and details on how to apply Microsoft Enterprise Search products in these areas to social search and BI.

This book sheds light on search in the enterprise and will provide the reader with in-depth knowledge of the new Microsoft Search platforms. It has material on *why* — the business value and applications of search and of particular features — as well as *what* and *how*. However, it is first and foremost a technical book focused on the details of new technology and how to work with it as an IT professional or developer.

The book contains detailed examples of how to implement solutions to real-world search problems. It provides code examples that are downloadable from Wrox.com. The authors also have a site for the book at www.microsoftsearchbook.com, which will provide incremental updates to the information presented in the book. Our goal is to provide enough material that readers can make intelligent choices in deciding to implement Search Server, SharePoint Server, FAST Search for SharePoint, or FAST Search for Internet Sites and be successful in the process. This includes:

➤ Common applications and application patterns for search and which Microsoft Enterprise Search products to use for each

➤ Architecture, capability, and management details and perspective on how to successfully deploy and run search

➤ Development patterns and code samples to help customize search and build search-driven applications

The Wrox website and the authors' website make it possible to add material over time. This was particularly important for this book as the timing kept us from including full coverage of the exciting new IMS and CTS components. While there is material about these in Part 2 of this book, there is additional material to be found on the websites.

HOW THIS BOOK IS STRUCTURED

Since the readership of this book is broad and the technology is varied, we have organized the book into four parts. Each part has three chapters, and a specific focus. There is something for everyone and it is not essential to read all the parts deeply to benefit from this book. However, the material in each chapter does build on previous chapters, so it is useful to at least skim Part I if you jump directly to Part II or Part III. Within each part, the chapters are meant to be read in order.

➤ **Part I, Introduction** — These chapters provide a business and application perspective. It will be useful for all readers, but particularly so for business analysts, IT managers, and marketing managers involved with search.

   ➤ Chapter 1 starts with an overview of Enterprise Search and how it differs from public search sites. It covers the capabilities that are enabling search, and how search can serve as the glue to all of the collaborative initiatives corporations are beginning to adopt. A section on frequently asked questions is meant to directly help those communicating to their organizations about Enterprise Search.

   ➤ Chapter 2 includes background on creating an internal business plan for search, including the planning of an Enterprise Search deployment and developing a successful strategy for the ongoing management of search. We discuss all of the skills required to make search work, and how successful companies organize their search operations.

   ➤ Chapter 3 ends Part I with an overview of all the Microsoft Enterprise Search options, where they are best applied, and how they fit with other Microsoft products, such as desktop search, exchange, SQL, and Bing.

➤ **Part II, Implementing Search** — These chapters focus on the products built from the SharePoint 2010 codebase or the new FAST Search for SharePoint codebase. This will be of particular interest to those experienced with SharePoint.

> ➤ Chapter 4 covers the search built into SharePoint Server 2010, including capabilities, architecture, and how to deploy it.
>
> ➤ Chapter 5 covers the new FAST Search Server 2010 for SharePoint product, which extends on the shared capabilities covered in Chapter 4.
>
> ➤ Chapter 6 is meant for developers; it goes through the ways to extend and customize search for all the products discussed in Part II from these codebases.

➤ **Part III, Implementing Search with** ESP — These chapters focus on the products built from the FAST Enterprise Search Platform (ESP) codebase with a brief introduction to the new Content Transformation Services (CTS) and Interaction Management Services (IMS) components. It is of particular interest for those planning on deploying standalone high-end search or extending their existing FAST ESP installations.

> ➤ Chapter 7 covers the product capabilities and architecture, including how to deploy and manage a simple topology.
>
> ➤ Chapter 8 focuses on multinode and multiplatform deployment in particular, since this is not well-covered in other pubic material and is essential to most installations.
>
> ➤ Chapter 9 includes advanced topics related to the products from these codebases, especially scalability, working with taxonomies, and specialized advanced linguistics techniques.

➤ **Part IV, Enterprise Search 2.0** — These chapters cover new directions in Enterprise Search. This applies to all products, so it is relevant whether your focus is on Part II or Part III. Each chapter also includes the why, as well as the what and the how, so some readers might read Parts I and IV while skimming the rest.

> ➤ Chapter 10 covers social search, both the elements that are built into the new Microsoft products as well as general techniques and trends.
>
> ➤ Chapter 11 is about the convergence of Enterprise Search and business intelligence. It provides an orientation to the Microsoft BI stack, covers the new capabilities from Microsoft that integrate search and BI, and also gives an overview of the bigger picture.
>
> ➤ Chapter 12 takes a look at the technologies and capabilities that are likely to be common in Enterprise Search in the future. Like the first three chapters of the book, Chapter 12 is not as deep technically as the rest of the book, but it offers a perspective useful for all audiences with advice about what you can do today.

WHAT YOU NEED TO USE THIS BOOK

To get the most from this book, you will want copies of SharePoint Server 2010, FAST Search for SharePoint, and FAST Search for Internet Sites. One easy way to get evaluation copies is to download virtual hard drives (VHDs) from MSDN. You can find a link to these at the Enterprise Search resource center at technet.microsoft.com/enterprisesearch. These virtual machines, while large, are preconfigured for you so that you can start working with the technologies without having to install all the software and configure it.

CONVENTIONS

To help you get the most from the text and keep track of what's happening, we've used a number of conventions throughout the book.

 The pencil icon indicates notes, tips, hints, tricks, or asides to the current discussion.

As for styles in the text:

➤ We *highlight* new terms and important words when we introduce them.

➤ We show filenames, URLs, and code within the text like so: persistence.properties.

➤ We present code in a different font:

```
We use a monofont type with no highlighting for most code examples.
```

SOURCE CODE

As you work through the examples in this book, you may choose either to type in all the code manually, or to use the source code files that accompany the book. All the source code used in this book is available for download at www.wrox.com. When at the site, simply locate the book's title (use the Search box or one of the title lists) and click the Download Code link on the book's detail page to obtain all the source code for the book. Code that is included on the Web site is highlighted by the following icon:

Available for download on Wrox.com

Listings include the filename in the title. If it is just a code snippet, you'll find the filename in a code note such as this:

Code snippet filename

 Because many books have similar titles, you may find it easiest to search by ISBN; this book's ISBN is 978-0-470-58466-8.

Once you download the code, just decompress it with your favorite compression tool. Alternately, you can go to the main Wrox code download page at `www.wrox.com/dynamic/books/download.aspx` to see the code available for this book and all other Wrox books.

ERRATA

We make every effort to ensure that there are no errors in the text or in the code. However, no one is perfect, and mistakes do occur. If you find an error in one of our books, like a spelling mistake or faulty piece of code, we would be very grateful for your feedback. By sending in errata, you may save another reader hours of frustration, and at the same time, you will be helping us provide even higher quality information.

To find the errata page for this book, go to `www.wrox.com` and locate the title using the Search box or one of the title lists. Then, on the book details page, click the Book Errata link. On this page, you can view all errata that has been submitted for this book and posted by Wrox editors. A complete book list, including links to each book's errata, is also available at `www.wrox.com/misc-pages/booklist.shtml`.

If you don't spot "your" error on the Book Errata page, go to `www.wrox.com/contact/techsupport.shtml` and complete the form there to send us the error you have found. We'll check the information and, if appropriate, post a message to the book's errata page and fix the problem in subsequent editions of the book.

P2P.WROX.COM

For author and peer discussion, join the P2P forums at `p2p.wrox.com`. The forums are a Web-based system for you to post messages relating to Wrox books and related technologies and interact with other readers and technology users. The forums offer a subscription feature to e-mail you topics of interest of your choosing when new posts are made to the forums. Wrox authors, editors, other industry experts, and your fellow readers are present on these forums.

At `http://p2p.wrox.com`, you will find a number of different forums that will help you, not only as you read this book, but also as you develop your own applications. To join the forums, just follow these steps:

1. Go to `p2p.wrox.com` and click the Register link.

2. Read the terms of use and click Agree.

3. Complete the required information to join, as well as any optional information you wish to provide, and click Submit.

4. You will receive an e-mail with information describing how to verify your account and complete the joining process.

 You can read messages in the forums without joining P2P, but in order to post your own messages, you must join.

Once you join, you can post new messages and respond to messages other users post. You can read messages at any time on the Web. If you would like to have new messages from a particular forum e-mailed to you, click the Subscribe to this Forum icon by the forum name in the forum listing.

For more information about how to use the Wrox P2P, be sure to read the P2P FAQs for answers to questions about how the forum software works, as well as many common questions specific to P2P and Wrox books. To read the FAQs, click the FAQ link on any P2P page.

PART I
Introduction

1

What Is Enterprise Search?

WHAT'S IN THIS CHAPTER?

➤ Defining Enterprise Search, and how it differs from Internet search portals

➤ Giving an overview of Enterprise Search architecture and the Microsoft Search lineup

➤ Characterizing the use of search within an organization.

➤ Exploring Search ROI and SCOE

➤ Answering common questions about Enterprise Search

Many people assume that "Enterprise Search" refers to search behind a corporate firewall. Although it certainly includes that, in this book we'll use a broader definition and consider Enterprise Search to be the search technology that your organization owns and controls, as opposed to the giant Internet search portals like Yahoo!, Google, or MSN/Bing.

This broad definition allows us to include and cover other search systems that power customer-facing applications and web properties that the company itself owns and controls. Such applications could include the search on a company's website home page and Tech Support area, or eCommerce shopping sites, which are also heavy users of search.

Organizations have different business objectives, and they implement search to help achieve those goals. As you'll see, Microsoft offers a wide range of products to power internal and customer-facing applications. But if you add up all the things that different organizations use search for, you come up with a pretty long list! Over the years, we've seen an amazing variety of ideas and projects, and about the only thing they have in common is being controlled by a specific company or agency, as opposed to being under the control of the giant web portals. This control issue is key; we'll come back to it again and again. If you are not happy with how Yahoo! or Google indexes your public site, there's a limited number of things you can do about it.

But if you own it (or lease it), and it's not working, you can change it. You can adjust it, tweak it, audit it, enhance it, or rip the whole darn thing out and start over! Ownership equals control!

Broadly, Enterprise Search could be thought of as all search engines *except* the public Yahoo!, Google, and MSN ones, since you *do* own and control the search engine that powers your public website or online store. And again, your usage patterns and priorities are likely different from those of the Internet portals.

This chapter introduces the concept of Enterprise Search, discussing its origins and how it differs from Internet search. It then provides a brief history of searching and discusses Microsoft's continuing commitment to improving its Search technologies, including a discussion of why Microsoft acquired the FAST ESP technologies and the current road map for integrating these technologies. You'll learn why a company would want to invest in Microsoft Enterprise Search and what some of the key components are.

WHY ENTERPRISE SEARCH?

Enterprise Search applications deliver content for the benefit of employees, customers, partners, or affiliates of a single company or organization. You're reading this book, so we imagine you already "get it." But if you didn't, we could say something like "if your company can afford to have search that's broken, either driving potential customers away or wasting countless hours of employees' time, perhaps you don't!"

Companies, government agencies, and other organizations maintain huge amounts of information in electronic form, including spreadsheets, policy manuals, and web pages, to mention just a few. Contemporary private data sets can now exceed the size of the entire Internet in the 1990s, although some organizations do not publicize their stores. The content may be stored in file shares, websites, content management systems (CMSs), or databases, but without the ability to find this corporate knowledge, managing even a small company would be difficult.

HOW ENTERPRISE SEARCH DIFFERS FROM WEB SEARCH

Search on the Internet is good; everyone knows that. But Enterprise Search often draws complaints for not performing up to expectations, and there are some fundamental reasons why.

The Enterprise Is Not Just a Small Internet

Many Enterprise Search offerings began life as a search engines to power generic Internet portal searching. You'd assume that, if you could handle the Internet, then of course you could handle a relatively puny private network; it just makes sense!

This seems like a perfectly sane and compelling argument, and this model has worked at some companies. If your Intranet has a few dozen (to a few thousand) company portals and departmental websites, which mostly contain HTML and PDF documents, this could possibly work for you.

But this assumption is usually false, and such engines have had to be adjusted to work well in the distinctly non-Internet-like corporate and government networks. To be fair, most vendors have responded to these differences with enhancements to their enterprise offerings. However, the underlying architecture and design may prove to be a fundamental mismatch for some specific search applications.

Technical Differences in Search Requirements and Technologies

Aside from data volume, there are a number of other technical differences between a company's private intranet and the Internet. There are also differences in how the infrastructure is used and functional requirements. These differences are the seeds for different software implementations. Here are some of the significant differences:

➤ **There is usually a right document** — Whereas Google finds tens of thousands of pages relevant to almost any search you could imagine, corporate searchers prefer fewer highly relevant results for a given search, and often there is only one "right" document: a project status report, a client profile, or a specific policy. If Google misses a few thousand documents, few people notice; if your corporate search misses one, users may consider it a failure.

➤ **Security is critical** — On the Internet, content is public for anyone and everyone who may find it. Companies often have many specific security requirements, from "Company Confidential" to "Limited Distribution." There may even be legal implications if a document is released to the public before a specific time and date.

➤ **Taxonomies and vocabularies are important** — Companies often have a specific vocabulary, such as project and product names, procedures, and policies. Corporations often have invested significant resources to build and maintain a taxonomy to categorize and retrieve content, often from content management systems. Taking advantage of these terms unique to an organization is critical to making retrieval work better.

➤ **Dates are important** — Internet search is generally unaware of document dates, because content on the Internet often lacks this information. If a corporate search for "annual report" doesn't return the most recent document, your users will be unhappy.

➤ **Corporate data has structure** — In corporate databases, and even in web content, companies have fields specific to the structure of corporate data. A large consulting firm may include human-authored abstracts in each report, and corporate search technology has to be able to boost documents based on relevant terms in the abstract.

The public Internet was the inspiration and proving ground for a majority of the commercial and open source search engines out there. Creating a system to index the Internet has influenced both the architecture and implementation as engineers have made hundreds of assumptions about data and usage patterns — assumptions that do not always apply behind the firewalls of corporations and agencies. There are dozens of things that make Enterprise Search surprisingly difficult and that sometimes flummox the engines that were created to power the public web.

When vendors talk about their products, features, and patents, they are usually talking about technology that was not specifically designed for the enterprise. This isn't just academic theory; as you'll see, these assumptions can actually break Enterprise Search, if not adjusted properly.

Every Intranet Search Project Is Unique

Although some engines were not created for the Internet, they were still usually targeted at specific business applications. For example, imagine an engine that was created to serve a complex parts database. Perhaps a spider and HTML filters were later added, but that was not its genesis. That engine could have certain intrinsic behaviors and limitations that don't align with other search projects, such as a heavy-duty versioned CMS search application. This doesn't mean that the engine is "bad"; it's just a question of mismatch.

ENTERPRISE SEARCH TECHNOLOGY OVERVIEW

At the most basic level, search engines share these four logical components:

➤   Spider and/or indexer process (AKA data prep)

➤   Binary full-text index (AKA the index)

➤   The engine that runs the searches and gives back results (AKA the engine)

➤   Administration and reporting

Each one of these systems is dependent on the previous one to function properly, except for administration, which controls the other three. A search engine can't run searches if there is no full-text index, and there won't be any full-text index if the documents are never fetched and indexed.

Search Components Outline

Modern search engines have further subdivided the data prep, index, and search functions into additional subsystems to achieve better modularity and extreme scalability.

An exploded component view might look like this:

> **Data Prep**
> > Spider
> > > Cross-Page Links Database
> > > Document Cache
> > > Fetch Web Pages
> > > Extract Links to Other Pages
> > > Scheduling Fetches and Refetching
> > Processing
> > > Determine Mime Type
> > > Filter Document
> > > Parse Meta Data
> > > Entity Extraction

Indexing

Determine Document Language

Separate into Paragraphs, Sentences, and Words

Calculate Stemming, Thesaurus, etc.

Write to Full-Text Index

Full-Text Index

Word Inversion Index

Special Indexes (i.e., Soundex, Casedex, etc.)

Metadata Index

Word Vector Data, N-Gram

User Ratings and Tags

Periodically Validate and Optimize Full-Text Indexes

Replicate Full-Text Indexes

Search Engine

Accept initial Query from the User

Preprocess Query (thesaurus, relevancy, recall, etc.)

Distributed Query

Check Actual Full-Text Index

Merge Intermediate Query Results

Calculate Relevancy

Sorting and Grouping

Calculate and Render Navigators

Render Results to User

Gather User Feedback and Tags

Administration and Reporting

Managing the search platform

Even this outline is oversimplified for larger, more complex engines.

Vendor Vocabulary

Vendors use different names and buzzwords for these search functions. For example, the act of fetching a web page, looking at the links on it, and then downloading those pages is called "spidering" by some and "crawling" by others. ESP (FAST/Microsoft's Enterprise Search Platform) further subdivides this into the fetching of the web pages and the indexing of the pages once they have been downloaded, so in ESP the enterprise crawler, document pipeline, and indexer are distinct subsystems and often reside on different machines.

Scalability

In the early days of search software, if you needed to handle more data, you upgraded the machine's memory or hard drives, or upgraded to a faster machine. Most modern engines scale by adding more machines and then dividing the work among them. This division of labor is usually done by distributing these subsystems across these multiple machines, so this is an additional motivation for you to understand the various subsystems in your engine.

Federated Search

Federated search is the practice of having the central search engine actually not do all the work, instead "outsourcing" the user's query to other search engines and then combining the results with its own.

Vendors don't always highlight this feature. Many search licenses have a component related to the number of indexed documents, total size of indexed content, and so forth. When a search is deferred to another engine, the license doesn't include those other documents. We suspect that, in general, this is why federated search isn't pushed more heavily by vendors.

One final note here on federated search, which is itself quite a broad topic, is that Enterprise Federated Search has more intense requirements than the general federated search demos that many vendors perform. Federated Enterprise Search needs to maintain document-level security as searches are passed to other engines. This may involve mapping user credentials from one security system or domain to another. This is something that generic federated demos, which often just show combining results from two or three public web portals, don't address. There are other in-depth technical issues with enterprise-class federated search as well. Our advice is generally to go with a solution that is extensible via some type of API, so that new and unusual business requirements can be accommodated. ESP does offer such an API.

MICROSOFT'S 2010 SEARCH TECHNOLOGY ROAD MAP

In short you'll have a number of good choices:

➤ **Entry-level** — Search Server 2010 Express

➤ **Midlevel** — SharePoint Server 2010

➤ **High-end** — FAST Search for SharePoint 2010

➤ **Multi-platform** — The existing FAST ESP product line

➤ And, of course, the ancillary search engines embedded in various desktop applications and OSs

Microsoft is also positioning these products according to employee- versus customer-facing uses, although these are not hard and fast rules.

Microsoft's Explanation

Microsoft will continue to embed search in specific products such as Windows and Office applications. For server-based search, however, Microsoft will offer different products designed for customer- and employee-facing applications. Customer-facing applications will include site search and eCommerce, where engaging search experiences drive revenue (hard ROI).

SharePoint and ESP will also target employee-facing applications, helping process vast amounts of information so that employees can get things done efficiently and effectively.

> *"With SharePoint Server 2010, Microsoft has made a major leap forward in Enterprise Search. This includes a range of choices — since great search is not a 'one-size-fits-all' endeavor."*
>
> MICROSOFT, 2009

Options include:

➤ **Entry-level** — Search Server 2010 Express is a free, downloadable standalone search offering. It incorporates many enhancements over its predecessor, Search Server 2008 Express.

➤ **Infrastructure** — SharePoint Server 2010 includes a robust search capability out of the box with many improvements from the previous version.

➤ **High-End** — Along with SharePoint Server 2010, a new product, FAST Search for SharePoint 2010, is being introduced; it uses technology from a strategic acquisition of FAST, an industry-leading search technology company.

➤ **Multi-Platform** — Another new offering, FAST Search for Internet Business 2010, is being introduced. This expands the FAST ESP product, and adds new modules for content and query processing. This offering is available for Linux as well as Windows.

The introduction of FAST Search for SharePoint provides a new choice: best-in-market Enterprise Search capabilities (based on FAST's premier search product, FAST ESP), closely integrated with SharePoint, with the TCO and ecosystem of Microsoft.

CATEGORIZING YOUR ORGANIZATION'S USE OF SEARCH — EXAMPLES

Everybody who writes about search claims that it's core, but really, how core is it? Although we also believe it's incredibly important, it's clear that it's more important to some organizations than others. The reality is there's a spectrum here. Since no two companies are exactly alike, their use of search will never be exactly the same. However, honestly evaluating your company's use of search might help with decision making down the line.

Instead of spouting all kinds of abstract rules, let's dive into some concrete examples.

The following are examples of companies where search is absolutely key:

➤ Internet search engines or yellow pages (a "no-brainer")

➤ eCommerce sites (shopping, travel, B2B, etc.)

➤ Knowledge worker–driven businesses (R&D, legal, medical, financial, intelligence agencies, etc.)

➤ Large customer service organizations

➤ Media organizations and online reference sites

The following are examples of companies where search might be secondary:

➤ Small to midsized manufacturers with stable product lines

➤ Small or domestic shipping lines

➤ Local blue collar service centers (plumbing, electrical, HVAC)

➤ A small company Intranet portal — yes, it would have search, but it might not be a driver

➤ Small brick-and-mortar businesses with relatively stable inventory and no online presence

A hard-core search purist could argue any of these into a scenario where search is key.

The Gray Area: Where Search Might Be Misranked

In many of these cases, a casual observer might think that search is secondary. While we would agree that current reality is that the companies in many of these scenarios are not primary users of search, we would argue that they *should* be. This would take a lot of work to do well enough to be of primary usefulness.

A Local Sales Office

Most field sales offices are small or midsized and have many isolated systems. Employees there connect to the main office systems for some information, use a variety of mobile devices, live in their voice mail, and talk to the local receptionist for the most up-to-date information.

Imagine if there were a single search box that went across all systems, both at corporate and local levels; it would include all customer records, product information, phone lists, personal and shared calendars, email, and voice mail. It would let the user quickly move between different data sources in the results, or do so by date. Imagine this search box is everywhere — on employees' desks, on their phones, in all conference rooms — and when customers called in, their inbound phone number was immediately run through a quick search to pull up account information on a nearby device, ready for immediate editing. Imagine that salespeople and administrators could effortlessly save important searches that would run constantly against all inbound information and keep them up to date without pestering them.

This is a very tall order. The global search could just as easily bring back obsolete junk, and saved searches could turn the already beeping cell phone into a nightmare. This implementation could be done very badly. If it were done well, however, it could enable that sales office to run like an incredibly efficient machine.

A Contract Manufacturer

A contract manufacturer handles a larger variety of jobs, with considerably more designs, machinery, and materials involved. They also have more direct interaction with customers, who tend to have technical and time-sensitive questions. As they handle more types of materials and serve customers from many jurisdictions, they need to keep track of a lot more environmental, shipping, and regulatory information.

Now imagine a unified one-box system, similar to the sales office system described previously. If done well, it could dramatically improve productivity and responsiveness. We're getting close to where these types of systems might be feasible.

A Midsized to Large Energy Producer

Energy producers drill for oil or put up giant wind turbine farms; why would they ever have search as a core asset? Like the contract manufacturer, energy companies have an incredible amount of regulatory and technical information to keep track of. Imagine all those trucks, all those pipelines, all those pumps and wires! Large energy companies typically span multiple countries and multiple languages, and energy producers actually have quite a few scientists and analysts involved in technical and market research. Imagine all those maps, all those energy futures, and the need for employees to get correct information, in 12 languages, about fixing a specific pump. Also, if some type of industrial accident should happen, there might be a large amount of eDiscovery requests to respond to.

It's harder to imagine what the ultimate search system might look for that company. Something involving lots more mobile terminals, in multiple languages, and possibly including image search, so employees can visually identify a part they need to replace. Of course, managers would want proactive notification of weather, transit issues, regulatory changes, you name it. Although hard to imagine, such an uber-search-system could really make a difference.

THE ROI OF SEARCH

Although a detailed explanation of the return on investment of search is beyond the scope of this chapter and has been written about by other authors before, a brief summary is certainly in order.

Improvements that can be measured are considered hard ROI, such as a change that directly increases sales. Whereas the more intangible benefits would be soft ROI, for example, the general agreement that a new search engine has made employees more productive but the exact value of which might be harder to quantify.

Predicting and accurately measuring how much money you'll earn or save can be difficult. Some of the popular ROI studies were done in the late 1990s, and even studies that appear to be newer are often citing the earlier work, so much of the ROI data is almost 10 years old!

While we do believe in ROI, the idea that if you improve search, you may very well earn more money from increased sales, or save money by improving employee efficiency and customer retention, results in a bit of a paradox. Although these gains are often hard to measure, capturing such numbers is more important than now than when idea of search ROI was popularized. Money is tighter now than 10 years ago, so many organizations will simply not spend any money on fixing systems unless there's a perceived critical need and a predictable way to address it and realize gains. So planners who do not proactively put these estimates together may not get funded, or teams that didn't meet these objectives before may be met with resistance on new projects.

So, do think about ROI in your planning, no matter how inaccurate it may be. Don't fret about absolute numbers as much as being able to at least capture trends. Estimates that are consistently 100% off may still be able to detect a trend.

And, finally, do beware of vendor ROI figures for improved employee productivity. When vendors present their ROI calculations, they usually multiply the hours per day spent searching times the number of employees, and the like, to arrive at some astronomical annual amount of wasted time. The implied and flawed assumption is that if you upgraded to their solution you would magically recapture all of that lost productivity — which is simply not true. A good search engine might save 5 to 10% of that wasted time, maybe in the extreme case 30%, but the point is that it's not 100%! Of recent note, Q-Go stands apart in modern search engine ROI in offering an ROI money back guarantee to qualifying customers. We'd like to see other vendors be so confident in their ROI numbers.

To summarize the commonly cited ROI benefits of improving search:

➤ Increases revenue from helping customers find things to buy quicker

➤ Increases revenue from using search to suggest additional related products

➤ Reduces support costs through self-service, reducing emails and phone calls

➤ Saves time by helping employees find information faster

➤ Saves time by not having employees recreate things that already exist

➤ Improves customer and employee satisfaction and retention

The Business Intelligence Benefits of Search

Most people just think of search in terms of helping users find things. A businessperson may then consider the ROI impacts of search, using it to sell more inventory or saving employees' time. Search has benefits, however, at a more strategic level as well, which appeal to marketing and corporate management.

We say that search has three levels of benefits:

1. **The direct benefit to users:** With a good search engine, employees or customers can find what they're looking for quickly. This is the aspect of search that everybody is aware of.

2. **Financial benefits/ROI:** These can be the result of the direct generation of additional revenue and cost savings, improving efficiency, and so forth — hard ROI versus soft ROI. We talked about this in the previous section. Although the ROI of search gets mentioned quite a bit in the press, we don't think it always justifies new search projects to management, except in the case of a customer-facing B2C or B2B commerce site.

3. **Strategic/BI (business intelligence):** This includes spotting search and content trends, and being able to respond more quickly. We believe this is a frequently untapped benefit of good search technology.

Here are some examples of the potential BI benefits of search:

➤ Learning what users are looking for and the *changes* in these interests over time.

➤ Finding what they are not finding, because of either misspellings, vocabulary mismatch issues (where the words used in the content don't match up with the search terms users type in), or perhaps the search relating to products that you don't yet offer.

➤ Customer service can spot a spike in complaints about a particular product glitch or searches from an important customer.

➤ Getting a handle on the content you own. Spiders and their related tools can actually teach you things about your data that you didn't know. Preparing for search can also inspire an audit of silos and metadata.

➤ Content owners can check that the terminology they are using is matching up with the search terms being used.

➤ Improving site navigation.

➤ Keeping track of competitors.

➤ Achieving more consistent compliance, which can also improve eDiscovery if it's ever required.

Old-school click-tracking of website analytics shows you which links a user follows and the number of seconds spent on each page, leaving you to guess why a user clicked on certain links and whether it answered his or her question or not. The more modern approach uses search analytics to obtain a much clearer view. Search analytics shows you exactly what the user wanted, because you know what he or she typed in! You can certainly see which searches produced zero results, which is a very good indicator that the customer was not satisfied. These analytics can also spot trends and changes in behavior and spot vocabulary mismatches between the search terms typed in and the language used on your web pages.

Modern search engines can look at search terms, phrases, and sentences at a statistical level. This functionality can be applied to both submitted searches and to recently authored content, possibly including tech support incident descriptions and bug reports, mailing list and blog postings, and other highly dynamic internal content. Modern software can also detect statistically significant changes, but assigning meaning and action to these changes is still best left to human experts within the company. We have ideas about how this can all be coordinated and turned into concrete actions, but most organizations are still busy working on more basic search upgrades.

When justifying search projects, we encourage clients to think in terms of all three levels of benefits. When thinking about the BI benefits of search, try to include additional stakeholders in the earliest parts of planning. Most companies already involve IT and site designers in their planning process. These BI benefits, however, will also be of interest to upper management, content creators, customer service/tech support, and marketing. The planning of Enterprise Search projects (behind the firewall) should also include human resources, helpdesk staff, corporate librarians, sales engineers and professional services, security and compliance officers, the CFO and legal staff, and any knowledge workers central to the company's core competence.

THE SEARCH CENTER OF EXCELLENCE

In short, a Search Center of Excellence (SCOE) is a team within an organization that specializes, at least in part, in search and related technologies.

Before SCOE

In the past, search was seen as tactical or infrastructure, almost like email or DNS. Someone within a company would recognize the need to "add search" to a portal project or website, or an edict would be handed down to "fix search." IT would be given some basic requirements and tasked with picking a vendor and making the system work. In other companies, the task was handed to the database team with similar sparse requirements. If an engine wasn't too expensive, and if it installed and ran without setting off alarms, it was considered to be working, and the busy IT folks would move on to fight new higher-priority fires.

We actually had one IT department tell us they didn't need to inventory the content being indexed by their search engine. They reasoned that if something important was missing, then somebody would eventually complain about it and they'd fix it then. This isn't about being reckless; it's just a question of infrastructure priorities. If search is viewed as just another piece of infrastructure then this is a very reasonable approach.

In a few larger companies, it was the corporate librarians who inherited the responsibility for search. Corporate librarians have been trained in search for years, along with categorizing and organizing information, so it seemed a small matter of bringing in some IT resources to get some software up and running. The benefit of a corporate library having responsibility is that librarians do know their content and are generally quite thorough. However, corporate librarians may not necessarily be thinking about things like business intelligence, search analytics, security, compliance, customer retention, and so forth. This is another case where the bigger strategic role of search might not be fully realized.

The Birth of SCOE

Over the last five years, companies have started to realize the strategic importance of great search, both within the company/intranet and on their public sites. Fortune 500 companies typically saw their intranets growing to the size that the entire Internet was back in the mid-1990, and they saw that deflecting customer service and IT helpdesk questions had a direct beneficial impact on staffing expenses — great search saved money!

At the same time, Internet retailers realized that, without really good search, customers would abandon their site. Jakob Nielsen, in his well-known 1999 study, found that half of site visitors would use search if there were a search box. We also all learned that a poor search results page is probably the last thing a frustrated site user sees before he or she leaves the site for one with better search. Conversely good search keeps customers happy and coming back for more. Great search increased sales!

Although there were two very different business drivers (cost savings and increased revenue), both groups started to reorganize their staff to focus on better search. These new teams became known as Search Centers of Excellence. Where these Search Centers of Excellence fit in the corporate organization chart depended on how the corporation approached search.

Centralized SCOE

In companies that view search as a primary way to drive revenue, the manager of the SCOE is often a high-level executive who reports directly to the CEO. The SCOE is charged with implementing search for all brands or lines of business (LOB), and typically all staff for search and search analytic management report to the chief search officer — the CSO. The SCOE in these companies includes IT and network responsibility for search as well, even if there is a separate IT operation for web operations; the search servers belong to the SCOE.

Distributed SCOE

Although search is important, many companies have grown into search over the years, and each department already had staff that directly managed search, or had business drivers related to it. In these organizations, a majority of the formal head count stayed where it originally was, but a federation of employees who dealt with search, from either a technical or business level, formed informal SCOEs. Some organizations later formalized and funded this activity. These SCOEs are typically championed by a high-level manager, perhaps at the VP level, who reports to the CIO. The SCOE may also still have some dedicated core staff.

In larger companies that use multiple search engines, these groups have become even more important. Although some technical practices aren't directly applicable to other engines, many business practices are. Coordinating search optimization and reporting efforts can be handled by a distributed SCOE. Having a high-level knowledge of multiple vendors' offerings can also help in terms of renewal and expansion negotiations, and can provide sanity checks on customer service and equipment requirements.

Examples of SCOE Tasks

A centralized SCOE will typically have well-defined projects, with a mix of funding sources and direct control over critical search systems. Even in the distributed SCOE model, however, tasks would include:

➤ Ongoing monitoring and tuning of various systems, or consulting with the staff directly tasked to do this

- Maintaining corporate knowledge of existing systems and the content they serve
- Serve as a sounding board for reported problems or newly proposed projects
- Cataloguing agreed-to search best practices
- Maintaining relationships with key vendors
- General industry awareness
- In-house training
- Helping to maintain controlled vocabularies or taxonomies

SCOE Staffing and Skills

Here are some general areas that an ideal SCOE would have covered:

- Executive sponsor
- Business domain expert
- Marketing staff
- Project management
- Information architects
- Librarians
- IT, operations, and networking staff
- Linguistic experts (taxonomies/synonyms/etc.)
- Content experts
- UI/HTML engineers
- Search expert developers
- Search quality assessment
- Search analytics specialists
- Business intelligence staff
- Search quality specialists
- Search evangelist

See Chapter 2 to learn more about SCOE.

Questions That Everybody Asks

Here are a few questions that come up in the course of most projects. We figured we might as well address them right up front.

WHY NOT JUST BUY A GOOGLE APPLIANCE?

Even if you're not seriously considering a Google appliance, or believe you understand fully why you'd select a Microsoft/FAST engine instead, make sure you understand what the Google appliance represents. We can almost guarantee that at some point in the purchasing process, some high-level executive at your company is going to ask about it, possibly more than once, and possibly very late in the process. Lately executives are also inquiring about open source alternatives. If IT departments don't have a complete justification readily in hand, they can find their carefully planned purchase process derailed at the eleventh hour.

As you may know, Google has packaged their world-famous search engine in a variety of sealed rack-mountable appliances. The Google Search Appliance, sometimes referred as the "GSA" or "Google Box," comes in various configurations. Most of the higher-end offerings are housed in bright yellow rack mounted cases, whereas the lower-end "light" version is a thin rack-mounted blue box, called The Google Mini.

We promise we're not going to engage in Google bashing here. Commercial buyers of search technology are generally tired of the tone taken by some of Google's competitors, and as a matter of full disclosure, some of the authors of this book are actually Google partners! For years we've been saying that there aren't really any bad engines left on the market. When we find unhappy clients it's often more about a mismatch between their business requirements or staffing levels and the engine that they selected, as opposed to a truly "bad" engine.

The truth is that some companies have chosen the Google Appliance and are happy with it. Employees and partners tend to respond positively to the brand name, and this may factor in their overall assessment and confidence. Some large companies have widely distributed sets of small intranet web servers, and contrary to our earlier statements, their network might very well resemble a small Internet. The Google box can certainly perform well in such environments. Some IT managers are also attracted to the perceived shorter learning curve and lower maintenance staffing requirements, responding to the "appliance" aspect of the product offering.

To Google's credit, they have been releasing new versions with more and more features, including some control over relevancy. Even the Google Mini, the lightweight end of the product line, has inherited some of these features. If you happen read a bad review of the GSA you might check the date on the article, and if it's an important feature, check Google's site for updated information.

Google has also tried to foster a network of partners and third-party vendors to give their customers lots of choices in service providers and add-ons. However, other companies have not been satisfied with the Google appliance after using it. This isn't a shocker, and you can find horror stories involving almost any vendor. All major search vendors have failed deployments or dissatisfied customers at some point in time, so even that is not a smoking gun.

When we've encountered companies who have been dissatisfied with the Google Appliance it's usually been due to their particular business priorities not meshing well with the Google feature set or licensing. These issues can be generally summarized into business and technical concerns.

Business Considerations

There are differences in licensing between the Google Appliance and the FAST/Microsoft offerings. This is not to say that Google is necessarily more expensive, and as most corporate buyers know, the prices for hardware, software, and services can vary because of many factors. Regardless of which engine you select, you will generally pay more to index and search larger amounts of content, because of either direct licensing fees or other, indirect costs. It's also important to understand your data-indexing requirements (size/number of docs) as opposed to your query volume (number of searches/users). Other requirements, such as advanced features or premium support plans, can also affect price.

For some time, Google did not offer telephone support for nonurgent issues. If this is a factor, please check with all of your vendors for clarification, as these policies are certainly subject to change over time.

For advanced document processing we found the FAST ESP document pipeline to be a more controlled environment. FAST ESP has long supported advanced features such as taxonomies, federated search, scoped searching, faceted navigation, advanced entity extraction and unsupervised clustering. Not every application needs all these features, and Google is adding many of them.

FAST ESP has generally provided more APIs and adjustments than almost any other major commercial vendor; of course the open source search engines also now offer many APIs. Whether your application needs all of those capabilities is another matter.

Technical Considerations

Some projects require much more control over search relevancy, or the ability to completely debug relevancy calculations. Google does allow some control over relevancy, and it has continued to improve on this. However, customers who need extreme control over relevancy may want to consider other solutions.

For high-security environments, there was a belief that Google either required dial-up access or required the return of the physical appliance upon termination of a contract. Although we cannot officially comment on such rumors, Google does list various government agencies as references, and presumably these items were addressed to their satisfaction. Again, if this is a concern, a diligent Google sales rep should be able to address them. FAST's Security Access module has also been at the forefront of document-level search engine security, although Google certainly offers document-level security as well, albeit with a different implementation.

The final common business factor is that some companies really are "A Microsoft shop." Virtually every company has some computers running Microsoft software; that's not what we mean. Some companies run their entire infrastructure on Microsoft Back Office applications and operating systems, including SharePoint. Those IT departments might feel right at home running a Microsoft search engine, no matter how good a Google Appliance might work. For companies with extremely strict compliance requirements for search, all search vendors should be thoroughly questioned; we're not singling out Google on this issue.

Why Not Just Use an Open-Source Engine Like Lucene?

We are truly impressed with the amount of technology that used to be very expensive and that is now available "for free" to technically inclined IT staff and programmers. Some of the authors have also worked with and written about these various offerings, including Lucene, Solr, and Nutch.

As with what we've said about the Google Appliance, this certainly isn't about "good" or "bad" engines. These open source engines are very impressive for what they do! In their current incarnations, however, these offerings are aimed squarely at programmers and tinkerers, not busy IT departments. We refer to this as "enterprise packaging." As of this writing (Spring 2010), all of these offerings assume that administrators will write command line scripts or Java programs to index data.

Nutch, the one offering that includes a spider, ships sample scripts in written only in Unix shell scripting language dialect. Yes, you can install Unix shell scripting on a Windows server or rewrite them in Windows shell scripting. The point is not whether these applications can be run on Windows; they certainly can! But if your IT department is used to commercial installers and Windows-driven administration, then these tools will be very different from what they are used to.

I Have Search Inside SharePoint; Do I Need Anything Else?

Maybe you don't! Microsoft has put lots of effort into making a formidable entry-level system, one capable of serving smaller data sets and light search usage.

While we've talked about scalability in terms of number of gigabytes of text or queries per second, this is not the only reason companies outgrow those basic engines. We've already explained how it's not reasonable to expect a search engine to put the document you're looking for in the top 10 search results all the time.

If search is getting more heavily used in your organization, and the amount of data it serves is increasing, then, by that very usage, search is becoming more important. If employees are doing lots of searches and starting to talk about the search engine in meetings, then it's time to inventory the work being done that involves search, and whether the current engine is getting the job done. Don't wait to hit some particular gigabytes or queries per second limit!

As search is used more and data grows, people will want to drill down into their results or save their searches, or perhaps particular fields in your documents are becoming more critical, such as custom part numbers or model numbers or order numbers. The list goes on. As you start to need more and more of these features, it's time to start thinking about an upgrade.

Why Is Search so Hard?

Basic search may not be very hard, depending on your application, the engine you're using, and the data source it's coming from. Firms like Microsoft and Google are working on making basic search easier and easier.

Like many other technologies there's not much "magic" in search engines; it's more about having dozens or hundreds of little things set up just right. Knowing what all those things are called by each vendor, how to set them, the symptoms of something not being set right, and exactly how to adjust something that's incorrect, are the bane of most search engine managers. When an engine packages up these little details well, with good documentation and debugging tools, they may have a hit on their hands.

The first area of complexity that creeps up is spidering. When the data to be searched lives on multiple web servers, a spider is sent to download the web pages and index them. A spider is often used on private websites behind its own company's firewall, not just against public websites. We won't go into details here, but getting this "just right" can be an iterative process. This is also the first stumbling block for some of the open source solutions. Getting data out of databases and other content repositories can be a challenge, depending on the engine and the corporate infrastructure.

Other things that tend to multiply the seeming complexity include:

➤ Staff that's not particularly familiar with web and database technologies.

➤ Staff that's not familiar with search engine terms and technology.

➤ Conversely, overly zealous staff creating "The RFP from Hell," with virtually every search engine feature ever imagined, all marked as "A Priority - Phase 1."

➤ Unreasonable management, IT, or user expectations.

➤ Getting data in from multiple sources.

➤ Complex metadata, normalizing, cleansing, and parsing. For example, industrial databases with electronic or machine parts can easily have hundreds of attributes, and if the data comes from various sources, or was entered via disparate processes, then getting this into a search engine *correctly* will take some time. The reward is having much better access to the inventory.

➤ Integrating search into existing web application frameworks.

➤ Integrating search with some eCommerce systems.

➤ Moderate- to high-level security requirements or requirements for heavy compliance, eDiscovery, or adherence to data retention mandates.

➤ Systems that require more complex search engine features, such as taxonomies, clustering or web 2.0-style user feedback.

➤ High data volume and/or search traffic. When search moves from an individual machine to a cluster, some additional complexity is likely.

➤ Systems where the authors and users tend to use very different vocabularies. For example, content that is prepared by expert government employees but is searched by average citizens. Medical and legal applications can also have this problem.

➤ Multilingual systems, especially if there are also strong testing or certification mandates.

➤ Systems with emphasis on nontextual data.

➤ Embedded or atypical search applications; for example, search embedded inside an email application, or search used for intelligence gathering or investigation.

We've Upgraded Search, and Users Are Unhappy.

Why would another upgrade be any different? Sadly this scenario is more common than you might imagine, and this can impact funding of future projects and the team's credibility, so it's something important to keep in mind! One possibility is that the new system *is* better, and there's no search engine that can read users' minds the way they expected (or were implicitly promised). As attractive as this rationalization might be, don't hang your paycheck on it. As the lead-in question suggests, even if this were the case, what's to keep it from happening again? A proactive approach is to measure various parameters and try to quantify the improvement. Presenting "before and after" five-digit decimal numbers to management, based on these measurements, may not be very compelling, but the staff involved with the search engines should be learning from these measurements.

Another possibility is that, although money was spent and vendors were swapped out, the new engine isn't really much better. This can happen if the staff selecting an engine simply got caught up in vendor hype and buzzwords, or perhaps very compelling customer references. The reality is that most vendors have decent search engines, if they are properly configured and monitored and adjusted over time.

Relating to the previous two paragraphs, give some thought to what process was followed (or skipped!) in the previous search engine upgrades. Borrowing from realtors, we like to say the three keys to good advanced search are "process, process, process!" It's very unlikely that a single missing feature or poorly worded RFP item is entirely responsible for a perceived failure. Was a thorough inventory of data repositories conducted? Were stakeholders interviewed and use cases discussed? Was the new engine monitored and adjusted, on an ongoing basis, to ensure that it was returning decent results? Was there a POC and phased implementation? Or did the selection process simply consist of a list of features and check boxes, and then perhaps were all the defaults accepted and the search engine summarily stuffed into an IT closet and forgotten?

If search is critical to your business, then it warrants some ongoing attention. Instead of "we've fixed search," a more reasonable expectation might be "we've moved to an engine we can continuously monitor and improve."

Do I Need a Taxonomy?

Generally, if your data or business or organization makes use of a well-defined taxonomy, then possibly yes. On the other hand, if the only reason you're considering one is that you've heard of taxonomies and really want something that will "fix search," then probably not. This is an incredibly broad topic to discuss. Some readers might not even be sure what a taxonomy is (don't worry, even the experts don't precisely agree!)

The good news is that, if you need one, Microsoft does support this. FAST ESP has supported this feature for years. Also SharePoint 2010 has added taxonomy and vocabulary management to its foundation. See Chapter 6 for information on enterprise content management.

A few key points to keep in mind with taxonomies include:

➤ Implementing a good taxonomy takes some work (doing a bad one, not so much!).

➤ Although most search engines "support" a taxonomy, actually implementing one is a completely different matter. This trips up lots of folks who are relying on feature checklists.

➤ Modern search engines offer alternatives to taxonomies that might fill a similar role but be easier to implement. Engines that offer faceted navigation and clustering should be considered.

➤ Beware of vendors offering totally automatic taxonomy generation. While this is possible in some contexts, ask careful questions about how taxonomy rules are maintained and adjusted. Also, we strongly advise using a POC.

And as a quick review, generally a taxonomy attempts to organize data in a hierarchy. Yahoo! is probably most widely known example. A taxonomy can be organized by subject, like the way Yahoo and your local library's card catalog do; this would be a subject or subject "domain" based taxonomy. Alternately, it can be arranged by grouping and subgrouping the data you already have into different segments. We call this a content- or corpus-based taxonomy, and some vendors do have tools that assist in doing this. Some vendors also call this auto-categorization. The third general type of taxonomy is the behavior- or user-based taxonomy, where the focus is organizing things by how users are searching for them, or perhaps even letting users directly tag documents.

Taxonomies can be used to limit the scope of a search, so a user can drill down into a large results set and focus in on a particular subset of results. The classic usage model of a taxonomy, that users will spend hours browsing around and discovering new data, is not as common as once thought. Most users are busy and looking for a particular document or answer, and they may not spend much time "just browsing." Taxonomies can also be used in various discovery and alerting applications.

If taxonomies really do fit your data and usage models, please do your homework or seek professional help. However, do not delay all search engine improvements while you carefully ponder taxonomies; this is a trap that some fall prey to.

Do I Need Facets or Entity Extraction?

Possible to likely, depending on your data and planned application, though by now that probably sounds like our answer to everything. First off, the good news: ESP supports both facets and entity extraction, and these are discussed a bit more in Chapters 3, 5, 7, and 8.

A quick reminder about facets. They are clickable links presented in search results that users can click on to drill down and target their search. For example, if searching for an automobile, perhaps facets would be presented for various nearby cities that have auto listings. Instead of looking at 5,000 results, a user can click and see just the 200 matches in their city of interest. We're strongly in favor of results list navigators of some sort, and facets are often one of the easier ones to implement, assuming the data can provide it.

It is not true that all clickable hyperlinks presented in results are facets. Links can also represent other search navigators such as automatic clusters, related searches, user tags, or even branches of a taxonomy tree. Facets are usually the clickable items based on well-defined document metadata such as locations, people, companies, ranges of dates, amounts of money or other numeric data, or internal classifications.

Since facets represent clickable filters based on well-defined data, the documents must contain those attributes. If the source data is from a database, then those facets will come from database fields. Data from XML feeds may have custom elements or attributes with values the facets can use.

However, if data does have attributes, but they are not stored in database fields, the case for facets gets a little hazier. This is where entity extraction can be considered. Entity extraction can sometimes bridge the gap between nondatabase content and faceted navigation. Entity extraction attempts to pull reasonably well-defined people, places, and things out of the full text of a document and store them as document metadata, which is then available to the search engine for facets, searching, and sorting.

In summary, if your source data is very structured, such as that from a database or XML feed, then you should consider facets. They will provide a good navigation aid for users. If your source data is not structured, but it does have people, places, and other well-defined items within its text, then consider using entity extraction to mine that text to form data that facets can run against. We do suggest using a POC. As with many advanced search features, the details can sometimes get involved.

And if your source data really doesn't have metadata or extractable items, then consider other result list navigation methods, such as clustering or taxonomies.

What Is Clustering?

Clustering means several different things in the search industry, depending on which vendor you're talking to. ESP supports the two types of clustering discussed here, and is discussed in Chapter 9.

The fancy totally automatic clustering is referred to as "unsupervised clustering" in ESP. It looks at the short phrases and sentence fragments in the matching documents and displays statistically significant phrases in the results. For example, if a user typed in the word "kidney," some of the clusters might have to do with "kidney bean recipes" as opposed to others about "kidney dialysis." These links prompt the user to think a bit more about the context they had in mind (food versus medical conditions), and clicking on one of those phrases focuses the search engine on that that topic.

There's a similar looking but slightly different feature often called "related searches." The difference is that the classic clusters discussed above really do drill down into the results. They will bring back a subset of the currently matching documents, whereas related searches will bring back a different set of documents, with only some overlap and not necessarily a smaller set. Above, if a user typed "kidney" and then clicked on the "kidney beans recipes cluster," he or she would see the subset of results that contained that phrase. However, related searches for "kidney" might include "vegetarian alternatives" and "organs of the body." The food-related search might also bring back documents about tofu and seitan, and the health-related search, those about the heart, lungs, and liver.

As you may have guessed, the other type of clustering is what ESP calls "supervised clustering," which is really just a fancier name for the facets, or refiners, we've already discussed. Clusters can also mean showing a few results from a group of documents, such as three documents from each matching site.

Although we admire the mathematics and coding that goes into unsupervised clustering, we normally advise clients that this is a workaround, a backup plan if none of the other result list navigation tools can be used.

Can't I Just Have Users Tag Everything?

Probably not, or at least not as your sole source of input, unless you have a *lot* of search activity, or have nontextual content and have absolutely no other choice. We do like user tagging, and it can be a valuable adjunct to other methods, just not the primary method; it's a question of numbers. SharePoint 2010 does have user tagging, which is discussed in Chapter 10.

The biggest factor in user tagging is user participation rates. With a small percentage of users tagging, and a relatively small number of users to begin with (compared to large public sites), it's often difficult to get a critical mass of tagging to happen.

If you run through the numbers, you can see this very clearly. If a large public website with 1 billion visitors gets 1% of them to tag documents, that's 10 million taggers, which is great. A private search application with 1,000 daily users, however, might have only 10 active taggers. You might get more than 1% of users to tag something once in a while, but the numbers still tend to be small.

When a user does take the time to tag a document with a particular word, this should be taken into consideration. You might, for example, weight user tags higher than text in the document.

There's another possible way to boost tagging, by using both explicit and implicit tagging. When casual users search for specific terms and then open a document from the results, you can also consider that an implicit tagging event. That user, after typing specific key words, clicked on this document, so there's likely some relationship. However, it could be that the document's title interested the user for some other reason, and they were just curious. Or, perhaps when they opened the document it was not relevant after all or had obsolete or incorrect information. Implicit tagging is still a bit speculative, and you certainly wouldn't weight such word associations as high as explicit tagging.

Can We Do It in Phases?

Yes! We strongly recommend not trying to do everything in one grand implementation. This subject is discussed more in Chapter 2.

A phased implementation has several advantages:

➤ Allows for some early wins in the overall project

➤ Spots unanticipated problems earlier on

➤ Builds some confidence between customer and vendors

➤ Is consistent with doing a POC and is also consistent with the more agile methods of rapid prototyping and versioning

➤ Allows the designers and architects to more easily modify later phases based on user feedback

➤ Helps cement the mindset that search is never "finished," that search engines need monitoring and periodic tuning

➤ May fit in more easily with longer-term budgeting and ROI goals

How Much Is This Going to Cost?

This is impossible to answer in a few sentences of a book's introductory chapter!

On the cost side, especially with higher-end search applications, it's not just about the licensing. Design, implementation, and ongoing maintenance can be significant, depending on the requirements.

Ironically, these other costs can be particularly surprising to companies who go with "free" open source software. Although there may not be any upfront licensing, the implementation costs can vary widely.

If an application must scale to hundreds of millions of documents or hundreds of queries per second, equipment and operation costs can go up. Meeting extremely high failover and redundancy quality of service goals can also get very expensive. Fortunately virtualization and cloud technologies may keep these costs from growing unbounded.

How long it will take is perhaps easier for us answer here: longer than you'd expect. However, a phased approach mitigates this to some extent. Gathering data ahead of time can also speed things up. However, we feel there is a diminishing return on specifying applications in a vacuum, before vendors and integrators are brought in.

Information that's usually good to gather up front includes:

> ➤ A thorough content repository inventory, preferably including a metadata audit
> ➤ Lists of key stakeholders
> ➤ Summaries of previously successful and failed projects
> ➤ Previous interviews and comments
> ➤ Pertinent use cases
> ➤ Some early mockups
> ➤ A prioritized set of desired features, and the reasons for each
> ➤ Staff and skill set matrix, and expected future staffing and job requirements
> ➤ Preliminary timeline, budgeting, and ROI goals

You'll notice that we didn't include a detailed implementation plan or other extremely specific materials. These items will evolve as engine selection and earlier phases are worked on. Making key decisions too early can actually hinder later design ideas or cost more money to correct.

What Type of Staffing Do I Need for Search?

Given its importance and complexity, search technology infrastructure is generally understaffed at most companies. Don't fall into this trap. If you can't devote a full-time person, then factor in at least three people at half time. Unless your use of search is extremely trivial, you'll want to have at least two "heads" allocated to it, to maintain continuity and foster an ongoing dialog about search. For larger projects, you may want to consider search staffing more along the lines of database staffing levels.

Even if you'll be outsourcing the initial implementation, most search engines still need ongoing maintenance from staff that is "web technology literate"; they understand what web servers are; what an application stack, a spider, and a database are; the difference between your private network and the Internet; and, hopefully, the difference between HTTP and HTML. If you'll be using ESP or one of the open source engines, you'll also need at least one person who can write shell scripts or similar code. This is the case for most of the larger enterprise engines.

If you'll be doing the implementation in-house, you'll usually need coders. If you're sticking with the Microsoft framework, then generally this means .NET developers. Most other engines typically require Java. Implementation usually requires some scripting, either Windows or Unix based. You'll also want some user interface design resources.

Many of the other roles surrounding search can be performed as a part time activity by staff with other duties, as long as they are done consistently. You'll want to have contact with administrators for the repositories you'll be searching. You'll typically want one or two businesspeople to be involved, looking at the search activity reports. If you'll be getting involved with taxonomies or a specialized vocabulary, you'll need somebody to work with that.

We also remind clients to include manual and automated testing in their project lifecycle. One issue is that relevancy testing isn't as easy to automate. Staffing plans should include at least a quarterly review of search engine activity. If search is absolutely key to your business, then this may need to be a weekly or daily activity, and it needs to include both technical and business resources.

Isn't Enterprise Search Dead?

We've been hearing these claims in one form or another for at least 15 years. In that time search has grown and grown and grown, and it's not going away any time soon. Some analysts have defined Enterprise Search in very specific ways and then predicted stagnation or declines in that metric. Our crystal ball is at the shop, but even if any of these carefully worded predictions came true, we could probably tweak the wording enough to change the outcome. So, search in the enterprise is not going away, not by a long shot!

The industry continues to see mergers and acquisitions, including Microsoft's purchase of FAST, which is part of a healthy, maturing industry. Basic search functionality is being included in more and more business applications. This fact, along with open source and hosted software, has put some pricing pressure on the lower end of the market. This is not "death," however, far from it; it indicates a very broad adoption of a technology.

And some vendors simply consider search as one component of their overall product offerings. For example, IBM has a number of enterprise-class search engines, and yet they tend to not market heavily to the "Enterprise Search market." If a company is a heavy user of IBM's software, and they have need of full-text search, then IBM can fill that requirement. Does that make IBM a primary player in Enterprise Search? That answer is entirely dependent on how you define the question. We would say "yes," but if your company doesn't use much IBM software, they are very unlikely to be on your "short list."

Even the "pure" search companies have repositioned themselves a bit. Autonomy now talks about search and compliance/eDiscovery. Endeca talks about eCommerce and Enterprise Search. Google has a search appliance, but their main search application is their public search portal. Some of the tier-2 vendors, such as Exalead, Attivio, Vivisimio, Dieselpoint, and the like, are still very focused on pure search.

How Important Is the Gartner Magic Quadrant?

The Gartner Magic Quadrant, and similar assessments, such as the Forrester Wave, are interesting to take a look at and can provide a cross-check on your vendor "short list." Not to worry, Microsoft does well in these rankings.

Here are some points to keep in mind:

➤ These lists include quite a few vendors, and most of the larger ones are already listed in the upper-right "magic" quadrant. So, hopping 1/4 inch from one of these vendors to another isn't going to magically fix anything.

➤ Generally, these lists don't directly compare things like implementation time, pricing, or customer service metrics. These are usually huge factors for a successful project.

➤ As we've said, most search engines on the market these days are at least decent, if configured and maintained properly. Using the Gartner Magic Quadrant to justify random vendor changes is a recipe for disaster, and a very expensive one at that.

➤ In some cases a tier-2 or tier-3 vendor might have a more specific product offering for particular set of requirements. Or, they may be more flexible on pricing or enhancements. Some projects might actually be better served by one of these other vendors. The point is that focusing only on industry behemoths might lead you to miss these opportunities.

Use these resources to cross-check your research but not to replace it.

SUMMARY

Enterprise Search is any employee- or customer-facing search that you own and control. If your favorite content management system already has search built in and it works well for the users, then that's great, but you're unlikely to be reading this.

As data grows, so does the size of results lists, and this tends to make specific documents harder to find. Although relevancy can be tweaked, you should also consider results list navigators, which lets users drill down in their results, to home in on what they need.

And unlike Internet content, data in the enterprise is complex. This tends to make search complex. Although some users are content to search within one system, your hard-core knowledge workers and managers are going to need access to broad sets of content on a somewhat unpredictable schedule. They need industrial strength search to slice and dice their way through thousands of matching documents from their desktops and mobile devices.

Advanced enterprise search systems provide a platform for building custom search applications. The same search engine can supply results in different forms to different applications. When you buy Oracle's database software, it isn't automatically an inventory control system or project management tool — those applications are built on top of Oracle. This is analogous to enterprise search technology — it's not a shrink-wrapped finished application; instead it's a set of tools for building applications.

2

Developing a Strategy — The Business Process of Search

WHAT'S IN THIS CHAPTER?

➤ Fundamentals of creating the search project plan

➤ The evaluation and acquisition process

➤ Gathering requirements

➤ How to plan a successful deployment

Search touches just about every part of your information infrastructure, and while great search can help defray expenses, sell product, or ensure regulatory compliance, bad search can have repercussions far beyond your website or intranet site.

This chapter looks at the basics of an Enterprise Search project plan. It covers the types of applications where Enterprise Search can make a difference, and a looks at how companies organize for success using search centers of excellence. Then it digs into the actual process of acquiring an enterprise platform, which is more than just the search-box application people used to associate with Enterprise Search.

We will talk about building a business case, the role external analysts and consultants can play in your success, and the process of identifying content and gathering user requirements. Next, we'll get into the actual purchasing, prototyping, deployment, and roll out. Finally we give some pointers about how you can help ensure that search will work well and provide you all the business intelligence it can.

After you read this chapter, you should be able to confidently begin the process of managing an Enterprise Search initiative and have an understanding of the real-world challenges and tasks — and some tricks you can use along the way to ensure the successful outcome of the project.

DEVELOPING THE SEARCH PROJECT PLAN

Companies purchase and deploy search for a number of different uses, and each potential application can have different objectives, requirements, features, and implementations. This section helps you identify how to create your project plan based on the type of search application you deploy.

When most people talk about Enterprise Search, they mean search owned and typically managed by an organization for the benefit of its employees, divisions, partners, affiliates, and customers. As you've seen, Enterprise Search is rather a broad term, and how you approach your business plan depends on the scope of your project.

eCommerce Search

Many organizations use the web as a means of reaching customers and consumers. If your search project is to be deployed in an environment where you are directly selling a product or service, you have special needs and capabilities, and planning requires participation from the group in your organization whose responsibility it is to market and sell your products.

eCommerce sites many people use include Amazon.com, Dell.com, and LandsEnd.com, and these all utilize web-facing Enterprise Search to power their sites and their business.

Search is a powerful tool in an eCommerce environment: not only does search show products that meet the end user's requirements, but it also delivers suggestions for related products, can upsell by suggesting related products, and delivers the "people like you" functionality that is often used on large Internet sites.

Relevance in eCommerce applications is different than relevance in most other search environments. Rather than deliver results that are most popular or that contain the highest frequency of the search terms provided by the user, eCommerce search has to consider, first, whether a particular product is in stock (and hence can be sold immediately). Second, eCommerce relevancy evaluates the margin on each item, typically displaying the item(s) with the largest margin at the top of the result list. Finally, the products displayed have to meet the user's requirements. Let's see how this works in practice.

Suppose that I am looking for a high-resolution digital camera. I start my search by typing "5 megapixel camera." The search engine has to first retrieve all products that meet my requirements, but a smart company will also include related products in the results. This smart retailer, however, will not include products that it cannot sell to me today, because if the consumer has to wait, he or she may decide to look at a competitor's site to get something right now. This smart eCommerce company will also show the consumer cameras with both higher and lower resolution, especially if the price might be attractive. Finally, before displaying the list of products, the search engine sorts the results based on the margin the eCommerce site gets from the manufacturer on each product, so that the product with the highest profit margin will rank highest.

To begin an implementation plan for eCommerce search, it's clear that having a capable product is not sufficient. You need access to a number of systems throughout the organization, and you should make sure that the departments that control those systems are tightly involved with your project plan. Some of the resources you will need may include:

➤ Inventory management, order processing, and purchasing systems

➤ Business line managers and staff

➤ Executive management and staff

➤ IT and operations specialists

➤ Application and search developers

➤ Web design specialists

➤ Product specialists

Intranet and Extranet Search

Companies are seeing growth in the amount of digital content they own, and this is the kind of data that makes up intranets and extranets.

Your intranet is where you store content intended for use only by your employees. It may include databases and content management systems such as SharePoint, CRM and accounting systems, and database, file shares on servers or even on company desktop and laptop computers.

Not all companies have extranets, which are usually an extension of the Internet site(s) that is visible to trusted customers, partners, and consultants who work closely with the company. This may be a secure site, where trusted nonemployees can enter and track orders or support requests, or otherwise have access to data that is not available to the general public.

Some characteristics of intranet and extranet content that makes it different — and sometimes harder to search well — include the following:

➤ **Security** — One thing that is unique to intranet and extranet content is that it is almost always content that should not be visible to the public. In fact, there may be different access levels within the company: managers may have access to content not meant for general consumption; there may be regulatory restrictions on content such as pending mergers, financial reports, and legal issues.

➤ **File formats** — While most of the public web textual content is HTML or PDF, inside the corporation there are often a significant number of different file formats, including Microsoft Office, text files, and many others. If you've had your intranets running for a few years, you probably have archival content in file formats that are no longer supported and that may be hard to access. These may include WordPerfect, VisiCalc, and even WordStar if you go back far enough.

Although public search engines are beginning to do a better job when they find these other formats, Enterprise Search engines have to display results in high fidelity, even within a browser.

➤ **Database content** — Much of corporate content is maintained in databases. They may be customer relationship management, order processing, or customer support systems; in any case, Enterprise Search has to understand not only the raw format, it has to understand the nature of the data to search logical documents, not just database rows.

➤ **Special vocabularies** — Chances are your corporation uses a special vocabulary that may include things like divisions, procedure names, or special acronyms that have meaning to employees but are not part of standard vocabularies that public search engines understand.

Enterprise Search, on the other hand, has to recognize these special terms, recognize potential misspellings, and even treat them as entities that may need to be extracted for advanced features like faceted navigation.

➤ **Unique content** — on the Internet, thousands of sites will often have content that addresses the same topic. If Google or Bing miss a few hundred sites, or a few thousands pages, it's no big deal; there are plenty more just like them. In the enterprise, however, there is only one current annual report, final project plan, or lunch menu, and there is typically only one corporate HR site. If an Enterprise Search engine misses the right content, employees become frustrated with search.

As you can see, Enterprise Search is more difficult to implement than Internet search in a number of ways. The good news is context: in the enterprise, you know more about the person doing the search, more about the content repositories, and more about the vocabulary in use.

To begin an implementation plan for intranet or extranet search, you'll need access to a number of systems throughout the organization. As with eCommerce search, you'll want to involve other groups within your company with your project plan. Some of the skills you will need may include:

➤ Business line managers and staff

➤ Executive management and staff

➤ IT and operations specialists

➤ Application and search developers

➤ Web design specialists

➤ Product specialists

File Share Search

Most people think of file share search as a subset of intranet search, but it has enough unique characteristics that we're covering it here as its own topic. Many people think of file shares as a bit out of date, given the growing acceptance of formal content management systems such as SharePoint. Nonetheless, many of the companies we work with provide a network directory for their employees to use in lieu of their local disk drives. Some benefits of these network directories feature automated nightly backups, which are generally not available for local drives, and they provide the capability for employees to access their files no matter which workstation they may want to connect from, not just from their desks.

Some file shares are archival in nature and contain hundreds or thousands of files. A number of companies continue to use Novell NetWare and Open Enterprise Server, as well as other commercial and open source products, and these are typical of the types of file shares that companies want to search-enable.

Some of the characteristics of network drives and file shares that make them challenging for Enterprise Search include:

➤ **Poor metadata** — On the Internet, content owners add metadata so search engines can find it. Enterprise software often allows users to add simple complete metadata to documents — Microsoft Word, for example, lets you add author, subject, and other properties to help Enterprise Search find the content. Unfortunately, many employees don't go to the trouble of adding useful and meaningful metadata. In fact, much enterprise content has the wrong metadata: rather than start with a new, blank document, many employees will often start with a copy of a previous document. A sales presentation, for example, might start with a copy of a previous presentation with just a few slides changed to reflect the customer's name or requirements. Unfortunately, the metadata from the previous presentation stays with the new one, which has the effect of making the document more difficult to find.

➤ **File-based security** — Unlike content management systems or databases, files on network drives are often protected by simple file system security. Depending on the way an Enterprise Search product handles security, this could lead to less-than-desirable performance at search time.

➤ **Duplicate content** — As if the problem of unique content isn't tough enough, Enterprise Search also has to deal with identical, or nearly identical, content. If you're like most people, you may save three or more different versions of a report before you're finished with it, and an Enterprise Search has to find the right one when you search for it months later.

➤ **Wide variety of file formats** — One last characteristic of file shares is that they often contain older, archival content. This means that files may have been saved by programs that have been obsolete for years, or files may be in formats not supported by modern search technologies. Of course, because network drives tend to not run out of space, these file shares are also used to store content that is only now becoming supported by Enterprise Search, including video and audio content. In both cases, it's hard for many search products to handle these varied file formats well.

Public Site Search

A final element of Enterprise Search that we'll address here is the search that companies operate on their own web properties. These public-facing sites each have their own challenges: companies use the public web to provide information to customers, prospects, investors, reporters, and even casual browsers. These people have widely divergent needs and interests, and some people — typically customers and investors — are willing to invest a great deal of time exploring your content. Other visitors, less vested in the relationship with your company, might spend no more than a few seconds; if they can't find what they are looking for, you lose them.

You'd think it would be easy to search-enable your public website. Most Internet websites generally contain HTM or HTML files (Hypertext Markup Language) or Adobe's PDF (Portable Document Format) files, and you've probably expended some effort to add meaningful descriptions, or metadata, to your content. After all, you want public web search engines to find your content. In fact, there is an entire industry providing help with this search engine optimization, known generically as search engine optimization (SEO).

The bad news is that the metadata you use to help Google and Bing find your site can often have a negative impact on your own search engine: SEO often tags virtually all of your content with terms about your site, not about the specific page. This lets companies find your site, but it can impact the ability of your own search engine to determine relevant content for a particular subject.

Tuning your own search technology is as important as the SEO you're doing; in fact, this enterprise effort is often called eSEO. Tuning for Enterprise Search technology is different, however, and many companies spend far less time and money tuning their own content. The problem can be solved, but it takes effort: Enterprise Search is not a "fire-and-forget" technology.

To begin an implementation plan for public site search, you'll need access to a number of systems throughout the organization. As with other Enterprise Search applications, you'll want to involve other groups within your company with your project plan. Some of those with the skills you will need may include the following:

➤ Business line managers and staff

➤ Executive management and staff

➤ IT and operations specialists

➤ Application and search developers

➤ Web design specialists

➤ Usability specialists

➤ Product marketing

➤ Corporate legal

➤ SEO and eSEO specialists

➤ Analytics specialists

ORGANIZING FOR SUCCESS: THE SEARCH CENTER OF EXCELLENCE

Many of the best companies have long used Centers of Excellence for infrastructure initiatives, and we've seen companies begin to form Search Centers of Excellence (SCOE), regardless of their management style. The SCOE can be a formal unit in the organization or be made up of distributed staff from a number of different departments who report informally to a SCOE manager. In both cases, the skills that go into making search work are the same. Chapter 1 provided some background into how Search Centers of Excellence have been organized, and some of the roles involved. In this section we'll talk about how SCOEs differ depending on the type of company and different problems search needs to solve.

Centers of Excellence

How companies choose to organize a SCOE depends on a number of variables, including the type of business, the size of the organization, and to some extent the company personality and management style.

Companies that use the web to make money — for example, eCommerce sites such as Amazon.com and Dell — organize an SCEO at a high level. The head of the SCOE is typically an executive of the company and often has the title of chief search officer.

Companies that use search as an infrastructure tool to make it easier to find content or to deflect customer service calls often organize a SCOE under the office of the CIO, either as a standalone unit or as part of IT. The head of the SEO typically reports to the IT manager or to the CIO.

There is one other twist in the way companies organize for success in search. When it comes to managing enterprise scale technology, every organization has its own style. Some large companies often manage — or attempt to manage — new technology initiatives centrally. This often enables technology standardization and efficient vendor price negotiations. It also facilitates the ability to maintain lessons learned and best practices.

Other companies distribute responsibility and authority to operating divisions, perhaps with limited support from corporate headquarters. This model enables each division to select the tools that best meet its disparate requirements, but at the cost of any critical mass when dealing with vendors, and lessons learned tend to remain in each division or business unit. This model can also increase company expenses, since there is often overlap of expertise across the organization.

Smaller organizations may not have a formal SCOE at all. In these cases, search is often one more responsibility for IT, perhaps with some limited input from marketing or sales.

Chapter 1 includes a discussion about the skills required in a successful SCOE. Since these skills are sometimes needed for only a brief period, or can be filled using outside consultants or staff from elsewhere in an organization, some companies are using a hybrid approach: the Virtual SCOE.

Building a Virtual SCOE

Unless your organization is large and centralized, you may wonder where you're going to find the resources to staff a new entity, the SCOE. Budgets are always tight, and justifying new bureaucracy is never easy.

The good news is that you may have all of the required skills in your organization: the trick may be to find the right people and bring them into the Virtual SCOE.

This Virtual SCOE can include people from all around your organization who can contribute to the SCOE on a part-time, dotted-line basis. You can also take advantage of trusted external consulting firms with specialized skills that can complement your internal staff. Together, these give your organization the benefit of a wide range of skills and viewpoints, and still meet the requirements of evaluating, selecting, implementing, and operating a world-class search operation.

THE PROCESS OF ACQUIRING A SEARCH PLATFORM

Once you have an idea of what kind of search you're looking for, and have organized a team to work with you, it's time to start considering the process you'll go through as you build the business case for search.

Building a Business Case

When reviewing capital purchase requests, the first thing most senior managers like to see is the financial return on investment (ROI). Sadly, this is one of the most difficult things to do when it comes to Enterprise Search. In almost all cases, the ROI for search is soft. For example, it improves employee productivity; it helps deflect customer service calls by enabling self-service; or it saves the company money. Unfortunately, there are no senior managers responsible for these nice "feel good" kinds of returns, so it's hard to justify search in hard currency.

About the only two areas of the company that can demonstrate hard ROI: eCommerce and regulatory/ compliance. Interestingly, both of these areas will often have a high level manager or VP whose job it is to worry about such things, and, more importantly, who has responsibility and budget.

Hard ROI

Let's start with the use cases that have hard justification. There are generally two types of hard ROI: a verifiable increase in sales and profitability or a hedge against potential legal issues in the event of a lawsuit or other investigation. Let's take a look at these two different scenarios.

eCommerce

If your company sells products on the Internet, you're a good candidate for an eCommerce search engine. What are the benefits?

➤ **Increased sales** — Your products are more visible, are easier for your customers to find, and are available to a worldwide audience, since your eCommerce website is selling 24x7. A caveat: you'll want an active SEO/ad placement/agency to push and promote your products and monitor the web to keep track of what people are saying, the buzz. It's not cheap but anything you can do to promote your products and understand how people react to them on the web is money well spent.

➤ **Higher profitability** — A successful eCommerce site doesn't replace a sales force on the phone — or in the field — taking orders, but a simple sales support call center can handle most of the heavy lifting. Consider successful eCommerce sites like Amazon.com, which handle just about all of the sales customer service electronically — no more rental cars or hotels to pay for.

➤ **Better understand your customer** — What do they buy and when? What do they buy together? The grocery industry generally has found that odd couples of products go together — for example, beer and diapers. What will you learn about your product line? Are your prospects price sensitive? Where do they live? How did they find you? There is an element of BI to track and use all this new data that can help you be even more profitable, but again, it's worth the extra cost to generate the additional revenue — and additional profit.

eDiscovery

The term eDiscovery covers a wide range of sins, and few people really understand what it means. Generally people use the term when they are considering search technology that can help the organization conform to and audit compliance with various government regulations, from Sarbanes-Oxley to various privacy and confidentiality requirements. The term is also used as a basis for providing a defense for an organization should it be sued by other parties: shareholders, competitors, suppliers, and vendors. eDiscovery can help your organization document discovery dates and internal communications about an alleged product design flaw, and help prove ownership and invention when your company needs to prove original discovery of new products or technologies.

eDiscovery, while sometimes considered a suitable application for Enterprise Search technology, encompasses a narrow range of requirements, and usually requires specific application capabilities provided by vertical applications based on search. Common search requirements in thorough eDiscovery environments include the ability to log all incoming and outgoing emails, any text messages from inside or outside the company, all electronic documents, and just about any digital assets an organization may have. Sometimes "light" eDiscovery can be handled by general Enterprise Search platforms, but enterprise-scale legal solutions provide much greater depth and application-specific solutions when it comes to eDiscovery, litigation support, Sarbanes-Oxley compliance, and other legal processes. These may well be best left to the specific applications that utilize search to provide the wide benefit of eDiscovery and compliance applications.

The Soft ROI

Soft ROI includes all the things you sense will occur but that you just can't prove in advance. You may hear arguments for search based on a soft ROI — soft because it's difficult, if not impossible, to prove. It's basically all the things you sense will come as a benefit of better search, but you can't be sure in advance. Search may well have merit: it's just that you cannot reliably expect to see some of the numbers that you may hear from some vendors and analysts.

One argument you may hear goes like this: Your employees spend half of their time searching for information. Since most employees report they find the right content only half of the time, each of your employees wastes two hours a day — 25% of their time! If your average employee cost is $100,000 a year, you can save $25,000 per employee per year. Multiply that by the 5,000 employees you have and you can see how this search product will save you $125 million dollars. All you need to do it buy this search engine. (Sign here.)

Don't! Not yet at least!

The problems here are many: Do your employees really spend four hours a day searching your corporate website? They may spend time searching, but we suspect that at least some of that time is looking through their paper files, or asking a coworker or manager for information. And if you have 5,000 employees, I suspect some folks are not the "knowledge workers" these numbers are often based on. After all, you have receptionists, a shipping department, drivers, and other employees who contribute to your bottom line but who don't depend on search 4 hours a day.

Because this kind of ROI is hard to calculate doesn't mean that you shouldn't try to figure out what impact great search will have on your bottom line. Soft ROI usually involves a few possible areas you can consider:

➤ **Enable customer self-service** — Deflect expensive calls that otherwise will require someone in your call center to spend time talking with your customers to solve a problem, modify an order, or answer a question before the order is placed. Great search won't eliminate your call center; but it may be that you can put those employees to more productive — and satisfying — use.

➤ **Expert finder** — Help employees find other people in your company who may have experience with an area of business. This works best when your company is geographically distributed and is one of the things people think of when they talk about "social search," which we discuss in Chapter 9.

➤ **Productivity improvements** — Even though we hope we've deflated some of the hype, great search will help your people — specifically those whose job is based on having access to your corporate knowledge: sales contracts, company policies and procedures, and marketing information. These folks are your knowledge workers, and they certainly should be represented when you're considering your search requirements. Who knows, you might also find they have more time to engage in activities that can impact your top line after all!

Defining Your Requirements

Defining your search requirements may seem pretty easy. Your boss probably has said something like "make our content easy to find" — an honorable objective. But when you are considering what you really need, you want to get into the details. If you don't know what you need to do with search, not only will you pay too much, but you may also find that you picked the wrong search.

The first things to do are to identify the scope of the project and document what you're using now. Many companies have acquired and implemented solutions like content management systems, customer relationship management systems, and even call center solutions. You'll need to determine whether your Enterprise Search initiative is to encompass all of these other systems or whether it will be sufficient to integrate the results from these external systems into your overall solution.

You'll also want to understand your users and their needs. Enterprise Search often covers a wide range of content, from the lunch menu at the headquarters cafeteria to molecular interactions and how they impact the efficacy of a new drug under test. Your users may type one or two simple words, or they may type complex questions and be quite comfortable with Boolean search operators.

How can you tell what the requirements are? Ask your users. Even better, organize a small Search Center of Excellence.

Remember: search touches everything in your organization. Search also grows beyond your initial expectation, however, and you'll find requirements and repositories long after you thought you had a complete understanding of what was needed. This means that growth and flexibility need to be part of your ultimate solution, so planning for it up front will save time and money later on.

An Overall Approach

The process of gathering requirements for a new search platform can differ depending on whether you are new to search, or whether your organization is replacing an existing operational platform.

In the former case, Enterprise Search may be an unknown quantity and your users — and management — may have expectations that far exceed the state of the technology. Worse still, your organization may have little in-house expertise, and you may find yourself susceptible to vendor hype. Working with a well-known partner is critical to your success; plan time to learn what you need and what is realistically available early on in the project.

In the latter case, your organization has been using search, so management and users know something about search. Sometimes search platforms are replaced for good reasons: the organization has outgrown the capacity of the technology, or the vendor no longer supports the technology in use.

At other times, organizations replace an existing platform because it just doesn't work: the results are awful; no one can find anything; and content is missing. Maybe the relationship has deteriorated to the point where remaining with the vendor is not an option.

In both cases, your organization enters the selection process with a better understanding of the requirements for a new search platform, and you can take advantage of that knowledge in the evaluation process. However, if the new project is happening because of dissatisfaction with the current vendor, you may want to consider whether the differences are irreconcilable. Why?

The easy answer is that change is exciting. But before you cut the cord, consider that most modern Enterprise Search platforms have many comparable capabilities. If you look at the leading analyst's graphic vendor comparisons, you'll see most are very close. What makes you think that spending money to move a vendor whose product is side by side with your old vendor will make all the difference? Often, the difference between successful search and mediocre search is the implementation, not the technology.

Consider the sage wisdom seldom heard in real-world technology decisions: If you don't have the resources to make it work now, what makes you think you have the resources to do it over?

If the relationship is beyond salvation by all means look for a new vendor; but it can't hurt to invest time in trying to get it right before you jump. Gather all the learning and experience you can from your current implementation, and get it right next time around!

High-Level Questions

As you set out on your quest for a new search platform be aware that detailed planning is critical to your ultimate success. You have to satisfy a number of constituencies, often with conflicting requirements and expectations. This is one reason we encourage organizations to organize Search Centers of Excellence, so you can ensure all of these conflicting constituencies have representation and participate in the section. In the process, you will likely find requirements you had not considered and content sources that you were never aware of; including these in your final selection will help ensure the success of the project in the long term.

In this section, we'll look at the kinds of questions you will need to answer in three generalized areas: business requirements, technical requirements, and hybrid requirements that involve technical, business, and content issues. In the next section, we'll discuss the kinds of questions you need specific answers to by stakeholder.

Business Requirements

Your directive to make stuff easy to find is a bit too vague to be useful in the search selection process. Consider these questions as a starting point to the kinds of questions the search business owner should answer.

- ➤ What business problem(s) are you trying to solve? Some of the answers might include:
  - ➤ Reduce support costs
  - ➤ Improved productivity
  - ➤ Increased sales
  - ➤ More effective use of resources
- ➤ Who will be the primary users? Identify for each unique search application you intend to deploy:
  - ➤ Customers
  - ➤ Company sales team

- ➤ Company employees

- ➤ Research and development staff

- ➤ Partners

➤ What do they expect to find with the search application? This may vary among different search applications deployed.

- ➤ (Specific) known content and reports

- ➤ Tech support, internal and external

- ➤ Internal proposals and sales quotations

- ➤ Product features, capabilities, and prices

- ➤ Company financials

- ➤ Company policies and procedures

- ➤ Awareness of subject matter experts in the organization

➤ What is the risk of not finding content? Answers to these can help identify the real drivers behind search.

- ➤ Lost sales

- ➤ Duplicate effort throughout the organization

- ➤ Unsatisfied customers, employees, partners

- ➤ Liability exposure

➤ What resources will you have in each stage of the project? Ensure that funding is planned for the entire project lifecycle.

- ➤ Investigation/requirements

- ➤ Vendor evaluation and selection

- ➤ Proof of concept

- ➤ Licensing

- ➤ Training costs

- ➤ Development of the search application(s)

- ➤ Hardware and infrastructure

- ➤ Deployment

- ➤ Ongoing vendor support

- ➤ Funding for SCOE search team

This entire process is easier for organizations already using Enterprise Search, but to be safe, survey your users, business line owners, content owners, and IT staff to verify your experience. Find out what works and what does not.

Technical Requirements

In the same way that you have business drivers for search, there are technical drivers to be considered and understood. Typically the IT and development resources on your SCOE can help provide answers to these topics.

- Platform: The systems your infrastructure uses:
  - Hardware
  - Operating system
  - Virtual or physical systems
  - Preferred programming language and environment
- Data repositories: Systems that impact your enterprise content
- Database and CMS systems
- Web servers and file shares
- Security infrastructure and settings
- Differences in security across various content sources
- Current search environment: The following statistics from your current search platform can also be quite helpful as you evaluate new solutions:
  - How much content is indexed
  - What document formats are searchable and in what proportion
  - What is the peak and average query activity?
  - How often do documents change (adds/updates/deletes)?
  - Search activity reports: top queries; no hits results
  - Synonyms and thesauri in use
  - Any taxonomies in use
  - Current maintenance and support costs
  - Network topology (failover, load balancing, and so on)

Note that from a search point of view, a simple change to a single metadata field may require a full reindex of the document; for large documents that may introduce load on the server.

Hybrid Requirements

Some of the requirements that impact your Enterprise Search selection cross traditional areas of responsibility, and often are the area that a SCOE can make the largest contribution to success. You'll find a sample of the type of content you should gather in Figure 2-1. The content is discussed in the following list:

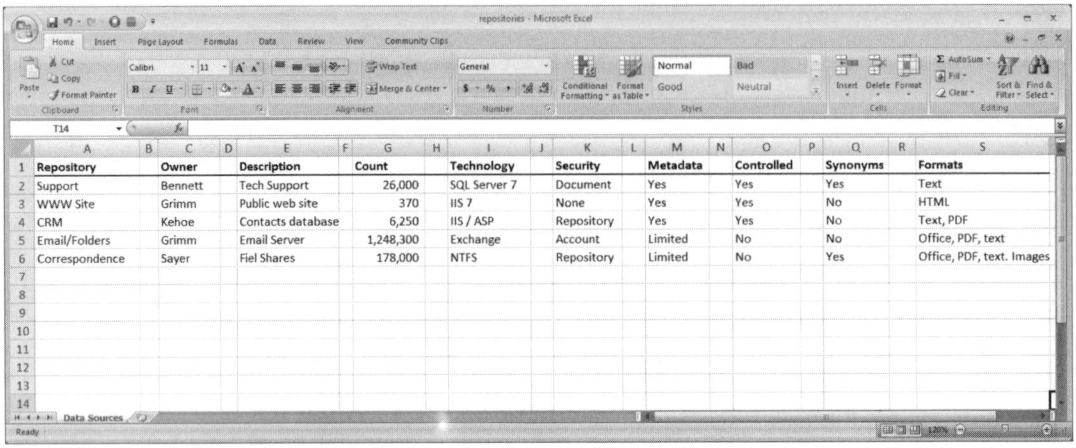

Repository	Owner	Description	Count	Technology	Security	Metadata	Controlled	Synonyms	Formats
Support	Bennett	Tech Support	26,000	SQL Server 7	Document	Yes	Yes	Yes	Text
WWW Site	Grimm	Public web site	370	IIS 7	None	Yes	Yes	No	HTML
CRM	Kehoe	Contacts database	6,250	IIS / ASP	Repository	Yes	Yes	No	Text, PDF
Email/Folders	Grimm	Email Server	1,248,300	Exchange	Account	Limited	No	No	Office, PDF, text
Correspondence	Sayer	Fiel Shares	178,000	NTFS	Repository	Limited	No	Yes	Office, PDF, text. Images

FIGURE 2-1

> **Repository information** — The left column contains the name, owner, and description of the repositories to be search-enabled. The columns correspond to the information that needs to be captured for each repository, critical in planning your Enterprise Search implementation.

> Why it's important — This exercise ensures that you identify all the content that needs to be search-enabled. It's not as easy as it might seem; we've actually sees implementations within large organizations where significant new sources of content were discovered during the initial content crawl and the differences in the new repositories required re-working of the original data scope.

> **Document properties** — Document Count is the next field in this simplified spreadsheet. Some other properties you may want to capture include the following:

>> Average document size and/or the size of each document.

>> How often does the content change: monthly, weekly, daily, or hourly?

>> Index latency: how quickly after an update does the search index need to reflect the change?

Knowing the document count may be required in licensing for some vendors, and it provides a metric by which you can measure the success of each search engine in your proof of concept. The IT and content staffs can also use this number, updated over time, to confirm that the full content repository is indexed properly.

The document size can be critical because some search engines have hard limits on how large the files can be that it will index; and others will not index all of a large document by default. The average size lets you determine the license cost for search engines that charge by total document repository size.

The latency can be important in some cases. The document churn — how often documents change in average — can have an impact on index time, which can then impact latency, the delay between a document being added, updated, or deleted until it is searchable.

One organization that was in a quite public legal battle over a patent dispute wanted to push its spin on each legal milestone as it happened; to them, having a new press release that presented their interpretation of the consequences of each finding was critical. If the new document took 24 hours to be visible, that represented a major concern to the legal team.

➤ **Security** — Information about the type of security and identity verification can be critical in maintained corporate data security and access. In Figure 2-1, only the type of security is shown, including Document, Repository and login Account level access. In a more complex environment, the list may include cookies, policy-based authentication, and single sign on (SSO), or other challenge-response methods.

Why it's important: The organization has implemented security for a reason: not everyone may have access. Poor security on content including corporate financials, HR records, and future product schedules may have financial, legal, and regulatory consequences for companies. And security has to extend to recommendations as well as to refiners and facets: A search result reporting zero of 1 document about an IPO pretty much violates security, even if the document itself is never displayed. And a sales by region query that shows sales range facets for an upcoming quarterly report may violate SEC regulations, even if no actual documents are displayed.

➤ **Metadata, Controlled Vocabulary, and Synonyms** — Companies go to great lengths to provide accurate metadata for content in corporate content management systems (CMS). Some fields allow free-form input by entry personnel; while others require metadata be selected from a pull-down list, controlling the values for each field. Some organizations even allow search users to enter metadata, a process usually known as document tagging.

Why it's important: If you have high quality metadata, not only are you the exception, but you're ahead. Companies also apply structured taxonomies to their content, often in an attempt to improve search results or to offer an alternate method of browsing content (by category). Synonyms are used at either index time (good) or at query time (bad) to expand the user query to include related synonymous terms: a search for "vacation schedule" might also return documents with the phrase "holiday schedule."

Note that these methodologies are likely to increase the number of documents returned from any given query which may harm more than help. For example, if thousands of docs are tagged "Important," is that a good way to limit search?

User tagging — a popular aspect of social search — lets users provide terms that they believe are relevant to a particular document. While the technology has proven widely popular on the Internet as a whole, within the organization there just may not be enough users tagging content to make it valuable for retrieval except in a few cases.

➤ **Document Formats** — Understanding the types of content that need to be searchable lets you select a search platform that provides support for your top content formats, ensuring that all of your documents can be properly searched. Some typical file formats include:

➤ Office formats (Word, Excel, PowerPoint, etc.)

➤ PDF

➤ Text

➤ Scanned images and documents

➤ HTML/XML

➤ Images/Video

Enterprise Search technologies perform search on textual content, so search platform has to convert your content format, often binary (i.e., Office, etc.) into a stream of text. If your content includes scanned documents, you have two additional potential issues: scanned images that are not processed through optical character recognition (OCR) are generally not full-text searchable. Instead, only keywords entered to your content management system will retrieve the document. The scanning process for large volumes of archival data is expensive: be sure to include OCR for each document as well for which the incremental cost is minimal.

Note that even OCR'd documents present an issue: depending on the quality of the source document, the OCR process may convert some letters and numbers. For example, it is not uncommon for an OCR file to treat the letters "o" and "l" as the digits zero and one. Hence you may find words that can be read by a user are not useful within search. Some search platforms handle this better than others; and there are ways to try to get around the problem by using synonyms. Still, having high quality OCR is worth the effort for archival search content.

One last point: if you're going to enable video or multimedia content, can it find scenes? Imagine the frustration of retrieving a large document and not being able to find the search terms you used until the very end of this large document. Video and audio content without scenes dooms the user to viewing or listening to minutes — or more — of content before knowing whether it is really relevant.

Stakeholders

The stakeholders in any technology implementation are the groups that share the responsibility and often the benefits of the implementation. The actual staff in each of the following categories of stakeholders might change between different search applications, but the responsibilities and interests are typically the same.

Business Case Owner

In successful implementations of Enterprise Search, the person representing the business case for search often assumes the lead in the process of evaluation, selection, and ongoing operations of the search application. Working with other key stakeholders, the business case owner helps define requirements and typically defines the user experience, the data sources and indexing requirements, and the ongoing operation of the search application.

One key question the business case owner needs to address is whether a single search front end will be sufficient for all users, such as on a storefront? Or will some advanced users need specialized search interfaces? For example, customers may search the knowledge base with a simple user interface, but tech support engineers, who use the system all day, might need more options, or have the search embedded inside of the case management system.

For the user experience, some of the decisions to be managed by the business case owner include:

➤ The search application:

  ➤ Is it a program that needs to be installed is or/it an embedded application inside of an existing application or portal?

  ➤ Is it a web-based application accessed via a standard browser?

- The search form:
    - Is it a simple search box or an advanced search form?
    - Do all users see the same form by default?
- The results list:
    - Is the layout fixed, or can users customize the layout to suit their preferences?
    - Are the document summaries — the "teasers" — static or dynamic and contextual?
    - Should search terms be highlighted in the result list?
    - Are there refiners/facets? Are they deep refiners showing facets for all documents, or shallow refiners showing facets that apply only to the current result set?
- Viewing documents:
    - When a user opens a document, does it open in the native application or does it display in the application windows/browser?
    - If displayed in the browser, does it need to look as much like the native document as possible?
    - Should search terms be highlighted in the viewer?
    - Can the user jump from term to term in the document?
    - Can the user provide tags associated with the document?
- Language support:
    - What languages need to be supported for user input?
    - Are users expecting search in one language to return documents in only that language, or in all languages?

When it comes to the data sources and indexing requirements, the business case owner has to address the following:

- Index latency:
    - How soon after a document is added or modified does it need to be searchable?
    - Do documents need to be removed from the index when your organization's document retention period is reached?
- Data sources:
    - What repositories should be indexed in each search application?
    - Do you need to federate content from other sources?
    - How does the user authenticate to confirm security is maintained?

Finally, the operational issues the business case owner must settle include the following:

- Ongoing management:
    - Does the search technology support distributed management?

➤ Can site owners control best bets and vocabulary for their own sites?

➤ Can a site owner add search to a website without central assistance?

➤ Are there controls that site managers can use to modify relevance models, or is programming required?

➤ Quality of service (QOS):

➤ What is the cost of search being down?

➤ Does search require multiple geographically distributed sites?

➤ What level of support is required from the search vendor? Form the implementation partner?

➤ Best bets:

➤ How do you implement best bets?

➤ Can they be defined for specific time periods (useful within organizations besides for simply eCommerce)?

➤ Are clicks on a best bet recorded in search reports? Should they be?

➤ Reporting:

➤ What reports are needed beyond top queries and "no hits"?

➤ How do you solve "no hits" if the users apply different vocabulary than your site implements (misspelled terms, and so on)?

➤ Can you track user behavior through your site including searches and documents viewed?

➤ Can you identify and adjust for seasonal variations in the type of search activity?

➤ Can you create a best bet directly from the activity reports?

Content Owner

Organizations often have groups specifically responsible for the content, whether it is for the corporate intranet, public web site, or a content management system (CMS). For each search application, the group that has responsibility will need to be involved to ensure success. There may be some overlap with other areas, but some of the issues that need to be addressed by the content owner include:

➤ Document language:

➤ What languages are used in the content repository?

➤ Are there documents that are essentially duplicates written in different languages?

➤ Access:

➤ Which documents are public and which require secure access?

➤ Is access based on an access control list (ACL)?

➤ Metadata:

> ➤ What repositories have quality metadata?
>
> ➤ Is there a controlled vocabulary for tagging documents?
>
> ➤ What metadata is available in each document and/or repository?
>
> ➤ How is metadata added to content?
>
> ➤ Who decides what metadata terms to apply to each document?
>
> ➤ What date formats are used?
>
> ➤ Are there multiple date fields? (i.e., create date, publish date, archive date)
>
> ➤ Are the document date(s) accurate?
>
> ➤ How does metadata for public web SEO impact the internal search relevancy?

➤ Index coverage:

> ➤ How many documents are in each repository? Are they searchable?
>
> ➤ What security level should apply to each document?
>
> ➤ How do you use search activity reports to identify missing or unclear content?

IT/Development

The IT staff in most organizations is responsible for infrastructure and sometimes for developing and implementing new technologies. As such, when it comes to Enterprise Search, development and IT have responsibilities to be acknowledged and assumed. Some of these include:

➤ Technology:

> ➤ What platforms are supported?
>
> ➤ What development language and environment are supported?
>
> ➤ How does search interact with monitoring systems?
>
> ➤ How does the technology scale? What are its limits?

➤ Security:

> ➤ Is security implemented at index time (early binding) or at search time (late binding)? Is security a hybrid of both?
>
> ➤ How does the search platform interact with security infrastructure at index time? Cookies? Active Directory?

➤ Operations:

> ➤ How can monitoring systems report index problems?
>
> ➤ Are document deleted when a page is no longer available? What happens if a web server is down temporarily when the indexer runs?

➤ What level of support do the vendor and partner offer, and what level do similar companies require? 5x8? 7x24?

➤ How does the organization grow the infrastructure as content and search applications grow?

➤ What licensing options are available as search applications grow?

➤ What is the ratio between source data size and index size, and what variables impact this ratio?

➤ Can the system be backed up or replicated while search and indexing are live?

➤ Quality of service:

➤ What QOS does the vendor claim to provide?

➤ Does it support load balancing?

➤ Can the search platform index and search at the same time?

➤ Does concurrent indexing impact search performance?

➤ Does system performance degrade during indexing?

➤ Do the licensing costs vary based on how the systems are set up (i.e., failover versus load balancing)?

➤ What symptoms tell operations that something is wrong?

Senior Management

Because search acquisitions are often implemented across the enterprise, senior management is often involved in the process if for nothing more than purchasing approval. They will be involved, sometimes actively, in the search selection and roll-out process, so addressing their questions up front will help the SCOE and search succeed.

Senior management questions typically include questions like:

➤ Business success:

➤ How will this technology be a strategic advantage in our primary businesses?

➤ How will we measure success three months after deployment? After one year?

➤ Is this product from a company that will be a long term technology partner?

➤ Are there other options or technologies to accomplish the same objectives? Why are we picking this one?

➤ Infrastructure/corporate plans:

➤ Does this technology align with our long term requirements?

➤ Is the staffing required to operate and manage this technology reasonable given current budget constraints?

➤ Cost:

    ➤ Is a perpetual license better than a term license for our organization and budget?

    ➤ What is the ratio of initial license and fees versus the overall total cost of ownership (TCO)?

The Role of Analysts

Many companies maintain relationships with large industry analyst firms for advice when it comes to big-budget projects like Enterprise Search. Most of these firms have excellent people who know the market and who talk with vendors and other companies who are implementing solutions. These analysts work hard to deliver good value, but remember that most analysis firms are paid by vendors and by clients like you. Recently, there was a lawsuit against an analyst firm by a vendor who claims the ratings are not based on technological capabilities but on revenue and market presence. Ironically, the analysis firm's initial defense is that they are just reporting the facts and don't claim their report is qualitative in any way — a significantly different position than their sales literature takes.

Some analyst firms fund their business based on subscribed revenue only and do not accept payment from vendors. This approach, which sounds more altruistic, doesn't guarantee more reliable information, but it helps. We like to see companies take advantage of analyst firms that have active implementation teams as well.

All analysis firms are different; make sure you're comfortable with the one you select, and make sure you understand where they make their money. Buyer beware.

Priorities

As you gather your list of requirements, try to get an idea of the relative priority for each of them. When you begin to look at solutions and implementations, you may find many of your requirements are standard features; others require some customization, and others still may require extensive programming and effort to make work. With a list of priorities up front, you'll have a much better idea of where you need to spend your budget and where you can take a pass.

For each feature on your list, include a priority — consider must have, nice to have, and will not need. Also since chances are good that your implementation will take place in two or more phases, indicate in which stage of the implementation process you'd like to see each feature implemented. And be concise regarding each feature or capability so you and your implementation team will not have any misunderstandings.

Pre-Enterprise Search

Some leading analysts are beginning to see that some clients are just not ready for full Enterprise Search solutions. In some cases, their content is not organized in a way that supports the kinds of integration Enterprise Search needs to be a competitive advantage. Other companies don't appreciate the effort that is required for a full-blown Enterprise Search platform. Still others may just benefit from some initial departmental search initiatives before jumping in all the way.

Microsoft offers two different search technologies that are pretty well integrated yet provide different levels of complexity. As part of your implementation, you may want to consider pilot projects to build up expertise in-house and give your SCOE time to build up internal best practices, implementation skills, and an understanding of what search can and cannot do for you. Search will grow far beyond its original application, and having that experience in-house will help ensure you're not the company that goes out to buy the magic beans some companies will sell you.

Plan for a Staged Implementation

Few large enterprise systems — and even fewer successful enterprise deployments — roll out all at once. In the same way you've prioritized the feature set and capabilities, you should also have an idea of which repositories will come up in what order. Some companies like to roll out a smaller application first, so they can get a better idea of implementation, work with users in small groups, and design a solution that may evolve based on user feedback and accumulated experience with the product. In the computer programming world, this technique is known as agile programming: on a fixed development schedule, design a capability, roll it out to test, and gather feedback. It sounds like it's more difficult to manage these kinds of projects, but an experienced team can actually create better final code in less time with happier users than the code produced in monolithic projects managed centrally to specifications defined in advance.

Creating the RFI or RFP

Whether you use a single vendor for all your technology needs, or use the best vendor for each technology you acquire, one of the first things you'll want to do is prepare a written Request for Information (RFI) and/or a Request for Proposal (RFP). Either way, do your homework with the help of a vendor-neutral company that can help you understand what features you can expect from a modern Enterprise Search platform and help map your requirements into the language the search vendors use. Whether you will work with a specific vendor or issue an RFI or an RFP, you know you're asking for the right response to your requirements in the language they will understand.

An RFI, in specific terms, defines your Enterprise Search requirements and asks potential vendors to provide you with a solution that will meet your needs. Generally speaking, an RFI is not asking for a firm price quotation, but it should include some ballpark pricing information that can help you determine which requirements are cost-effective and which might be overkill.

After you review the responses from vendors, you would typically issue a request for formal proposal — the RFP. Really, an RFI and an RFP are quite similar in scope and purpose, but the RFP is typically asking for a specific product and services price to implement each of your requirements. Some companies may find the RFP is the only document they need, but some organizations may have regulatory requirements that dictate an RFI precede an RFP, while other organizations just like to window shop before they buy.

We encourage you to keep license and implementation distinct. Few vendors have large in-house consulting groups, so there's some chance that the implementation team your vendor brings in is actually from one of their smaller partner companies. While the vendor will stand behind their work, hiring an independent implementation team makes sense for a couple of reasons. First, you usually pay a high markup on the implementation costs, and you can probably hire a team with comparable skills — perhaps even the same team of individuals — for much less money by negotiating with a third-party implementation team directly. The other benefit is that an implementation team working directly for the vendor is generally unable to advise a solution that may not include a product the vendor offers. We actually saw this not too long ago, where the software vendor was selling a solution that had a major bug in interfacing to infrastructure. The vendor proposed waiting 6 months for a solution, whereas the independent implementation provider was able to write a custom connector to the infrastructure that met the customer's needs for much less money and was able to deliver it in weeks. The customer met their original roll-out date, and saved a few thousand dollars on the final solution.

Collecting Your Content

Most organizations that want to implement Enterprise Search don't spend much time worrying about the nature of the content they have. Companies tend to have a number of data repositories — web servers, content management systems, databases — and leave it at that.

Because search touches everything, if you've got anything unusual in any of your repositories, search will find it and cause pain. In this section, we'll point out some of the more common problems and what you can do to avoid the suffering that many of your peers in the industry have experienced.

Identify Your Content and Repositories

Depending on your role, it may be tough to figure out all of the repositories in your organization. The good news is that content repository initiatives are typically big events and known to most people in the organization. Here we're looking for any software that stores, manages, or provides access to documents. You may be looking for databases like SQL Server, Oracle, or MySQL, or commercial content management systems like SharePoint or Documentum. IT and purchasing staff can be useful sources of information, as can the folks you've been talking with about your Search Center of Excellence.

When you begin using an Enterprise Search platform, ideally, you include all your enterprise content in the search index. However, there are some content repositories you won't want to — or cannot — index. Some sources include obsolete content, or content beyond your organization's retention policy. You may even find some repositories have a content owner who is uncomfortable with having an index of their content outside of their control. Finally, you may have some external content — say a content publisher — where you have rights only to view the material.

In these cases, you may be able to combine results from these sources into your search result lists by using a process called federation.

Understanding Your Users and Their Needs

An important element in the success of your Enterprise Search initiative is your ability to provide access to the documents that your users need to find. This means that before you can really understand the repositories you need to include, you have to know what your users want. This means that you need to identify your eventual users, talk to them about what kinds of information they need to do their jobs, and understand where they go to get the answers now.

If you are charged with bringing up your first Enterprise Search initiative, you are facing an exciting and challenging opportunity. Users will no doubt be excited to have the opportunity to find the content they need to do their work electronically. On the other hand, they may have very high expectations — perhaps too high — based on their favorable experiences using web search technology. Users tend to see the great results but don't realize the effort and attention — not to mention daily monitoring — that goes into running a successful public search engine.

If you are replacing an existing search technology or combining several search applications into a single instance, you already have good starting point. Identify top users and talk with them. Find out what they are usually looking for, whether they are successful in finding it, and what additional content and capabilities would make their jobs easier. At the same time, see if you can identify groups or departments that are underutilizing the current search technology, and talk to users in those areas. It may be that search isn't that important to them, but it may just be that the content they need isn't available through search or that their experience with poor search has lead them to find alternative strategies to find the information they need.

It may seem counterintuitive, but Enterprise Search is harder than web search. Consider a few points we've made earlier in the chapter:

➤ On the web, there are thousands, and perhaps even millions, of sites on any subject you can imagine. On your intranet, there may well be a single document that contains the information a user needs. Miss that one document and your search sucks.

➤ The people who run those public websites spend significant money and effort making their content easy for the search engines to find. Users who create much of the content you'll find indexed by Enterprise Search tend to ignore metadata, and in fact, often have wrong metadata in their documents. While formal content management systems typically do better, enterprise metadata has a long way to go.

➤ On the public web, content wants to be free, but organizations require levels of security. Managers can see salary data, but only for their own employees. Access to preliminary financial information is limited by law, and a publicly traded company violates the law — with severe penalties — if the information is made public prior to formal public disclosure.

Our point is that you need to manage your users' expectations. Search is not going to blow your users away unless you put ongoing time and effort into making it great. Also, remember that an active and participating user community is a plus for your initiative, and you may consider inviting some representative folks to join your SCOE.

The Acquisition Process

When you've completed your business plan and researched the data stores and requirements you have, it's time to begin the process of acquiring search. This often involves meeting with companies that sell and implement search. If you don't know what you need, you risk picking a company that may not be able to deliver what you really need. Worse, you may start the project and find out you've built a solution that doesn't meet your requirements, and you'll have to start over at significantly higher cost. We've got your answers here.

Meeting with Suppliers

After you have defined your requirements, it's time to find a company that can deliver a solution. You will have certainly identified likely software vendors as you worked with analysts or search consulting firms, or just attended a trade show or two.

If you are in a large organization, you may find your IT department already has established relationships with one or more of the vendors, which can often be a help in getting things done. If, on the other hand, your organization is small, it may be more difficult to get the attention of large software vendors. There are at least two solutions you might try.

First, ask the search software vendors to put you in touch with a partner who can help you select and implement your solution. Most have working relationships with a number of local and national partners, and they would be happy to introduce you to one. Remember, you're sending your RFI/RFP out to a few firms, so you should be able to get a decent cross-section of the market.

A second choice is to find a search consulting firm that works with many different vendors. That's harder to do, because software vendors like partners to work exclusively with them, but remember, it's your money.

One thing coauthor Mark Bennett has said hits home: "If you want to buy magic beans, there are a lot of vendors out there willing to sell them to you."

The Proof of Concept

When you're evaluating vendors and partners, you're likely to see a number of cool demos that show off the capabilities of the search engine, whether your requirements are relatively straightforward or quite complex. Remember, no matter how flashy a demo you may see, if the product doesn't meet your requirements, it's not going to do the job. While you want a technology that can grow with you, if a product exceeds your requirements, you may end up paying for cool you won't use.

The other thing to be aware of is best summed up in a warning we can confirm is true: "Any sufficiently advanced demo is indistinguishable from product." Even if the company doing the demo is a long-trusted partner, you want to be sure that the software will work great in your environment. The proof of concept, or POC, is going to give you an idea of what you can expect with the product using your content.

 Differences between technologies often reveal themselves when it comes to accessing data stores, dealing with security, and integrating with other applications. A POC helps insure that you will understand how the candidate technology will work in your environment.

Now, few companies are in the business of doing work for free. If your search application is simple — say indexing a public website — you may find your potential vendor is willing to do the POC for free. If your environment is complex, however, or has special security or indexing requirements, or if you want a complex, customer search interface, it's not unreasonable for a vendor to ask for a paid POC. Since complex search applications can be expensive, spending a small sum in advance that will demonstrate that your new search application will meet your needs is a worthwhile investment.

If your requirements are complex, or include custom indexing or search interfaces, the POC may well include much of your eventual application. You may find it helpful to negotiate the POC as part of the overall sale.

Clearly define the scope of the POC, and define acceptance criteria so you and your vendor will know when you've got sufficient confidence to go ahead and make the purchase. Don't hesitate to include failure criteria as well, so that there will be no question as to whether the POC met or failed to meet your expectations.

Negotiating the Purchase

Even if software license is fixed, few search installations are trivial and there will probably be some customization, and this may give you room to negotiate a better total cost. You may even seek out bids from one or two vendors, as long as they are equally qualified to deliver the solution you want. Remember, if you use price as the only measure, you may find that quality suffers and your project ends up less successful than you had expected.

Gathering Information: Training and References

Search is not a fire-and-forget technology. It may look easy on the public web, but you don't see all the work Microsoft, Google, Yahoo!, and others put into making your Internet search experience a good one.

Buying and deploying your application is only the first step in a long process of having a successful search implementation. Search applications have lots of dials and levers, and you want to adjust then from time to time to keep search in top shape. Find a company that's happy with its search, and you'll find a company that mines search activity and performance periodically to keep it in top shape.

Learning how to manage search takes knowledge, and most companies find that training is the best way to come up to speed. Talk with your vendor before you buy, and make sure that you'll get the right kind of training for your staff. There is a good argument for sending your staff to training even before you buy: you'll be amazed what you can learn about a product in a class with people from other companies that have implemented search already, and that knowledge may pay off for you.

Remember when you spend a week in class, you've got a theoretical understanding of the basics on which you can make smart choices, but that knowledge cannot compare to real-world experience you'll pick up as you implement and manage the search technology. Make sure that you've got help from your vendor while you build up that expertise in house.

Make sure that your implementation vendor will provide transfer of information (TOI) as part of the implementation engagement that covers both the base product and any customizations they may have included. In addition, when you've finished the project, plan on sending a few more folks to basic and advanced training to make sure that you have deep, real-world understanding of the search technology.

PLANNING YOUR DEPLOYMENT

Once the acquisition process is complete, it's time to get started on the implementation and deployment. Your vendor may have proposed that they participate in the implementation, or you may be doing the work yourself in-house, but successful deployments present a new set of options and decisions.

We like to use an implementation philosophy that is modeled on agile development practices. Certainly start with a plan, but as soon as the software is up and running, we like to get the content indexed. This serves a couple of purposes:

➤ It validates your content survey and helps identify any unexpected content problems up front. Maybe a data repository, or part of it, requires unique security that never came up in the content survey. Maybe there are links between tables that are handled by views in your database system but that don't work quite the same for your search technology.

➤ A quick index of all your content provides a way to show your management team that you're making progress. After spending all that money, managers like to see some progress sooner rather than later. If you can show your management team that most of your enterprise content is searchable a week after installation, they feel better about the decision to spend money, and that usually makes your life much easier.

➤ Looking at default results helps you understand how the search engine's relevance works out of the box and lets your team start working on corporate vocabulary for a lightweight thesaurus, or for clustering, or just for boosting content.

➤ Once people can see progress, then you can get down to designing the user interface and other capabilities you'll want in the final product — after having already established credibility by having a working search even if it is a prototype. It buys you time.

Optimizing the Roll-Out

When your search is ready, employ a controlled roll-out. Pick a small group in the organization and ask them to start using the new search. Sit with them. Make them your new best friends. Talk with them. Listen to them. When you've made the tuning or cosmetic changes they suggested, go back and show them, and listen again.

Once you have one small group on your side, bring up another group or two. Spend time with them. Listen to them. Make changes.

After you have a group of users who have used your new search technology, you're ready for the big event: the roll-out. Actually, you're not. We favor the small, quiet roll-out. Far better to quietly add major new search capability to your site and let people find it themselves, than to roll it out with a big splash, only to find that it doesn't meet some users' needs. As in so many cases, slow and quiet trumps fast and furious.

Tuning Relevance

You want your Enterprise Search to return relevant documents for every query, but relevance is hard to define. Most people know it when they see it but have a hard time putting it into words.

Once you've seen your searches in action, you can start tuning the relevance engine in the search platform to produce better results. You may find relevance is different depending on the kinds of content people search for in different departments.

You can start by tuning for general content. For example, a research firm might have really high-quality abstracts with each document, so a query term that shows up in the abstract indicates a potentially relevant result. This kind of tuning is algorithmic in that it applies to all of your content, or at least to content in a single repository. This kind of tuning defines the shape of your search histogram, as shown in Figure 2-2.

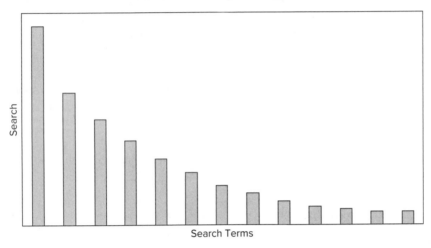

FIGURE 2-2

While this type of tuning is important, consider these other ways to tune:

➤ **Query terms** — Sometimes, you can tell what the user wants by examining the search terms. And sometimes these searches apply to a single document. When you see a query like "building 3 lunch menu" or "annual report," you know exactly which document your user is looking for.

➤ **Query structure** — You can tell a lot about users' intent by looking at how they type the query. On the public web, if you type a FedEx tracking number, Google knows to suggest "Track This Package" with a link to FedEx.com. How? Google knows that FedEx tracking numbers are 12 digit numbers in a certain numeric range. On your search platform, provide the same smarts: if it looks like a product number, make sure that product page shows up at the top of the result list. If the query matches one of your employee's names, put that person's name, email address, and phone number at the top of the result list.

➤ **User background** — Different words mean different things to different people. "ATM" to you may mean automated teller machine, but it may mean asynchronous transfer mode to an engineer. Since it's generally easy to know who your searcher is — in the enterprise, at least — bias your search results to the user's specialty. Microsoft SharePoint 2010 search offers this ability to search profiles automatically, so that helps solve this problem for you.

Most Enterprise Search technologies don't have these features out of the box, but they will. You can't afford to wait, however. In the meantime, you can attack these kinds of problem by using best bets or featured content, which most search technologies today provide. Algorithmic tuning defines the general shape of your search histogram: using specific "best bets" solves the problem for your top searches.

One more point: you must deal with unexpected vocabulary. You make your best guess at the kinds of terms your users will search for, and you make sure your thesaurus and/or synonym list matches your expectations. Then, out of the blue, users get creative and use an entirely different vocabulary! What do you do? Watch your query logs, and be prepared.

There is a story we've heard that provides a great learning opportunity for us. The Swedish electronics company Ericsson manufactures electronic devices. Ericsson calls one of their product lines "mobile phones." We've heard that, on first roll-out, Ericsson discovered by monitoring their search logs that the top no-hits query was "cell phones," the term we use for that type of product here in North America. If Ericsson had not been watching their search logs, they might have missed the opportunity to get their story out worldwide. Don't have that happen to you.

AFTER THE ROLL-OUT

After you've deployed your new search, there may be people in your organization who think the job is done. How hard can it be to have a search just like Google?

The reality is that the job has just started. Like most other enterprise software, search is not a fire-and-forget technology. Successful Enterprise Search is a story of ongoing and continuous improvement. Great Enterprise Search is easy. Start by checking your search logs every day. Look for zero-hits search terms that don't seem right and watch for new vocabulary. Your search logs may reveal opportunities for new products or services, or they may reveal content that needs to be added to your site.

Try to spot trends over time. If your site is an eCommerce one, selling products, you'll be looking at search logs every day, at least once, for a long, long time. If yours is not an eCommerce site, you can start to check your logs. We'd suggest this schedule for at least the first few months. If things look good, then you can go to quarterly search reviews, and plan on them on an ongoing basis. Why?

First, user vocabulary changes over time. Your organization will introduce new products or services, or hire new executives, and those terms may start showing up. And trust me, every executive, early on in a deployment, will search for his or her name to see what comes up. By the way, executives' names make excellent best bets going in!

Next, search activity is often cyclical. In the spring, you'll see queries about vacation policy or about seasonal product lines. In the fall, benefits need to be updated. And that search — "annual report" — has to be updated every year. Not to mention "holiday sales" for eCommerce sites.

Finally, search logs can provide early warning for potential problems, from product defects to sexual harassment. Our understanding is that courts have determined liability in cases where an organization should have known it had a problem. We're not lawyers, but we wouldn't be surprised if, before too long, a company's search logs will be used as evidence in a lawsuit.

Search Sucks!

We're firm believers in continuous process improvement over time. That's why we suggest you roll out to small groups at first, and, when you think you're ready, roll out quietly. Once search has rolled out, however, you will have fans who love what you've done, and doubters who don't like it at all. Don't be too surprised, and don't be hurt. Great search is easy: tune, measure, repeat.

How do you do it? Mine your search logs. Don't be afraid to update your tuning algorithms — to change the shape of the histogram. But use best bets heavily. Here are some ideas:

➤ Look at your search logs, and identify the top 20 queries. Make darned sure those 20 queries return really great results, or define best bets to put them at the top. When you have those 20 handled, move to the next 20. Check every few months and update as necessary.

➤ If one term always shows up on the top, make room on your home page to address the subject. We worked with a firm where the term "blackberry" was consistently the top query. They put a big headline neat to the search box that linked directly to the BlackBerry phone policy. Guess what? Blackberry remained the top query, but at least the search results were good.

➤ If many of your users are looking for information you don't have indexed, investigate federating content from an appropriate internal or external site. If the content is from a repository that you were not permitted to include, approach the content owner about reconsidering the decision to omit that content, or consider creating a landing page that points a user to the sources of that information.

➤ Encourage feedback. Users will probably not tell you what a great job the search platform did when it's right, but trust us, they will tell you when it's wrong. Ask how you could have done better; talk to the user directly. Turn an unhappy user into a fan. All it takes it time.

Get these working and you're well down the path to search nirvana.

Theory and Practice

We've talked a lot about the practice of search in this chapter, and it boils down to this: be involved and get help from others who will assist with search, either in a formal or informal search center of excellence. In the same way that vendor training is a good start, what we've talked about here is good theory: it's your task to put it into practice. We'd suggest that, either within your own organization or with outside specialist companies, keep measuring and improving your search over time. We've seen far too many companies fail simply because they rolled search out and left it to die. Don't let that happen to you.

SUMMARY

A successful implementation of Enterprise Search requires a process for successfully evaluating, selecting, and deploying a new search engine platform. This chapter covered the details to allow the reader to understand the process and to begin building a business plan for the process. Included in the chapter was a discussion of the most common types of search predicts, and an endorsement of forming a Search Center of Excellence as an ongoing project to insure initial — and continued — success with search in your organization.

The chapter also included the details for acquiring search, including defining requirements, identifying key stakeholders, and identifying the area of responsibility for each. It then discussed Proof of Concept, planning and executing the deployment, and managing the ongoing operation of an Enterprise Search application.

No chapter — or book — can replace the depth of experience that experienced Enterprise Search experts can provide. If you select any of the powerful Microsoft search platforms, which we introduce in the next chapter, chances are good you'll be working with a Microsoft partner; pick one with in-depth understanding of search and experience implementing it in organizations like yours. If you decide to use a different commercial or open source search platform, we strongly urge you to consider working with a company that partners with the leading search platforms so you can be sure you have the right technology and that the implementation and roll-out will go smoothly.

Great search is a journey, not a destination; and takes time to iterate into a successful search experience for your users. Good luck!

3

Overview of Microsoft Enterprise Search Products

WHAT'S IN THIS CHAPTER?

➤ Overview of the new Enterprise Search product line, with guidance on which product to use for a given situation

➤ Comparing features between SharePoint Server 2010 search and FAST Search Server 2010 for SharePoint

➤ Exploring typical Enterprise Search applications and which Microsoft product to use for each one

➤ Touring search in other Microsoft products — desktop search, SQL, Exchange, and Bing, — and how to tie them together with OpenSearch federation

Microsoft has been in the Enterprise Search business for a long time. The last two years have seen an increased focus in this area, including the introduction of Search Server 2008 and the acquisition of FAST Search and Transfer. Search is becoming strategic to many businesses, and Microsoft's investments reflect this. In 2010, Microsoft has added new Enterprise Search products and updated existing ones. The result is a set of products that accommodate pretty much any Enterprise Search need, although the lineup can be confusing at times.

Microsoft also has search offerings in several other areas: Windows has desktop search, Bing is focused on web search, and both SQL Server and Exchange have embedded search capabilities. Each of these has independent road maps and versions, and new capabilities worth knowing about. There are licensing variants plus hosted "OnLine" offerings. It can seem overwhelming. But if you understand a bit about the heritage of these offerings, the picture becomes much clearer.

For the sake of completeness, we will talk a bit about all of the available search offerings in this chapter. The rest of this book is focused on Enterprise Search offerings — either those associated with SharePoint or their standalone siblings. It will also cover desktop search integration in more depth in Chapter 5.

This chapter starts with a description of the Microsoft product lineup for Enterprise Search, describing each offering. It specifically analyzes the difference between SharePoint Server 2010 search and FAST Search Server 2010 for SharePoint and then covers typical search applications and which products apply to them. It then covers the broader picture — the wide range of other search capabilities found in Microsoft products and how federation (in particular, using OpenSearch) is now a unifying capability across all of them. Finally, it summarizes the search offerings and gives some advice about choosing the right Enterprise Search product.

UNDERSTANDING THE 2010 ENTERPRISE SEARCH PRODUCT LINE

In 2010, Microsoft is introducing a number of related products, with different products coming out at different times. The 2010 Enterprise Search products bring a *lot* of new capabilities. Some of these are brand new, some are evolutions of the SharePoint 2007 search capabilities, and some are capabilities brought from FAST. There are options for every search need — a blessing because you can solve any search problem with technology from a single vendor.

Figure 3-1 shows the Enterprise Search products in 2010. There are many options; in fact there are nine choices for Enterprise Search. This is a reflection of the attention Microsoft is paying to search, but it is also a byproduct of a large acquisition in midstride.

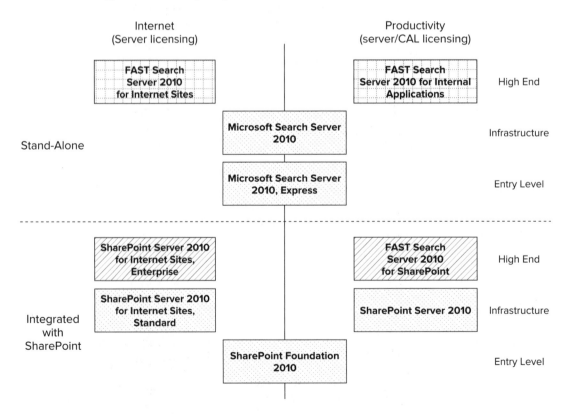

FIGURE 3-1

This lineup might seem confusing at first, but there is some method to this madness. For most purposes, you will be considering only one or two of these.

Looking at the lineup from different angles helps in understanding it. There are three main dimensions to consider:

➤ **Tier** (along the right side of Figure 3-1) — Microsoft adopted a three-tier approach in 2008 when they introduced Search Server 2008 Express and acquired FAST. These tiers are entry *level*, *infrastructure*, and *high-end*. Search Server 2010 Express, and the search in SharePoint Foundation 2010 are entry level; SharePoint Server 2010, SharePoint Server 2010 for Internet Sites (FIS), and Search Server 2010 cover the infrastructure tier, and any option labeled "FAST" is high-end.

➤ **Integrated with SharePoint or standalone** (along the left side of Figure 3-1) — Search options integrated with SharePoint have features like social search, which are based on other parts of SharePoint. Standalone search options don't require SharePoint but lack these features.

➤ **Application** (across the top of Figure 3-1) — Microsoft divides applications into customer-facing (Internet) and employee-facing (Productivity) categories. For the most part, the distinction between these is a pure licensing distinction. For Productivity search applications (inside the firewall), products are licensed by server and by client access license (CAL). For Internet search applications (outside the firewall), it isn't possible to license clients, so products are licensed by server. The media, documentation, support, and architecture are the same across these applications (e.g., horizontally across Figure 3-1). There are a few minor feature differences, which are called out in this chapter where relevant.

There is another perspective useful in understanding this lineup: codebase. The acquisition of FAST brought a large codebase of high-end search code, different from the SharePoint search codebase. As the integration of FAST proceeds, ultimately all Enterprise Search options will be derived from a single common codebase.

At the moment there are three separate codebases from which Enterprise Search products are derived, as shown in Figure 3-2. Full code integration, with all options built from the same base, is on Microsoft's road map. But in 2010, there is a mixed set of products, which can make understanding the differences tricky! The "combined" codebase used in FAST Search for SharePoint is, in many ways, a brand-new animal, pulling the best from FAST and SharePoint.

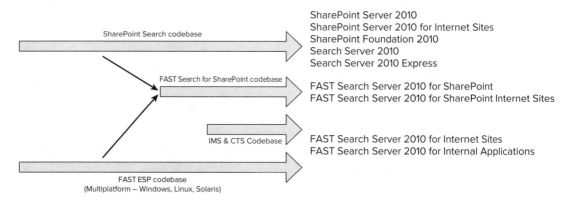

FIGURE 3-2

Options based on the legacy FAST codebase are multi-platform; they run on Linux and Solaris x86, as well as Windows. This is a unique situation for Microsoft products! However, these options are available only through FAST as a subsidiary. This means having a separate set of contracts, support options, and so forth. Also note that Microsoft has announced that this set of products will be the last major multi-platform releases; even though support horizons on them are quite long, new installations are better off starting in Windows for this reason.

Products in this lineup are being introduced in two sets: most of these were released along with SharePoint 2010. The two standalone high-end options (based on the legacy FAST codebase) are being released at a later time.

SIZE MATTERS

Although scale isn't the main difference between search options, it's the easiest to understand. (We'll talk more about scale in Chapters 4, 5, and 7.) For Microsoft Enterprise Search, the amount of content that can be searchable is defined in terms of items. An *item* is something you'd see in a line on a search result; it is most often a document, but it could be a database record, a chapter of a longer document, or something created by joining multiple records or documents.

➤ Entry-level search is limited to 300,000 searchable items

➤ Infrastructure-tier search is limited to 100,000,000 searchable items

➤ High-end search can scale to an unlimited number of searchable items

---

SharePoint Foundation 2010

Microsoft SharePoint Foundation 2010 (SPF) is a free, downloadable platform that includes search capabilities. The search is pretty basic — limited to content within SharePoint, no search scopes, no refinement, or the like. In the categories described above, SPF is in the entry-level tier and is integrated with SharePoint.

If you are using SharePoint Foundation and care about search (likely since you are reading this book!), forget about the built-in search capability and use one of the other options. Most likely this will be Search Server Express, since it is also free.

Search Server 2010 Express

Microsoft Search Server 2010 Express (MSS Express or MSSX) is a free, downloadable standalone search offering. It is intended for tactical, small-scale search applications (such as departmental sites) requiring little or no cost and IT effort. Search Server Express 2008 was a very popular product — Microsoft reported that there have been over 100,000 downloads. There is a lot added in 2010 — better connectivity, faceted search navigation, improved relevance, and much more.

Search Server 2010 Express is an entry-level standalone product. It is limited to one server with up to 300,000 items. It lacks many of the capabilities of SharePoint Server, such as taxonomy and people and expertise search, not to mention the capabilities of FAST. But it can be a good enough option for many departments that require a straightforward site search.

If you have little or no budget and an immediate, simple, tactical search need, use MSS Express. It is quick to deploy, easy to manage, and free. You can always move to one of the other options later.

Search Server 2010

Microsoft Search Server 2010 (MSS) has the same functional capabilities as MSS Express (MSS-X), with full scale — up to about 10 million items per server and 100 million items in a system using multiple servers. It's not free, but the per-server license cost is low. MSS is a great way to scale up for applications that start with MSS Express and grow (as they often do).

MSS is an infrastructure-tier standalone product. Both MSS and MSS Express lack some search capabilities that are available in SharePoint Server 2010, such as taxonomy support, people and expertise search, social tagging, and social search (where search results improve because of social behavior), to name a few. And, of course, MSS does not have any of the other SharePoint Server capabilities (BI, workflow, etc.) that are often mixed together with search in applications.

If you have no other applications for SharePoint Server and need general intranet search or site search capability, MSS can be a good choice. But in most cases it makes more sense to use SharePoint Server 2010.

SharePoint Server 2010

Microsoft SharePoint Server 2010 (SP) includes a complete intranet search solution that provides a robust search capability out of the box. There are many significant improvements over its predecessor, Microsoft Office SharePoint Server 2007 search. New capabilities include faceted navigation, people and expertise search with phonetic matching, social tagging, social search, query suggestions, editing directly in a browser, and many more. Connectivity is much broader and simpler, for both indexing and federation. SharePoint Server 2010 also has a markedly improved scale-out architecture, providing flexibility for different scale and performance needs. These capabilities will be detailed in Chapter 4.

SharePoint Server has three license variants in 2010 — all with precisely the same search functionality. With all of them, Enterprise Search is a component or workload, not a separate license. SharePoint Server 2010 is licensed in a typical Microsoft server/CAL model. Each server needs a server license, and each user needs a client access license (CAL). For applications where CALs don't apply (typically outside the firewall in customer-facing sites), there is SharePoint Server 2010 for Internet Sites, Standard (FIS-S), and SharePoint Server 2010 for Internet Sites, Enterprise (FIS-E).

For the rest of the book, these licensing variants will be ignored, and we will refer to all of them as SharePoint Server 2010 or SP. All of them are infrastructure-tier, integrated offerings.

SharePoint Server 2010 is a good choice for general intranet search, people search, and site search applications. It is a fully functional search solution and should cover the scale and connectivity needs of most organizations. It also supports light customization so it can be tailored for some applications. However, it isn't the best option for developing search-driven applications of the type covered in Chapter 6. Even for general-purpose intranet search, it is no longer the best search option offered with SharePoint, now that FAST has been integrated.

FAST Search Server 2010 for SharePoint

Microsoft FAST Search Server 2010 for SharePoint (FS4SP) is a brand-new product. It is a high-end Enterprise Search product, providing an excellent search experience out of box and the flexibility to customize search for very diverse needs at essentially unlimited scale. FS4SP is notably simple to deploy and operate compared to other high-end search offerings. It provides high-end search, integrated with SharePoint.

Fast Search for SharePoint is essentially a combination of SharePoint search and FAST search technology in a hybrid form, plus several new elements and capabilities. As discussed in Chapter 4, this means that it shares APIs, system management, and search management with SP. They are not precisely the same; there are differences, such as extensions to the query object model (OM), to accommodate the additional capabilities of FAST. But the biggest differences are in the functionality available: a visual and "contextual" search experience; advanced content processing, including metadata extraction; multiple relevance profiles and sorting options available to users; more control of the user experience; extreme scale capabilities; and much more.

Just as with SharePoint Server 2010, there are licensing variants for internal and external use. FAST Search Server 2010 for SharePoint is licensed per server, requires Enterprise Client Access Licenses (e-CALs) for each user, and requires SharePoint Server 2010 as a prerequisite. FAST Search Server 2010 for SharePoint Internet Sites (FS4SP-IS) is for situations where CALs don't apply, typically Internet-facing sites with various search applications. In these situations, SP-FIS-E is a prerequisite. In fact, everything carries an SP-FIS-E license in this situation. There isn't anything officially called FS4SP-IS — it is an SP-FIS-E license applied in a search role.

For the purposes of this book, we will use the FS4SP-IS acronym if there is a specific reason to discuss this software in this role. However, FS4SP and FS4SP-IS have basically the same search functionality — variations are due to how a given feature does or doesn't apply outside the firewall. Unless otherwise noted, we will ignore these differences and refer to both licensing variants as FAST Search for SharePoint or FS4SP.

FAST Search for SharePoint handles general intranet search, people search, and site search applications, providing more capability than SharePoint Server does, including the ability to give different groups using the same site different experiences via a user context. FS4SP is particularly well suited for high-value search applications, such as those covered in Chapter 6.

FAST Search Server for Internet Sites

Microsoft FAST Search Server 2010 for Internet Sites (FSIS) is another new offering. It combines FAST ESP with new elements (Interaction Management Services and Content Transformation Services, which are described in Chapter 8), and provides these in a new licensing framework with a new name. FSIS is intended for customer-facing applications and is licensed per server.

A variant of FSIS, called FAST Search Server 2010 for Internet Applications (FSIA), is also available. This is intended for internally facing applications and is licensed in a server/CAL model (with its own CALs, not SharePoint CALs). Unlike FSIS, FSIA does not include Interaction Management Services and Content Transformation Services. This means that it is the same as FAST ESP, with a new name and new, simpler licensing. Both FSIS and FSIA are high-end, standalone search offerings, like FAST ESP.

FSIS and FSIA are the direct migration path for FAST ESP customers. For those running the latest ESP version (5.3), it looks like a minor version upgrade and a new license. Although Microsoft is offering license grants for ESP customers who wish to move to FAST Search for SharePoint, there is no direct technical migration path. (Migration is covered in more detail in Chapter 11.) There are some compelling reasons to make this move, but as of Spring 2010, there isn't much experience in the migration. If you are currently happy with FAST ESP, staying with FSIS or FSIA is most likely the best path, at least for now.

For the most demanding and advanced Internet sites, FAST Search for Internet Sites is the natural choice. IMS and CTS provide developers with an ability to build engaging, search-driven experiences quickly. If you are running a high-volume e-commerce site, a top-tier content-publishing site, or a complex online support site, FSIS is likely to be the appropriate search option.

Summary of Enterprise Search Options

There are a *lot* of different search options in the new lineup. The breakdown of the nine options is as follows (refer to Figure 3-1):

➤ Two entry-level (SPF, MSS-X), three infrastructure-tier (SP, SP-FIS, MSS), four high-end (FS4SP, FS4SP-IS, FSIA, FSIS)

➤ Four standalone (MSS-X, MSS, FSIA, FSIS), five integrated with SharePoint (SPF, SP, SP-FIS, FS4SP, FS4SP-IS)

➤ Three intended/licensed for internally facing applications (SP, FSIA, FS4SP), three intended/licensed for externally facing applications (SP-FIS, FS4SP-IS, FSIS)

➤ Six different images/media sets (SPF, MSS/MSS-X, SP/SP-FIS/SP/FIS-E, FS4SP/FS4SP-IS, FSIA, FSIS)

Of course, this is a book about advanced search. Therefore, for practical purposes, there are only three options to consider: SharePoint Server 2010, FAST Search for SharePoint, and FAST Search for Internet Sites. These are the focus of the rest of this book. Entry-level needs are well covered by MSS-X, and this product is straightforward enough that you don't need the rest of this book. You can use the orientation from Chapter 1, the planning principles from Chapter 2, and the context of this chapter, and then do a simple deployment.

As mentioned, FAST Search for Internet Sites (FSIS) is the natural choice for the most demanding and advanced Internet sites (unless they are powered by SharePoint). If this is clearly your focus, you can jump right to Part III.

For most other purposes, the choice is between SharePoint Server 2010's search capabilities and FAST Search for SharePoint. The next section outlines the differences between these two in relatively high-level tables, which let you understand the key capabilities. The section after that covers the most common applications for search and provides a sense of where you would use different Microsoft Enterprise Search products. After a tour of the search offerings beyond those strictly intended for Enterprise Search (such as exchange, SQL, Windows7, and Bing search), we will return to the question of "What product should I use?"

WHAT ARE ALL THESE ACRONYMS AGAIN?

Microsoft tends to use long product names, and search is no exception. That's why we are using shorter names and acronyms in this book. We use the same short names and standard acronyms that Microsoft uses. (Yes, some of these acronyms have numbers in them, too.) Here's a review:

TABLE 3-1: Search Product Names and Acronyms

ACRONYM	FULL NAME	SHORT NAME
MOSS	Microsoft Office SharePoint Server 2007	MOSS 2007
MOSS-FIS	Microsoft Office SharePoint Server 2007 for Internet Sites	MOSS 2007 FIS
WSS	Microsoft Windows SharePoint Services 2007	WSS 2007
SP	Microsoft SharePoint Server 2010	SharePoint Server 2010
SPF	Microsoft SharePoint Foundation 2010	SharePoint Foundation 2010
MSS	Microsoft Search Server 2010	Search Server 2010
MSS-X	Microsoft Search Server 2010 Express	MSS Express; Search Server 2010 Express
SP-FIS	Microsoft SharePoint Server 2010 for Internet Sites, Standard	SharePoint Server 2010 FIS
SP-FIS-E	Microsoft SharePoint Server 2010 for Internet Sites, Enterprise	SharePoint Server 2010 FIS-E
FS4SP	Microsoft FAST Search Server 2010 for SharePoint	FAST Search for SharePoint
FS4SP-IS	Microsoft FAST Search Server 2010 for SharePoint Internet Sites	FAST Search for SharePoint IS
FSIS	Microsoft FAST Search Server 2010 for Internet Sites	FAST Search for Internet Sites
FSIA	Microsoft FAST Search Server 2010 for Internal Applications	FAST Search for Internal Applications

Some of these names and acronyms are very close to each other; luckily you are typically thinking about only one or two of them at a time. The naming of the FAST variants can be particularly confusing — especially as there are two different FAST code bases right now! And there is no name for "the search that comes built into SharePoint Server 2010"; we call that SharePoint Server 2010 search or SP in this book.

All of the new products have "2010" in the full name, but many of them are new products or names so they don't need to include '2010' in the short name.

FS4SP-IS is the only acronym that isn't an official name — you won't find it on a price list or licensing document. Microsoft has only one license for SP-FIS-E and FS4SP-IS, and you use that in either a "SharePoint Server" role or a "FAST Search" role. So FS4SP-IS technically means a SP-FIS-E license in the FAST Search role. This was changed late in the product cycle to reduce confusion.

SHAREPOINT SERVER SEARCH VERSUS FAST SEARCH FOR SHAREPOINT

Most commonly, organizations implementing a Microsoft Enterprise Search product will choose between SharePoint Server 2010's search capabilities and FAST Search for SharePoint. SharePoint Server's search has improved significantly since 2007, so it is worth a close look, especially if you are already running SharePoint 2007's search. FAST Search for SharePoint has many capabilities beyond SharePoint Server 2010's search, but it also carries additional licensing costs. By understanding the feature differences and the applications that can be addressed by each, you can determine whether you need the additional capabilities offered by FAST.

FAST Search Server 2010 for SharePoint builds on SharePoint Server 2010 and provides significant enhancements to the Enterprise Search capabilities. The frameworks and tools used by IT professionals and developers have been kept as common as possible across the product lines, given the additional capabilities in FAST Search Server 2010 for SharePoint.

FAST Search Server 2010 for SharePoint can be used to solve a variety of search problems, but it is designed with "high-value" search applications in mind. SharePoint Server 2010's built-in search, on the other hand, is targeted at "general productivity search." General productivity search solutions increase employee efficiency by connecting a broad set of people to a broad set of information. Intranet search is the most common example of a general productivity search solution. High-value search applications drive measurable returns on investment (ROI) by helping a specific set of people make the most of a specific set of information. Common examples include product support applications, research portals, and customer record locators.

Since SP and FS4SP largely share the same APIs, connectors, and management consoles, it is relatively straightforward to move from SP to FS4SP, but this also reduces the difference between them. In general, you won't find big differences in connectors or security, which traditionally are areas where search engines have differentiated themselves. Instead, you see big differences in content processing, user experience, and advanced query capabilities. Examples of these capabilities are:

➤ Content-processing pipeline

➤ Metadata extraction

➤ Structured data search

➤ Deep refinement

➤ Visual search

➤ Advanced linguistics

➤ Visual best bets

➤ Development platform flexibility

➤ Ease of creating custom search experiences

➤ Extreme scale and performance

Summary of Feature Differences Between SP and FS4SP

The following tables provide an overview of the differences, from the perspective of the end user searching for information, the IT pro deploying and operating search, and the developer building applications that include search. In these tables, you will find:

➤ Capabilities that are the *same* in FS4SP as those in SP

➤ Capabilities that are *better* in FS4SP than those in SP

➤ Capabilities that are *unique* to FS4SP

People using search will see a big difference between SharePoint Server 2010 and FAST Search for SharePoint, as outlined in this Table 3-2:

TABLE 3-2: End-User Perspective — Feature Summary

	SHAREPOINT SERVER 2010 (SP)	FAST SEARCH SERVER 2010 FOR SHAREPOINT (FS4SP)
One-stop search center	Excellent OOB relevance, federated results, PC, phone, or browser access	Same capabilities, plus broader and better language support, broader query syntax
Exploration/Conversational Search	Metadata-based shallow refiners, related searches, view in browser	Same capabilities, plus deep refiners with counts, similarity search, and sorting on any property

	SHAREPOINT SERVER 2010 (SP)	FAST SEARCH SERVER 2010 FOR SHAREPOINT (FS4SP)
Social search (people and expertise)	Phonetic and nickname matching, relevance and refiners, and integrated presence	Same capabilities
Search gets better with use	Click-through drives relevance, colleague and expertise suggestions, and query suggestions	Same capabilities
Visual cues		Thumbnails and scrolling previews, and visual best bets
Contextual search		User context from user profile, and multiple relevance profiles

The most noticeable differences are the visual and contextual features. There are also differences in the area of conversational search-faceted navigation with accurate counts, similarity search, and the like. Differences in search essentials, like query syntax and language support, will be important to some users.

Those who deploy and maintain search as part of their daily work certainly care about the end-user perspective, but they are more likely to care about the kind of differences outlined in this table:

TABLE 3-3: IT Professional Perspective — Feature Summary

	SHAREPOINT SERVER 2010 (SP)	FAST SEARCH SERVER 2010 FOR SHAREPOINT (FS4SP)
Scale-out and performance	Enterprise scale-out (to 100M items) Full fault tolerance Native 64 bit Full Hyper-V support	Same capabilities, plus extreme scale-out (billions of items)
Easy deployment	Wizard-driven installation Consolidated search dashboard	Same capabilities
Enterprise-class manageability	PowerShell support SCOM support Full search reporting	Same capabilities, plus deeper SCOM support
Secure, broad connectivity	Full set of connectors Add new sources via BDC Strong security	Same capabilities, plus FAST-Specific connectors (Enterprise Web Crawler, JDBC connector)

continues

TABLE 3-3 *(continued)*

	SHAREPOINT SERVER 2010 (SP)	FAST SEARCH SERVER 2010 FOR SHAREPOINT (FS4SP)
Advanced content processing OOB		Content-processing pipeline Metadata extraction
Easy-to-configure high-end user experiences		Easy setup of user context, visual best bets, and promotion Gives end users control over sorting, ranking, and navigation

The most distinctive capabilities IT professional will notice come from FAST Search for SharePoint's advanced content processing. There are also significant differences in scale, additional connectors, and an additional set of search administration screens and capabilities.

Developers will find many things to love in SharePoint 2010 overall. Search inherits these, and adds a few more (as covered in Chapter 6). The main differences between SP and FS4SP for developers are outlined in Table 3-4:

TABLE 3-4: Developer Perspective — Feature Summary

	SHAREPOINT SERVER 2010 (SP)	FAST SEARCH SERVER 2010 FOR SHAREPOINT (FS4SP)
Customize the OOB user experience using web parts	Unsealed web parts	Same capabilities, based on the most powerful user experience
Extend connectivity using the BDC and federation	New connector framework Integrated with BCS	Same capabilities
Combine search with other SharePoint capabilities	Integrate Search with Business Intelligence, Workflow, Social Computing, and collaboration	Same capabilities, applying high-end search capabilities
Use familiar tools built for developer productivity	BDC tooling built into SharePoint Designer (SPD) Application tooling in VS2010	Same capabilities
Leverage advanced content processing		Add custom property extractors Extend content processing
Customize relevance		Include external data in relevance Build multiple relevance profiles Extend user context
Use advanced query capabilities to create powerful applications		Leverage FAST Query Language (FQL) to create geosearch, user-selected influencers, and much more

In addition to the advanced content processing, there are distinctive relevance and query capabilities provided with FS4SP. These are the things that make FS4SP the recommended platform for search-driven applications.

Capabilities Found Only in SharePoint Server 2010 Search

FAST Search for SharePoint is designed to deliver a superset of SharePoint search, but there are a few things FAST Search for SharePoint doesn't do out of the box in this release. The top five include:

➤ Alerting (saved searches)

➤ Refinement and relevance based on social tags

➤ Definition extraction

➤ Index mirroring across data centers

➤ Out-of-the-box monitoring (FAST Search for SharePoint requires SCOM)

There are ways to accomplish all of these with FAST Search for SharePoint (see Chapter 5), but they take extra effort and in some cases extra cost.

Between SharePoint Server 2010 search and FAST Search for SharePoint, there is more in common than there is different. As you will see in Part II, the APIs and management frameworks are common between them. But there are also significant differences, which are worth understanding in detail as you plan a search deployment or application.

At this point, you should have a general understanding of the Microsoft Enterprise Search product line in 2010, and a sense of the differences between SP and FS4SP features. The next section describes common search scenarios and gives you a sense of how different products apply to them.

TYPICAL SEARCH SCENARIOS

Chapter 1 and 2 provided some examples of how Enterprise Search is used. Typically, organizations find many different search applications in-house. This section illustrates how different applications use search features and gives general guidelines on what Microsoft products are best suited for these applications.

There is a wide range of search applications and a spectrum of what is possible with different degrees of customization. The examples that follow are not a full list, of course, but are meant to give you a sense of what capabilities are typically important for this type of application.

Some search applications are general purpose — often used by everybody in an organization. Others are special purpose — usually used by an identified group of people with a specific purpose (for example, researchers). General-purpose search applications usually have broader, less specific requirements, and often have a less crisp business case. Special-purpose search applications tend to have an identifiable business value and ROI — although it may not always be obvious that they are "search-based applications."

The general purpose versus special purpose distinction is particularly useful for employee-facing (productivity) applications. General-purpose productivity search solutions increase employee efficiency by connecting a broad set of people to a broad set of information. Intranet search is the most common example of a general productivity search solution. Special-purpose productivity search applications drive measurable returns on investment (ROI) by helping a specific set of people make the most of a specific set of information. Common examples include product support applications, research portals, and customer record locators. These are sometimes called "search-driven applications." They are like other enterprise applications but they incorporate the strengths of search (familiar, intuitive user interaction; broad information reach and flexible integration, etc). In Chapter 6, we will show how search-driven applications are built.

You can use this distinction in planning your search application and also in choosing the appropriate Microsoft product. For example, SharePoint Server 2010's built-in search is targeted at general-purpose productivity search applications. FAST Search Server 2010 for SharePoint, on the other hand, is designed with special-purpose search applications in mind, although it can be used to solve general-purpose search problems as well.

Intranet Search

Intranets cover a wide range of scope, size, and sophistication — and search is essential across the whole range. Increasingly, intranets are being used to deliver tools and applications, facilitate collaboration, and as corporate culture-change platforms. Individual departments often have their own sections of the corporate intranet, their own sites, and their own portals. At the same time, there are parts of the corporate intranet which are meant for all users — enterprise wide. That's why we consider intranet search to be a general-purpose application; some authors call all employee-facing search "intranet search", which is misleading.

Several of the Microsoft Enterprise Search products apply to intranet search, reflecting the diversity of scenarios and needs. Small, basic intranet search can be handled with little or no budget using Search Server 2010 Express. Strong enterprise-wide intranet search can be provided using SharePoint Server 2010. The best intranet search — in terms of both user experience and platform capabilities — is provided by FAST Search for SharePoint.

How do you know which platform to use? Use the approach from Chapter 2: understand your users' needs and level of sophistication, and consult your budget. If this project is tactical, you can likely work with SP (or even MSS-X, for small projects). But if your intranet is considered a strategic resource, try out FAST Search for SharePoint (FS4SP).

People Search

A big part of most jobs is connecting with the right people and expertise. Knowing who to consult is a search problem — as is seeing if your question is already answered in that person's documents. People search is often associated with knowledge management, but it is a big part of nearly any search application these days. As you will learn in Chapter 10, the social search capabilities of SharePoint Server 2010 are very strong, well integrated, and easy to deploy and manage.

If searching for people and expertise is an important part of your needs, this simplifies the product choice. The products that are integrated with SharePoint Server 2010 (SP, FS4SP, SP-FIS, and SP-FIS-E) have integrated people search; the other offerings (SPF, MSS-X, MSS, FSIA, and FSIS) don't.

Site Search

Just as there is a broad range of intranets, there is a spectrum of approaches and needs for site search. You may need only a simple site presence that lets your customers know who you are; you might field a complete self-service application for customer support as part of your site, or you might use your site as the centerpiece of your online brand and business strategy. In any of these scenarios, search is a central component for a great site experience.

Several of the Microsoft Enterprise Search products apply to site search, reflecting the diversity of scenarios and needs. Small, basic site search can be handled with little or no budget using Search Server 2010 Express (MSSX). Beyond this, the main determiner is whether SharePoint is a big part of your site or not. Since the capabilities of SharePoint for creating and managing great websites are greatly enhanced with SharePoint 2010, it is likely that you will want to look at this first.

If you are using SharePoint to power your website, then you have two choices: SharePoint Server 2010 FIS or SharePoint Server 2010 FIS Enterprise (which includes FAST Search for SharePoint IS). Either can provide great site searching; if you have a large site, a need for navigation across many items, are crawling sites that include JavaScript, or want different relevance profiles for different audiences or parts of your site, choose SharePoint Server 2010 FIS Enterprise (SP-FIS-E).

If you are not using SharePoint to power your website, your choices are Search Server 2010 (MSS) or FAST Search for Internet Sites (FSIS). Any high-end site will want FSIS, for the reasons given earlier and for the general ability to field and control a high-end search experience.

Research Portals

Research applications are found in many places within most organizations: market research, competitive research, product research, financial research, and so forth. What they share is a set of users who spend most of their time exploring and synthesizing information. In these applications, the ability to find better answers faster has big payoff — in competitive advantage, lower costs, better returns, and so forth. For example, in product development, researchers can leverage the power of search to gain access to the silos of R&D, engineering, partners, and intellectual property data to avoid reworking past initiatives that have failed, avoid compliance penalties, and accelerate time to market for new products/services to capitalize on the revenue opportunities and beat the competition.

FAST Search for SharePoint (FS4SP) is the appropriate choice for any of these applications — both for high-end search capabilities and for tight integration with SharePoint. Researchers benefit from tailored relevance, the ability to have multiple relevance profiles they can pick from, visual and conversational elements in the search experience, and other high-end search capabilities — in fact, they often demand these capabilities. In many cases, a research portal also includes BI, authoring and publishing workflows, and collaboration capabilities as well as search.

Customer Management

Do you know what your customers think of your products/services? Who are your most profitable or costly customers? Is your value proposition resonating with your customer base? Quite often it is very difficult to measure and manage this effectively, without a lot of manual intervention and analysis across a myriad of systems and applications. Imagine an environment where search can collate relevant customer information across all internal systems and external sources, enabling your marketing teams to analyze messaging and product effectiveness across your customer demographic. Access to detailed customer and competitor insights gives them the power to innovate and refine customer messaging and product/service positioning to drive significant revenue for the business and leapfrog the competition.

Applications like these are found in many forms and under many names: call center portal, sales portal, voice of the customer, Customer Relationship Management (CRM) portal, sales assistant, and so forth. They may be focused on insight (like voice of the customer projects), on intelligence (like customer context and events), or on action (like pipeline management or collateral portals). There is a growing movement in the CRM world to extend CRM to Social Media, generally known as "Social CRM." (Microsoft has a new hosted service called LookingGlass which monitors social media and provides a dashboard as well as a feed into SharePoint. We describe this in Chapter 9.)

FAST Search for SharePoint (FS4SP) is the appropriate choice for these applications, since they require capabilities like:

➤ Unified access/aggregation to all customer data across multiple CRM systems and difficult-to-access systems

➤ The capability to combine structured and unstructured data

➤ The capability to collect and make available external data (such as product or market information)

➤ Advanced content processing, tagging, and classification

➤ Deep refinement (navigation over the entire result set with exact counts on each facet)

Parts Search

Structured data often contains codes, symbols, and patterns (part numbers like CX-65N-433-2T, diagnostic codes like Y333.44, Social Security numbers, phone numbers, zip codes, etc.). While exact matches on these can be done with any search technology, users struggle to enter them accurately, and both data and queries are prone to error.

Applications for search on symbols arise in many places: the shop floor, manufacturing operations, shipping, logistics centers, and applications with scientific or technology names such as chemicals or genomes. These applications are a good fit for high-end search, since FAST supports "fuzzy" matches, such as "find parts in stock like CX-65M433-2y."

For this kind of application, you should choose either FAST Search for SharePoint (FS4SP) or FAST Search for Internal Applications (FSIA). The main determiner is whether you have a SharePoint infrastructure in place for these groups or not. If you don't use SharePoint, use FSIA. But consider using SharePoint Server 2010 for these applications, since there are a lot of benefits from content management and collaboration — and the people search and expertise search and visual search elements that come with FS4SP boost productivity in these scenarios.

Intelligence and Investigation

Intelligence applications are most often associated with governments and appear under names such as Analyst Workbench, Law Enforcement Information Center, Fusion Center, Competitive Intelligence Analyzer, and the like. But these applications are found in every industry, characterized by the presence of analysts that are tasked with keeping aware of particular domains and being responsive to new information from many different sources. The most common issue in this kind of organization is the inability to bring information from different parts of the organization together quickly and effectively. These applications make heavy use of entity extraction and bring together information from many different sources in many different types, so they are definitely FAST territory.

For this kind of application, the same considerations from the discussion of parts search apply, even more strongly. If you don't use SharePoint, or don't use Windows, use FSIA. But consider using SharePoint Server 2010 and FAST Search for SharePoint (FS4SP) for these applications, since there are a lot of benefits from content management and collaboration. Finding people and expertise is particularly important in intelligence, as is the ability to log and control workflow — both are elements that come with FS4SP. Most of Microsoft's integration work, like the FusionX initiative, are based around SharePoint Server 2010 and FS4SP.

Intellectual Property Protection

Intellectual Property (IP) protection applications are found in areas such as patent search, trademarks, copyrights, and research and development, which often involve collaboration with other organizations such as outside legal counsel. Applications are also found in the entertainment and media industries, protecting rights to music, photos, films, and other media. High-end search capabilities, including relevance control, are essential to these applications, since missing something in a search can cost millions of dollars. FAST Search for SharePoint (FS4SP) is the appropriate tool for this kind of application.

Compliance

Compliance is a very broad subject and can range from IT auditing and compliance with the Sarbannes-Oxley (often shortened to SOX) Act through drug approval, to compliance with e-discovery regulations such as the Federal Rules of Civil Procedure (FRCP). Ensuring compliance by leveraging IT tools is a deep subject, worthy of several books in its own right. Search is a key component for compliance, but it is only one of several components. For example, e-discovery solutions typically need content management, integrated policy management, email archiving, desktop and server discovery and search, and domain-specific workflow. Great high-end search, such as that provided by FAST, is incredibly valuable, but you will find yourself either building custom applications or working with third-party vendors and Microsoft partners to do a complete job. The federation capabilities, scale, and text analytics provided by Exchange Server 2010, SharePoint Server 2010, and FAST Search for SharePoint (FS4SP) are often the main ingredients in solutions of this type.

E-Commerce

If you are a retailer or wholesaler, you need e-commerce as part of your web presence. Search for online commerce is a specialized area and needs faceted navigation, tight control of relevance, and the ability to feature specific content according to business rules. For this kind of application, either FAST Search for Internet Sites (FSIS) or SharePoint Server 2010 FIS-E (SP-FIS-E) is an option. The choice depends primarily on whether your site is powered by SharePoint. If it is (or if it uses Commerce Server), then use SP-FIS-E. Otherwise, use FSIS. In either case, there are some specialized additional modules that apply, which are discussed in Chapter 11.

Search is found in many different applications within most organizations. Microsoft now has offerings that cover the full range of search applications; different applications may require different members of the family. You now have a feel for the types of applications and which Enterprise Search products to use with them. At a high level, general-purpose applications can use products from any tier (entry-level, infrastructure, or high-end), while special-purpose applications require high-end search products.

Having a diversity of applications is a good argument for establishing a Search Center of Excellence (as described in Chapter 2). Some applications use multiple products together — both Enterprise Search products and other products, ranging from desktop search through servers with search capabilities through web search. The next section covers other search offerings from Microsoft at a high level — enough to give you context for what to use when and how to integrate these into a solution.

MY STUFF, OUR STUFF, THE WORLD'S STUFF

Search is found in many different forms. This book is about Enterprise Search, but there are three overall levels:

➤ **Desktop Search** — Designed for getting at "my stuff"; there can be variants for servers versus desktops or laptops, personal "assistants" that collect or track local information, and variants specifically tailored for desktop applications like email clients.

➤ **Enterprise Search** — Designed for getting at "our stuff", such as information shared in a group or organization; there are variants optimized for and integrated with databases and email servers, and sometimes embedded search within content management and storage systems.

➤ **Web Search** — Designed for getting at the Internet as a whole; there can be variants for different "slices" of the web or for particular audiences.

Microsoft has offerings at all three levels. These all work together, as we discuss in the section on Federation and OpenSearch.

WINDOWS DESKTOP SEARCH

In addition to the Enterprise Search products, Microsoft offers desktop search software. This has evolved substantially from early days, and search is now built into both client and server operating systems.

There are some special considerations with desktop search. There is no need for extensive connectors or for special security trimmers. When you change a file on your desktop, copy a folder, or archive your mail, however, you want to be able to find content in them as soon as possible.

More searches are done on the desktop than on enterprise portals. Roughly as many desktop searches are done as web searches! But desktop search has been a relatively weak offering until recently.

Microsoft has maintained a consistent development effort on desktop search over the years. Historically, most serious search zealots added separate desktop search programs, even though search was available with the operating system. With the most recent revision of Microsoft's desktop search, users will have less need for this, since the search capability, speed, and user interface is dramatically improved.

The Role of the Desktop in Enterprise Search

No matter how much we try to manage content centrally, most of it ends up on individual desktops and servers. The amount of content and the variety of comment types is growing like crazy, filling up storage just as fast as users expand it. Finding information has become a difficult task.

The end user is typically concerned with finding content wherever it may be, so desktop search is a big part of the picture. Information is stored in many locations, such as the local PC, network file shares, line of business systems, the internet, and other online repositories. End users constantly ask for more intuitive ways to search for their content across these locations — whether it's "my stuff," "our stuff," or "the world's stuff."

Desktop applications increasingly include search as well. Most desktop search programs, including Microsoft's, are designed as components you can build on. So desktop search is increasingly a part of Enterprise Search, and ways to tie these two worlds together seamlessly are emerging.

Windows Desktop Search 4: XP and Vista

The most common desktop search program is not X1 or Google desktop — it's Windows Desktop Search 4 (WDS4). This was developed and initially released as Windows Vista Search, but it is also available for Windows XP as well as Windows Server 2003 and 2008.

WDS 4 has all the features found in its predecessor, WDS 3.01, but also introduces many additional capabilities, including:

➤ Crawling and indexing a number of different formats, including Word, Excel, PowerPoint, OneNote, and Outlook

➤ Integrated search experience with "word wheeling" (search as you type)

➤ Full windows actions on search results (such as copy, move, delete, etc.)

➤ Integration with Office 2007, especially Outlook, to speed searches of email, calendar, contacts, and tasks

Figure 3-3 shows the Windows Search default experience. The search experience is functional and easily understandable, and is very familiar if you have ever used Outlook search folders.

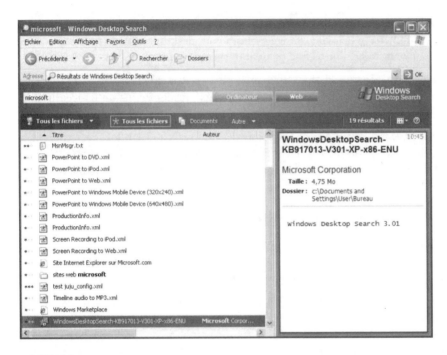

FIGURE 3-3

Windows 7 Desktop Search

Although it's not officially named "WDS 5," there is a new and improved desktop search capability in Windows 7 and Windows Server 2008 R2. Figure 3-4 shows the search experience for search in Windows 7. This is improved in many respects, notably:

> ➤ The user experience is integrated with Windows Explorer.

> ➤ It has faster indexing, which is less intrusive on desktop operations.

> ➤ It has built-in federation.

In Windows 7, Microsoft introduced a new experience — fully integrated with Windows Explorer — that uses search as the primary method of navigating through information on the user's PC, as well as shared resources on other PCs and servers. Windows Explorer organizes this information into libraries, which represent different types of content (documents, pictures, etc.). For instance, My Documents can now include documents from multiple locations and devices and now uses search as the way to aggregate and navigate through your documents. The entire search user interface is based on Explorer and provides a very familiar way to find files and email messages located on your PC and connected resources. The Windows integration has been extended to provide one-click access to move, delete, copy, burn, attach, or drag and drop files where you need them.

The performance and "citizenship" of WDS 5 is markedly better than WDS 4. Indexing throughput and latency are much better, even with the additional indexing work involved with providing better relevance. You will *not* notice the load of WDS 5 indexing your machine — it is now truly a well-behaved background task.

FIGURE 3-4

A lot of attention has been placed on the administration and development aspects of WDS 5. This is a true sign that desktop search from Microsoft has come of age. Robust Group Policy support gives IT professionals control over every aspect of search functionality — including the types of files indexed and the locations that are indexed. Windows Search is also extensible for third-party developers and IT professionals to build upon, offering comprehensive APIs for developers to display user search query results in custom applications and tools using the .NET Framework or a Common Object Model (COM) interface.

Federation is built in to WDS and is an integral part of the user experience. This makes the desktop part of Enterprise Search in a big way, as you will see later in this chapter when we discuss OpenSearch.

SEARCH IN EXCHANGE AND SQL

Microsoft has search capabilities in other server products as well, notably Exchange Server and SQL Server. These two products are based on the same infrastructure as SharePoint search technology, so the iFilters provided in the Microsoft Filter Pack 2010 work on these two servers as well. However, each of them is maintained by a different group at Microsoft. They are specialized for the application each is integrated with (email search and database search respectively).

The full-text search in Exchange and SQL are product-specific and cannot crawl other repositories, while Enterprise Search offerings crawl across many different datasources. Of course, the administrative UI, backup and restore functions, and other administrative capabilities are integrated into each server product.

SQL Server 2008

SQL Server Integrated Full Text Search (SQL iFTS) is the full-text search technology in Microsoft SQL Server. It provides features for indexing and searching the contents of character-based, XML, and binary data stored in SQL Server databases.

Figure 3-5 shows an overview of the SQL iFTS search architecture, composed of the FTS crawler and the FTS query engine. The FTS crawler works on the content side. It streams tokenized words from full-text indexed documents and data stored in the database, manages word breaker components that use language-based rules to determine word boundaries during the tokenization process, removes stopwords, and updates the full-text index. The FTS query engine handles the query side. It parses the incoming client full-text search request, expands the query according to a language-specific XML thesaurus, locates matches in the full-text search index, and passes off the IDs of matching documents to the SQL Server query engine so that it can return relevant documents and data from the database.

In SQL Server 2005 and prior, the FTS query engine was a separate service that existed outside of the SQL Server process space. Beginning with SQL Server 2008, the FTS query engine is closely integrated directly with the SQL Server query engine and is not a separate service, hence the designation "iFTS."

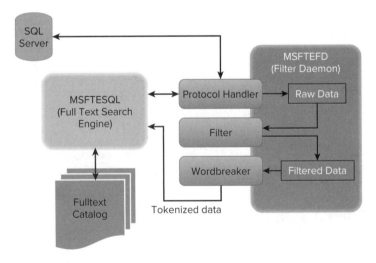

FIGURE 3-5

The way to access FTS is through SQL, using an FTS query language that can be used within FTS-specific predicates and functions to perform full-text queries. SQL Server provides the predicates and functions listed in the Table 3-5, each of which can accept FTS query strings.

TABLE 3-5: SQL Server Predicates and Functions

KEYWORD	MEANING	RETURNS
CONTAINS	Supports complex syntax to search for a word or phrase using Boolean operators, prefix terms, weighted terms, phrase search, thesaurus expansions/replacements, and proximity search	Boolean
CONTAINSTABLE	Supports the full CONTAINS syntax and returns document IDs with rank scores for matches	Table
FREETEXT	Accepts a simplified FTS query syntax and automatically performs thesaurus expansions and replacements	Boolean
FREETEXTTABLE	Supports simplified FREETEXT syntax and returns document IDs and rank scores for matches	Table

FTS includes capabilities for doing proximity search (using NEAR), user-defined proximity weights (using ISABOUT), inflectional language forms, and prefix searches. It does not include all the capabilities of SharePoint search, let alone FAST. But it is a very robust engine that understands the nuances of searching SQL Server data.

Exchange 2010

Microsoft Exchange Server 2010 Search allows users to perform full-text searches across documents and attachments in messages that are stored in their mailboxes. *Exchange Search* (also known as full-text indexing) creates the initial index by crawling all messages in mailboxes within an Exchange 2010 database. As new messages arrive, Exchange Search updates the index based on notifications from the Microsoft Exchange Information Store service.

Figure 3-6 shows an overview of the Exchange Search architecture. Full-text indexes are not stored in your Exchange databases. The search index data for a particular mailbox database is stored in a directory that resides in the same location as the database files.

Exchange Search replaces content indexing (the search functionality in Exchange Server 2003 and 2007) and provides a variety of improvements over content indexing:

➤ Utilization of system resources such as CPU, memory, disk I/O, and disk space required for its indexes is improved, which significantly increases overall performance.

➤ New messages are typically indexed within 10 seconds of arrival, and query results are returned within seconds.

➤ Exchange Search is automatically enabled upon installation and does not require any configuration.

➤ Attachments can now be indexed. Several attachment types are supported, including Microsoft Office documents, text attachments, and HTML attachments.

➤ Indexing is automatically withheld for a specific mailbox database, which reduces the disk I/O load. Also, indexing is automatically withheld for the entire Mailbox server, which reduces both disk I/O and CPU utilization for Exchange Search.

➤ There is an easily accessible search bar in Microsoft Outlook Web Access 2007 or 2010 and query builder support in Microsoft Office Outlook 2007 or 2010.

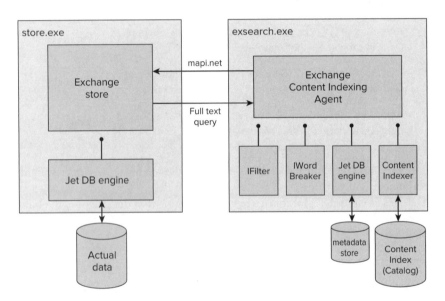

FIGURE 3-6

BING

Bing.com launched in May 2009, offering Internet search customers a more interactive search experience — a significant step up from Live.com. Part of this was based on Microsoft's acquisition of Powerset. Bing.com added semantic analysis and features such as query completion, search history, related searches, and top-level categories to navigate through results.

Bing is probably best known for its photo-of-the-day approach to the home page. It is definitely the underdog in the web search wars, and has developed a different approach, branded a *decision* engine.

On the main search page, some key features are the listing of search suggestions as queries are entered and a list of related searches (called the Explorer pane) based on semantic technology from Powerset.

Bing is not standing still. A number of new capabilities came with the second version of Bing, including real-time search, enhanced previews, Bing Mobile, the Bing Bar, visual search, search sharing, streetside viewing in Bing Maps, and many more. Partnerships with Yahoo! (powering yahoo.com with the Bing search engine), and with Wolfrom Alpha (in a new health and diet section) have been established in as well. And there is a string of new releases providing search of Twitter and other social media, including Bing Twitter and Bing Twitter Maps.

The Bing Exploration Approach

The basic approach to Bing is to provide great core search results for general search, and to extend these into guided explorations. These explorations provide guided experiences that help people make informed decisions. In specific scenarios, people aren't looking for a single answer to a question but would rather know what options are available and the key factors involved in each — for instance:

> *What digital camera should I buy?* Bing.com presents faceted navigation of brands and price ranges, while the result summaries describe features and distinguish between user review and expert review ratings.

> *What flight should I take to San Francisco?* Bing.com recommends the cheapest fares on a calendar of possible departure and arrival times. It also indicates whether prices are likely to rise or fall and maps that price trend over time. When you've selected your preferred flight, Bing will take you directly to the transaction page of the travel provider to close the purchase.

Sections of Bing

As of May 2010, Bing provides the search explorations shown in Table 3-6.

TABLE 3-6: Search Explorations in Bing

SERVICE	DESCRIPTION
Health	Bing Health refines health searches using related medical concepts to get relevant health information and to allow users to navigate complex medical topics with inline article results from experts. This feature is based on the Medstory acquisition.
Images	Bing Images enables the user to quickly search and display most relevant photos and images of interest. The infinite scroll feature allows browsing a large number of images quickly. The advanced filters allows refining search results in terms of properties such as image size, aspect ratio, color or black and white, photo or illustration, and facial feature recognition.
Local	Bing Local searches local business listings with business details and reviews, allowing users to make more informed decisions.
Maps	Bing Maps enables the user to search for businesses, addresses, landmarks, and street names worldwide, and to select from a road-map style view, a satellite view or a hybrid of the two. Also available are bird's-eye images for many cities worldwide, and 3D maps, which include virtual 3D navigation and to-scale terrain and 3D buildings. For business users, it will be available as "Bing Maps For Enterprise."

continues

TABLE 3-6 *(continued)*

SERVICE	DESCRIPTION
News	Bing News is a news aggregator and provides news results relevant to the search query from a wide range of online news and information services.
Reference	Bing Reference semantically indexes Wikipedia content and displays it in an enhanced view within Bing. It also allow users to input search queries that resembles full questions and highlights the answer within search results. This feature is based on the Powerset acquisition.
Shopping	Bing Shopping lets users search from a wide range of online suppliers and marketer's merchandise for all types of products and goods. This service also integrates with Bing cashback offering money back for certain purchases made through the site. This feature is based on the Jellyfish.com acquisition.
Translator	Bing Translator lets users translate texts or entire web pages into different languages.
Travel	Bing Travel searches for airfare and hotel reservations online and predicts the best time to purchase them. This feature is based on the Farecast acquisition.
Twitter	Bing Twitter search allows users to search for and retrieve real-time information from the Twitter service. Bing Twitter search also provides "best match" and "social captions" functionalities that prioritizes results based on relevance and contexts. Only public feeds from the past seven days are displayed in Bing Twitter search results.
Videos	Bing Videos enables the user to quickly search and view videos online from various websites. The Smart Preview feature allows the user to instantly watch a short preview of an original video. Bing Videos also allow users to access editorial video contents from MSN Video.
Visual Search	Bing Visual Search allows users to refine their search queries for structured results through data-grouping image galleries that resembles large online catalogues, powered by Silverlight.
xRank	Bing xRank lets users search for celebrities, musicians, politicians, and bloggers; read short biographies and news about them; and track their trends or popularity rankings.

Voice Search: Bing and Tellme

Microsoft uses Tellme, its voice technology subsidiary, to power a set of upgraded mobile services that are voice accessible. Voice is now available for Live Search services on Windows phones at www .tellme.com/you. Along with Windows Mobile 6.5, phones and other devices will offer people a dedicated button that can trigger three voice-driven tasks: search, contacts, and text messaging. Users just click the button and say "pizza," and the phone will find pizza restaurants near their location via GPS. Or they can say "San Francisco Giants," and they'll be taken to a web page with information on the baseball team. Tellme's voice search is not integrated with Microsoft Enterprise Search today, but it can be integrated into enterprise solutions by partners or services.

FEDERATION ACROSS PRODUCTS

Microsoft has search offerings that span the desktop, enterprise, and web. This is important since nearly every user needs to find and explore across "my stuff, our stuff, and the world's stuff." Given the breadth of their offerings and their use of open standards, Microsoft is able to combine desktop, web, and intranet search experiences together for hundreds of millions of users.

Federation and OpenSearch

OpenSearch is a standard for search federation, originally developed by Amazon.com for syndicating and aggregating search queries and results. It is now supported by a broad community. OpenSearch is in common use among online information service providers (such as Bing, Yahoo!, Wikipedia, and Dow Jones-Factiva) and is becoming more common in business applications. Since Microsoft's introduction of OpenSearch into its Enterprise Search products, partners have built OpenSearch connectors to applications such as EMC Documentum, IBM FileNet, and OpenText Hummingbird.

The operation of OpenSearch is shown in Figure 3-7. It is a standard used throughout the industry. The basic operation involves a search Client — which could be a desktop (Windows 7), a browser (Internet Explorer 8), or a server (SharePoint 2010). It also involves a Search Provider — which is any server with a searchable RSS feed, meaning that it accepts a query as a URL parameter and returns results in RSS/Atom. OpenSearch uses XML for search results. Since search results are structurally lists of documents or URLs, similar to lists of blog postings, OpenSearch simply extends the RSS and ATM XML dialects.

How OpenSearch federation works

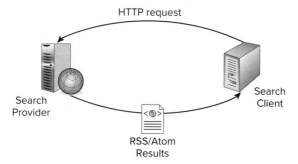

- HTTP request with query in the URL:
  - http://www.site.com/srchrss.aspx?q={searchTerms}
- RSS / Atom results:
  - RSS results with <title>, <link>, <description>
  - Best sources also include:
    <pubdate>, <author>, <category>, <media:thumbnail>
  - Optionally include custom metadata:
    <recordid>, <projectname>, <contactnumber>

FIGURE 3-7

Microsoft began supporting OpenSearch in 2008 with the introduction of Search Server 2008. Now all of Microsoft's Enterprise Search products support OpenSearch, and all of them have implemented comprehensive support for federation with out-of-the-box federation connectors to a range of search interfaces. Federation is built to be extremely easy to set up, taking less than five minutes for an administrator add a federated connector and see federated results appear in search queries. Further flexibility and control over the use of federated connectors come from triggering, presentation, and security features. Enterprise Search offerings can act as OpenSearch Providers, OpenSearch clients, or both.

Support for OpenSearch at Microsoft goes broader. Bing offers an OpenSearch provider. WDS is an OpenSearch client. Internet Explorer 8 also plugs into OpenSearch providers and offers automatic search suggestions based on federated results. OpenSearch providers can also be created easily for Exchange and SQL Server (see Chapter 11).

Federation is now a very powerful way to hook different search products together — both multiple Microsoft products and software from other vendors. A common configuration involves Windows 7 search as a client, with SharePoint, FAST, Bing, and other web applications as providers — making access to FAST search a natural part of search from the desktop desktops.

Windows 7 and Federation

Federated search allows you to search Microsoft Office SharePoint Server 2007 without using a web browser to search to the SharePoint site. Federated search results are presented in Windows Explorer with the same fidelity as local files — including rich previews, file details, and file operations. Users can select the scope of their search using the same kinds of interactions they use to select folders and libraries on their PC. Organizations can populate the list of federated search locations using Group Policy.

From a user perspective, there are a number of advantages to using Windows 7 search federation along with Microsoft Enterprise Search offerings:

➤ By using a federated search connector that can be easily created by an IT Professional or a developer, the information worker can search the SharePoint site directly from Windows Explorer and the Start menu in Windows 7.

➤ Searching for information though federated search can also take fewer steps since users don't have to go to the SharePoint site and execute the search, which can make information workers more productive.

➤ If information workers discover that they need to use the advanced searching and filtering capabilities of SharePoint after they run the search via federated search, they can easily click one button to view the search results on the website and have access to all the capabilities that SharePoint provides.

➤ Windows 7 can also make it easy to re-scope a local search on your PC to SharePoint without having to reenter the search string by leveraging Enterprise Search Scopes, which can be set up by an IT professional.

Integrated search allows information workers (also known as knowledge workers) to stay in their current application and search SharePoint for the content they need. For example, if you were in

Microsoft Office PowerPoint 2007 and wanted to insert a picture from SharePoint into your slide, you would normally open your web browser, go to the SharePoint search page, and enter your query. Once you found the picture, you would save the file locally to your PC and then go back into PowerPoint and insert the file that you had just saved locally. With federated search in Windows 7, you can go into the Insert tab inside of PowerPoint and choose the picture option. The dialog box that opens gives you access to your federated search connectors so that you can search for the image you are looking for in SharePoint without ever leaving PowerPoint.

Your federated search content is also actionable, since it leverages the Windows Explorer interface. Many of the common Windows Explorer functions like copy, paste, and print can be used with the content returned from a federated search query. The preview pane in Windows Explorer is also available to help you review your content before you decide to take action on it. If you want to make a copy of the file from SharePoint, you can use the drag and drop capabilities from your federated search results to easily copy the file from SharePoint to your local PC.

Choosing a Product for Your Application

Understanding the Microsoft Enterprise Search offerings is important, especially if you are choosing the appropriate option for a particular situation. Although we won't offer a definitive recipe, we can offer some guidelines that are more prescriptive than Microsoft's published material.

➤ If the content you want to search is held completely in one source and that source is Exchange, SQL Server, or individual desktops, you should consider using the built-in search capabilities of the respective product. (This is very rare, but worth mentioning for completeness.) Otherwise you should use one of the Enterprise Search products — perhaps in combination with Exchange, SQL, and/or WDS via federation.

➤ If you are planning a simple, low-volume departmental or site search, try Search Server Express 2010. It is a free download, simple to set up, and more than adequate for basic entry-level search.

➤ If you are currently running MOSS 2007 search for intranet, extranet, or site search, and are happy with it, upgrade to SharePoint Server 2010. You can enjoy the benefit of a lot of enhancements and new capabilities at no extra cost. You can always upgrade to FAST Search for SharePoint later.

➤ If you want high-end search and have any familiarity with SharePoint, try FAST Search for SharePoint. This could be for intranet, extranet, or site search, for specialized search applications (such as research portals, sales applications, etc.), or for customer-facing sites powered by SharePoint (including e-commerce and customer support sites that may use other Microsoft servers as well).

➤ If you are running a high-traffic customer-facing site *not* powered by SharePoint, consider FAST Search for Internet Sites. This provides extreme scale and flexibility in standalone high-end search.

You are likely to find that you will use several of these products in your organization, either separately or in combination. Since all of these products support federation, you can tie different search installations together relatively easily.

SUMMARY

Microsoft has introduced lots of new search capabilities and *lots* of choices in the 2010. There are options for every search need — so you can be confident in your ability to solve any search problem. The sheer number of options can be confusing, but by reading this chapter you now have an understanding of the different options and what to use for different applications.

There are two main groups of Enterprise Search products from Microsoft in 2010, which we cover in the next two sections of this book:

➤   Part II covers products built from the SharePoint 2010 code or the new FAST Search for SharePoint codebase (MSS-X, MSS, SPF, SP, SP-FIS, SP-FIS-E, FS4SP, FS4SP-IS).

➤   Part III covers products built from the FAST ESP codebase (FSIA, FSIS).

As you will see in subsequent chapters, there are many differences between these products, especially between the two groups covered in these two sections. But there is more in common than there is different — most of the core concepts and techniques involved are common across all Microsoft search products.

PART II
Implementing Search

Search within SharePoint 2010

WHAT'S IN THIS CHAPTER?

- ➤ Overviewing SharePoint Search 2010 and other Microsoft search technologies
- ➤ Understanding SharePoint Search key components and architecture
- ➤ Planning deployment and understanding information architecture best practices
- ➤ Installing and configuring SharePoint Search 2010 and search deployment scalability
- ➤ Enhancing the search user experience

This chapter is intended to introduce you to the key differences between SharePoint Foundation Search 2010, Search Server 2010, and Search for SharePoint 2010. Content in this chapter covers planning for search, installation, and prerequisites, as well as configuration, ongoing operations, and search deployment best practices guidance for deployment of the SharePoint Search 2010.

Fast Search for SharePoint, while a big part of the overall SharePoint search offering, will be briefly discussed in this chapter only from features comparison standpoint to give you a better idea of the options available from within the SharePoint-based search offering. Fast Search for SharePoint will be covered in more detail in Chapter 5.

SEARCHING WITH SHAREPOINT 2010

With the release of SharePoint 2010, Microsoft has made a clear and serious investment in Enterprise Search, and with it has introduced several platform options to meet a very broad range of requirements. In this chapter and the next, we will cover the installation, initial configuration, and administration of three of the new search products: SharePoint Search 2010 and FAST Search for SharePoint 2010 (both based on the same code base and architecture), and Search Server 2010.

The FAST family of offerings represents a major rewrite and upgrade of the FAST ESP 5.3 product, which has been commercially available for a while. The family comprises two new products that front powerful, advanced search capabilities for the SharePoint platform and represent a major thrust into the Enterprise Search market by Microsoft, which we'll discuss in depth in Chapters 8 and 9.

SharePoint 2010 Overview

SharePoint 2010 platform is a business collaboration platform for the enterprise and the web. This platform has become an ultimate portal solution among Microsoft offerings and has gained business adoption rapidly for its ability to connect and allow users to make educated business decisions using its feature set. With powerful collaboration features, it allows teams to stay connected and aware of the expertise of those in the enterprise. Document and web content management are the core enterprise content management features of SharePoint 2010, which delivers controlled presentation and content, enhanced authoring, document management, records management, and publishing and policy management. The flexibility and extensibility of the platform permit IT professionals to build powerful business solutions that address ever-growing business needs in a timely fashion. But most of all, through its extensive functionality and highly customizable and reusable presentation layer, SharePoint 2010 has enhanced user productivity as a direct result of providing a centralized location for accessing disparate content sources and knowledge repositories, regardless of users' geographical location and the location of the original source of the information, with a unified yet personalized user experience.

With the evolution of the SharePoint platform and the ever-growing accumulation of data and information, the SharePoint search offering had to surpass the boundaries of SharePoint as an information container in order to make SharePoint the "go to" search solution for all enterprise content, regardless of its format and location, by indexing enterprise data from multiple systems. This includes shared data stored in SharePoint; file shares; websites; line-of-business applications (LOB), such as Customer Relationship Management (CRM) databases; Enterprise Resource Planning (ERP) solutions; and so on.

The SharePoint 2010 platform is more or less divided into two separate products: SharePoint Foundation Server and SharePoint Server 2010. While both have search capabilities, the feature set for each is quite different. Out of the box, SharePoint Foundation 2010 search provides only basic SharePoint site search for sites within the same farm. This base search functionality can be extended by adding Search Server 2010 (either the Express or full version).

The following sections provide a summary of the three core search offerings available with the release of the SharePoint 2010 platform.

Search Server 2010

For those familiar with Microsoft Search Server 2008, Microsoft Search Server 2010, as the name implies, is essentially an upgrade, offering all the Enterprise Search features and functionality that currently ship with the product. There are also several new features and capabilities that allow search administrators to configure an optimal, secure, search infrastructure that enables users to find information in the enterprise quickly and efficiently. The following list provides an overview of new features offered in Search Server 2010:

- ➤ Support for Boolean queries (such as AND, OR and NOT)
- ➤ Wildcard prefixes

➤ Query completion (suggestions while typing search queries)

➤ Suggestions to the user after a query has been run

➤ Did you mean this? suggestions for search query variations

➤ Connectors for Enterprise Search in Windows 7

➤ Refinement panels for users to refine search results

➤ Enhancements for relevance of search results

➤ Ranking based on search results history

➤ Relevance based on inferred metadata

➤ Relevancy tuning by document promotion and/or site promotion

➤ Best bets

➤ Shallow results refinement

➤ Query federation (OpenSearch specification)

➤ PowerShell support

In addition to the full version of Search Server 2010, there is also an Express version of the product. The only fundamental difference between the versions is scalability: The full version is able to handle larger volumes of information.

SharePoint Search 2010

SharePoint Search 2010 represents a core shift in Microsoft Enterprise Search technology. The previous search platforms and this new breed of search truly diverge. SharePoint Search 2010 includes a healthy repertoire of new features and is at its core, a completely re-architected platform compared to the SharePoint we've all grown to know and love. We will devote a significant amount of time discussing the SharePoint Search 2010 architecture in detail in the next section; however, the following is a taste of the more prominent features it provides beyond what comes with Search Server 2010:

➤ Socially aware search — people search

    ➤ Search by location, skills, projects, expertise

    ➤ Higher ranking for people names and social tagging

    ➤ Self-search and My Sites search

➤ User experience improvements:

    ➤ Best bets

    ➤ Query federation

    ➤ Query completion based on previously executed queries

    ➤ Improved query language with support for complex queries, such as and/or operators, wildcard searching capabilities, and the Did You Mean This? feature

➤ Phonetic search (currently only available for the following languages: English, Spanish, French, German, Italian, Korean, Portuguese (Brazil), and Russian)

➤ Click-through relevance

➤ Taxonomy integration

➤ Search administration:

➤ PowerShell scriptable deployments and operation

➤ GUI-based administration

➤ Microsoft System Center Operations Management Pack

➤ Health monitoring

➤ PowerShell configuration cmdlets

➤ Usage Reporting

Fast Search for SharePoint 2010

Fast Search for SharePoint 2010 is the workhorse of the new Microsoft Enterprise Search Suite. It offers some significant enhancements to core SharePoint 2010 functionality:

➤ Updated, one-stop Search Center to find answers quickly

➤ Deep refiners, allowing quick, visual exploration of results

➤ Added web parts for easy, out-of-the-box user experience customization

➤ Enterprise-class manageability, scalability and performance of the system

It also provides a unique and powerful set of functionality all its own, including:

➤ Visual cues through presentation of visual best bets, document preview, and document thumbnails for rapid recognition of information

➤ Contextual search to meet the needs of diverse groups

➤ Customizable relevance-ranking models

➤ Advanced content processing that allows complex entity extraction and content enhancements

➤ Easy-to-configure end user experiences

➤ Advanced query capabilities, which enable creation of powerful applications

Chapter 5 covers the features of the FAST Search for SharePoint 2010 in more detail.

SHAREPOINT 2010 SEARCH ARCHITECTURE OVERVIEW

In the previous version of SharePoint, search was offered as a service within a shared service provider (SSP), where services such as User Profiles, Excel, and Search were bundled together and could not be decoupled. Additionally, web applications were bound to a specific SSP, making it challenging to share these services across farms. In the new SharePoint 2010 architecture, all services are offered à la carte, making it easy to share them across multiple farms and scale them. SharePoint Search 2010 is provided to web applications as a search application, with querying and indexing componentized to allow you to run multiple search service instances or to have a completely dedicated search farm that provides a search service to other SharePoint farms in the environment. The advantage of having a separate search farm is that you can tune this farm to meet particular search needs without affecting other farms.

The new platform architecture offers an extended connectors framework that can crawl through a wide range of repositories out of the box, such as exchange folders, file shares, websites, People profiles, Lotus Notes, database content for LOB applications, and other third-party applications that can be made available through connector framework. Powerful federation features allow SharePoint Enterprise Search 2010 to surface search results from non-SharePoint indexes that are OpenSearch industry standards (for example, Bing and Yahoo!) and to be extended to the Windows 7 desktop (through connector framework) with the Windows native search interface, with drag-and-drop functionality and file preview support. It includes an updated services architecture that enables farms to connect to multiple farms to consume cross-farm services and provides the option of having a dedicated search farm that is optimized for search only.

Key Components

The SharePoint search 2010 componentized architecture allows you to create greater redundancy within a single farm and to scale in numerous directions. You can separately scale the components that make up the query and the crawling architecture based on volume of content, performance, redundancy, and the search availability needs of an organization.

Administration

Every search application has one, and only one, administration component. It is responsible for the overall configuration of the search application and can be run on any server in the farm. It is also the only element in the search topology that cannot be scaled out to multiple instances.

Crawler

The job of the crawler component is to orchestrate how disparate content sources are accessed and how retrieved content is brought back into the search engine. Depending on where the information originally resides, the crawler component will use the appropriate connector to handle the specific source data. The following content sources can be traversed by the SharePoint 2010 Crawler using out-of-the-box connectors:

➤ SharePoint Sites and People profiles

➤ Windows file shares

➤ Exchange Public folders

➤ Databases through Java DataBase Connector (JDBC)

➤ Non-SharePoint websites

➤ Line-of-business applications through the content integration options available with SharePoint 2010.

Crawler instances are entirely stateless and do not depend on each other for the exchange of information. They depend on the crawl database to look up the data to be indexed, retrieve source data utilizing protocol handlers, then record crawled items in the crawl search database. In this way, all configuration rules are applied through the crawl database residing in SQL server, ensuring the true independence and redundancy of crawler instances, and further ensuring high availability and scalability.

There are a number of databases that are associated with the search application and the crawler:

➤ **Search Service Application DB** — This is a master database for the search application. In Microsoft Office SharePoint Server (MOSS) 2007, search was provided as a part of Shared Services. In SharePoint 2010 however, search is an entirely independent application, of which there can be multiple configured within the same farm. Each search application is associated with only one search application database. This database stores search application configuration information, crawler configuration data associated with the search application, and Access Control Lists (ACLs) for crawled content.

➤ **Crawl Database** — While multiple crawlers can be configured within a single search application, each crawler component is associated with at least one crawl database. The crawl database stores detailed information about the content updates, crawler schedules, and timestamps for the last crawler run. Crawl databases can exist within a single SQL server, or be distributed over multiple SQL servers for improved I/O performance. Similarly, crawlers associated with a given crawl database can be scattered across multiple index servers for high availability and load sharing.

➤ **Property Database** — The Property database, even though considered part of the Crawler component, is also part of the Query server. The crawler discovers metadata and records it into the Property database; from there, it is later exposed to the end user at query time. The Query server then gathers these properties and displays them within the search interface. These crawled properties are also used to calculate the relevancy of the results.

Administrators can control the behavior of the crawler by applying sets of rules that define how the crawler traverses content in disparate data repositories. The crawler search element can also be scaled to provide crawl distribution across the SharePoint farm with built-in load balancing by creating multiple crawler instances. Later on, within the "Topologies and Federation" section of this chapter, we will discuss different models of search component distribution in greater detail.

Query and Index

After content is discovered and fetched by the crawler, it is then passed to the indexing engine where it is analyzed and stored in a physical file. Based on the type of content delivered by the crawler, the indexing engine first checks whether the content is an update to what already exists in the index or if it is in fact new content to be added to the index. It further optimizes the index file by removing noise words; manages word breaking, identifying how and in which index to store the data; and, finally, propagates updates to the index or index partitions held by query server.

When a user submits a search query, the request is forwarded to the query components of all index partitions. Once the query has been processed by all partitions and the results come back, the query processor combines the results into a single result set, applies security trimming based on the ACLs, detects and eliminates duplicates, and, finally, displays those results to the user.

Unlike in MOSS 2007, in SharePoint 2010 there are several options for configuring how much of the index is stored by an individual query server. For instance, it is possible to have multiple query servers, each storing only a portion, or partition, of the entire index. (See Figure 4-1.)

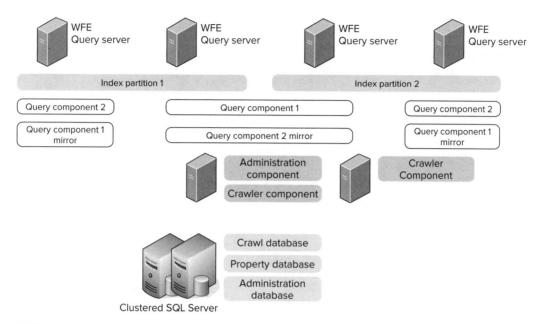

FIGURE 4-1

In the search application configuration, at least one server must be configured to perform the Query role. Additional query servers may be added for redundancy and/or performance. Scaling options for the query component will be discussed in more detail next.

DEPLOYMENT PLANNING

Just as with previous versions of SharePoint, SharePoint Server 2010 Search application deployment requires thoughtful planning. While the SharePoint 2010 Search platform is greatly extensible and can be scaled out over time to meet an organization's growing capacity, performance, and resiliency needs, it is highly advisable to take the time to create a road map of where and how far search will be extended, and what business problems it should solve.

Going through a thorough planning exercise prior to deployment helps you anticipate resource needs so that you can respond in a controlled and timely manner, which makes managing expectations easier, and also lays the foundation for creating a more manageable, phased approach. Approaching deployment in this way also allows for clearly defined milestones, allowing you to demonstrate progress, and, ultimately, the success of the deployment. You also have arguments to justify further investment in the effort should that be necessary.

Capacity Planning

The volume of data (size), as well as the count of items (sites, lists, items in document libraries, database records, files, and web pages) determines the storage requirements and plays a key role in determining architectural requirements for search.

As a starting point for determining potential hardware and architecture requirements, you can use the metrics provided in the following table, which summarizes how the number of items you plan to crawl affects the size of your farm. (See Table 4-1)

TABLE 4-1: Effect of Number of Items on Your Farm

NUMBER OF ITEMS TO BE INDEXED	SIZE OF THE FARM
0 to 10 million	Small farm (See Figure 4-2)
10 to 20 million	Medium farm with shared resources
20 to 40 million	Medium farm dedicated to search application (See Figure 4-3)
40 to approximately 100 million	Large dedicated farm topology (See Figure 4-4)

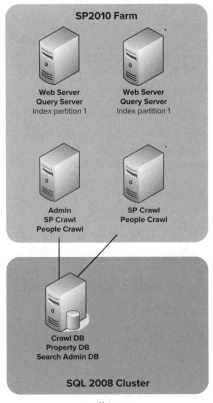

Small Farm Architecture

Scope:
- Query rate: < 10 QPS
- Content: < 10M items
- Standard configuration

FIGURE 4-2

While this table is a good start to determining minimum requirements, you need to consider other factors when designing your production topology. For instance, if requirements dictate that certain content sources must be frequently updated because having fresh search results is imperative to the business, multiple crawl servers and crawlers may be needed to facilitate a higher crawl speed and faster indexing to maximize the freshness of query results.

Medium Dedicated Search Farm

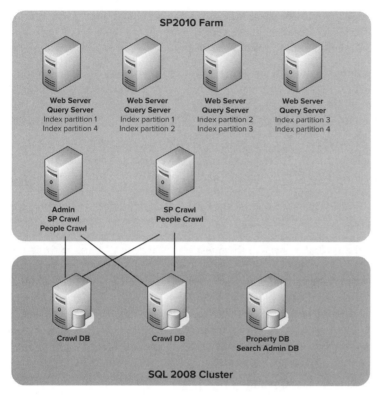

Scope:
- Query rate: < 10 QPS
- Content: < 40M items
- Standard configuration

FIGURE 4-3

Large Dedicated Search Farm

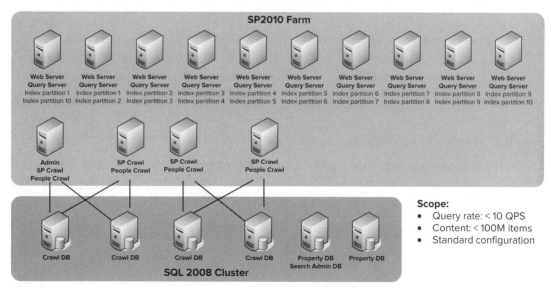

Scope:
- Query rate: < 10 QPS
- Content: < 100M items
- Standard configuration

FIGURE 4-4

Distribution Considerations (Location, Location, Location . . .)

In geographically dispersed or global deployment scenarios, the physical location of users and content within the enterprise dictates to some extent the rudimentary plan for deployment to best meet users' needs across a specific region and/or around the globe.

Bandwidth and latency will undoubtedly impact how long it takes to crawl content, the perceived time it takes to execute queries, and the speed with which results are returned. When connections are slow because of limited bandwidth, you might consider either limiting the body of content that you include in your index by excluding this data from the crawl altogether or federating the search of these content sources.

Another option would be to deploy multiple SharePoint farms. However, this approach also increases the complexity of maintaining such a topology, increases deployment and operating costs, and will likely produce overhead in imposing an effective enterprise governance plan.

Information Architecture

"Garbage in, garbage out" was the typical answer to the question "Why can't I find anything I'm looking for?" posed by many users of SharePoint 2007. This answer simply meant that the quality and relevance of search results were directly related to the initial quality and/or understanding of the data indexed. Taking this a step further, it also suggests that proper planning of your information architecture, as well as an adequate understanding of your external content sources and structure, can greatly reduce the level of frustration that results from the search experience. It will also drive stronger and wider adoption of your enterprise search solution by displaying a deeper and more effective understanding of how content relates to the goals of individuals within the company.

Some of the key decisions that will drive better quality of content are:

➤ Exclude expired, no longer relevant content from the crawl, for example: old announcements, events, expired policies, and the like.

➤ When indexing databases, take advantage of the relational structure of records. Instead of indexing entire tables and fields therein, define your entities or "documents" efficiently, omitting unnecessary fields and relationships.

➤ Indexing files automatically provides some basic information about them, such as filename, format, date, and extension. It is beneficial to understand the structure of files and their internal metadata when mapping to document properties in SharePoint, for example: the title tag or property, MIME type, date, keywords, and author.

Crawled Properties and Managed Properties

Crawled properties are simply the metadata discovered and retrieved by the crawler, from defined content sources, such as SharePoint lists and libraries, and external sources. Managed properties are an additional layer that offers a powerful way to unify and standardize metadata across the entire body of enterprise data.

By exposing managed properties to end users, you can enable them to more easily understand and use this information without requiring any knowledge of the underlying information architecture.

Managed properties further improve end user experience by providing the ability to create complex, highly focused search queries on the fly without special knowledge of the search query language. These searches can also be scoped to a particular document or item property. For example, by selecting Created By as managed property filter and executing a query against a person's name, the user would receive a result set containing documents and/or items that were created by the person they searched for.

Managed properties can be created through the Search Service Administration (SSA) Interface by mapping crawled properties to them. Single or multiple crawled properties can be mapped to a single managed property. This is particularly useful in cases where there is more than one metadata field that carries the same or similar piece of information, and should be treated and searched as one entity.

Consider the following scenario. Within your SharePoint environment, you have multiple document libraries, each containing a Description field, which you use to describe the content of any given document. You also have other libraries in your installation that use a doc comments field to store descriptions. Even further, you index external content repositories, which define a document purpose metadata field, to provide the same bit of data — the document description. Using managed properties, you can map all of these fields to a single property — Document Description — and expose it from within the search interface, giving end users the capability to select Document Description and execute a single query against it, retrieving all documents where there is a match against their respective description field.

Content types

The notion of *content types* was first introduced in Microsoft Office SharePoint Server 2007. While planning for content types is outside of the scope of this book, it is beneficial to understand the concept and the role content types play in the overall SharePoint information architecture design, specifically their impact on the quality of search results.

Content types enable you to apply a set of metadata and define the behavior of a document or item in a centralized, reusable way. They provide for standardization and a controlled way of enforcing presentation, management, and governance rules on the information stored within the SharePoint, thus reinforcing the integrity and quality of the content. The inheritance model of content types provides parent-level grouping of metadata, which allows the sharing subsets of properties across child content types.

Table 4-2 lists a number of advantages to using content types as they relate specifically to search.

TABLE 4-2: Advantages of Using Content Types

AREA OF IMPACT	DESCRIPTION
Content quality	Content types allow you to define and enforce required/mandatory metadata. By requiring this metadata, the quality and relevance of content becomes richer.
Content relevance and accuracy	You can create rules on the content source to index specific content types only. This provides the ability to define a much narrower and targeted index, which can increase relevancy of searches.
User experience	Content types can be exposed as refiners, which provides end users with the ability to filter search results in a highly targeted way.
User experience	Searches can be scoped to specific content types.

Using SharePoint Designer 2010 and Visual Studio 2010, you can integrate SharePoint 2010 with external data sources by creating and crawling external content types and entities for databases or Web Services.

When integrating with data systems that implement dynamic data models, you can implement .NET types for Business Connectivity Services and use either Visual Studio 2010 or SharePoint Designer 2010 to create external content types and entities for the .NET type.

INSTALLATION AND CONFIGURATION

SharePoint Server 2010 deployment can vary in complexity and size, depending on your business requirements. It can be installed on a single machine or multiple servers that would compose your SharePoint farm. When you install SharePoint Server 2010 on a single server farm, you can configure SharePoint Server 2010 to meet your specific needs by provisioning service applications on SharePoint. This section will concentrate on installation and configuration steps as they apply to the search application; for more information on the installation procedure for SharePoint 2010, refer to the SharePoint installation guide.

SharePoint 2010 is available only for 64-bit edition of Windows Server 2008 Standard with SP2. If you are running Windows Server 2008 with SP1, during the install, Microsoft SharePoint 2010 Products Preparation Tool will install SP2 automatically.

Following is the list of minimum system requirements for the installation of SharePoint 2010:

➤ Hardware Requirements:

  ➤ Processor — 64-bit, four-core, 2.5-GHz minimum per core

  ➤ RAM — 4-GB minimum, 8 GB preferred

  ➤ Disk space — 80 GB for installation

➤ Software Requirements:

  ➤ Microsoft .NET Framework version 3.5 SP1

  ➤ Microsoft "Geneva" Framework

  ➤ Microsoft Sync Framework Runtime v1.0 (x64)

  ➤ Microsoft Filter Pack 2.0

  ➤ Microsoft Chart Controls for the Microsoft .NET Framework 3.5

  ➤ Windows PowerShell 2.0 CTP3

  ➤ SQL Server 2008 Native Client

  ➤ Microsoft SQL Server 2008 Analysis Services ADOMD.NET

  ➤ ADO.NET Data Services v1.5 CTP2

Single Node

A single-node farm typically consists of one server that runs both SQL Server and SharePoint Server 2010. This configuration is also useful if you want to configure a farm to meet your immediate search needs first and then add servers to the farm later.

When running the Farm Configuration Wizard — which is shown in Figure 4-5 — during installation to provision the search application on the SharePoint server, make sure that Search check box is not cleared. The search application is configured by default in single-node deployments, and the default content access account that will be used to crawl content is set to NT Authority\ Local Service. The contact email address is then set to the default value *someone@example.com* and can be changed at a later stage. The installation process for the search application is very simple in a single-node scenario, as the search application is installed with the SharePoint 2010 installation.

FIGURE 4-5

Multiple Nodes

To set up SharePoint in a multi-node environment, the SharePoint platform has to be installed on all servers in the farm. After the SharePoint Products Configuration Wizard has been completed, you will have installed binaries, configured security permissions, and the configuration and content databases, as well as SharePoint Central Administration site. As the next step, you will have to run the Farm Configuration Wizard to configure the farm settings and select the search service application:

1. From the Application Management section of Central Administration, click Manage service applications. This page lists all services running on the server. Click the Search Application link to get to Search administration page.

2. From the Ribbon menu on the Search Administration page, click New and select Search Service Application.

3. On the Create New Search Service Application page, accept the default value for Name, or specify a new name that will be used for the search service application.

4. In the Search Service Account section, accept the default account for the farm, or create a new one. The default account that will be used is the farm administration account; it is recommended that you change this account to a less privileged account to avoid having a crawler discover and index draft documents and serve them in the search results.

5. For the Application Pool for the Search Admin Web Service, you can accept the default or create a new application pool that will be used by the search application.

6. In the Application Pool for Search Query and Site Settings Web Service section, click Use Existing Application Pool, and select the application pool that is used for the Search Admin Web Service. Table 4-3 lists search application and setup configuration information.

TABLE 4-3: Search Application Setup and Configuration Parameters

NAME	DESCRIPTION	RECOMMENDATION	MANDATORY?
Default content access account	Service account to be used by crawler for content sources that do not explicitly specify a different account to be used	Specify a domain user account that has read access to the content that is going to be crawled. This account can be changed at any time.	Yes
Contact e-mail address	This is the email address that is written into log files of crawled servers	Change this to the account that an external administrator can contact when a crawl might be contributing to a problem, such as performance degradation, on a server that the system is crawling.	Yes
Proxy Server	The proxy server address to be used by index server when crawling content that is external to the server farm	By default, there is no proxy selected on the search application. Specify the proxy server if it is needed.	No

NAME	DESCRIPTION	RECOMMENDATION	MANDATORY?
Search Time-out	Connection — amount of time in seconds that the search application will wait when connecting to a content repository Request acknowledgment — amount of time in seconds that the search application will wait until the request for content is acknowledged by the content source	Extend this time when crawling over slow connections.	No
SSL warnings	Specifies whether SSL certificate warnings should be ignored by the system		No

Proxy server, Search Time-out, and SSL warning settings are farmwide search settings and can be modified from the Search Administration page: from the Quick Launch menu, click Farm-Wide Search Administration, and click on the link with name of the setting to be modified.

Scaling a Search Application in a Farm

While all other search components can be mirrored for redundancy or moved from one server to another within a farm to provide better load spread, search administration is an exception. This is the only component that cannot be moved and will reside on the server where the search application was created initially.

After the first search server in the farm is provisioned, the topology of the search is simple, resulting in crawl and query components residing on the same server. To scale out your search topology, you will have to join additional SharePoint servers to the farm and move search components to the joined servers. The following is a list of steps to move a query component to another server:

1. From the Search Service Application page of the Central administration site, in the Search Application Topology section, click Modify.

2. Click Query Component 0 from in the Index Partition section, and select Edit Properties from the drop-down menu.

3. On the Edit Query Component page, select one of the front-end web servers from the Server drop-down list. You can optionally specify if you want to use this server as a failover query component. In this case, the server will start serving queries only in the case of the failure of the primary query server in the same index partition.

4. Click OK.

   You can also add a mirror of the query component by selecting the Add Mirror option from the Query Component 0 drop-down menu. When a mirror is added, the mirror server will have a replica of the index partition.

5. On the Add Mirror Query Component page, in the Server drop-down list, select the server that you identified on the Edit Query Component page, and click OK.

Configuration

When a standalone or basic installation of SharePoint Server 2010 is performed, a local SharePoint site's content source is automatically created and a full crawl is automatically performed following the installation procedure. An incremental crawl is scheduled to occur every 20 minutes after that. In an advanced installation of SharePoint Server 2010, since crawling content requires at least one content source, a local SharePoint site's content source is also automatically created, but no crawls are performed or scheduled. Crawling of content sources can be manually started for a one-time crawl or scheduled to perform full and incremental crawls at specified time intervals. You can review and modify the settings for already created content sources from the Search Services Administration page by clicking on the link of the content source listed in the Content Sources section. (See Figure 4-6.)

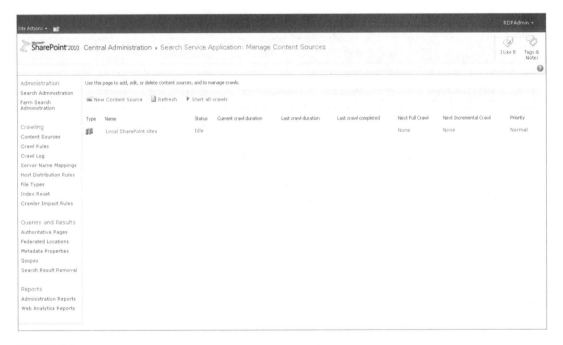

FIGURE 4-6

To create a content source, click the content source link from the Quick Launch section of the SSA page.

1. On the Manage Content Sources page, click add Content Source page, and in the Name field, type a name for the new content source.

2. Select the type of content that you want to crawl.

3. In the Start Addresses section, type the URLs from which the crawler should begin crawling.

4. Select desired crawling behavior in the Crawl Settings section.

5. Define the crawling schedules in the Crawl Schedules section:

    ➤ **Full crawl** — Specify the schedule for a full crawl by clicking Create Schedule. A full crawl crawls all content that is specified by the content source, regardless of whether the content has changed.

➤ **Incremental crawl** — Specifies the schedule at which an incremental crawl of the content is performed. An incremental crawl crawls content that is specified by the content source that has changed since the last crawl. To define a schedule, click Create schedule. You can change a defined schedule by clicking Edit Schedule.

6. To prioritize the content source for the crawler, on the Priority list, select Normal or High. You can click "Start full crawl of this content" to immediately begin a full crawl.

7. Click OK.

You can edit a content source to change the schedule on which the content is crawled, the crawl start addresses, the content source priority, or the name of the crawl. Crawl settings and content type cannot be changed when editing a content source.

You can create external data sources to crawl with SharePoint. External data sources are crawled with connectors. SharePoint ships with a number of connectors that allow you to connect to the most popular data sources out of the box. You can manage connectors by using the Search Service application in SharePoint Central Administration. To configure indexing of external data sources, navigate to the Manage Service Applications section of Central Administration and go to Search Service Applications. From this interface, you will create a new content source and select the connector that will be used to index the external repository.

People Search

The user profile application is the data source for people search. People profile information can be drawn from AD/LDAP (Lightweight Directory Access Protocol) or other repositories storing data about employees. To enable people search, user profiles, and managed metadata, the search application itself has to be started and configured.

The User Profile Service application is an important part of people search because it stores much of the information that appears in results for people search. For example, information for My Site sites and LDAP stores, such as Active Directory Domain Services (AD DS), are stored by the User Profile Service application.

The Managed Metadata application provides a way to store relationships between metadata values, and allows administrators to have some control over the health of the data in the profile store. The Search Service application features tuned results, refinement, and ranking to take advantage of the data coming from the User Profile application and the Managed Metadata application.

The following steps explain how to verify the existence of the service applications that people search depends on. It also will help you to create the service applications if they do not exist. To verify that service applications exist, the account that is used to log in to the central administration site has to be a member of the Farm Administrators SharePoint group.

1. Click the Manage Service Applications link from the Home page of the Central Administration website, in the Application Management section.

2. Verify that Managed Metadata Service, Search Service Application, and User Profile Service are listed in the name column on the Manage Service Applications page. (See Figure 4-7.)

FAST Search Query	Search Service Application Proxy	Started
Managed Metadata Service	Managed Metadata Service	Started
Managed Metadata Service	Managed Metadata Service Connection	Started
PerformancePoint Service Application	PerformancePoint Service Application	Started
PerformancePoint Service Application	PerformancePoint Service Application Proxy	Started
Search Administration Web Service for FAST Search Content	Search Administration Web Service Application	Started
Search Administration Web Service for FAST Search Query	Search Administration Web Service Application	Started
Search Administration Web Service for Search Service Application	Search Administration Web Service Application	Started
Search Service Application	Search Service Application	Started
Search Service Application	Search Service Application Proxy	Started
Secure Store Service	Secure Store Service Application	Started
Secure Store Service	Secure Store Service Application Proxy	Started
Security Token Service Application	Security Token Service Application	Started
State Service	State Service	Started
State Service	State Service Proxy	Started
Usage and Health data collection	Usage and Health Data Collection Service Application	Started
Usage and Health data collection	Usage and Health Data Collection Proxy	Started
User Profile Service Application	User Profile Service Application	Started
User Profile Service Application	User Profile Service Application Proxy	Started

FIGURE 4-7

If any of these service application names does not exist, use the following list of steps to create necessary service applications:

1. From the home page of the Central Administration website, in the Quick Launch Toolbar, click Configuration Wizards.

2. Click Launch the Farm Configuration Wizard from the Configuration Wizards page.

3. On the next page select Walk Me Through the Settings Using This Wizard, and then click Next.

4. On the Configure Your SharePoint Farm page, in the Service Account section, select Use an Existing Account.

5. Select the check boxes for the service applications that need to be created, and click Next.

6. Skip the Create Site Collection page.

7. Click Finish.

Ensure that the Managed Metadata Service application is started by clicking Manage Service Applications in the Application Management section. Make sure that the Status column for the Managed Metadata Service application shows Started. In cases when the services are created manually without using the Farm Configuration Wizard, the Managed Metadata Web Service might not be running.

To expose the people search to the end user, a Search Center site has to be created as well. You will find more information about setting up and configuring Search Center later in this chapter.

Reporting

SharePoint 2010 OOB provides robust Administration and Web Analytics reports that can be used to monitor the overall health and usage of the search application.

Search Administration Reports

Search Administration reports come in a variety of flavors and are aimed at helping to determine the health of search service application components in a SharePoint farm. Health and performance monitoring features enable an administrator to monitor the activities of search operations in the farm and are especially helpful for monitoring the crawl and query components' status. Reports provided with the search aid in the analysis of search system operations and query performance-tuning activities. For example, these reports can help you determine the best scheduling for crawls and the overall search application topology by providing information on how many queries are issued during certain time periods, and peak query times.

 To enable Search Web Analytics reports, you must have a SharePoint environment that contains crawled data with a Search Center and the State Service enabled through the Farm Configuration Wizard.

Administration reports are enabled by default and show high-level, as well as in-depth, monitoring information that is collected from all components for the selected Search Service application. When the verbose query monitoring is enabled for search, verbose search administration reports can use per-query data to derive query latency percentiles.

You can also run the Health Analysis tool to check for problems automatically, by setting it to run on a predefined schedule and to automatically alert the administrator if problems are found. To access reports in the Search administration reports folder, you must be logged in as a member of the Farm Administrators SharePoint group on the computer running the SharePoint Central Administration website and ensure that the Web Analytics Service application is running.

IMPLEMENTING SECURITY

Search results' security is important in any search application, but when it comes to Enterprise Search it is imperative to ensure that content is served in a manner that is compliant with the security require-ments. Search results' security trimming is managed through the query component, where the query engine performs an access check for the user's identity against the security descriptor stored in the content index for each item in the search results and then removes any items in the search results that the user does not have access to, so that the user never sees these results. The query engine caches access check results for each unique security descriptor. However, this only works when SharePoint knows who has access to the content and who doesn't.

Out-of-the-box, you can configure SharePoint to crawl content and index ACL information via a protocol handler for a number of sources, including file shares, SharePoint content, and other sources that can be crawled through available connectors. During the content-crawling process, the protocol handler for a content source extracts the security information for a content item and stores this in the index.

When building new connectors for content integration with the Business Connectivity Services, the security is straightforward and can be easily implemented. On the other hand, the claims-based authentication that SharePoint 2010 relies on can provide a wide range of options for securing content from diverse environments.

CAPACITY AND LIMITATIONS

SharePoint Foundation Search can index and search items only within the local farm and is limited to indexing up to 10 million items. When the organization does not require an enterprise-wide search solution or need to index external data sources, SharePoint Foundation Search might fit the bill. The feature set does not allow you to search beyond a site collection level, but it is extendable with Search Server 2010. Search Server 2010 Express is a low-end, standalone search product that is limited to one server deployment with up to 300,000 documents if deployed with SQL Express, and up to 10 million with SQL server. This product is offered at no license cost and is great for a low or no budget search deployment project. It can be a good enough search option when the search need is a immediate and straightforward and availability is not a big issue; for example, when there is a need to enable department-level search or add more capabilities on top of the SharePoint Foundation Search.

Microsoft Search Server 2010 Express is a free downloadable product that provides searching over enterprise content. This product can crawl external data sources, including SharePoint sites, websites, Windows file shares, Exchange Public Folders, Business Data Catalog connections, and Lotus Notes. But the deployment is limited and cannot be scaled to multiple database or application servers for redundancy or to increase capacity or performance. However, if you install it using the Advanced option, you can add web servers.

Search Server 2010

Microsoft Search Server 2010 (MSS) is an upgraded version of Search Server 2008. It offers all of the Enterprise Search features and functionality that exist in Microsoft Search Server 2008 and more. It is considered to be a medium to low-end Enterprise Search solution that can scale to multiple servers. With MSS, search administrators can configure the most beneficial, secure search infrastructure, which enables end users to find information in the enterprise quickly and efficiently.

MSS is an easy-to-deploy search solution that can crawl local SharePoint sites in the farm immediately after the Farm Configuration Wizard finishes running. While MSS greatly extends the functionality of a basic search and comes with its own Search Center preconfigured site template, it is still limited in its extensibility options through BCS. Consider using Search Server 2010 if you need an enterprise-scale search solution that supports multiple crawl servers and query servers.

SharePoint Search 2010

A scaled-out SharePoint Server 2010 farm can serve searches for up to 100 million items. SharePoint Server 2010 is a good choice for an Enterprise Search solution, as it provides high availability through the redundancy of its search components. It can be easily extended to index external data sources, people search, and site search applications. It is a fully functional search solution and should cover the data volume and performance needs of most companies.

TOPOLOGIES

The main values of a true Enterprise Search solution are its ability to scale to support large volumes of content and its high query rate with low query latency. The scalability is achieved through the addition of query servers to the farm. The new search architecture has introduced the concept of index partitioning, where subsets of the full index are propagated to different query servers, thus spreading the load of queries across multiple query servers. In the multiple index partitions scenario, each partition must be associated with at least one query server, but multiple query servers can be associated with the same partition and hold a mirror of the index partition.

SharePoint Server 2010 uses a hash of each document's ID to identify the partition that stores index entries for this document. At the query time, each query server is contacted by the query object model so that results from all partitions are returned. For optimal performance, a query server should be allocated to no more than 10 million items. A subsecond query latency and high volume of queries to be executed concurrently are good indicators of a need for multiple query servers, and possibly multiple index partitions. From the indexing perspective, performance and the results' freshness depend on the crawl time. The time it takes to crawl items largely depends on the following factors: number of data sources, latency, size and type of files, and the query load while crawling is occurring.

It is important not to underestimate the role of SQL server when scaling your SharePoint Search application. There are two databases that play key role in the topology planning: the crawl database and the properties database. Each query component is associated with a property database; this database is used for retrieving managed properties and Access Security Lists (ACLs) for query components. The crawl database contains crawled content and should be located on a separate hard disk from the property database as a best practice to prevent I/O contention. If the crawling is in progress when end users are executing queries or several crawler connections are concurrently established to the crawl database, it is best to deploy crawl databases to separate SQL servers.

The following are general rules of thumb for search component scaling:

> If query throughput is low, add multiple query components with mirror index partitions.

> If SQL server is memory/CPU bound, add an additional SQL Server with additional crawl databases.

> When query availability is the key, deploy redundant query servers and use clustered or mirrored database servers to host property databases.

> If you have multiple content locations for crawling, use multiple crawlers on redundant index servers and add crawl databases.

> If query latency is caused by high peak query load, add query servers and index partitions. Each index partition can contain up to approximately 10 million items; the query throughput increases when you add index partition instances.

> If query latency is caused by database load, isolate the property database from crawl databases by moving it to a separate database server.

Refer to the Figure 4-4 for different topologies' deployment options.

FEDERATION

Federation is a powerful way of providing a unified search experience while avoiding the cost of indexing content that is distributed across multiple repositories where search already exists or the crawling of this content is not feasible to begin with. Federation enables end users to issue a query against multiple sources and renders result sets in separate web part on a single results page. These searches can be executed against enterprise content repositories, portions of your Search Server index, and other search engines. SharePoint Server 2010 out-of-the-box search provides federation of the following:

➤ SharePoint People Search

➤ Related Searches

➤ OpenSearch providers such as Bing and Yahoo!

➤ Windows 7 and IE8 searching SharePoint 2010

➤ Rich RSS feeds and the federation generator

One of the points of Enterprise Search is creating a central point of access to the data; people don't want to search several different places to find information. Federating results saves time and frustration, and it makes people more productive. Tables 4-5 and 4-6 summarize and explain the advantages of indexing content versus using the federation of search results.

TABLE 4-4: Indexing Versus Federation

INDEXING THE CONTENT	FEDERATION OF SEARCH RESULTS
Aggregated results set with common relevance and ranking model.	Certain level of aggregation is possible through during run time.
Control over the scope of the searchable body of data.	Up to the provider, but might be scoped by constructing more complex queries.
Property extraction for the refinement of search results.	Refinement available through custom code
Ability to control and expand the metadata extraction.	Only through custom code.
Better system performance and fault tolerance	No control over availability and performance of the search; up to the provider.
Full control over document and item security and security trimming.	Up to the provider.

 Federation is not an option and the indexing of content will be mandatory to enable searching of the repositories where search is not available.

The following table explains advantages of using federation over indexing.

TABLE 4-5: Advantages of Federation over Indexing

INDEXING THE CONTENT	FEDERATING SEARCH RESULTS
Storage cost.	Allows you to reduce the storage cost by utilizing the index stored in third-party system.
Crawling is not feasible because of geographical distribution, performance of crawling and indexing, or legal restrictions.	Query results are served by third-party query services, bypassing the limitation on indexing the content, and providing fresh results sets.
Security-trimmed search results.	Nothing built into OpenSearch.

SEARCH USER EXPERIENCE

The Search Center enhances the search experience for end users by providing a centralized and greatly customizable user interface to perform search queries and discover information. Search Center template availability depends on the template originally chosen for site collection site. It comes with a preset number of web parts and can be customized through the web parts toolbox by modifying its configuration settings or through XSLT. The default home page of the Search Center site allows searching with either the All sites scope, so that users can search across all content in the index, or navigating to people search through the tabular navigation above the search box, and provides links to the current user's search preferences and advanced search options. Administrators can choose to add tabs to the navigation options available and associate them with custom scopes that users can use to query different subsets of the content index. The Advanced Search page allows users to construct advanced search queries. Queries can be fairly complex, with inclusion and exclusion rules for keywords and search phrases. Users can also select property restrictions to limit the searchable scope of the body of a document or an item to a specific managed property.

When a user performs a search, the results are displayed on a search core results page, which offers a very user-friendly and intuitive, rich user interface with an easy-to-navigate layout. On the left side of the page, users can drill down into the results, refining the result set, by clicking on the value of a refiner fetched by search. Refiners allow end users to build complex queries on the fly, without knowledge of the search query language, and let people more easily understand the structure of the information without any knowledge of custom metadata. The right side of the results page presents federated searches results web parts, such as people search and similar searches. The core results web part is located in the center of the page; the look and feel of the result items' presentation is easily customizable through the application of custom XSLT and the configuration of the results web part properties. You can refer to Chapter 6 in this book for more customization options available.

If you do not have a Search Center site, use the following procedure to create a site collection based on the Search Center template:

1. In the Application Management section of the central administration site, click Create Site Collections.
2. On the Create Site Collection page, provide the title and description for this site collection.

3. Type in the URL for the site.

4. In the Template Selection section, click the Enterprise tab, and then select either the Enterprise Search Center or Basic Search Center template.

 Only the Enterprise Search Center template includes people search.

5. Select the username for the Primary Site Collection Administrator.

6. Click OK.

People Search

SharePoint Server 2010 provides an address-book-style name lookup experience and will search for all variations of common names, including nicknames, with better name matching through phonetic search, which returns names that sound similar to what the user has typed in a query. Refiners built into the people search results page allow users to browse and filter out people by name, title, and other fields defined in the user profile.

The value of people search lies in finding those with particular expertise and talents within the enterprise, and this value increases as users add data to their profiles. The first thing that most people try to search for when presented with a people search option is their name. In people search, when a user performs a search for him- or herself, the system treats it as a "self-search" and displays information that pertains to the searches that have led to the user. This information includes the number of times the My Site profile was viewed and the keywords that other people used to get to the person's profile. The self-search feature provides a good start in creating an incentive for people to populate their profile, by showing the number of searches that led to their profiles and the associated search keywords. This can encourage users to add information to their profile pages to help people with common business interests, expertise, and responsibilities find them, and it increases productivity by connecting the community.

Users can manually submit or automatically generate a list of colleagues mined from Outlook as a way of rapidly inferring social relationships throughout the organization, which speeds the adoption and usefulness of people search results. SharePoint Server 2010 also infers expertise by automatically suggesting topics mined from the user's Outlook inbox and suggesting additions to their expertise profile in their My Site. This makes it easy to populate My Site profiles and means that more people have well-populated profiles and get the benefits of this in both search and communities.

People search results can also include real-time presence through Office Communication Server, making it easy to immediately connect with people once they are found through search. The more information that people share about their projects, responsibilities, and areas of expertise, the more relevant and focused a people search becomes.

OPERATIONS

SharePoint Server 2010 provides new capabilities for monitoring farm operations and customizing reports for Enterprise Search. Specifically, administrators can review status information and topology information in the search administration pages of the Central Administration website. They can also review crawl logs, as well as health reports, and can use the Systems Center Operations Manager to monitor and troubleshoot the search system. The SharePoint administration interface can be extended by PowerShell cmdlets that allow the scripting of many operational tasks.

Relevance Tuning

"You will be done once it is built" is not applicable to good search solutions. Just as content is constantly changing and business needs are always evolving, so too should your Enterprise Search. Enterprise Search has greatly evolved and is not just about searching; it is a company's business intelligence tool, which gleans information from the vast pool of data. To deliver the right information, you need to ensure that the system continues to meet users' needs by providing them with relevant result sets. The concept of relevancy is important to search, as it is a direct result of a sorting order in which results that are most significant as answers to the executed query appear first in the result set. For example, when you search for a document and the query finds a match in the title of one document and the body of another, the document with the matching title is considered a better match. In SharePoint Search 2010, there is a predefined ranking model, which cannot be changed, but you can influence relevancy of documents by defining keywords, best bets, synonyms, search scopes, managed properties, and site promotions.

Initial relevance tuning provides a good start, but as part of ongoing operations, further adapting the out-of-the-box experience by analyzing user search behavior will drive higher end user satisfaction and productivity. The quality-of-search tuning cycle can make the search experience even better.

SharePoint 2010 comes with a number of reports that aid in search pattern analysis. Site Analytics reports identify popular queries — the queries that should work well and can be good candidates for best bets keywords — or provide an indication as to which queries need keyword management — best bets queries that failed (which queries didn't work well). Failed queries are the queries that returned zero search results and can provide hints as to what content sources should be added to the crawl or be indicators that there are crawl issues. The first thing to check, in this case, would be crawl sources and crawl logs, to identify if documents that should match the query were actually crawled.

SUMMARY

Enterprise Search always been meant to be in the center of SharePoint platform, and a key element of the value proposition for deploying SharePoint into organizations. But only SharePoint version 2010 has offered a true Enterprise Search solution to complement the wide variety of SharePoint features. This chapter introduced you to key components of the search architecture, administration, and installation options as well as end-user experience.

5

FAST Search within SharePoint 2010

WHAT'S IN THIS CHAPTER?

➤ Exploring the new Microsoft Enterprise Search offering, FAST Search for SharePoint 2010

➤ Understanding key search features, components, and the search engine architecture

➤ Examining installation and configuration procedures as well as capacity and scaling scenarios

➤ Overviewing search administration and monitoring options with FAST Search for SharePoint

➤ Understanding relevance tuning, the Search Center, and the end-user experience

This chapter covers the installation details (but not customization) of FAST Search for SharePoint 2010. It includes product details, hardware prerequisites, the OS platform, and recommended configurations to fit business needs. Key components, such as the indexing server and search query server, are discussed in detail. It also discusses product features, relevance tuning, the end user experience, and some customization options. This chapter supplements Chapter 4, given that SharePoint Server 2010 Search represents an important upgrade to the existing search in SharePoint, while FAST Search for SharePoint 2010 is a completely new offering and the first new product based on the FAST technology since FAST was acquired by Microsoft in April 2008. FAST Search for SharePoint 2010 adds a whole new level of search capabilities that are a superset of what comes in the out-of-the-box SharePoint 2010 Search product.

SEARCH WITH FAST SEARCH FOR SHAREPOINT 2010

This new product truly attests to Microsoft's years of investment in the Enterprise Search platform. By combining SharePoint and FAST platforms, Microsoft has brought the best of both worlds together to create an unparalleled content management, collaboration, document management, and Enterprise Search platform. FAST Search for SharePoint 2010 builds on the comprehensive development framework of SharePoint 2010. The customization options range from configuring out-of-the-box search behavior and web parts to extending existing functionality using web part code and SharePoint Designer to creating brand new components and functionality with the available APIs.

FAST Search for SharePoint 2010 Product Overview

FAST Search for SharePoint 2010 is a new product that was completely re-architected from its predecessor, FAST ESP 5.3. It is designed to be installed and operated on top of the SharePoint 2010 platform and takes full advantage of the content and document management features of SharePoint. The newly architected platform, while still retaining the majority of the architectural flexibility and functionality of FAST ESP 5.3, shares a common set of APIs with SharePoint 2010. It enriches the end-user search experience by providing conversational search capabilities and enhances the impact of knowledge and expertise searches through its social search features. It allows you to take advantage of extensible content processing to get the best of enterprise data without compromising the security and data source structure. It empowers developers to build great search-driven applications and shape the end user experience to maximize productivity. It enables IT professionals to deploy and manage an industrial-strength scale and manageability Enterprise Search platform. Integration with System Center Operations Manager (SCOM) gives administrators a granular overview of the system and the capability to monitor the system's performance, and it supports standard Windows monitoring services.

When FAST Search for SharePoint 2010 (FS4SP 2010) is deployed in addition to the SharePoint 2010, it greatly enhances some of the core SharePoint search features and adds some unique features on top of SharePoint search — features that are available only through FAST. The following list gives a clearer picture of significant enhancements to core SharePoint 2010 functionality:

➤ Updated, one-stop Search Center to find answers quickly

➤ Deep refiners, allowing quick, visual exploration of results

> *The difference between shallow refiners that are available with SharePoint Search 2010 and the deep refiners offered with FS4SP2010 is that shallow refiners do not offer the exact count of the matched occurrences of a term, they only provide a count of up to 50 occurrences. Deep refiners do provide the exact count of all occurrences of the term in the result set.*
>
> *For those familiar with the FAST ESP platform, the term "refiner" in the SharePoint vernacular is the same as the term "navigator" in FAST ESP.*

➤ Added web parts for easy, out-of-the-box user experience customization

➤ Enterprise-class manageability, scalability, and performance of the system

FAST also provides unique and powerful functionality all its own, including the following features:

➤ Visual cues through presentation of visual best bets, document preview, and document thumbnails for rapid recognition of information

➤ Contextual search to meet the needs of diverse groups

➤ Customizable relevance ranking models

➤ Advanced content processing that allows complex entity extraction and content enhancements

➤ Easy to configure end user experiences

➤ Advanced query capabilities that enable the creation of powerful applications

The following section covers the features of the FAST Search for SharePoint 2010 in more detail.

 Even though FAST Search for SharePoint 2010 was built on concepts similar to those introduced by FAST ESP Search, there is no upgrade path from FAST ESP to FAST Search for SharePoint 2010 at this time, as they are considered to be two different products.

The integration of FAST with the SharePoint platform allows developers to build search solutions to support search engines and extend the functionality of SharePoint search by taking advantage of more advanced features available with FAST Search.

Key Search Engine Components

All the different services within the search system are performed by search components. Some of the components work in synch with each other, while others work independently. For example, query-matching services coordinate with the query processing services, whereas the crawler component works independently, crawling the content. The following sections describe in more detail all the search components that make up the search engine.

Administration

In every FAST Search for SharePoint deployment, there is one *administration* component. This is the only component that does not scale to multiple nodes in the system for redundancy. The administration component provides services such as logging and contains functionality to control the search experience, such as determining how to perform property extraction, which synonyms to use, and which items to use as best bets.

Another important function that this component provides is the communication middleware that facilitates synchronous function calls as well as asynchronous message callbacks across different services in the search system. The Index Schema service manages the index schema for the search system. The index schema contains all the configuration entities that are needed to generate the configuration files related to the index schema for all the other services in the system. The index schema service exposes an API through which protocol clients can view and modify the index schema. The index schema controls which managed properties of an item will be indexed, how the properties will be indexed, and which properties can be returned in the query hit list. The index schema also includes a rank profile. The rank profile controls how the rank will be calculated for each item in a query hit list. Most changes to the configuration of the index schema trigger updates to item processing, indexing, query matching, and query processing.

Content Gathering

SharePoint Search 2010 and FAST Search for SharePoint both use indexing connectors to discover, enumerate, and index the content contained in content sources that are hosting the information. If the content is not crawled, it is not indexed, which means that the content is not searchable. The FAST Search Content application gathers content for indexing through the utilization of indexing connectors that "understand" how to connect to the content source and recognize the content structure with respect to the repository, for example, hierarchical versus link traversing.

Although the connector framework is the same for SharePoint search and FAST Search for SharePoint, the following connectors come only with the FAST Search for SharePoint 2010 installation.

➤   JDBC connector
➤   Lotus Notes

Indexing connectors also have a mechanism to provide incremental versus full crawling to reduce the load on the repository when the full crawling is not required. Another important feature of connectors is recognition of the security descriptors or Access Control Lists (ACLs) from the content source, so, based on the user's permissions, the query processor can provide security trimmed results to the end user.

Content-Processing Pipeline

When the content is fetched from the content source and properties are extracted by the indexing connector, it is being passed to the content-processing pipeline before it is placed into an index. The pipeline consists of sequential processing stages that provide normalization of content, further content analysis, and manipulation based on linguistic features and extractors. The content-processing pipeline can be extended with custom processing stages to provide more sophisticated processing that includes business rules specific to an organization.

Index

When the content exits the content-processing pipeline, it is passed to the indexing dispatcher. The indexing dispatcher determines which index partition to place the content into, thus providing seamless handling of index partitioning, which is useful for handling large volumes of data. If the indexing is deployed on multiple nodes, the index dispatcher and the indexing component will also be deployed on multiple nodes.

The index itself is an inverted index that contains a list of indexed words and references to their location in the document and/or list item. (See Figure 5-1.) The index is designed to scale according to the number of items to be indexed. To scale the indexing service up, it is possible to deploy it across more than one index column. Each index column will contain one part of the index, and the combined set of index columns will constitute the entire index. In this case, each indexing node handles only a fraction of the entire index, thus scaling the indexing service up in terms of the number of items that it can index per second and the total number of items that can be placed in the index.

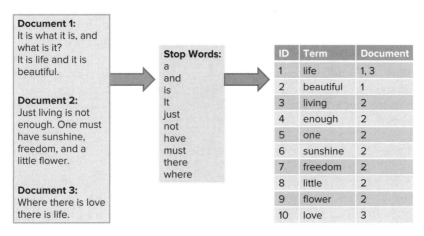

FIGURE 5-1

The indexing is defined by the index schema object model. The index schema defines the mapping of managed properties to the searchable index structures, and how relevancy ranking is to be performed based on the managed properties configuration.

FAST Search Authorization

The FAST Search Authorization Manager service receives security updates from indexing connectors and then pushes the updates to all the query-processing nodes in the system. In addition, the service keeps the security-related configuration of these nodes consistent and synchronizes such configuration changes across multiple query-processing nodes. It is the responsibility of the query-processing service to make sure that end users performing a query receive only the results for which they are authorized. The query-processing service, thus, checks the access rights of the user and rewrites the incoming query with an access filter that corresponds to the current user. The FAST Search Authorization (FSA) Manager regularly pushes the information that is needed for the rewrite, and the query-processing service combines this information with information from Active Directory Data Store (AD DS) and Active Directory or other Lightweight Directory Access Protocol (LDAP) directory services.

To generate the user's security filter, the FSA worker component needs to know which groups the user is a member of. For users in a local cache user store, the FSA worker component uses that user store for the groups. Some users have identities in multiple user stores. For example, an Active Directory user may have a corresponding account under Lotus Notes. To generate the user's security filter, the FSA worker component requires the user's identities and groups in all user stores. Because the security principal identifier may not be the same in all user stores, the FSA worker component uses principal aliasing to map users and groups from one user store into another; the same concept is currently used in Security Access Module for FAST ESP (SAM).

Query Component

When the query is submitted to the search engine, the query-processing function performs preliminary query analysis, including query-language parsing and linguistic processing. It also determines the identity of the user executing the query and rewrites the query to include an access filter that corresponds to the current user and group membership to ensure that the result set returned to the end user is security trimmed. This ensures that the end user does not see any items that he or she should not have access to. After this is done, the query-matching service accesses the index to find matches to the search terms and provides the result set to the query-processing service, which then formats the query hit list and query refinement data, and removes duplicates. When there are multiple index partitions in the environment, query processing is also responsible for merging the result set from multiple partitions.

Web Analyzer

The Web Analyzer or Web Link Analysis component examines the hyperlink structure of the web pages and provides important information about the significance of a web page. If a large number of pages are linking to a specific page, this page is considered more important than a page that is being linked to only few or no pages. Specifically, links to a page from pages that are considered important already indicate higher importance and play significant role in the relevance ranking of the page.

Another important function of the web Analyzer component is the analysis of the click-through log. The click-through log provides information on how many times the link was clicked from the search results page, thus identifying this link as a possible answer to the query and signifying its importance in relevance to the links that were not recorded in the click-through log. The more times the link was clicked, the higher ranking the page will receive in the search results. Web analyzer component stores its information in the lookup database created as a result of configuration of this component.

Installation and Configuration

To install and configure FAST Search for SharePoint 2010, first you have to prepare the server for installation by installing SharePoint 2010 and making sure that the SQL database is available. The document preview in the search results set for Word and PowerPoint presentations is dependent on the Microsoft Office web applications, which have to be installed prior to running the Configuration Wizard. Before proceeding with the FAST Search for SharePoint 2010 installation all the prerequisites have to be satisfied.

 The installation instructions covered in this section are based on the beta release of the SharePoint 2010 and FAST Search for SharePoint. The installation procedure might change significantly by the Release To Manufacturing (RTM) release of both products.

Prerequisites

The following are the minimum and recommended hardware requirements to deploy FAST Search Server 2010 for SharePoint.

Hardware Requirements

Following are the minimum and recommended hardware requirements:

Minimum

> ➤ 4 GB RAM

> ➤ 4 CPU cores, 2.0 GHz CPU

> ➤ At least 50 GB disk space

Recommended

> ➤ 16 GB RAM

> ➤ 8 CPU cores, 2.0 GHz CPU

> ➤ 1 TB disk space on RAID 5 for optimum combination of performance and reliability

Operating System Requirements

The installation of FAST Search for SharePoint 2010 should be performed on a server with a clean installation of Windows Server 2008 SP2 x64. (The 32-bit version is not supported.)

All regular 64-bit Standard, Enterprise, or Datacenter versions are supported. The server must be fully updated with the service packs and patches and restarted before you proceed with the installation of FAST Search for SharePoint 2010.

 Even though Fast Search for SharePoint may coexist with other products, the server should not be used for anything other than FAST Search for SharePoint 2010.

Turn off automatic adjustment of daylight saving time (DST) in the system.

Permissions

Do not run the installation under local system account; ensure that the user who runs the installation is a domain user member of the Administrators group on the server.

Create a domain user for running the FAST Search for SharePoint 2010, for example "fastadmin." This user must have sysadmin and dbcreator permissions in Microsoft SQL Server, which will be used for the administrative database.

Prerequisite Installer

The Prerequisite Installer checks your server for the components and updates that are required to install and run FAST Search for SharePoint 2010. If any of the components are missing, the installer will download and install them.

For the Prerequisite Installer to automatically download necessary components, the server must have the Internet access firewall open on port 80. The user performing these actions must also be a member of the Administrators group on the server. In a multiple server deployment scenario the Prerequisite Installer must be run on all servers that will run FAST Search for SharePoint 2010. Windows Update service must also be running, otherwise the prerequisite installer will fail.

Here are the installation steps:

1. Double-click the `prerequisiteinstaller.exe` file. The Welcome to the FAST Search for SharePoint Prerequisite Installer screen appears.

2. Click Next. The prerequisites for FAST Search will be installed and you will see the progress bar informing on the status of the installation.

3. Click Finish. (See Figure 5-2.)

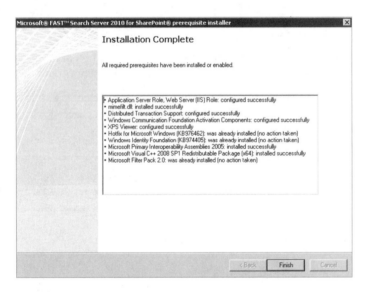

FIGURE 5-2

You can also install software prerequisites from the `splash.hta` page by double clicking the splash file and clicking the Install software prerequisites menu option. The `splash.hta` file can be found under the root directory of the installation location.

 The Prerequisite Installer may require restarting the server during installation.

Installation

After installing all the prerequisites you are ready to start the installation of FAST on the machine. Run the installer by double clicking on the splash.hta file and selecting the Install FAST Search Server 2010 for SharePoint link to start the installation. It will create a new directory called `C:\FASTSearch` by default. You can optionally specify a different path for the installation where all files necessary for the installation will be unpackaged.

After that, follow these steps:

1. Click Install to initiate the installation (see Figure 5-3). The installation process might take some time, but you will be informed of the progress by the status bar displayed on the screen.

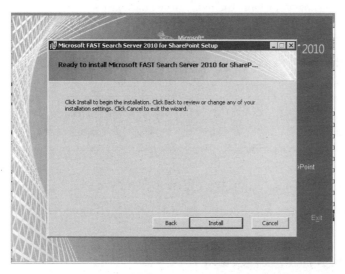

FIGURE 5-3

2. Click Finish once the installation is complete.

As the next step, you will have to run the Configuration Wizard that can be found from the Start menu.

 You will have to run the wizard under a user name with local administrator privileges.

1. On the Configuration Wizard Welcome screen, select the deployment type, for example, Single Server, and then click Next.

2. Enter the user name and password for the FAST Search Server 2010, and click Next.

You must use an existing Windows account.

3. On the next screen, enter the password to be used for certificate that will be used to secure communications between servers and click Next.

4. Enter the Fully Qualified Domain Name (FQDN) of the server and select the base port number. Click Next.

The port number that you select for the FAST search services must be above 13000.

5. On the database settings page, provide the name of the database server that is already existing in the following format *[server name]\[instance name]*, and click Next.

6. The next screen allows you to configure click-through relevancy. If this is not desired in the deployment, select the Do Not Enable Click-Through Relevancy option and click Next.

 Click-through relevancy enables automatic relevancy tuning based on how search users click results.

7. Review the configuration summary and click Configure.

8. On the Post-setup configuration was Successful screen, click Finish and restart the server. (See Figure 5-4.)

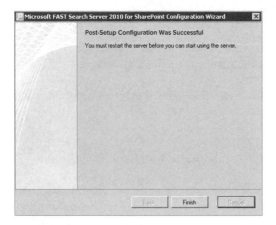

FIGURE 5-4

9. To verify that the installation was in fact successful, run the Microsoft FAST Search Server 2010 for SharePoint shell from the Start menu. Type in the **nctrl status** command to view the status of all FAST search components. See Figure 5-5.

FIGURE 5-5

Configuration

To make FAST deployment operational several services have to be configured. To continue with the configuration, open the Services Console and ensure that the following services are started:

- ➤ FAST Search for SharePoint

- ➤ FAST Search for SharePoint Browser Engine

- ➤ FAST Search for SharePoint Monitoring

- ➤ FAST Search for SharePoint QRProxy

- ➤ FAST Search for SharePoint Sam Admin

- ➤ FAST Search for SharePoint Sam Worker SharePoint Server Search 14

- ➤ SharePoint Foundation Search V4

After you have installed and configured FAST Search Server 2010 for SharePoint, you must add FAST Search Server 2010 for SharePoint by creating and setting up the Content Search Service Application (SSA) and Query Search Service Application (SSA for your FAST Search Server 2010 for SharePoint.)

The Content SSA crawls the content and feeds it into the index. The Query SSA provides query results from the content that is crawled by the Content SSA.

Setup FAST Search Query Service

From the Start menu, open the Central Administration site, click Manage Service Applications, and then follow these steps:

1. Click New and select Search Service. (See Figure 5-6.)

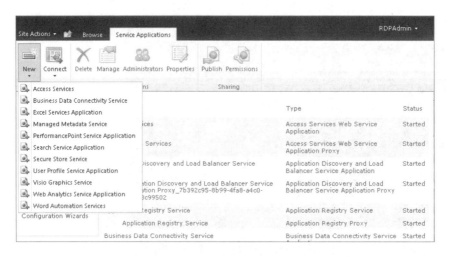

FIGURE 5-6

2. In the Name field, type **FAST Search Query**.

3. For the type, select FAST Search Query.

4. Type in the application pool name for admin server, for example, **FASTSearchAdmin**.

5. Type in the application pool name for search query and site settings, for example, **FASTSearchQuery**.

6. For Query Service Location, type `https://<Domain>:<port#>`.

7. For Administration Service Location, type `net.tcp://<Domain>:<port#>`.

8. For Resource Store Location, type `http://<Domain>:<port#>`.

 The port numbers are in `C:\FASTSearch\Install_Info.txt` *and must be above port 13000.*

9. Fill in the user account information.

10. Click OK.

Set up Content Search Service Application (SSA)

For the FAST Search Connector to start crawling content, the Content Search Application must be configured. Through the Content SSA, the FAST Search Connector crawls the content and feeds it into the FAST Search Server 2010 for SharePoint back end. To configure the Content SSA, follow these steps:

1. From the Central Administration site, click Application Management.

2. Click Manage Service Applications.

3. Click New, and select Search Service.

4. Fill out the name fields, for example, **FAST Search Connector.**

5. Select FAST Search Connector as the type.

6. Provide a name for the application pool, for example, **FASTConnectorPool.**

7. For content distributor, type **<Domain>:<port#>**.

> *The server name and port number are specified in your* `Install_Info.txt` *file in the root of the FAST installation directory.*

8. Type in the name for the content collection.

9. Click OK.

Configure SSL-enabled Communication

To enable content feeding from SharePoint 2010 to FAST Search Server 2010 it is required to configure Content SSA to use a Secure Sockets Layer (SSL). certificate. During the installation step the self-signed certificate was created and encrypted by the password provided during the installation steps. The following steps must be performed to enable SSL communication for the Content SSA:

1. From the FAST installation directory under `installer\scripts` of the FAST administration server (in a multiple server deployment scenario), copy the `securefastsearchconnector.ps1` script to the SharePoint Server 2010 administration server.

2. From the FAST installation directory under `data\data_security\cert` folder copy certificate file `FASTSearchCert.pfx` to the SharePoint administration server.

3. On the SharePoint 2010 administration server open a Microsoft SharePoint 2010 Administration shell with the Run as Administrator option, navigate to the directory where you placed the `securefastsearchconnector.ps1` script, and run it, replacing the necessary parameters with the values for your environment.

> *The domain and user name should be the domain and user name used by the SharePoint Server Search 14 (OSearch14) service.*

Available for download on Wrox.com

```
.\SecureFASTSearchConnector.ps1 -certPath
"path of the certificate\certificatename.pfx"
-ssaName "name of your content SSA"
-username `domain\username"
```

CodeSnippet snippet_ch05_01

4. When prompted to enter the certificate password, enter the certificate password that you supplied when you ran the post-setup configuration of FAST Search Server 2010 for SharePoint.

Now you have finished the deployment of the FAST Server 2010. As the next step, reindex content:

1. From the SharePoint Central Administration site, click Application Management.

2. Go to Manage Service Applications.

3. Click FAST Content Application, and then go to Content Sources.

4. Click New Content Source.

5. Follow the instructions for the configuration of the new content source.

6. Check the Start Full Crawl of This Content Source box.

7. Click OK.

Configure FAST Search Authorization (FSA)

After the Microsoft SharePoint server is configured to use either HTTP or HTTPS, you must finish the configuration of all query servers, if you have more than one, by enabling the security access module. FAST Search Authorization (FSA) provides item-level security for FAST Search for SharePoint 2010 queries. It implements security trimming on search results, making sure that users can see only information that they are authorized to see.

Open the Microsoft FAST Search Server 2010 for SharePoint Shell under the user account of a user who is a member of the local Administrators group, and run the following commands:

```
New-FASTSearchSecurityClaimsUserStore -id win
Set-FASTSearchSecurityDefaultUserStore -DefaultUserStoreId win
```

CodeSnippet snippet_ch05_02

 You will have to run the commands on all query servers in the farm.

Configure Claims-Based Authentication

To finish the configuration of the FAST Search and to enable queries from the Web Front Ends (WFEs), you need configure claims authentication by executing the following sequence of steps:

1. From the Start menu, right-click SharePoint 2010 Management Shell, and select Run As Administrator.

2. Type in the following command:

```
$stsCert = (Get-SPSecurityTokenServiceConfig).LocalLoginProvider.SigningCertificate
$stsCert.Export("cert") | Set-Content  -encoding byte MOSS_STS.cer
```

The file MOSS_STS.cer will be created in the directory from which you run the commands.

3. Copy MOSS_STS.cer to a location that is accessible by the FAST Search Server 2010 for SharePoint query servers.

4. On each FAST Search Server 2010 for SharePoint query server, import the SharePoint STS certificate by right-clicking Microsoft FAST Search Server 2010 for SharePoint shell and select Run As Administrator.

5. At the prompt, browse to the FAST installation directory installer\scripts\, and type the following command:

```
.\InstallSTSCertificateForClaims.ps1 -certPath [full path of MOSS STS certificate]
```

After finishing these steps, you have completed the configuration of the FAST Search Server 2010 for SharePoint Query Server. Repeat for all query servers if you have more than one. Now you can test search from the FAST Search Center site.

Multinode

In a multiple-server deployment scenario, one server must perform the administrative role. The admin server is the server where the administrative services are installed and run. The deployment is scaled out by adding one or more nonadmin servers to the farm. All nonadmin servers connect to the running admin server in a multiple-server deployment, and the admin server is the first one added to the deployment. Before the postconfiguration step is carried out on the first server (admin server), a deployment file has to be prepared, since it is a required input parameter for the postconfiguration command and will be used to configure the multiple-server installation.

The deployment file is an XML file that specifies the distribution of components and services across servers. Each FAST Search for SharePoint 2010 deployment has a deployment file that is read by each server to determine the services that run locally on that server and the location of other services with which it communicates.

The completed `deployment.xml` file to be used for the installation must be named `deployment.xml`. Do not save it in the deployment folder; instead, save it to a folder that you created.

The FAST Search Server 2010 for SharePoint administrator can reconfigure the deployment by adding or removing servers or services in the deployment file.

Capacity and Limitations

FAST Search for SharePoint is a true heavy-duty lifter in the Enterprise Search arena. With its high-performance and highly distributed architecture, you can scale the system in multiple dimensions to achieve the desired performance and fault-tolerance needs, as well as handle large content indexing. A large-scale deployment can handle way over 100 million items, which is the limit for SharePoint Search 2010, and handle billions of items in the index. (See Figure 5-7.)

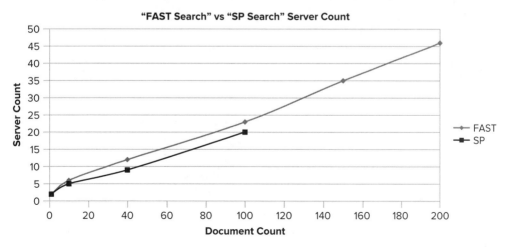

FIGURE 5-7

All components and databases that are significant in improvement of indexing, document processing, and query performance can scale out. Whereas index distribution model allows scaling, passive mirrors provide failover, and active mirrors of components increase the throughput. We talk more about the different scenarios of the component scale-out in the next section. Figure 5-8 represents capacity limitation per component:

Component	Capacity
SharePoint Crawler w/SQL server	~25 mil items per crawler/SQL server
Web Analyzer	~30 mil items per web analyzer node
Indexer/search node	~15 mil items per crawler, including document processing

FIGURE 5-8

Topologies and Federation

Depending on the volume, performance, and redundancy needed for the search application, the farm topology can be scaled out. FAST Search for SharePoint 2010 uses SharePoint Servers 2010 for query servers and for crawling content, but adds servers in a FAST farm. The additional servers process content, produce index columns, and process queries. A single FAST farm can be shared across multiple SharePoint farms. A wide range of topologies are possible that cover both simple and demanding Enterprise Search solutions. Small or limited deployment farms usually consist of from one to seven servers and are acceptable options when redundancy, query performance, and content volume are not big concerns. See Figure 5-9 and 5-10, where the small deployment farm would provide the query rate of up to 10 queries per second and the content volume of up to 15 million items.

FS4SP—Minimum Deployment

Single-tier setup

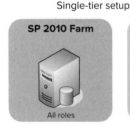

Two-tier setup

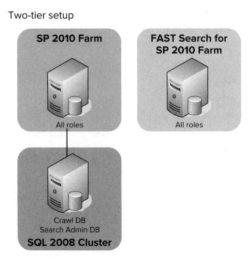

Note:
None of these environments are redundant. For a production environment, you should at a minimum consider running the SharePoint and FAST servers in a virtual environment and with a mirrored or clustered SQL server.

FIGURE 5-9

The first components to consider for scaling out would be SharePoint Crawler with the SQL server, Web Analyzer, and Indexer/search node.

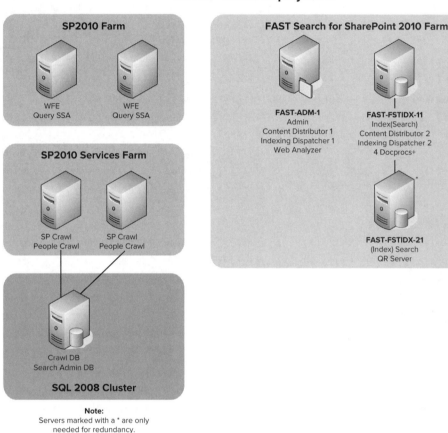

FS4SP—Small Deployment

FIGURE 5-10

The size of the SharePoint 2010 farm should be based on overall needs for SharePoint Server services but has to take into consideration the volume of content to be crawled. Additional FAST servers can take some load off the query servers as well. The medium-sized farms usually include up 8–12 servers and have a redundant query component to distribute the load of the queries across servers. (See Figure 5-11.) This implementation is capable of handling a query rate of up to 10 queries per second and content volume of up to 40 million items.

Large or dedicated search farms would provide the most reliability and best performance for the search application. When deciding on the desired topology, performance metrics and business requirements should be applied to the specific choice of topology. (See Figure 5-12.) For larger environments, FAST Search Server 2010 for SharePoint uses rows and columns of servers to scale out to an unlimited content size and query volume, and includes built-in fault tolerance.

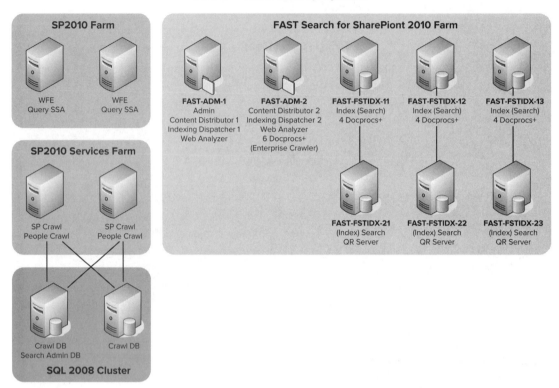

FIGURE 5-11

Adding more columns of servers increases content processing capacity linearly. Adding more rows of servers increases the query processing ability. Fault tolerance is provided by deploying a minimum of two rows. (See Figure 5-13.)

To improve crawl performance, additional crawl servers, crawlers, and crawl databases should be added to the farm. Each crawl database can contain content from different sources and have several crawlers associated with it. Multiple crawlers and associated databases allow concurrent crawling of content.

To resolve query latency issues that might be caused by a high peak query load, additional query servers with index partitions and mirror copies can be added for each query component for a given index and placed on a different server. In general, query throughput increases when additional index partition instances are added. Query latency might also be caused by the database load and can be mitigated by moving the property database to a different SQL server, thus isolating those databases. Deployment of redundant query components for each index partition will also provide higher availability for querying.

Large deployment model

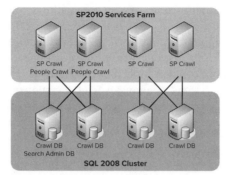

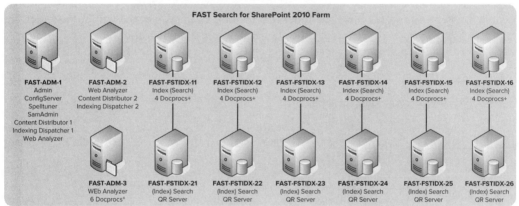

FIGURE 5-12

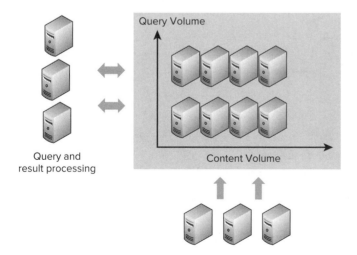

FIGURE 5-13

Search Cluster Columns and Rows

The concept of a search cluster originally came from the FAST ESP search engine and provides the main topology structure for indexing and query matching. Scaling the indexing capacity and the query capacity require a different approach, since this cluster architecture model introduces the concept of rows and columns. The indexing and query matching components that comprise the search cluster architecture use a row/column configuration. The index row is the full searchable body of the index that is split into multiple sections (columns) when the complete index becomes too big for one server to handle. In the multi-column scenario each query is sent to all index columns and the result set from them is merged into one search result set. Primary indexers are the active indexers in the cluster and backup indexers provide the passive mirror index for fault tolerance where both contain the same set of indexes, but only active nodes distribute indexes to the search nodes within the search row.

A search row represents a set of search nodes that contain all items indexed within the search cluster. A search row consists of one search node per each index column within the cluster. Multiple search rows allow for performance load sharing and fault-tolerance. (See Figure 5-14.)

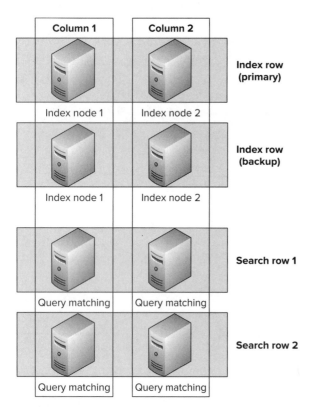

FIGURE 5-14

Topology Design Considerations

While not all servers in the farm have the same specifications and can host multiple application components, Tables 5-1, 5-2, and 5-3 can guide you when designing the topology in terms of the system resources that are consumed by FAST components.

TABLE 5-1: Content Gathering Resources Utilization

RESOURCES	ENTERPRISE CRAWLER	WEB ANALYZER	DATABASE CONNECTOR
CPU Usage	Moderate	High	Low
Memory	Moderate	Low	Low
Disk Space	Moderate	Moderate	Low

TABLE 5-2: Document-Processing Resource Utilization

RESOURCES	CONTENT DISTRIBUTOR	CONTENT PROCESSOR	INDEXING DISPATCHER
CPU Usage	Low	High	Moderate
Memory	Moderate	Moderate	Moderate
Disk Space	Low	Low	Low

TABLE 5-3: Index and Query Resource Utilization

RESOURCES	INDEX/SEARCH	QUERY RESULTS
CPU Usage	High	Moderate
Memory	High	Moderate
Disk Space	High	Low

The administration component consists of three main services: the Name Service, the Administrative Service, and FAST Search Authorization (FSA). FSA consumes a moderate amount of the CPU resources of the server where it is residing, but overall the administration component does not produce much load on system resources.

The following number of servers estimation matrix makes the assumption that it is planned for the intranet search where the 70 percent of the content is made of items and the remaining 30 percent is documents to be indexed, with an average size of 10–100KB. It supports up to 10 queries per second. (See Figure 5-15.)

Server Calculation Matrix

Max item count (in Millions)	Adm + WA	Indexers (1 row)	SharePoint (crawlers)	Crawl DB Server	Redundancy	Total
1	0	1	0	0	1	2
10	1	1	1	1	2	6
40	2	3	2	2	3	12
100	3	6	4	4	6	23
150	5	9	6	6	9	35
200	6	12	8	8	12	46
500	10	25	14	14	25	88

FIGURE 5-15

The disk space estimation matrix shown in Figure 5-16 is helpful in the initial estimation of the hardware resources required for the installation or the FAST Search 2010.

Max item count (in Millions)	Adm	Web Analyzer	Crawl DB Server	Indexer
1	1 x 72 GB	1 x 5 GB	1 x 9 GB	1 x 120 GB
10	1 x 72 GB	1 x 50 GB	1 x 85 GB	1 x 1.2 TB
40	1 x 72 GB	1 x 60 GB	2 x 170 GB	3 x 2.0 TB
100	1 x 72 GB	2 x 75 GB	4 x 210 GB	6 x 2.0 TB
150	1 x 72 GB	4 x 75 GB	6 x 210 GB	9 x 2.0 TB
200	1 x 72 GB	5 x 75 GB	8 x 210 GB	12 x 2.0 TB
500	1 x 72 GB	9 x 75 GB	14 x 210 GB	25 x 2.0 TB

FIGURE 5-16

When allocating the disk space for servers follow these rules of thumb:

➤ Admin nodes only need disk for swap and log

➤ Web Analyzer component needs approximately 4.5 GB disk space per million documents

➤ Crawl Database servers need approximately 3GB log + 5.5GB data disk space per million documents

➤ Indexers need approximately 120 GB per million documents

Federation

Federation is a new search object model in SharePoint 2010; it is not FAST Search for SharePoint–specific. It provides a unified interface for querying against different search providers, giving developers of search-driven web parts a way to implement end user experiences that are independent of the underlying search engine. The object model (OM) also allows for the combining and merging of results from different search providers. Out-of-the-box web parts in SharePoint 2010 are based on this OM, and SharePoint 2010 ships with three different types of locations: SharePoint Search, FAST Search, and OpenSearch. The Federation OM is also extensible, should you want or need to implement a custom search location outside of the supported types.

Content Processing

Content processing is one of the most powerful features of the FAST Search for SharePoint 2010. It allows the content that is fed into the systems to go through a fairly complex pipeline that consists of different stages that ensure that the content is properly recognized and further split into content entity and entity elements. The entity is the original document or item, which can, for example, be a database record, and the elements are supplemental pieces of information about the entity, such as title, date created, author, or modified by. Keep in mind that the entity elements can come from an original document, as well as from assigned metadata or even an external source. For example, within the content-processing pipeline that you are using to process all corporate contracts before they are indexed, you might be extracting the customer code or ID from the document. In one of the later stages, you can fetch a customer name and description from a customer database and associate it with the original document as an additional element or metadata that can be used to provide more descriptive customer name refiners in the user interface, instead of customer codes.

FAST Search for SharePoint comes with a preset content-processing pipeline. Its stages include the following:

- **Format Conversion** — Contains iFilters, OutSideIn
- **Language and encoding detection** — Determines the language of the content
- **Lemmatizer** — Performs linguistics normalization
- **Tokenizer** — Breaks words
- **Entity Extraction** — Companies, locations, people names
- **DateTimeNormalizer** — Normalizes dates
- **Vectorizer** — Creates a document vector for similarity searching
- **WebAnalyzer** — Anchors text and performs link cardinality analysis
- **PropertiesMapper** — Maps to crawled properties
- **PropertiesReporter** — Reports detected properties

Tokenization, Normalization, and Lemmatization

It is important to understand what tokenization, normalization, and lemmatization are within the content-processing pipeline, as it is the pipeline's responsibility to ensure that the content is normalized and tokenization takes place.

Before content is tokenized, the language of the content is identified and the normalization identifies accented characters and maps them into unaccented characters to enable phonetic searches. The tokenization process treats characters such as spaces, question marks, and commas as word delimiters and splits the content into actual words that should be indexed and processed further. The lemmatization feature adds morphological and spelling variations to the content, as well as misspelled or phonetic variants. This allows searches to happen for all morphological and spelling variations as well as misspelled forms or phonetic variants when people execute search queries. Phonetic searching for names is available with SharePoint Search 2010 out of the box (OOTB), but FAST Search for SharePoint 2010 offers more advanced linguistic features.

There are several types of lemmatization:

➤ **Stemming** — The stem is identified and applied to a word, for example, "doing" has "do" as its stemma

➤ **Lemma** — The stem of the word "worst" would be missed by stemming, but the lemma of the word as "bad" would be identified.

➤ **Verbs** — The word "greeting" may be a form of a noun or can have a verb "to greet" as its base. Verb or noun dictionaries can provide the right level of lemmatization.

Lemmatization is language-specific; it allows you to provide more relevant search results to end users and enhances the recall of search results. Lemmatization stages within the content-processing pipeline result in expansion on the index side because all word variants will be written into the index itself. This approach, as compared to lemmatization on the query side, will not produce query performance degradation and will result in high-precision results because it is independent of query language and based on comprehensive morphological dictionaries. For languages with highly complex morphology such as Russian, it is better to apply baseform reduction, which records only the base form of the word and eliminates all possible variants that might cause the index to grow to an unreasonable size compared to the size of the actual content.

Entity Extraction

The FAST matching framework supports several ways of providing entity extraction. You can use a set of predefined terms that should be extracted from content by creating a dictionary; this is called a verbatim extractor. The dictionary can be contained in any SharePoint list, and as an item or document is being processed, its content in various formats will be parsed, and terms from the dictionary will be located in the content and mapped to managed properties. You can use managed properties to define search scopes, sorting order, and refiners from the search administrative interface. In the FAST Search for SharePoint, there are built-in entity extractors, such as People, Companies, and Locations. You can create a content-processing stage that extracts entities based on a specific business rule or a need, as well as entities by matching them to regular expressions. For example you can extract client names from a document where this information is not available as metadata and expose them as a managed property.

Query Component

The query component consists of Query Processing and Query Matching Services. They are equally important but perform different sets of functions. The high-level overview of the roles that both play in search is as follows: When the query is executed, either by the end user typing in the search terms and submitting them to the search engine or by a search application responding to a search request, the query-processing component parses the search expression and passes it to the query-matching component, which in turn finds all items that match the query in the index and passes the results back to the query-processing component. The query-processing component formats the search results, removes duplicates, applies security trimming, and renders the result set.

➤ **Query Matching** — This service, unlike the Query Processing Service, does access the index to find matches to the search terms passed from the query-processing component.

➤ **Query Processing** — This service does not access the index; it receives a search request that consists of a query expression and query parameters, where query parameters specify general aspects of the search expression. Parameters specify the natural language of the query and determine whether all conditions specified must be satisfied by the result set or if only a specific condition is applicable. It also identifies how to adjust dynamic ranking based on the similarity to a document vector and whether to correct the spelling of words in the search expression, as well as whether to apply query refinement.

FAST Query Language

FAST Query Language (FQL) is a structured query language that is used to describe search criteria. This is particularly useful in search application scenarios as it allows users to issue complicated and nested query expressions. A typical FQL expression consists of search tokens and operators.

➤ **Token** — A token consists of a value or range of values to search for.

➤ **Operator** — An operator specifies inclusion, exclusion, and rank for the search results.

The following table shows some of the operators, their effect on the query expression, and usage examples.

TABLE 5-4: FQL Operators

OPERATOR	FUNCTIONALITY	USAGE EXAMPLE
:	As with the `in` operator, the name of a managed property must precede this operator, and the token or search expression in parentheses must follow this operator. This specifies that search expression value must match in the specified managed property.	`description:car` Searches for all items that have "car" in the "description" managed property.
and	The query expression must contain two or more operands, and items in the search results must match all operands.	`and(car, track, sedan)` Searches for all words "car", "track" and "sedan" in the item.
or	The query expression must contain two or more operands, and the item should match one or the other operand.	`or(car, track, sedan)` Searches for any word such as "car", "track", or "sedan" in the item.
not	The expression must specify one operand, and the item must not match the operand.	`not(book)` All items that do not have the "book" keyword will match this expression.
andnot	The expression must specify more than one operand, and the item must match the first operand but not any subsequent operands.	`andnot(car, track, sedan)` Only items that match "car" but do not match "track" and "sedan" are returned.

continues

TABLE 5-4 *(continued)*

OPERATOR	FUNCTIONALITY	USAGE EXAMPLE
count	The expression can take three parameters: a string token to be searched for, a `from` parameter that specifies the minimum number of occurrences of the token, and a `to` parameter that specifies the number of occurrences of the item that are permitted to be included in the search results.	`count(train, from=2, to=5)` All items that have the word "train" repeated two or more times, but not more than four times, will match. If the `from` parameter does not exist, there is no low limit of the occurrences to match for. The `to` parameter specifies the unacceptable number of occurrences. Based on the example above, a document with five occurrences of the word "train" will be excluded from the result.
equals	The specified managed property must be an exact match to the search string.	`title:equals("The cook book")` Search will return only items that are titled "The cook book", but not "the cook book number 2".
near	Must specify two or more tokens that are not separated by more than four indexed tokens to search for.	`near(car, price)` Search will return item with "Search the largest selection to get the car you want at the price you want" but not "Search the largest selection to get the car you want without any worries about the price".
onear	Similar to the `near` operator, but the tokens that are searched for must appear in the specified order.	`onear(car, price)` Will match all occurrences of the word "car" as long as it is found before "price" and there are no more than four tokens separating them.

The FQL can also be used to affect the ranking of the items within the search results, thus affecting the relevance, by increasing or decreasing the dynamic rank of the item. The dynamic rank, as opposed to the static rank, of the document indicates how well the search query matches the indexed item. The two operators that are used for this purpose are `rank` and `xrank`. Neither of these operators contributes to the number of items returned in the search result; they just influence the dynamic ranking.

➤ rank — The `rank` operator must specify an expression operand in addition to one or more search strings. For example, `rank(car, certified)`.

This query boosts the rank of all items that have `car` and `certified` in them; for example, `and(title:car, rank(title:sedan, description:certified)`.

The previous example matches all items with `car` and `sedan` in the title and will increase the ranking for items that match `certified` in the managed property called `description`.

➤ `xrank` — The `xrank` operator is more flexible than the `rank` operator. Just as with the `rank` operator, `xrank` will be applied only to items that match the first parameter, and the boost will be applied to items that also match the subsequent parameters. This operator also allows users to specify the number by which to increase the boosting of the items. For example, `xrank(or(title:track, title:sedan), "new car", boost=300, boostall=yes)`.

This query matches all items that have `track` or `sedan` in the title of the items and will add a boost of 300 to all items regardless of whether or not they had a dynamic rank before.

FQL is a powerful query language that opens up a lot of possibilities to developers of search applications for programmatic query creation. It offers control of ranking at query time, advanced proximity operators (`near` and `onear`), nesting of queries, and wildcard support. The full set of features is too long to cover in this book, but the reference documentation is available on MSDN at `http://msdn.microsoft.com/en-us/library/ff394628.aspx`.

Relevance Tuning

Sophisticated relevance modeling is one of the key features that FAST search is adding to the SharePoint search core functionality. The previous chapter covered the importance of relevance and relevance tuning and some of the reporting features of SharePoint that can aid in identifying the necessity for relevance tuning. We also covered the importance of relevancy in end user satisfaction and productivity ratings.

This section concentrates on some of the tools that FAST provides for relevancy tuning and the different elements that affect relevancy. One element that determines relevancy within the search results is rank points. Rank points determine the importance of the searchable item, where the more points the item gets, the higher up it appears in the result list. The item receives its ranking points before it is indexed and during the query in the following ways:

➤ **Dynamic rank** — Ranks points are given to an item at query time. Points might be influenced through `rank` or `xrank` parameters in the FQL. The number of points given is related to the words used for searching.

➤ **Static rank** — These are points given to a searchable item before the item is indexed. The number of points is based on the importance that is calculated based on defined rules and classifications.

The rank profile is the collection of all configurations used to control the order of the items returned to the search front end. You can have multiple rank profiles in your search engine and expose them as a sorting criteria in the search front end.

To create the relevance model that satisfies the needs of the diverse groups in the enterprise, it is important to:

➤ Know the content that is being indexed.

➤ Understand the end users' expectations and their definition of the "good" search results.

➤ Provide an iterative relevance-tuning session that includes analysis of the query logs, and thorough testing and comparison of the results with a predefined query that will allow you to ensure that no harm is done.

➤ Not all the content is equally important, and some content should not be indexed at all. By excluding content that is of no interest, you prevent irrelevant content from appearing in the search results. Use the Crawl Rules option from the Crawling menu to provide crawl start addresses or regular expressions to include and exclude content from search.

➤ When building custom web pages, it is also possible to tag parts of the page with the tag `<noindex>`. When using this tag, only the relevant part of the page will be indexed and used for search. For example, you might consider using `<noindex>` for the menu, footer, and header, or any other information that is repeated on several pages and not something that should be searched for.

Text in the links that are created between different items contributes to rank points, both dynamic and static. Static points are given based on the link structure and on the managed property's `SiteRank` and `DocRank` parameters (see Figure 5-17.) The more the item is linked to from disparate places, the more static points that are assigned to it by the Web Analyzer component. Dynamic points are assigned at query time when the query words match the words used in the link text (anchor text).

```xml
<rank-profile default="yes" name="default" stop-word-threshold="2000000" position-stop-word-threshold="20000000" rank-model="default">
  <quality weight="50">
    <quality-component name="hwboost" weight="100" />
    <quality-component name="docrank" weight="100" />
    <quality-component name="siterank" weight="100" />
    <quality-component name="urldepthrank" weight="100" />
  </quality>
  <authority weight="0" field-ref="f8" />
  <query-authority weight="0" field-ref="f8" />
  <freshness weight="0" field-ref="write" resolution="second" />
  <field-boosts weight="100" />
  <composite-rank composite-field-ref="content">
    <proximity weight="50" />
    <context weight="50">
      <field-weight field-ref="f1" value="5" />
      <field-weight field-ref="f2" value="10" />
      <field-weight field-ref="f3" value="20" />
      <field-weight field-ref="f4" value="30" />
      <field-weight field-ref="f5" value="40" />
      <field-weight field-ref="f6" value="50" />
      <field-weight field-ref="f7" value="60" />
    </context>
  </composite-rank>
</rank-profile>
```

FIGURE 5-17

Managed Properties

Managed properties are an essential part of FAST Search for SharePoint 2010, as they provide the definition of searchable item elements and play an important role in the search results' relevancy. Multiple crawled properties can be mapped to a managed property, and different data types selected for the managed property can influence the relevance in different ways. Any managed properties defined as integers can be used as input to the static rank. The weight of the quality of the source data is set according to the scale used in the managed property.

In the Text Data Type properties, you can enable stemming; if you do, the query returns results for all the possible forms of a word that are found in the managed property. For example: a search for "walk" will include the results for a managed property that does not contain the "walk" keyword but contains "walking," since it matches the stem, "walk."

Sort Property indicates whether a property can be used as a sorting criterion. *Query Property* enables a managed property to be included in query operators and filters, thus increasing an item's relevance by allowing end users to run more focused search queries. The *Refine* property specifies whether the item should be included in the search results as a drill-down category to filter on the term found in this managed property.

Full-text index mapping defines the rank priority of the property, thus directly influencing the relevance. Properties can be mapped to different priority levels based on their importance and size. Small, relevant properties, such as document title and keywords, should be mapped to a high priority, while longer, less relevant properties, such as body, should be mapped to a lower priority.

The modifications to the static rank of the properties are available through the PowerShell. Use the following URL to access a list of steps and PowerShell commands to modify the static rank on managed properties: `http://technet.microsoft.com/en-us/library/ff453906.aspx`.

Rank Profile

The rank model and rank profiles provide configuration settings for the relevance within the search system, but only rank profiles are available for customization through PowerShell cmdlets. Rank profiles provide an advanced and flexible way of calculating the rank score for a document in relation to a query word used as a search term. The calculation of the rank score for the document is based on magnitude of calculations performed on the rank scores of the managed properties defined in the system.

By examining the default rank profile that is available out of the box, you can get a clearer picture of what it is and what you can do with it. (See Figure 5-18).

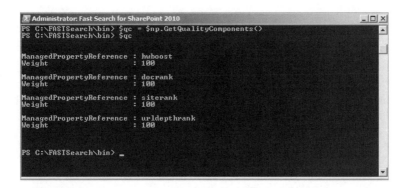

FIGURE 5-18

You can create new rank profiles that affect static and dynamic rank scores. The following list explains some of the profile properties and their impact on the rank profile.

➤ **Quality** — Static rank score for the item that is derived from multiple managed properties and their composite rank settings. The OOTB properties that influence the qualities are: hwboost, docrank, siterank, and urldepthrank.

➤ **Authority** — Specifies the rank of the item when the query keyword is matched to the anchor text.

➤ **Query-authority** — Rank that is given to the item if that item was previously found with the same query terms and clicked on through search results interface by end user.

➤ **Freshness** — Boosts documents based on their last modified date; the fresher the document the higher the boost value.

➤ **Proximity** — The document is boosted according to the distance between the query words within the item property where they are found.

➤ **Context** — The boost points that are assigned to the search item according to which managed property search words were hit. It is assigned as an overall weight and as a weight based on the different levels defined for managed properties, such as title and body. The properties are mapped to different levels, which means that a higher rank score will be given to a document when the search word is hit in title than when the hit occurs in the body.

➤ **Field-boosts** — You can specify a value for a managed property that can be used as input criteria for extra rank points for an item. For example, you can specify extra boost points for a specific document format, such as a PowerPoint presentation or Word document.

When creating new rank profiles, you can use custom-managed properties to increase or decrease the relevance of the searchable item by setting different rank score values on each specified managed property. To better illustrate the value of this, let's take a look at one example:

Available for download on Wrox.com

```
ManagedPropertyReference : title
Weight                   : 200
ManagedPropertyReference : body
Weight                   : 50
ManagedPropertyReference : description
Weight                   : 100
```

CodeSnippet snippet_ch05_03

In the preceding example, if the hit to the query is found in the title of the document, it will have higher relevance than if it is found in the description. Hits found in the body of the document will receive a lower relevance ranking than hits in the description. All rank profiles are exposed to the end user as a search result's sorting criteria, making it easier for the user to control the relevance profile that should be applied to the end results based on how he or she wants to receive the content.

See "Relevancy Tuning" under "Search Center" section of this chapter for more about the relevancy-tuning options that are available through the user interface.

Search Center

FAST Search site administrators can manage site settings from the Site Collection Settings page to improve search results. (See Figure 5-19.) Search site collection administrators can manage search keywords, best bets and visual best bets, and document promotion and demotion (in FAST ESP terms: boosting and blocking of documents to improve the relevance of the search results).

FAST Search keywords can have definitions and synonyms connected to them to improve relevance and create targeted communication. By defining keywords that are often used in searches as search terms, a site collection administrator can provide a standard glossary of names, processes, and concepts that are part of the "common knowledge" shared by members of an organization. When keywords have synonyms and associated best bets, visual best bets, or document promotions and demotions, they also become handy tools for guiding users toward recommended resources.

Site promotions or demotions also greatly improve the relevancy of the search results. By demoting a site with poor-quality content and promoting sites with high-quality content, administrators can make sure that items from sites with high-quality content appear higher on the results set and the low-quality content does not obscure the search results. Extra rank points are then added to the items found if they were promoted or subtracted if they were demoted. This can be done for sites or for individual items. By providing a URL for a site (without the `default.aspx` extension), all pages below the site will be boosted. If a full URL is provided, only that particular item is boosted.

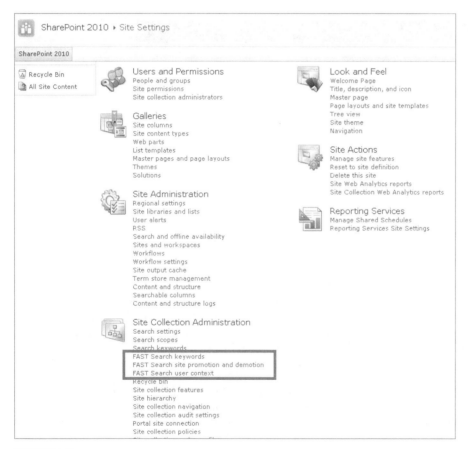

FIGURE 5-19

Since the 2007 version of the SharePoint, personalization of the content that appears to the end user has become an important functionality in targeting the relevant content to users based on their user profile information. FAST Search for SharePoint 2010 has adopted a similar strategy by delivering a relevance model that supports the use of user context for personalizing the end user search experience. Site collection administrators can define relevant user contexts for their site. The user contexts can then be associated with settings such as best bets and site promotions or demotions.

Search Administration

The Search Administration user interface in the Central Administration site offers a number of configuration settings that are available to authorized users for managing properties, property extraction, and spell checking. (See Figure 5-20.) You can access this page by navigating to the Manage Service application page from the home page of the Central Administration site, and clicking on the FAST Search Query application. From the FAST Search Query administration page, click the FAST Search Administration link.

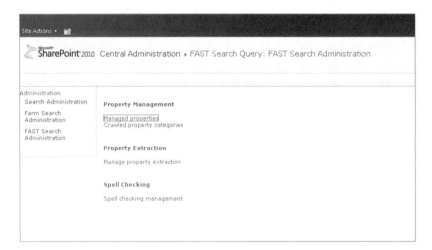

FIGURE 5-20

The Property Management section allows you to define new managed properties and edit existing ones. The managed properties extraction feature identifies key information, such as people's names, company names, and geographic names/locations in documents. You can use the properties to improve the search experience, for example, by providing search result refinement based on the properties.

Spell checking improves the search experience by adding spell checking exceptions. Spell checking exceptions are words or phrases that should be excluded from spell checking. For example, some acronyms that are used in the company might look like misspelled words to the search engine and should be added to the spell checking Exclude Words or Phrases list.

Monitoring

Fast Search for SharePoint provides a wide range of reporting options for tracking the performance of the query and crawl performance metrics. Regular analysis of those reports will clue in administrators in a timely fashion to the need to scale or tune the search application components.

Microsoft System Center Operations Manager (SCOM) provides a comprehensive monitoring suite for monitoring and managing all SharePoint applications that also include FAST Search for SharePoint and its related databases. FAST Search for SharePoint pushes the data by aggregating information from disparate logging services and technologies to provide a comprehensive report that includes information from Windows event logs, FAST Search–related performance counters, ULS trace logs, and log files in the FAST Search Server 2010 for SharePoint installation folder at `\var\ log\[syslog]`.

Through the SharePoint Server 2010 Search Health Monitoring Object Model, administrators and developers can customize and provide new administrative dashboards and reports, and pages that present snapshots of the overall health of the search system to identify problematic components and underlying issues.

PowerShell

Microsoft has released almost 500 PowerShell cmdlets that allow the administrator to configure and extend the SharePoint deployment. Some administrative tasks can be done on a Central Administration page, while other tasks can be run only with PowerShell cmdlets. Over 80 cmdlets are dedicated to administration actions in the areas of search management, index schema management, security, and administration for FAST Search for SharePoint 2010. They enable administrators to upload compiled dictionaries to the resource store, create a security user store, and map metadata to indexable fields. FAST Search for SharePoint 2010 uses a master Windows PowerShell snap-in called `Microsoft.FASTSearch.PowerShell.dll`. This DLL includes all the code for cmdlets. There are four categories of cmdlets:

- ➤ Administration
- ➤ Security
- ➤ Index schema
- ➤ Spell tuning

Developers also have an ability to create custom PowerShell cmdlets that can be deployed just like any other SharePoint solution using SharePoint Solution Packages (WSP) created with Visual Studio 2010.

Cmdlets can be used to perform simple and complex administrative tasks. PowerShell is becoming the preferred way to manage and automate administrative tasks, but it cannot be run unless you are running PowerShell. For more information on PowerShell, visit `http://technet.microsoft.com/ en-us/library/ee221100.aspx`.

Search Center

When FAST Search for SharePoint is installed, the new site template is also installed.

End User Search Experience

From the end user perspective, FAST Search for SharePoint 2010 offers a number of search interfaces that are very intuitive and easy to use. Visual search capabilities enhance the level of interaction that end users have with the search results by providing seamless but engaging and efficient ways to interact. Document thumbnails offer a quick glance at the documents. Word documents and PowerPoint presentations can be previewed directly on the search results page, which provides faster recognition of information, making the use of the search results more efficient. PowerPoint documents can also be previewed and browsed through the Silverlight web part. (See Figure 5-21.)

Visual best bets functionality, which is available only with FAST Search for SharePoint 2010, provides a great way for Search Center administrators to feature specific content by associating keywords with images. The conversational search capabilities guide end users through the process of refining search content and building complex queries through end user click-through interaction with search results. Sorting the search results through managed properties and rank profiles allows end users to apply a desired relevance and sort order, making it quicker to find information.

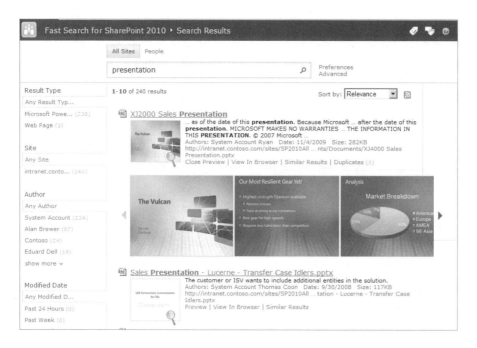

FIGURE 5-21

The SharePoint Search 2010 search results page offers shallow refinements on a managed property and, by default, only the first 50 results are displayed. FAST Search for SharePoint 2010 extends refiners by providing deep refiners on a managed property, which brings all results back on the search page. This functionality provides a deeper type of content discovery to end users and lets them see the total number of items that were found in the managed property. Data returned for numeric refinements can also be used as statistical information in other types of analysis. (See Figure 5-22.)

Similar results and result collapsing are also unique features found in FAST Search for SharePoint. Results collapsing displays all "duplicate" versions of the item found in the index that would not be displayed by default on the results page. Similar results functionality reruns the query to produce search results that are similar to the document in question by bring back documents with similar document vectors.

Did You Mean suggestions appear to help end users with misspelled and ambiguous queries, and acronyms are expanded in the related search sections.

People Search

The People search functionality is provided natively by SharePoint 2010. The FAST Search Center simply federates People search to the SharePoint 2010 search and displays the results on the search results page. End users can also access the People search page from the tabular navigation that is available in the FAST Search Center site.

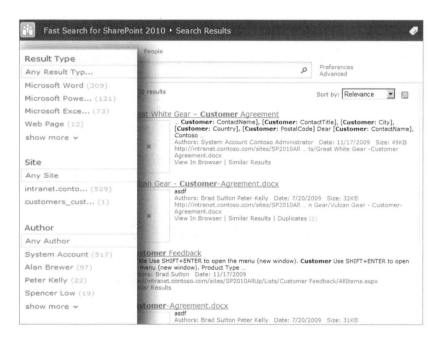

FIGURE 5-22

SharePoint Server 2010 provides an address book–style name lookup experience with better name matching, making it easier to find people by name, title, and organizational structure. This includes phonetic name matching, which will return names that sound similar to those the user has typed in a query. It will also return all variations of common names, including nicknames.

A number of refiners are also available on the People search results page, making it easier for end users to drill down into the results via name, title, and other fields that are available in the user profile.

UI Design Considerations

When developing enterprise portals, a number of things can influence a person's user experience and directly or indirectly affect the usability and end user adoption of the system. When it comes to search, answering the following questions will help to determine and guide UI design and experience.

➤ Who are the users, what do they know, and what can they learn?

➤ What do users want or need to do?

➤ What is the user's previous experience with search application?

➤ What is the context in which the users are working, and how do they expect to find information?

These are the questions are even more important to consider when creating search-driven applications.

The simplicity of the UI should be the key design factor. Even though you might be tempted to show everything that is available for the search page, keeping the search interface clean and simple might be a good starting point.

Web Parts

The SharePoint web parts framework provides users with the tools to build a personalized and easy-to-manage view of the contents. SharePoint web parts are the building blocks of many pages.

While the out-of-the-box FAST Search Center provides a predefined search page and search results page, the search experience can easily be modified through search web parts. SharePoint 2010 provides many search-related web parts that enable power users and developers to customize the end user search experiences by implementing best bets, a refinement panel, or featured content, or even running predefined search queries. The look and feel can be easily customized through XSL without the need for custom web part development. Web parts can be configured through the toolbox properties and reused throughout the site farm. (See Figure 5-23.)

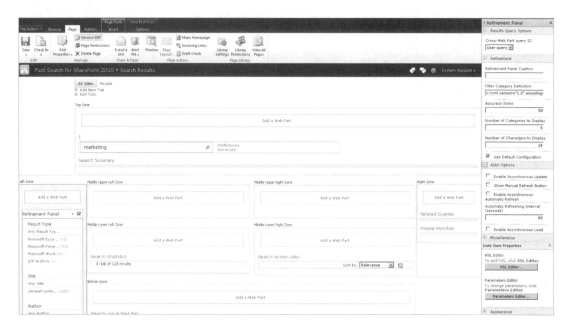

FIGURE 5-23

FAST Search for SharePoint 2010 web parts use the same unified object model as SharePoint Server 2010 web parts and the other search platforms from Microsoft.

User Context

The search results provided to end users based on the query they ran can vary from one person to another based on the user context. You can create FAST Search user contexts by using the site collection settings page. When you have created a user context, you can associate it with best bets, visual best bets, document promotions, document demotions, site promotions, and site demotions.

User context can be based on office location and/or person-specific knowledge. It provides a more focused and relevant search result set based on the information available in the user profile.

SUMMARY

FAST Search for SharePoint 2010 changes the way that enterprises are looking at the SharePoint search offering. FAST provides a powerful foundation for great Enterprise Search business solutions that are transforming the way people think about search.

FAST Search solves many technical problems that companies are facing and allows you to customize the search experience so that it fits how your business and your people work. It enables people to search enterprise content in the language of the business and delivers contextually relevant results tailored to their role and job function within the company. FAST Search 2010 enables search administrators to tune relevancy and improve accuracy and precision of the search results.

But most of all it provides a low total cost of ownership (TCO) and high return on investment (ROI) to the enterprise customers that are already utilizing SharePoint platform.

Customizing Search with SharePoint 2010

➤ Using common patterns for developing extensions and applications with Enterprise Search in SharePoint 2010

➤ Customizing all aspects of search, from user experience and social search to federation, connectors, and content processing

➤ Exploring examples you can use to get started on custom search projects

Enterprise Search applications are found throughout most enterprises — both in obvious places (like intranet search) and in less visible locations (search-driven applications often don't look like "search"). Search supports all of these applications and also complements all of the other workloads within SharePoint 2010 — Insights, Social, Composites, and the like — in powerful ways.

Learning to develop great applications, including search, will serve you and your organization very well. You can build more flexible, more powerful applications that bridge different information silos while providing a natural, simple user experience.

This chapter provides an introduction to developing with search in SharePoint 2010. First, it reviews the architecture of search at a process level and at a Shared Service Application (SSA) level. A section on the most common search customizations gives you a sense of what kind of development you are likely to run into. Next, you run through customization of different areas of search: social search, indexing connectors, federation, content processing, ranking and relevance, the UI, and administration. In each of these areas, this chapter provides a deeper look at the capabilities and how a developer can work with them, as well as an example. Finally, the summary gives an overview of the power of search and offers some ways to combine it with other workloads in SharePoint 2010.

SEARCH ARCHITECTURE AND TOPOLOGIES

The search architecture has been significantly enhanced with SharePoint Server 2010. The new architecture provides fault-tolerance options and scaling well beyond the limits of MOSS 2007 search (to 100M documents). Adding FAST provides even more flexibility and scale. Of course, these capabilities and flexibility add complexity. Understanding how search fits together architecturally will help you build applications that scale well and perform quickly.

SharePoint Search Key Components

Figure 6-1 provides an overview of the logical architecture for the Enterprise Search components in SharePoint Server 2010.

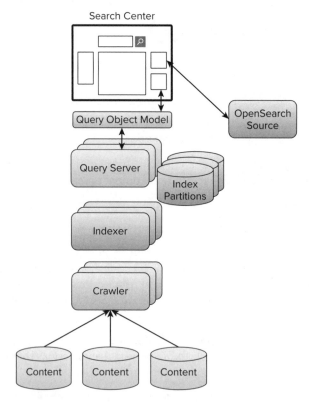

FIGURE 6-1

As shown in Figure 6-1, there are four main components that deliver the Enterprise Search features of SharePoint Server 2010:

➤ **Crawler** — This component invokes connectors that are capable of communicating with content sources. Because SharePoint Server 2010 can crawl different types of content sources (such as SharePoint sites, other websites, file shares, Lotus Notes databases, and data exposed by Business Connectivity Services), a specific connector is used to communicate with each type of source. The crawler then uses the connectors to connect to and traverse the content sources, according to crawl rules that an administrator can define. Connectors load specific iFilters to read the actual data contained in files. Standard iFilters are provided with SharePoint Server 2010, and an additional Advanced Filter Pack comes with FAST Search for SharePoint.

➤ **Indexer** — This component receives streams of data from the crawler and determines how to store that information in a physical, file-based index. (Note that SharePoint Server 2010 Search uses SQL Server for storing indexed properties, while FAST Search for SharePoint stores everything in a specialized data structure directly in the file system.) The indexing engine ensures that enterprise data from multiple systems can be indexed. This includes collaborative data stored in SharePoint sites, files in file shares, and data in custom business solutions, such as customer relationship management (CRM) databases, enterprises resource planning (ERP) solutions, and so on.

➤ **Query Server** — Indexed data that is generated by the indexing engine is propagated to query servers in the SharePoint farm, where it is stored in one or more index files. The query server is responsible for retrieving results from the index in response to a query received via the Query Object Model. The query sever is also responsible for the word breaking, noise-word removal, and stemming (if stemming is enabled) for the search terms provided by the Query Object Model.

➤ **Query Object Model** — Searches are formed and issued to query servers by the Query Object Model. This is typically done in response to a user performing a search from the user interface in a SharePoint site, but it may also be in response to a search from a custom solution (hosted either in or out of SharePoint Server 2010). Furthermore, the search might have been issued by custom code, for example, from a workflow or from a custom navigation component. In any case, the Query Object Model parses the search terms and issues the query to a query server in the SharePoint farm. The results of the query are returned from the query server to the Query Object Model, and the object model provides those results to the user interface components (or other components that may have issued the query).

Figure 6-2 shows a process view of SharePoint Server Search. The Shared Service Application (SSA) construct, new to SharePoint 2010, is used to provide a shareable and scalable service. A search SSA can work across multiple SharePoint farms and is administered on a service level.

FAST Architecture and Topology

FAST Search for SharePoint shares many architectural features with SharePoint Server 2010 search. It uses the same basic layers (crawl, index, query) architecturally. It uses the same crawler and query handlers, and the same people and expertise search. It uses the same object models (OMs) and the same administrative framework.

However, there are some major differences. FAST Search for SharePoint adds on to SharePoint server in a hybrid architecture (see Figure 6-3). This means that processing from multiple farms is used to make a single system. Understanding what processing happens in what farm can be confusing. Keep the hybrid architecture in mind and it will be much easier to understand system configuration and operations. The common components (crawlers, query OM) are on the edges of the system, while separate people and content search operate at the core.

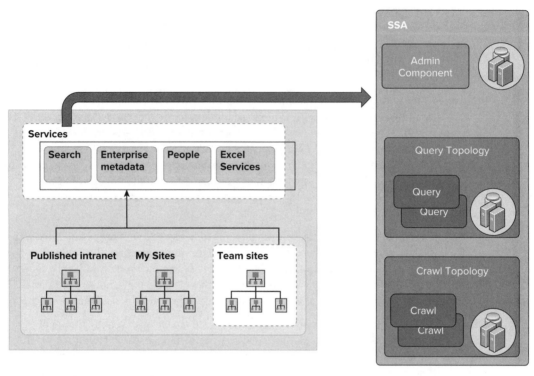

FIGURE 6-2

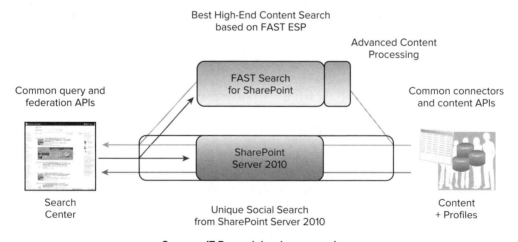

FIGURE 6-3

Figure 6-4 shows a high-level mapping of processing to farms. Boxes that cross-hatched represent the SharePoint farm, boxes with stipple (dots) represent the FAST back-end farm, and boxes with diagonal shading represent other systems such as the System Center Operations Manager (SCOM).

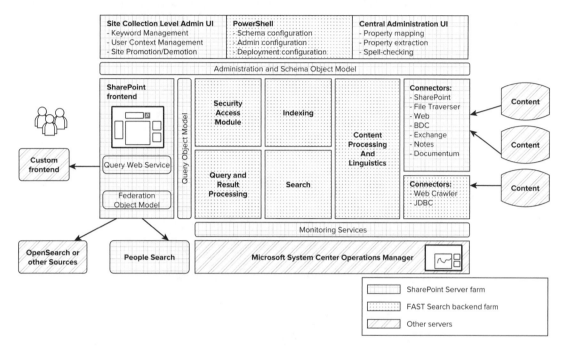

FIGURE 6-4

SharePoint 2010 provides shared service applications (SSAs) to serve common functions across multiple site collections and farms. SharePoint Server 2010 search uses one SSA (see Figure 6-2). FAST Search for SharePoint uses two SSAs: the FAST Query SSA and the FAST Content SSA. This is a result of the hybrid architecture (shown in Figure 6-3) with SharePoint servers providing people search and FAST servers providing content search. Both SSAs run on SharePoint farms and are administered from the SharePoint 2010 Central Administration console.

The FAST Query SSA handles all queries and also serves people search. If the queries are for content search, it routes them to a FAST Query Service (which resides on a FAST farm). Routing uses the default service provider property — or overrides this if you explicitly set a provider on the query request. The FAST Query SSA also handles crawling for people search content.

The FAST Content SSA (also called the FAST Connector SSA) handles all the content crawling that goes through the SharePoint connectors or connector framework. It feeds all content as crawled properties through to the FAST farm (specifically a FAST content distributor), using extended connector properties. The FAST Content SSA includes indexing connectors that can retrieve content from any source, including SharePoint farms, internal/external web servers, Exchange public folders, and line-of-business data and file shares.

The FAST farm (also called the FAST back end) includes a Query Service, document processors that provide advanced content processing, and FAST-specific indexing connectors used for advanced content retrieval. Configuration of the additional indexing connectors is performed via XML files and through Windows PowerShell cmdlets or command-line operations, and are not visible via SharePoint Central Administration. Figure 6-5 gives an overview of where the SSAs fit in the search architecture.

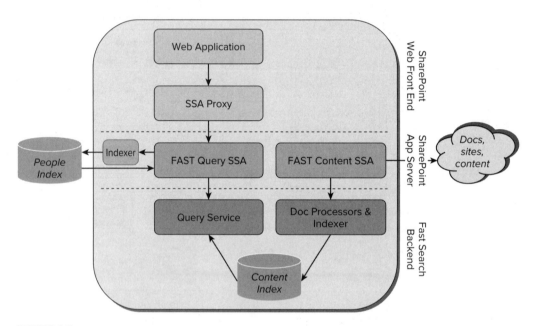

FIGURE 6-5

The use of multiple SSAs to provide one FAST Search for SharePoint system is probably the most awkward aspect of FAST Search for SharePoint and the area of the most confusion. In practice, this is pretty straightforward, but you need to get your mind around the hybrid architecture when you are architecting or administering a system. As a developer, you have to remember this when you are using the Administrative OM as well.

How Architecture Meets Applications

Capacity planning, scaling, and sizing are usually the domain of the IT pro; as a developer, you need only be aware that the architecture supports a much broader range of performance and availability than MOSS 2007. You can tackle the largest, most demanding applications, without worrying that your application won't be available at extreme scale.

Architecture is also important for applications that control configuration and performance. You may want to set up a specific recommended configuration — or implement self-adjusting performance based on the current topology, load, and performance. The architecture supports adding new processing on the fly — in fact, the Central Administration console makes it easy, as we described in Chapter 4. This means that your applications can scale broadly, ensure good performance, and meet a broad range of market needs.

DEVELOPING WITH ENTERPRISE SEARCH

Developing search-driven applications has traditionally been a difficult task. Even though search is simple on the outside, it is complicated on the inside. Many people aren't comfortable with the notion of a search-driven application until they see one. With the release of SharePoint 2010, however, developing search-driven applications is much simpler, and we expect many more interesting applications to emerge as a result.

Part of this comes for free with the developer enhancements in SharePoint 2010 as a whole. With SharePoint 2010, developers have a development platform that is *much* more powerful and simpler to work with than MOSS 2007. SharePoint 2010 includes many features that make the platform easier to use for developers. Most web parts are unsealed, Business Communication Services (BCS) provides easy access to external data, and LINQ has been added to the SharePoint platform. Developing and deploying applications on SharePoint is much easier, through the use of sandboxed deployment, the new developer dashboard, and many other enhancements for developers. Integration with Visual Studio 2010 and SharePoint Designer is built in, and you can now develop, deploy, and test directly from your desktop.

There are specific enhancements that make developing search-based applications easier as well. Through a combination of improvements to the ways in which developers can collect data from repositories, query that data from the search index, and display the results of those queries, SharePoint Server 2010 offers a variety of possibilities for more complex and flexible search applications that access data from a wide array of locations and repositories.

There are many areas where development has become simpler — where you can cover with configuration what you used to do with code, or where you can do more with search. The new connector framework provides a flexible standard for connecting to data repositories through managed code. This reduces the amount of time and work required to build and maintain code that connects to various content sources. Enhanced keyword query syntax makes it easier to build complex queries by using standard logical operators, and the newly public Federated Search runtime object model provides a standard way of invoking those queries across all relevant search locations and repositories. The changes enable a large number of more complex interactions among Search web parts and applications, and ultimately a richer set of tools for building search result pages and search-driven features.

Range of Customization

Customization of search falls into three main categories:

➤ **Configure** — Using configuration parameters alone, you can set up a tailored search system. Usually, you are working with web part configuration, XML, and PowerShell. Most of the operations are similar to what IT pros use in administering search — but packaged ahead of time by you as a developer.

➤ **Extend** — Using the SharePoint Designer (SPD), XSLT, and other "light" development tools, you can create vertical and role-specific search applications. Tools built into SPD let you build new UIs and new connectors without code.

➤ **Create** — Search can do amazing things in countless scenarios when controlled and integrated using custom code. Visual Studio 2010 has tooling built in that makes developing applications with SharePoint much easier. In many of these scenarios, search is one of many components in the overall application.

Figure 6-6 shows some of the kinds of customization that you can do in each of these categories. Of course, if you can configure something you can also extend it or create something new. For example, you can enable a federation source through configuration, extend an existing one to add new information or attributes, or create a new one.

Applications can be built at different levels of customization. A vertical search portal for a group (for example HR) might need only configuration, a research application might require some extension, and a patent search application might need custom code created. There are no hard rules here — general-purpose search applications, such as intranet search, can benefit from custom code and might be highly customized in some situations, even though intranet search works with no customization at all. However, most customization tends to be done on special-purpose applications with a well-identified set of users and a specific set of tasks they are trying to accomplish. Usually, these are the most valuable applications as well — ones that make customization well worth it.

Range of Search Customizations

Configure	Extend	Create
User Context	Relevance Profiles	Custom Elements
LOB Connectivity	UI & Web Parts	Work Environments
Content Processing	Result Rollup	New Innovations
Business Language	Visual Elements	....
Federation Sources	Workflows	
UI Look & Feel	Analytics	
.....	.....	

FIGURE 6-6

Top Customization Scenarios

Although there are no hard rules, there are common patterns found when customizing Enterprise Search. The most common customization scenarios are:

➤ **Modify the end user experience** — To create a specific experience and/or surface specific information. Examples include adding a new refinement category, showing results from federated locations, modifying the look and feel of the out-of-the-box end user experience, enabling sorting by custom metadata, adding a visual best bet for an upcoming sales event, and configuring different rankings for the human resources and engineering departments.

➤ **Create a new vertical search application** — For a specific industry or role. Examples include reaching and indexing specific new content, designing a custom search experience, and adding audio/video/image search.

➤ **Create new visual elements** — Add to the standard search. Examples include showing location refinement on charts/maps, showing tags in a tag cloud, enabling "export results to a spreadsheet," and summarizing financial information from customers in graphs.

➤ **Query and Result pipeline plug-ins** — Used to process questions and answers in more sophisticated ways. For example, you might want to create a new "single view of the customer" application that includes customer contact details, customer project details, customer correspondence, internal experts, and customer-related documents.

➤ **Query and indexing shims** — Add terms and custom information to the search experience. Examples include expanding query terms based on synonyms defined in the term store, augmenting customer results with project information, showing popular people inline with search results, or showing people results from other sources. Both the query OM and the connector framework provide a way to write "shims" — simple extensions of the .NET assembly where a developer can easily add custom data sources and/or do data mash-ups.

➤ **Create new search-driven sites and applications** — Create customized content exploration experiences. Examples include showing email results from a personal mailbox on Exchange Server through Exchange Web Services (EWS), indexing content from custom repositories like Siebel, and creating content-processing plug-ins to generate new metadata.

Search-Driven Applications

Search is generally not well understood or fully used by developers building significant applications. SharePoint 2010 will, hopefully, change all that. By making it easier to own and use high-end search capabilities, and by including tooling and hooks specifically for application developers, Microsoft has taken a big step forward in helping developers do more with search.

Search-driven applications are applications like any other, except that they take advantage of search technology in addition to other elements of SharePoint to create flexible and powerful user experiences. Table 6-1 summarizes search-driven features.

TABLE 6-1: Search-Driven Applications by Role

	SALES	MARKETING	RESEARCH & DEVELOPMENT	CUSTOMER SUPPORT	PROFESSIONAL SERVICES	MANUFACTURING / OPERATIONS	FINANCE	LEGAL	HUMAN RESOURCES	IT	EXECUTIVE
Research (example: patent research)		x	x	x	x	x	x	x			
360 degree (example: voice of the customer)	x	x	x	x	x					x	x
Awareness (example: competitor tracking)	x	x	x		x	x	x	x	x	x	x

continues

TABLE 6-1 *(continued)*

	SALES	MARKETING	RESEARCH & DEVELOPMENT	CUSTOMER SUPPORT	PROFESSIONAL SERVICES	MANUFACTURING / OPERATIONS	FINANCE	LEGAL	HUMAN RESOURCES	IT	EXECUTIVE
Knowledge Base (example: consultant KM)	x	x	x	x	x	x	x	x	x	x	x
Information discovery (example: pub center)	x	x	x	x	x		x	x		x	x
Action environment (example: Call Center Advisor)	x			x	x	x	x	x	x	x	
Authoring tool (example: proposal center)	x	x	x		x			x	x		x
Logistics and planning (example: production planner)	x	x				x				x	

Search-Driven Application Example

A mockup of an example search-driven application is shown in Figure 6-7. It is built through a combination of out-of-the-box parts (like the Federated Results web part), configuration settings that don't require code (like custom rank profiles), and extensions built SharePoint Designer and/or Visual Studio.

This example is similar to the out-of-the-box Search Center (refiners on the left, core results in the center, federated results on the right). It extends the out-of-the-box Refiner web part and combines it with the SharePoint Chart web part to create visual refiners. It uses a feature called result collapsing to organize results by customer, then drill into that customer with a single click. It brings in line-of-business data using Business Connectivity Services (BCS) and applies custom property extraction to it using the content processing pipeline.

Acting on search results, the user can create an email from selected results, schedule meetings, visit a team site, or even use the capabilities directly within SharePoint, such as social search, using SharePoint workflows.

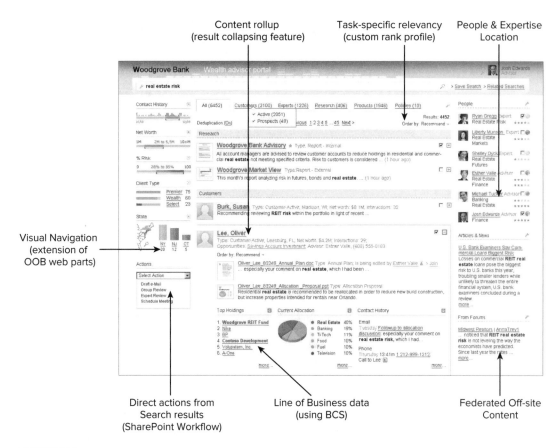

FIGURE 6-7

The rest of this chapter covers different aspects of search with SharePoint 2010, highlighting how you can customize them and how you can include them in search-driven applications.

CUSTOMIZING THE SEARCH USER EXPERIENCE

While the out-of-the-box user interface is very intuitive and useful for information workers, power users can create their own search experiences. SharePoint Server 2010 includes many search-related web parts for power users to create customized search experiences, including best bets, refinement panel extensions, featured content, and predefined queries. Figure 6-8 shows the Search web parts.

IT pros or developers can configure the built-in search web parts to tailor the search experience. As a developer, you can also extend the web parts, which makes it unnecessary to create web parts to change the behavior of built-in web parts on search results pages. Instead of building new web parts, developers can build onto the functionality of existing web parts.

In addition, query logging is now available from customized search web parts, and from any use of the `Query` object to query the Search Service.

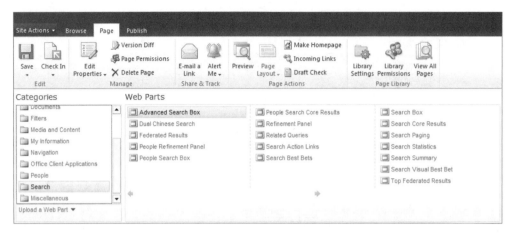

FIGURE 6-8

Web Parts with FAST

SharePoint search and FAST Search for SharePoint share the same UI framework. When you install FAST Search for SharePoint the same Search Centers and Small Search Box web parts apply; the main Result web part and Refiner web part are replaced with FAST-specific versions, and a Search Visual Best Bets web part is added. Otherwise, the web parts (like the Related Queries web part or Federated Results web part) remain the same.

Figure 6-9 shows several of the FAST-specific features visible to the user, notably deep refiners, thumbnails and previews, similarity search, and sorting. Because of the added capabilities of FAST, there are some additional configuration options. For example, the Core Results web part allows for configuration of thumbnails and scrolling previews — whether to show them or not, how many to render, and so forth. The search Action Links web part provides configuration of the Sorting pull-down (which can also be used to expose multiple ranking profiles to the user). The Refinement web part has additional options, and counts are returned with refiners (since they are deep refiners — over the whole result set).

The different web parts provided with FAST Search for SharePoint and the additional configuration options are fairly self-explanatory when you look at the web parts and their documentation. Since most web parts are now unsealed with SharePoint 2010, you can look at them directly and see the available configuration options within Visual Studio.

Inter-Web-Part Communication

The search web parts communicate among themselves. For example, a query is shared out to multiple web parts so that different federated web parts can work simultaneously with the core results web part. Federation was introduced with Search Server 2007 and included with SharePoint 2007 SP2, but it wasn't a first-class citizen until SharePoint 2010. Now the communication uses the Federation OM along with a public class called the SharedQueryManager. There is one instance of the SharedQueryManager per search page, shared by all the synchronous web parts. You get to the other classes that are part of the Federation OM through the SharedQueryManager.

Thumbnails   Similar Results   Sort on any field

Deep
Refinement

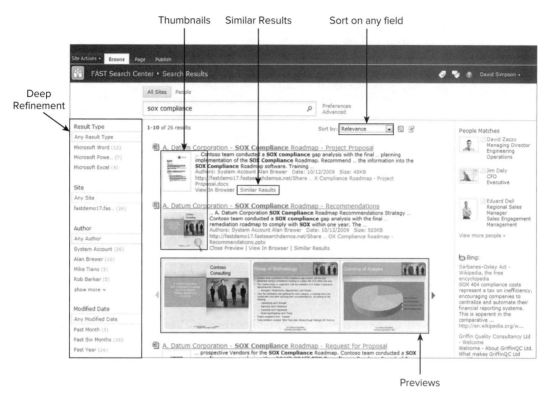

Previews

FIGURE 6-9

This new approach provides a lot of power. Using the Federation OM you can hook into the query path. You can fetch the search results after the query has been executed, or you can modify the query before submitting it for searching. You can apply the results of federation to any web part, and you can build modules that combine results from different sources into one result set. By leveraging the inter-web-part communication in SharePoint 2010 you can build exciting search experiences quite easily.

Example: Tag Cloud Web Part

Let's walk you through the customization of a search experience by adding a Word Cloud web part and using it to visually display the most important terms in a search result set.

To follow along, you can go to wrox.com and download the code. The full code is included with project_ch06_01 and is courtesy of Arnt Schoening. We also have portions of the code in snippets, which are in the text and also downloadable.

**Available for
download on
Wrox.com**

Code file project_ch06_01

We'll use the Federation OM to create the search experience shown in Figure 6-10.

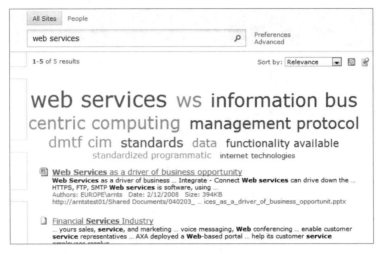

FIGURE 6-10

This example uses the document vectors of the first few results. These document vectors are created during document processing (before indexing) and are available in the managed property `docvector` when querying against FAST Search for SharePoint.

First, find and keep a reference to the `QueryManager` within the `SharedQueryManager` class in the `OnInit()` method:

Available for download on Wrox.com

```
protected override void OnInit(EventArgs e)
{
    queryManager = SharedQueryManager.GetInstance(this.Page).QueryManager;
    base.OnInit(e);
}
```

Code file snippet_ch06_01

You access the result set in the `OnPreRender()` method, and collect the document vectors you want.

```
LocationList locList = queryManager[0];

Location location = locList[0];

var nav = location.Result.CreateNavigator();
XPathNodeIterator iterResults =
 nav.Select("All_Results/Result");

string myContent = "";

// concatenate document vectors
foreach (XPathNavigator res in iterResults)
{
    var docVectorNode = res.SelectSingleNode("docvector");
```

```
            if (null != docVectorNode)
                myContent += docVectorNode.Value;
    // [term1, weight1]..[termN, weightN]
            }
```

Next, you remove the surrounding brackets from these vectors, and store the terms and associated weight in a dictionary:

```
dict.Clear();
if (myContent.StartsWith("["))
        {
            // remove surrounding brackets, and split term and weight
            myContent = myContent.Remove(0, 1);
            myContent = myContent.Remove(myContent.Length - 1, 1);

var array = myContent.Split(new string[] { "][" },
StringSplitOptions.RemoveEmptyEntries);

            for (int i = 0; i < array.Length; i++)
            {
                string[] keyvalue = array[i].Split(',');
                string key = keyvalue[0];
                string val = keyvalue[1];

                if (dict.ContainsKey(key))
                    dict[key] = dict[key] + Double.Parse(val);
                else
                    dict.Add(key, Double.Parse(val));

                // only keep 10 docvector items for each result
                if (i >= 10)
                    break;
            }
        }
```

Code file snippet_ch06_02

The last step happens in the RenderContents() method where you output the terms from the dictionary, sorted in descending order by weight:

```
if (dict.Count > 0)
{
    // order terms in dictionary by weight
    var words = from k in dict.Keys
                orderby dict[k] descending
                select k;

    int fontsize = 30;
    string color = "3333CC";

    int step = (30 - 8) / dict.Count;

    writer.Write("<p><center>");
    foreach(string word in words)
```

```
            {
                // output one term...
                writer.Write("<a href=\"results.aspx?k="
                + word + "\" title=\"" + word + "\" style=\"color:#"
                + color + ";font-size:" + fontsize + "pt\">" + word
                + "</a>    ");

                // ...set smaller font for next term
                fontsize = fontsize - step;

                // ...and alternate color
                if ("3333CC".Equals(color))
                    color = "9999FF";
                else
                    color = "3333CC";
            }
            writer.Write("</center></p>");

            base.RenderContents(writer);
        }
```

Code file snippet_ch06_03

Different font sizes and alternating colors visually tell the user the importance of each term.

SEARCH CONNECTORS AND SEARCHING LOB SYSTEMS

Acquiring content is essential for search: if it's not crawled, you can't find it! Typical enterprises have hundreds of repositories of dozens of different types. Bridging content silos in an intuitive UI is one of the primary values of search applications. SharePoint 2010 supports this through a set of precreated connectors, plus a framework and set of tools that make it much easier to create and administer connectivity to whatever source you like. There is already a rich set of partner-built connectors to choose from, and as a developer, you can easily leverage these or add to them.

SharePoint Server 2010 will support existing protocol handlers (custom interfaces written in unmanaged C++ code) used with MOSS 2003 and MOSS 2007. However, indexing connectors are now the primary way to create interfaces to data repositories. The connector framework uses .NET assemblies and supports the Business Connectivity Services (BCS) declarative methodology for creating and expressing connections. It also enables connector authoring by means of managed code. This increased flexibility, with enhanced APIs and a seamless end-to-end experience for creating, deploying, and managing connectors, makes the job of collecting and indexing data considerably easier.

A number of prebuilt connectors provide built-in access to some of the most popular types of data repositories (including SharePoint sites, websites, file shares, Exchange public folders, Documentum instances, and Lotus Notes databases). The same connectors can be configured to work with a wide range of custom databases and Web Services (via BCS). For complex repositories, custom code lets you access line-of-business data and make it searchable.

Search leverages BCS heavily in this release. BCS is a set of services and features that provide a way to connect SharePoint solutions to sources of external data and to define external content types that are based on that external data. External Content Types allow the presentation of and interaction with external data in SharePoint lists (known as external lists), web parts, Microsoft Outlook 2010, Microsoft SharePoint Workspace 2010, and Microsoft Word 2010 clients. External systems that Microsoft BCS can connect to include SQL Server databases, Enterprise Resource Planning (ERP) applications such as SAP , Web Services (including Windows Communication Foundation Web Services), custom applications, and websites based on SharePoint. By using Microsoft Business Connectivity Services, you can design and build solutions that extend SharePoint collaboration capabilities and the Microsoft Office user experience to include external business data and the processes that are associated with that data.

Microsoft BCS solutions use a set of standardized interfaces to provide access to business data. As a result, solutions developers don't have to learn programming practices that apply to a specific system or adapt to each external data source. Microsoft Business Connectivity Services also provide the runtime environment in which solutions that include external data are loaded, integrated, and executed in supported Office client applications and on the web server. Enterprise Search uses these same practices and framework, and connectors can make information available in SharePoint that is synchronized with the external line-of-business system, including writing back any changes. Search connectors can use other BCS features, such as external lists.

New Connector Framework Features

The connector framework, shown in Figure 6-11, provides improvements over the protocol handlers in previous versions of SharePoint Server. For example, connectors can now crawl attachments, as well as the content, in email messages. Also, item-level security descriptors can now be retrieved for external data exposed by Business Connectivity Services. Connectors also perform better than previous versions of protocol handlers, by implementing concepts such as inline caching and batching.

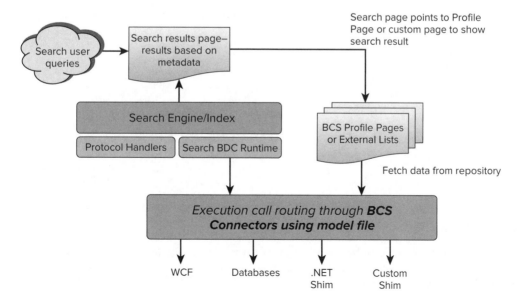

FIGURE 6-11

Connectors support richer crawl options than the protocol handlers in previous versions of SharePoint Server did. For example, they support the full crawl mode that was implemented in previous versions, and they support timestamp-based incremental crawls. However, they also support change log crawls that can remove items that have been deleted since the last crawl.

Crawling Associated Content

SharePoint Search 2010 ships with new features that enable crawling of Business Data Connectivity associations. For example, data from two SQL tables connected by a foreign key can be crawled and indexed together whenever either changes, or an email that contains attachments can be indexed as one item. By using search-specific metadata properties for crawling associations, you can provide some exciting capabilities without writing code.

From the search perspective, the source external content type of an association is referred to as the Parent external content type. Search can crawl external content types associated with the parent in two ways: as attachments or as child external content types. Attachments don't have their own result URLs and profile pages; they appear as part of the parent's. Child external content types do have their own result URLs and profile pages.

To mark an association to be crawled as attachment, add the `AttachmentAccessor` property to the association:

```
<Association Name="AttachmentsNavigate Association"
Type="AssociationNavigator" .........>
<Properties>
<Property Name="AttachmentAccessor"
Type="System.String">x</Property>
</Properties>
</Association>
```

To mark an association to be crawled as child external content type, add the `DirectoryLink` property to the association:

```
<Association Name="ChildrenNavigator Association"
Type="AssociationNavigator" ..........>
<Properties>
<Property Name="DirectoryLink"
Type="System.String">x</Property>
</Properties>
<DestinationEntity Namespace="Foo" Name="Child External Content Type" />
</Association>
```

Code file snippet_ch06_04

Creating Indexing Connectors

In previous versions of SharePoint Server, it was very difficult to create protocol handlers for new types of external systems. Protocol handlers were required to be coded in unmanaged C++ code and typically took a long time to test and stabilize.

With SharePoint Server 2010, you have many more options for crawling external systems:

➤ Use SharePoint Designer 2010 to create external content types and entities for databases or Web Services and then simply crawl those entities.

➤ Use Visual Studio 2010 to create external content types and entities for databases or Web Services, and then simply crawl those entities.

➤ Use Visual Studio 2010 to create .NET types for Business Connectivity Services (typically for back-end systems that implement dynamic data models, such as document management systems), and then use either SharePoint Designer 2010 or Visual Studio 2010 to create external content types and entities for the .NET type.

 You can still create protocol handlers (as in previous versions of SharePoint Server) if you need to.

If your external system has a static schema, it very likely can be covered by using Microsoft Business Connectivity Services (BCS) to crawl and index external data. You can expose your external system via Business Connectivity Services by writing code to create a Web service, a .NET connectivity assembly, or a custom indexing connector. If the entity model in the external system is dynamic, has custom types, and is large-scale, you should consider creating a custom connector for that data source type.

Model Files

Every indexing connector needs a model file (also called an application definition file) to express connection information and the structure of the back end, and a BCS connector for code to execute when accessing the back end (also called a "shim"). The model file tells the search indexer what information from the repository to index and identifies any custom-managed code that developers determine they must write (after consulting with their IT and database architects). The connector might require, for example, special methods for authenticating to a given repository and other methods for periodically picking up changes to the repository.

You can use OOB shims with the model file or write a custom shim. Either way, the deployment and connector management framework makes it easy — crawling content is no longer an obscure art. SharePoint 2010 also has great tooling support for connectors.

Tooling in SPD and VS2010

Both SharePoint Designer 2010 and Visual Studio 2010 have tooling that manages authoring connectors. You can use SharePoint Designer to create model files for out-of-box BCS connectors (such as a database), to import and export model files between BCS services applications, and to enable other SharePoint workloads such as External Lists. Use Visual Studio 2010 to implement methods for the .NET shim or to write a custom shim for your repository.

When you create a model file through SharePoint Designer, it is automatically configured for full-fidelity high performance crawling. This takes advantage of features of the new connector framework, including inline caching for better citizenship, and timestamp-based incremental crawling. You can specify the search click-through URL to go to the profile page, so that content includes writeback, integrated security, and other benefits of BCS. Crawl management is automatically enabled through the Search Management console.

Writing Custom Connectors

Custom connector code is written with .NET classes and compiled into a Dynamic Link Library (DLL). Each entity maps to a class in the DLL, and each BDC operation in that entity maps to a method inside that class. Once the code is done and the model file is uploaded, you can register the new connector either by adding DLLs to the global assembly cache (GAC) or by using PowerShell cmdlets to register the BCS connector and model file. Configuration of the connector is then available through the standard UI; the content sources, crawl rules, managed properties, crawl schedule, and crawl logs work as they do in any other repository.

If you chose to build a custom BCS connector, you implement the `ISystemUtility` interface for connectivity. For URL mapping, you implement the `ILobUri` and `INamingContainer` interfaces. Compile the code into a DLL and add DLL to the GAC, author a model file for the custom back end, register the connector using PowerShell, and you are done! The SharePoint Crawler invokes the `Execute()` method in the `ISystemUtility` class (as implemented by the custom shim), so you can put your special magic into this method.

Now let's walk through creating an example of a connector with a custom shim.

To follow along, you can go to `wrox.com` and download the code. The full code shows the walks through this example step by step. It is included with `project_ch06_02` and is courtesy of Todd Baginski.

Available for download on Wrox.com

Code file project_ch06_02

Assume that you have a file in an external system with names and addresses, and want to make it searchable. There are two types of custom connectors: a managed .NET Assembly BCS connector and a custom BCS connector. This case uses the .NET BCS connector approach. You need to create only two things: the URL parsing classes, and a model file.

Our example defines an entity (containing the schema of the file) and the entity service class which queries the data source and returns entities. The entity service class defines the methods used to return entities from the data source. The example also creates a BDC Model which defines the data source, how to connect to it, how to query it, and what type of information it returns.

Before creating a BDC Model, an entity must be defined. The `Entity1.cs` file defines an entity the BDC Model returns. We have to create an entity which maps to the data in the file:

```
namespace FlatFileBDCModel.BdcModel1
{

    public partial class FlatFileEntity
    {
```

Available for download on Wrox.com

```
        public string ID { get; set; }
        public string Company { get; set; }
        public string FirstName { get; set; }
        public string LastName { get; set; }
        public string Address { get; set; }
        public string City { get; set; }
        public string State { get; set; }
        public string ZipCode { get; set; }
        public string Phone { get; set; }
        public DateTime LastUpdated { get; set; }
    }
}
```

Code file snippet_06_05

Once the entity is defined, you create the entity service class. The entity service class defines the finder and specific finder methods used to return entities from the data source. The finder method is responsible for returning all the entities in the data source. This method returns an IEnumerable generic collection of entities. In this example the ReadList method returns an IEnumerable collection of FlatFileEntity objects (the entity class, created previously).

```
public static List<FlatFileEntity> GetAllEntities()
{
    List<FlatFileEntity> flatFileEntityList = new List<FlatFileEntity>();

    TextReader textReader =
new StreamReader(@"c:\data\flat-file-data-source.txt");

    string row;

    while ((row = textReader.ReadLine()) != null)
    {
        FlatFileEntity flatFileEntity = new FlatFileEntity();

        string[] entityData = row.Split(',');

        flatFileEntity.ID = entityData[0];
        flatFileEntity.Company = entityData[1];
        flatFileEntity.FirstName = entityData[2];
        flatFileEntity.LastName = entityData[3];
        flatFileEntity.Address = entityData[4];
        flatFileEntity.City = entityData[5];
        flatFileEntity.State = entityData[6];
        flatFileEntity.ZipCode = entityData[7];
        flatFileEntity.Phone = entityData[8];
        flatFileEntity.LastUpdated = DateTime.Parse(entityData[9]);
        flatFileEntityList.Add(flatFileEntity);
    }

    textReader.Close();

    return flatFileEntityList;
}
```

Code file snippet_06_06

A Few More Tips

The new connector framework takes care of a lot of things for you. There are a couple more new capabilities you might want to take advantage of:

➤ **Create item-level security** — Implement the `GetSecurityDescriptor()` method. For each entity, add a method instance property:

```
<Property Name = "WindowsSecurityDescriptorField"
Type ="System.Byte[]"> Field name </Property>
```

➤ **Crawl through entity associations** — For association navigators (foreign key relationships), add the following property:

```
<Property Name="DirectoryLink"
Type="System.String"> NotUsed </Property>
```

Deploying Connectors

Developers and administrators use the Windows SharePoint Services 3.0 solutions framework to deploy connectors. After authoring a solution, the developer creates a CAB (`.cab`) file that combines the application's definition file and the solution code. An administrator or a developer then creates a Windows SharePoint Services 3.0 solutions management consumable package — a manifest file that contains the CAB file, connection information, and other resources. When the CAB file is available, the administrator uses the Windows SharePoint Services `Stsadm` command-line tool to upload the file, placing the CAB file into the configuration database of the server farm. Then, the administrator deploys the solution in the Windows SharePoint Services solutions management interface. This step also registers the solution and puts its DLLs in the global assembly cache of all the index servers.

After the connector is installed, the associated repository can be managed and crawled via the Content Source type list in the administration UI.

FAST-Specific Indexing Connectors

The connector framework and all of the productized connectors work with FAST Search for SharePoint as well as SharePoint Server search. FAST also has three additional connectors.

The Enterprise crawler provides web crawling at high performance with more sophisticated capabilities than the default web crawler. It is good for large-scale crawling across multiple nodes and supports dynamic data, including JavaScript.

The Java Database Connectivity (JDBC) connector brings in content from any JDBC-compliant source. This connector supports simple configuration using SQL commands (joins, selects, and so on) inline. It supports push-based crawling, so that a source can force an item to be indexed immediately. The JDBC connector also supports change detection through checksums, and high-throughput performance. The FAST-specific Notes connector has additional capabilities for handling group-level security. If your Lotus Notes installation makes heavy use of groups this can be an important capability.

These three connectors don't use the connector framework and cannot be used with SharePoint Server 2010 Search. They are FAST-specific and provide high-end capabilities. You don't have to use them if you are creating applications for FAST Search for SharePoint, but it is worth seeing if they apply to your situation.

Customizing Connectivity

Using OOB shims (`Database/WCF/.NET`) is very straightforward with SharePoint 2010 and is recommended if the backend structure is static.

Writing a custom shim and a model file is the best approach for cases with dynamic back-end structures. One example of this is the Exchange public folders. This approach also provides a cleaner integration with search user interface.

To create and deploy a new connector, there are two parts: a model file and .NET classes. Whether you use OOB shims or custom shims, you can create and deploy the model file using SharePoint Designer (SPD). If you write a custom shim, you can create and deploy .NET classes using Visual Studio and also coordinate this with the model file. Either way, you use the search administration UI or the administrative OM to configure crawls.

WORKING WITH FEDERATION

In addition to indexing information, search can present information to the user via federation. This is a "scatter-gather" approach: the same query is sent to a variety of different places, and the results are displayed together on the same page. Federation is not a replacement for indexing, but it is an essential tool for situations in which indexing is impossible (web search engines have the whole web covered; you don't have the storage or computer power to keep up with that) or impractical (you have an existing vertical search application that you don't want to touch). Federation can also be a great mechanism for migration.

The following lists show some of the situations where you might use indexing and federation. Microsoft has embraced federation wholeheartedly, in particular the OpenSearch standard.

Use indexing in the following situations:

➤ If there is no way to search a repository.

➤ You want common relevance ranking.

➤ You want to extract full text and metadata.

➤ You want to be able to scope to an arbitrary subset of content.

➤ The source search performance/reliability is insufficient.

Use federation in the following situations:

➤ You need a quick, powerful way to bring together results across multiple search systems.

➤ Data is distributed across multiple repositories.

➤   Search already exists in the repository.

➤   Crawling is not feasible:

    ➤   Cost or integration difficulty.

    ➤   Geodistribution of systems.

    ➤   Proprietary and/or legal restrictions exist on source content access.

Microsoft began supporting OpenSearch in 2008 with the introduction of Search Server 2008. Now all of Microsoft's Enterprise Search products support OpenSearch, and all of them have implemented comprehensive support for federation with out-of-the-box federation connectors to a range of search interfaces. Federation is built to be extremely easy to set up. It takes less than five minutes for an administrator to add a federated connector and see federated results appear in search queries. Further flexibility and control over the use of federated connectors comes from triggering, presentation, and security features. Enterprise Search offerings can act as OpenSearch providers, OpenSearch clients, or both.

OpenSearch is a standard for search federation, originally developed by Amazon.com for syndicating and aggregating search queries and results. It is a standard used throughout the industry, and new OpenSearch providers are being created every day.

The operation of OpenSearch is shown in Figure 6-12. The basic operation involves a search client, which could be a desktop (Windows 7), a browser (Internet Explorer 8), or a server (SharePoint 2010). It also involves a search provider — which is any server with a searchable RSS feed, meaning that it accepts a query as a URL parameter and returns results in RSS/Atom.

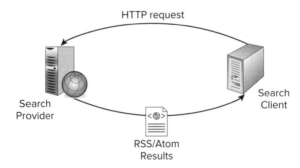

- HTTP request with query in the URL:
  - http://www.site.com/srchrss.aspx?q={searchTerms}
- RSS / Atom results:
  - RSS results with <title>, <link>, <description>
  - Best sources also include:
    <pubdate>, <author>, <category>, <media:thumbnail>
  - Optionally include custom metadata:
    <recordid>, <projectname>, <contactnumber>

FIGURE 6-12

OpenSearch is now supported by a broad community (see `Opensearch.org`) and is in common use among online information service providers (such as Bing, Yahoo!, Wikipedia, and Dow Jones-Factiva). It is becoming more and more common in business applications. Following Microsoft's introduction of OpenSearch into its Enterprise Search products, partners built OpenSearch connectors to applications such as EMC Documentum, IBM FileNet, and OpenText Hummingbird.

Microsoft Search Server 2008 supported OpenSearch and Local Index Federation. It included a federation administration UI and several Federation web parts, but federation was a bit of a side capability. The main Results web part, for example, couldn't be configured to work with federation.

With SharePoint Server 2010, all web parts are built on the federation OM. Connections to Windows 7, Bing, IE8, and third-party clients are built in. FAST Search for SharePoint and Search Server 2010 support federation in the same way, and the federation OM is now public — so you can create your own type of federated connector!

Custom Federation to FAST ESP

This section shows a custom OpenSearch provider that allows federation to FAST ESP from any OpenSearch client (such as a Windows 7 desktop or SharePoint Server 2010.)

To follow along, you can go to `wrox.com` and download the code. The full code includes the OpenSearch provider and also the OSDX file that defines the format for OpenSearch clients. It is included with `project_ch06_03`.

Code file project_ch06_03

The first part of the code is a script which creates a simple RSS feed from an ESP search result. Additional templates for headers, footers, no-results, error-result, and so on are included in the full listing. The code iterates through search hits and creates an RSS item for each of them:

```
_WHILE(<=,_CURRENTHIT_,_CURR:HITCNT_)<{
    _IF(>,_HIT:NO_,0)<{
        <item>
            <title>_HIT:[bsumtitle]_</title>
        <link>_HIT:[bsumurl]_</link>
            <description>_IF(>,_SIZE(HIT:[bsumbody])_,0)
                <{_DYNSUM_PLAIN(HIT:[bsumbody])_}>
                <{_HIT:[bsumteaser]_}>_</description>
        </item>
    }><{}>_
    _OP(add,_CURRENTHIT_,1)_
}>_
```

Code file snippet_06_07

The behavior of this OpenSearch provider is described in an OSDX file, which is included with `project_ch06_03` and also shown here:

 An OSDX file is simple XML, and clients like Windows 7 can incorporate this with one click. Of course, SharePoint 2010 also acts as an OpenSearch client (as well as an OpenSearch provider).

```xml
<?xml version="1.0" encoding="UTF-8"?>
<OpenSearchDescription xmlns="http://a9.com/-/spec/opensearch/1.1/"
xmlns:msose="http://schemas.microsoft.com/opensearchext/2009/">
<ShortName>FAST ESP</ShortName>
<Description>OpenSearch Federation to FAST ESP.</Description>
<Url type="application/rss+xml"
template="http://fastespenstance:15100/cgibin/opensearch?
query=string("{searchTerms}")&num=10&format=rss"/>
<Url type="text/html" template="http:// fastespenstance:15100/cgibin/opensearch?
query=string("{searchTerms}")&format=rss"/>
</OpenSearchDescription>
```

Code file snippet_06_08

Additional Considerations in Federation

There are a number of additional things to remember when using federation. First, ranking is up to the provider, so mixing results is not as dependable as you might think. Simple mixers that use a round-robin results presentation are okay for situations in which all the sources are of the same type and strong overall relevance ranking is not crucial. Second, OpenSearch does not support refinement OOB; use custom runtime code and OpenSearch extensions to pass refiners if you need to. You may want to translate the query syntax to match a given source system; use a custom web part or runtime code for that. Security also needs special handling with federation; there is nothing built into OpenSearch. Microsoft has provided extensions to OpenSearch and a framework that handles security on a wide range of authentication protocols. Implementing this, however, requires you to be aware of the security environments your application will run in.

When designing an application using federation, plan out synchronous and asynchronous federation approaches. If the federation is synchronous, it is only as strong as its weakest link — results will be returned only when the slowest system comes back, and relevance ranking will be worse than the worst system involved. If federation is asynchronous, pay careful attention to the number of different result sets and how they are laid out on the UI. If you want to make your solution available via desktop search, this is easy with Windows 7 and it works out of the box with standard SharePoint or FAST Search. You do this by creating an OpenSearch Description (`.osdx`) file, which can then be deployed to Windows 7 via Group Policy if you like.

We have noted a few common federation design patterns. The federation-based search vertical focuses on using federation with core results to provide a complete results experience. A lightweight preview of results, in contrast, would show a few (three or so) results to preview a source. The instant-answer-across-multiple-sources approach is supported by the top Federated Results web part, which is useful for finding an exact match or quick factoid. Last, a custom application using the Federation OM might use query alteration, refinement, and query steering across multiple sources.

Federation is a powerful tool in your arsenal, and SharePoint 2010 has made it easy to use it. It is not a panacea; if you can pragmatically index content, this is nearly always better. However, using the Federation OM and building OpenSearch providers can help in many situations.

WORKING WITH THE QUERY OM

Query processing is an essential part of search. Since effective search depends on getting good queries from the user, query processing is often used to improve the queries, by adding context or doing pre-processing. An example is location-aware searches, where the user is looking for results within a preferred distance of a particular location, and the location might be taken from the user's context (such as a GPS coordinate in a mobile phone). Query-side processing can be used to examine search results as they return and trigger more searches based on their contents. There is a huge range of things you can do using the SharePoint Query OM, and some very exciting applications you can build with it.

Query-Side APIs and OMs

Figure 6-13 shows the "stack" with query-side APIs and OMs with SharePoint Server 2010 search.

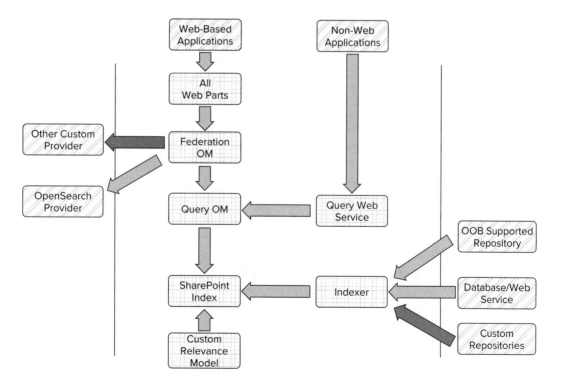

FIGURE 6-13

Figure 6-14 shows the same "stack" with FAST Search for SharePoint.

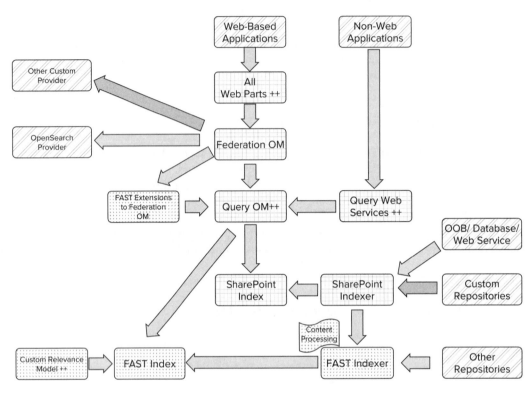

FIGURE 6-14

In these figures, boxes that are cross-hatched represent the SharePoint farm, boxes with stipple (dots) represent the FAST back-end farm, and boxes with diagonal shading represent other systems such as a full-custom front end. Content flow is also shown in these figures, so that you can see how the whole system fits together.

You can access queries and results in several ways, as shown in the figures. In addition to Web Parts, you can use the Federation OM, the Query Web Service, or even the Query RSS feed and Query OM. The next few sections go through each of these query-side OMs.

The Federation Object Model

This is a new search object model (OM) in SharePoint 2010. It provides a unified interface for querying against different locations (search providers), giving developers of search-driven web parts a way to implement end-user experiences that are independent of the underlying search engine. The object model also allows for combining and merging results from different search providers. Out-of-box web parts in SharePoint 2010 are based on this OM, and SharePoint 2010 ships with three different types of locations: SharePoint Search, FAST Search, and OpenSearch. The Federation OM is also extensible, should you want or need to implement a custom search location outside of the supported types.

The Federated Search runtime object model is now public, enabling developers to build custom web parts that search any federated location. This change, combined with richer keyword query syntax, provides a common and flexible interface for querying internal and external locations. The Federated Search Object Model now provides a consistent way to perform all queries from custom code, making it easier to write clean, reusable code.

An important enhancement of the Federated Search Object Model is the public `QueryManager` class, which makes it possible to customize the query pipeline. For example, developers can build a web part that passes search results from a given location or repository to other web parts. A single query can, therefore, serve multiple web parts.

The Query Web Service

This is the integration point for applications outside your SharePoint environment, such as stand-alone, non-web-based applications or Silverlight applications running in a browser. The Query Web Service is a SOAP-based Web Service and supports a number of operations, including:

➤ Querying and getting search results

➤ Getting query suggestions

➤ Getting metadata, for example managed properties

The same schema is shared by SharePoint Search and FAST Search, and both products support the same operations. For querying, clients can easily switch the search provider by setting a `ResultsProvider` element in the request XML. A number of extensions are available for FAST Search, for example, refinement results, advanced sorting using a formula, and issuing queries using the FAST Query Language.

The Query RSS Feed

Certain scenarios, such as simple mash-ups, may need only a simple search result list. The RSS feed is an alternative, lightweight integration point for supplying applications outside of SharePoint with a simple RSS result list. The Search Center — the default search front end in SharePoint 2010 — includes a link to a query-based RSS feed. Switching the engine to the RSS format is done simply by setting a URL provider. Because it was designed to be simple, there are some limitations to what can be returned and customized in the Query RSS feed. The use object models or Web Service integration scenarios are recommended for more advanced applications.

The Query Object Model

This is the lowest-level object model, used by the Federation Object Model, the Query Web Service, and the Query RSS feed. Both SharePoint Search and FAST Search support the `KeywordQuery` object in this object model. While the Federation OM returns XML (to web parts), the Query OM returns data types.

Figure 6-15 shows the newly customizable pipeline for queries that originate from SharePoint Server 2010. All objects in the figure can be customized with the exception of the rightmost one, Query Processing, which cannot be customized.

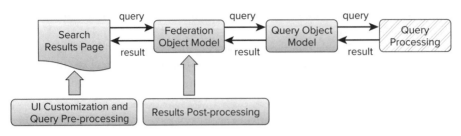

FIGURE 6-15

Query Syntax

The federation and query OM are the methods for submitting queries. The queries themselves are strings that you construct and pass to the Search Service. A query request from a query client normally contains the following main parts:

➤ **The user query** — This consists of the query terms that the user types into a query box found on the user interface. In most cases, the user simply types one or more words, but the user query may also include special characters, such as + and -. The user query is normally treated as a string that is passed transparently by the query client on the interface.

➤ **Property filters** — These are additional constraints on the query that are added by the query client to limit the result set. These may include filters limiting the results by creation date, file type, written language, or any other metadata associated with the indexed items.

➤ **Query features and options** — These are additional query parameters that specify how a query is executed and how the query result is to be returned. This includes linguistic options, refinement options, and relevancy options.

Search in SharePoint supports four types of search syntax for building search queries:

➤ KQL (Keyword Query Language) syntax (search terms are passed directly to the Search Service)

➤ SQL syntax (extension of SQL syntax for querying databases), for SharePoint search only

➤ FQL (FAST-specific Query Language syntax), for FAST only

➤ URL syntax (search parameters are encoded in URLs and posted directly to the search page)

KQL is the only syntax that end users would typically see. For developers, this syntax is simpler to use than the SQL search syntax because you do not have to parse search terms to build a SQL statement; you pass the search terms directly to the Search Service. You also have the advantage that KQL works across SharePoint and FAST, whereas SQL and FQL are codebase-specific. You can pass two types of terms in a Windows SharePoint Services Search keyword query: keywords (the actual query words for the search request) and property filters (the property constraints for the search request). KQL has been enhanced with SharePoint 2010 to include parametric search, so there should be very little need for SQL.

Keywords can be a word, a phrase, or a prefix. (With FAST you can also use full wildcards, so a keyword can be a partial word or phrase). These can be simple (contributes to the search as an OR), included (must be present — for example, AND, denoted by +), or excluded (must not be present — for example, AND NOT, denoted by -).

Property filters provide you with a way to narrow the focus of the keyword search based on managed properties. These are used for parametric search, which allows users to formulate queries by specifying a set of constraints on the managed property values. For example, searching for a wine with parameters of {Varietal: Red, Region: France, Rating: ≥90, Price: $10} is easy to achieve with property filters, and easy to explore using refiners.

KQL supports using multiple property filters within the same query. You can use multiple instances of the same property filter or different property filters. When you use multiple instances of the same filter, it means OR; for example, `author:"Charles Dickens" author:"Emily Bronte"` returns results with either author. When you use different property filters, it means AND; for example, `author:"Isaac Asimov" title:"Foundation*"` returns only results that match both. Property filters also allow you to collapse duplicates; for example, `duplicate:http://<displayUrl>` requests duplicate items for the specified URL (which would otherwise be collapsed).

With SharePoint Server 2010, enhancements to keyword query syntax enable more complex search queries that in the past were supported only by the SQL query syntax. These enhancements include support for wildcard suffix matching, grouping of query terms, parentheses, and logical operators, such as AND, OR, NOT, and NEAR. Improved operators now support regular expressions, case-sensitivity, and content source prioritization. KQL can express essentially anything you can say with SQL. The Advanced Search page, for example, now creates KQL rather than SQL.

FAST Query Language

FAST Search has a number of extensions beyond the standard SharePoint search that are available on both the Federation and Query Object Models, and also on the Query Web Service. Some examples are:

> The FAST Query Language (FQL), which supports advanced query operators, such as XRANK for dynamic (query-time) term weighting and ranking

> Deep refiners over the whole results set and the possibility of adding refiners over any managed property

> Advanced sorting using managed properties or a query-time sort formula

> Advanced duplicate trimming, with the ability to specify a custom property on which to base duplicate comparisons

> "Similar documents" matching

> The FAST Search Administrative Object Model for promoting documents or assigning visual best bets to query keywords/phrases

FQL is intended for programmatic creation of queries. It is a structured language and not intended to be exposed to the end users. The FAST Query Language can be used only with FAST Search for

SharePoint. The following FAST Search for SharePoint features may be accessed only using this query language:

➤ Detailed control of ranking at query time, using RANK/XRANK operators, query term weighting, and switching on/off ranking for parts of a query

➤ Complex wildcard and pattern matching

➤ Advanced proximity operators (ordered/unordered NEAR operators)

➤ Advanced sorting, using SORT/SORTFORMULA operators

➤ Complex combinations of query operators, such as nesting of Boolean operators

FQL opens a whole world of search operations to the developer. The full set of capabilities is too long to cover in this book, but the reference documentation is available on MSDN and is part of the SharePoint 2010 SDK. The next two sections illustrate just two of the FQL operators.

Using RANK and XRANK

FQL provides capabilities that allow you to control relevance ranking on a query-by-query basis. RANK and XRANK let you boost the placement of items in the results without changing which items match the query. Let's run through some examples, which are also included in snippet_06_09, which you can download from wrox.com.

RANK boosts items that match a specified term or phrase in the full-text index. The amount of boosting is based on the relevance of the term(s) used for boosting. For example:

```
rank(darwin, evolution)
```

returns all items that match darwin and boost those that also contain evolution, and

```
rank(darwin, evolution, title:origin)
```

returns all items that match darwin and boost those that contain evolution OR that have origin in the title.

XRANK boosts items based on information in the full-text index and also on information that might appear in managed properties that aren't included in the full-text index. The amount of boosting is a constant value given as a parameter, so you can add rank to items even if they are not otherwise used for relevance calculations. For example:

```
xrank(or(darwin, lamark), species, boost=500, boostall=yes)
```

returns items that contain either darwin or lamark, and boost every item containing species by 500 rather than by the default of 100, even for items that previously had no rank. With XRANK you can also move results further down the result list, simply by using a negative boost value.

After you get used to using RANK and XRANK, you will discover lots of applications for them. For example, if you want to use user comments, social tagging, or content rating to impact relevance of some items, you can do this with XRANK. The following query matches items containing "management" and boosts them by 5000 if there is a user tag that matches and by an additional 3000 if there is a comment that matches:

```
xrank(xrank(string("management",ANNOTATION_CLASS="USER"),
tag:string(" management "), boost=5000),
ratedcomment:string(" management "), boost=3000)"
```

Code file snippet_06_09

RANK and XRANK are great for applications where you want to provide extra control to users. You can use them to create "influencers," where the user controls ranking with a button, slider, or other control. If you want to show search results dynamically changing while you drag different objects around on the screen, based on the size of items or the distance between them, use RANK and XRANK. If you want social tagging to apply when someone is searching user-generated content but not when they are searching authoritative content, use RANK and XRANK. The possibilities are endless.

Using SortFormula

SortFormula also changes the order of results rather than the set of results returned. However, it doesn't work by boosting particular items. It orders the results according to a mathematical formula. This algorithmic sorting is an extension of the single- and multilevel sorting functionality that comes out of the box with FAST Search for SharePoint. But where simple single- and multilevel sorting are based on managed properties, SortFormula goes way beyond these in the hands of a clever developer.

You can use a full range of math operators, including rounding/bucketing, arithmetical operations (such as add, multiply and exponent), and trigonometry functions (such as cosine and arctangent). The following are examples of features that can be implemented using this feature:

➤ Classification and grouping of results using K-nearest neighbor algorithms

➤ Location-aware search using Euclidean distance, Manhattan distance, or "warped" geometries

➤ Closeness to target — sorting results based on how far a given managed property value is from a preferred value

Let's run through some examples of SortByProperties and SortFormula. These examples are also included in snippet_06_10, which you can download from wrox.com.

The sort direction in SortByProperties sets how you want results returned. For example,

```
<SortByProperties>
<SortByProperty name=title direction={Ascending} />
</SortByProperties>
```

sorts the search results in alphabetically ascending order based on the title managed property. SortFormula is invoked by setting the sort direction to FQLFormula. The expression

```
<SortByProperties>
<SortByProperty name= abs(20-height) direction={FQLFormula} />
</SortByProperties>
```

brings to the top the items that have the height managed property closest to 20.

You can do many interesting things with `SortByProperties` and `SortFormula`. Let's say that you want to present the results of a search in groups according to their size, and make this easy to use by getting rid of tiny differences in size. You could specify:

```
<SortByProperties>
<SortByProperty name=bucket(size,5,15,50,100)direction={FQLFormula} />
</SortByProperties>
```

This rounds the value of the `size` managed property down to one of the values 0, 5, 15, 50, or 100. Then, it presents the results in groups according to those buckets, using other ranking criteria to set the order within that bucket. If result collapsing is used on `size`, then the user sees a search result with five sets as well as any associated navigators. She can click a set to see all the items beneath it — a nice, intuitive, exploration experience.

Let's look at one final example, for a mobile search application where you might want to return results that are close to where the user is at the moment. You would first ensure that content was geotagged with the managed properties `latitude` and `longitude`. A lot of content already has geocoordinate metadata, but you can also use third-party or custom geotaggers to create this metadata at index time. (We discuss this in the section on extending the pipeline processing pipeline.) Then, you get the current geocoordinates (from the GPS or other locater capabilities of the mobile device). Say that you determine you are at latitude 50 N and longitude 100 W — somewhere in Manitoba. You could specify:

```
<SortByProperties>
<SortByProperty name= sqrt(pow(50-latitude,2)+pow(100-longitude,2))
direction={FQLFormula} />
</SortByProperties>
```

Code file snippet_06_10

and the search results would be ordered by 2D distance from your current location.

CONTENT ENHANCEMENT

As discussed in Chapter 5, FAST Search for SharePoint includes advanced content processing, which is applied to all content. This is configured and managed from the FAST Content SSA. It provides very powerful text analytics technology that prepares content for findability. This includes web link analysis, linguistics support for 84 languages, document format support for over 400 types, and property extraction (which creates metadata by machine, based on the content of each document).

Advanced Content Processing with FAST

The content-processing pipeline is a framework for refining content and preparing it for indexing. It encapsulates a range of technologies and has the following characteristics:

➤ The content-processing pipeline is composed of small simple stages, each of which does one thing. Stages identify attributes such as language, parse the structure of the document encodings (document format, language morphology, and syntax), extract metadata, manipulate properties and attributes, and so forth.

➤ A wide range of file formats are understood and made available for indexing by the pipeline. These are processed by the Advanced Filter Pack which adds over 400 file types to the standard Filter Pack.

➤ A wide range of human languages are detected and supported by the pipeline (84 languages detected, 45 languages with advanced linguistics features). This includes spell checking and synonyms (which improves the search experience) and lemmatization (which provides higher precision and recall than standard techniques like stemming).

➤ Property extraction creates and improves metadata by identifying words and phrases of particular types. Prebuilt extractors include Person, Location, Company, E-mail, Date, and Time. A unique offensive-content-filtering capability is also included.

Figure 6-16 shows the high-level structure of the content-processing pipeline.

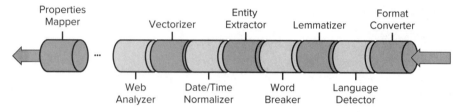

FIGURE 6-16

Content Pipeline Configuration

The content-processing pipeline in FAST Search for SharePoint can be configured and extended. It is different than the content processing pipeline in ESP, FSIS and FSIA — it's simpler, more robust, and less error prone. Configuration of each stage is done via graphical user interface (GUI) or XML configuration, and is available via PowerShell. In the pipeline, content is mapped into "crawled properties" (whatever is found in the content) and then into "managed properties" (mapped into a schema and made available for searching, sorting, and navigation). This schema is accessible via GUI or PowerShell.

Content Pipeline Extensibility

The Content Pipeline is destined to be extended. Figure 6-17 shows how pipeline extensibility works.

The extensibility in FAST Search for SharePoint is different from the mechanisms used with ESP, FSIS and FSIA. You cannot create custom stages and insert them into the content-processing pipeline. This eliminates the need to learn Python in order to create custom stages; you can write pipeline extensions in any language you wish and they run in a sandbox environment. This also eliminates many of the debugging and robustness issues associated with an open pipeline. However, there are more restrictions on the kind of processing you can do. You cannot, for example, create your own tokenizers and insert them into the pipeline. You can generally meet any requirement that comes your way. But if you are used to extending ESP pipelines, this is one of the biggest changes to learn.

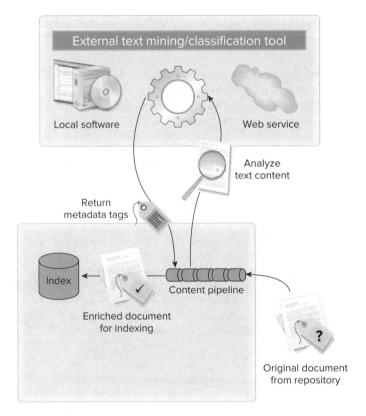

FIGURE 6-17

There are several ways for developers and partners to add value in content processing:

➤ Configure connectors, pipeline configurations, and the index schema to support specific search applications.

➤ Apply optional pipeline stages such as using the XML properties mapper, the Offensive Content Filter, and field collapsing (which allows grouping or folding results together).

➤ Create custom verbatim extractors (dictionary-driven identification terms and phrases); for example, to identify all product names or project names and extract these as managed properties for each document.

➤ Create custom connectors, using BCS (or other APIs) to bring in and index data from specific systems and applications.

➤ Process content prior to crawling — for some applications pre-processing content prior to crawling is useful (such as separating large reports into separate documents). This can be done externally to search or within a connector shim.

➤ Extend the pipeline by creating code that is called right before the `PropertiesMapper` stage. Specialized classifiers, entity extractors, or other processing elements can be used to support specialized scenarios, as illustrated in Figure 6-17.

Multilingual Search

If your organization is truly global, then the need for multilingual search is clear. But even if you initially think that all of your organization's search needs are English only, it is fairly common to discover that some percentage of users and content are non-English.

You should think carefully about the language-specific features of your search function. If people search only for content in their own language, or if there is wide variation in the language types used (English, Polish, and Chinese, for example), then it will help to have users specify their language in the query interface. Where there are common linguistic roots — on an e-commerce site featuring English and Dutch content, say — it may be easier to handle everything in the most common language, in this case, English.

A full description of linguistics and how you can use them to improve search is beyond the scope of this book. There are a few things, however, you should know about linguistics:

➤ Better use of linguistics will improve precision and recall.

➤ Industry and user knowledge are needed to optimize search systems.

➤ Linguistic choices can affect hardware and performance.

➤ Some sites should favor language independence.

➤ Bad queries can be turned into good queries with the proper linguistic tools.

For many search applications, the out-of-the-box search configuration is all you need. User language choices are set in the Preferences panel of the Search Center and, by default, are determined from the browser. Be aware, however, that linguistic processing can provide a lot of power in multilingual situations or in situations that demand particularly tuned recall and precision.

EXTENDING SEARCH USING THE ADMINISTRATIVE OM

SharePoint Server 2010 provides an extensible Search Health Monitoring Object Model. This object model enables administrators and developers to customize the administrative dashboards and pages that provide snapshots of the overall health of the search system, and to provide ways to troubleshoot and identify the underlying causes of any problems. The Search Health Monitoring user interface provides tools for monitoring the health of functional search subsystems (for example, crawling and indexing), search content sources, and key components (for example, databases) of the search system's topology.

Authentication and Security

Security in search is both a simple and a deep subject. Simply put, search uses the user's credentials and the entitlements on any content that has been indexed to ensure that users can see only content they are entitled to read. For OOB connectors and straightforward security environments, this just works. As you build custom connectors and work in heterogeneous and complex security environments, you also have the responsibility to extend security for search.

There are two major new security capabilities with SharePoint 2010. First, item-level security descriptors can now be retrieved for external data exposed by Business Connectivity Services. This means that search security is straightforward when building new connectors with BCS. Second, claims authentication (see Chapter 11) provides a wide range of security options for heterogeneous environments. Search benefits from these significantly, because search is often used as a "bridge" to look across information from many different systems.

Search Reports

The object model supports a reporting system that you can easily customize and extend. You can modify default alert rules and thresholds, for example, by changing the alert rules XML file. You can also upload new reporting applications developed by third parties to a standard search administration document library. The reports generated by these reporting applications are XML files in the standard Report Definition Language Client-Side (RDLC) format. For more information, see the Report Definition Language Specification, which is available on Microsoft TechNet.

SUMMARY

Building powerful search applications is easier than ever in SharePoint 2010. You can create a wide range of applications based on search, at various levels of customization. You can also combine search with other parts of SharePoint (Insights, Social, Composites, Sites, and Content) to create compelling solutions.

FAST Search is now integrated into the SharePoint platform, and developers of search-driven solutions and applications can leverage a common platform and common APIs for both SharePoint Search and FAST Search. This means you can build applications to support both search engines and then extend them if and when desired to take advantage of the more advanced features available with FAST Search, such as dynamic ranking, flexible sort formulae, or deep refiners for insight into the full result set. FAST Search Server 2010 for SharePoint web parts use the same unified object model as SharePoint Server 2010 and the other search platforms from Microsoft. The result is that if you develop a custom solution that uses the Query Object Model for SharePoint Server 2010, for example, then it will continue to work if you migrate your code to FAST Search Server 2010 for SharePoint.

PART III
Implementing Search with ESP

7

Introduction to FAST ESP

WHAT'S IN THIS CHAPTER?

➤ An Introduction to ESP

➤ Installing ESP

➤ Quick start: indexing and searching a website

➤ Managing ESP

➤ ESP Goodies

➤ Guide to ESP documentation by role

In the previous three chapters, our focus has been on the Microsoft search products that integrate tightly with SharePoint 2010. Those products, especially the new FAST Search for SharePoint 2010, represent a new and exciting direction for search on the Microsoft Windows platform.

In this chapter and in Chapter 8, we will discuss the technology inside of the only multi-platform search technology from Microsoft: FAST ESP, newly branded as FAST Search for Internal Applications and FAST Search for Internet Sites.

Microsoft continues to market the existing FAST Search and Transfer product, FAST ESP 5.3, on both Windows and non-Windows platforms. In this chapter, and in Chapter 8, our focus shifts into this newly branded product.

The FAST ESP 5.3 product is available from Microsoft under two different names, based primarily on the product licensing model.

FAST Search for Internal Applications (FSIA) is the new name for FAST ESP 5.3 for internally-facing search applications in customer organizations. FSIA is licensed based on servers and on Microsoft enterprise client access licenses (ECAL), a per-seat model. Remember, FSIA is intended for use for an organization's intranet and other internal systems, where the number of users is predictable.

FAST Search for Internet Sites (FSIS) includes FAST ESP 5.3 as a base component; but FSIS includes two new utilities intended to extend the capability of ESP for public-facing Internet applications and web sites. These capabilities are the Content Transformation Services (CTS) and Interaction Management Services (IMS).

CTS, which integrates with Microsoft Visual Studio 2010, is a graphical tool for manipulating content. CTS allows content flows to be created from multiple structured and unstructured content sources; processed; and routed to repositories like a search index or a data warehouse. It is an extensible framework, in that developers can modify the native CTS operators.

IMS is a framework for rapidly creating and managing intent-driven, conversational user search experiences. It facilitates the creation of search-driven interfaces, and provides much more control over query and result processing.

Because FSIS is intended for public-facing Internet sites, it is licensed based solely on the number of servers required. Licensing based on users could be prohibitively expensive; after all, a successful eCommerce site could have millions of visitors using search. Microsoft addresses these sites by using a server licensing charge.

Either way, it's important for the reader to remember that FSIA and FSIS are both based on what is essentially a repackaging of the FAST ESP 5.3 release. While there are additional tools bundled with FSIS, in both this chapter and in Chapter 8, we will use the term ESP for both products on all supported platforms, unless we specifically point out a difference.

Microsoft likes to make the analogy that the SharePoint-based FAST search products are like high-performance production cars, while the ESP-based products are more like racing cars. In reality, the differences are not quite that extreme. The SharePoint-based product lines offer powerful search technology with easy configuration and customization, while the ESP-based products provide more in the way of capacity and customization. All this flexibility requires a bit more effort to install, configure, and create applications, but ESP provides access to low-level capabilities that provide for extreme capacity, customization, performance, and flexibility. If your search requirements are demanding, ESP is probably the platform for you.

Again, FAST Search for Internal Applications (FSIA) and FAST Search for Internet Sites (FSIS with CTS and IMS) are both repackaged versions of the same FAST ESP 5.3 product. While there are some licensing and bundling differences between the two, for the purposes of the next two chapters, we'll refer to both products together as ESP.

Finally, the ESP components of both products are available on Solaris x86 and for several versions of Linux. Throughout these chapters, we'll simply use the term Linux to refer to both unless there are specific differences.

ESP PRODUCT OVERVIEW

ESP is built on technology that drives search for some of the most demanding web and intranet applications in the world in eCommerce, publishing, finance, and government, serving petabytes of content with thousands of queries per second. Many of its strengths have been incorporated into the SharePoint-based search products, including:

➤   Predictable scalability

➤   Entity extraction

➤ Deep refiners

➤ Flexible pipeline approach to indexing content

➤ Advanced query capabilities

➤ A dashboard for nontechnical users

Some capabilities unique to FSIA and FSIS include:

➤ High availability

➤ Multi-platform support

➤ Multi-language APIs (C#, Java, Python, Perl, and so on)

➤ Multiple language support (Latin and Unicode content)

➤ Minimum indexing latency

➤ Full redundancy capability for mission-critical applications

➤ Full control over security and access

FAST is a well-established technology that continues to provide the ultimate in power, flexibility, and capacity.

System Architecture and Administration

ESP started out as a Norwegian search for the then-new World Wide Web. Over the last two decades, it has evolved into a flexible, powerful, and scalable search platform that powers some of the most demanding intranet and web-facing Internet search environments throughout the world. FAST was one of the first companies to recognize that search was a platform for solutions powered by search, not an end unto itself.

The versions of ESP available now from Microsoft, FSIA and FSIS, continue to provide this power and flexibility, which we'll begin to drill into in this chapter and examine in a bit more depth in Chapter 8.

ESP Architecture and Key Components

At a high level, classic ESP architecture is similar to that of the versions bundled within SharePoint, but the actual low-level details are quite different. Figure 7-1 illustrates a simplified view of the components of FAST ESP. The components and the functions they provide are discussed next:

➤ **Content Sources,** on the left side of the figure, are the documents to be search-enabled. This content may be in documents located on file shares, housed in content management systems, or located on internal or external websites. Figure 7-1 illustrates just a few of the types of content repositories that are accessible to ESP.

➤ **Connector Crawler** — The first step in indexing any content is to be able to read the content wherever it may be located. While the actual details may differ from source to source, the crawler will fetch content — documents, database records, web pages, and the like. The crawler is typically specific to the nature of the content source — documents from a file system directory are accessed differently than web pages — and the crawler has to know how to process all documents in a given source. A file system crawler needs to be able to process each file in a starting directory and may even need to retrieve documents in subdirectories; a web crawler needs to fetch a starting document, and follow hyperlinks in that document to subsequent documents. In ESP, the rules for each connector crawler are defined via an administrative console.

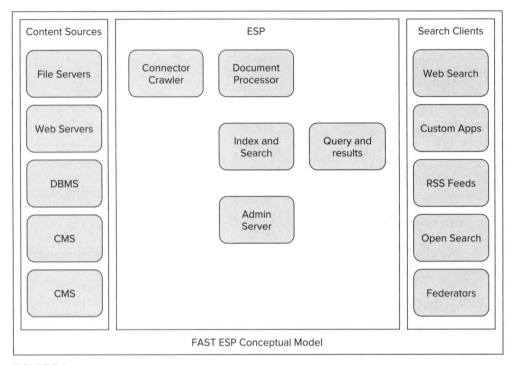

FIGURE 7-1

➤ **Document Processor** — Like virtually every Enterprise Search solution, the first step in search-enabling content is to feed the content into the search engine. The document processor performs perhaps the most complex task in ESP: preparing each document, web page, or database record for indexing. ESP uses an innovative content pipeline, which consists of several individual processes that can be assembled in a number of ways to perform the types of tasks required. Some of these include:

➤ Converting binary format text (Office, PDF, etc.) into a stream of text

➤ Recognizing the document language

➤ Performing any index-side lemmatization (stemming, etc.)

➤ Recognizing and extracting entities (people, places, and things)

➤ Applying synonyms and taxonomies

Actually, the indexing stage is one of the most important parts of a great implementation: if the content is not indexed properly, it's hard to have really great search experience. The indexing pipeline is one of the most flexible technologies out there, and in ESP, the developer has the maximum flexibility in terms of language, customizing elements ("stages") in the pipeline to provide the most relevant content to the search user.

➤ **Index and Search** — This element represents two of the functions that are really the core of the search engine. In reality, there are actually a number of components and processes related to the Index and Search element; they are discussed in greater depth in Chapter 8.

➤ **Query and Results** — The Query and Results element represents what most people think of as search: submitting a query to the search engine, and retrieving a result list of relevant documents. As with the Index and Search element, the Query and Results element includes a number of components and processes, which are discussed in Chapter 8.

➤ **Admin Server** — The ESP Admin Server is made up of a number of processes that supervise all of the other modules and provide the user interface for all of the administrative GUI tools. There are also command line management tools which can also be thought of as part of the Admin Server, but of course they are typically involved using direct command window input or via scripts initiated by the Windows Task Scheduler.

At the heart of the Admin Server is an Apache Tomcat web server, and, like much of ESP, it is implemented largely in Java, Python, and JSP pages. The most visible of these are the FAST Home, Search Business Console, and ESP GUI Admin console; but others include the Search Front End (SFE) and services on other ports.

Finally, Search Clients on the right are where the query is performed and the results displayed. Usually the client is a web browser or a custom search-derived application (SDA), but increasingly there are more special-purpose clients, including open search and RSS feeds, and often results are federated in with other search results lists by a different instance, or a different brand, of search engine.

The ESP Administrative Interface

FAST was one of the earlier companies to provide an easy-to-use graphical interface for administering Enterprise Search. A quick-start guide to using ESP is included later in this chapter, but this section provides the reader with a brief introduction to its administrative tools.

Viewing the Administrative Screens

There are three different screens associated with administration of ESP content. One, the ESP Admin GUI, primarily intended for use by developers and IT staff, provides access to the tasks associated with creating, managing, and validating ESP indexing and search activity. The other two — the FAST Home and Search Business console — use a softer interface and are intended for use by business line managers and content owners. They are the people responsible for the quality of the search results and who need tools to tweak relevance, best bets, synonyms, and search activity reports. Technical staff may access these tools as well, but they are designed for use by a less technical audience as well.

➤ **FAST Home** — FAST Home is the primary entry point into the graphic administration tools for ESP. Figure 7-2 shows a sample screen of a site with a single search profile with several collections.

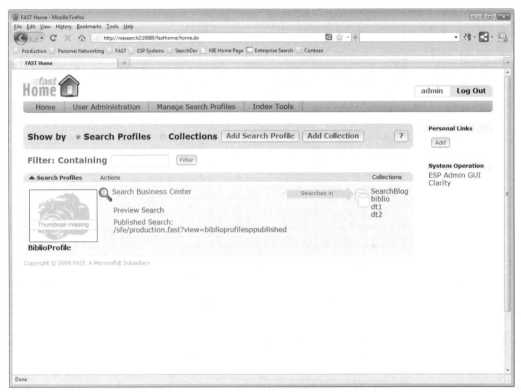

FIGURE 7-2

Think of the FAST Home as starting point for managing the ESP administrative tools and for creating search profiles, which are used to distribute management of the business-related components. On the main screen, you can see that a single search profile — a site — is defined.

Later in this chapter, you will learn more about the components of the FAST Home tool, but for now the links of interest are those to the ESP Admin GUI and to the Search Business Center.

➤ **Search Business Center** — The Search Business Center, or SBC, is accessed from the FAST Home screen for each individual search profile. It provides management for logical sites independent of the search platform itself. This means that the SBC allows the people who need to manage the business and marketing elements of Enterprise Search to do just that, without exposing the low-level operation of the search platform. A typical SBC main screen is shown in Figure 7-3.

Note that the Search Business Center link only appears after a search profile has been created; we'll discuss that process later in the chapter.

➤ **ESP Admin GUI** — Clicking the ESP Admin GUI link from FAST Home leads to a screen like the one in Figure 7-4. The ESP Admin GUI is the primary interface for creating, managing, and removing collections; for managing the ESP installation (whether on a single server or in a large cluster of hundreds of nodes); for checking system status; and for checking index and crawl activity.

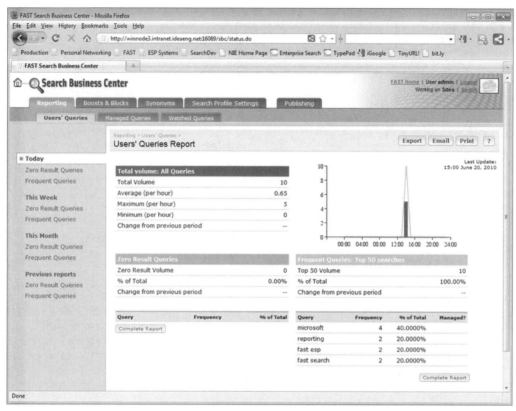

FIGURE 7-3

The Collection Overview in Figure 7-4 shows an installation with eight active collections; on a newly installed system none is defined. We'll discuss creating collections shortly.

Normally, IT and development staff, and occasionally content and business line owners, form the audience for the ESP Admin GUI.

Accessing The Search Front End

Related to the ESP Administrative Console — in fact, one of the links directly from the ESP Admin GUI — is the Search Front End, or SFE, which provides powerful search capabilities in a generic search application. The SFE can also be accessed directly via a browser by connecting to port 16089 on a system installed using the default parameters:

```
http://servername:16089/sfe
```

The screen in Figure 7-5 shows the SFE with a basic search result list.

The FAST SFE is not intended to provide a complete end user search application, but it does provide many of the advanced capabilities included with ESP, and it can be used by IT, experienced administrators, and business users to test collections and learn about many of the advanced capabilities in ESP.

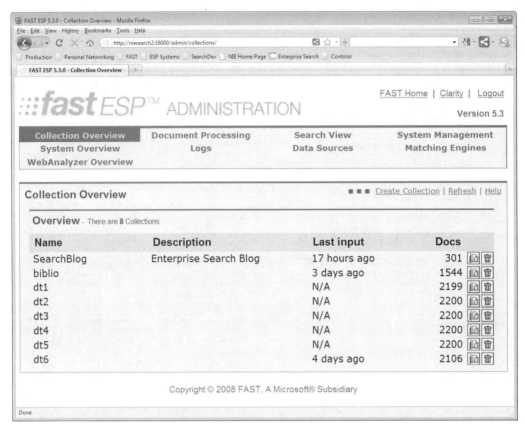

FIGURE 7-4

The SFE is driven by the integrated Apache Tomcat server, and it can be used as a template to drive some very nice search demo and prototype applications. Refer to the Search Front End user and developer guides for additional information about customizing the SFE.

Installation and Setup

With ESP, there are a number of details to address before you actually begin the installation: platforms, operating system, and supporting software, as well as the architecture and layout. In this chapter, the focus is primarily on single-node installations. Chapter 8 dives into detail about multinode installations on both Windows and Linux platforms.

Perhaps more than with many enterprise applications, reading the release notes and the *Installation Guide* are critical first steps: read them, and keep them handy.

Hardware

Generally speaking, ESP likes to run on server class systems with lots of memory. Supported configurations are listed in the *ESP Installation Guide*, but Microsoft does suggest 2GB of memory per core and a minimum of four cores; yet they suggest a minimum of 4GB of memory. In our experience, 8GB is really the minimum acceptable, and if you can go bigger, do it.

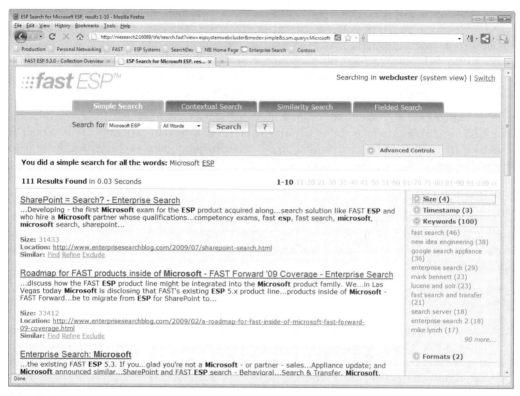

FIGURE 7-5

To efficiently use much over 3 gigs of RAM on Windows or Linux, you need to have a 64-bit system running a 64-bit operating system. These will run both 32- or 64-bit binaries; although individual 32-bit binaries are limited as to the amount of memory they can access, all processes still benefit from a 64-bit operating system in terms of the overall total memory that is available.

In the FSIS and FSIA releases, ESP must be installed while running 32-bit Java on Windows; however, ESP itself will run under 64-bit Java, so it seems to be an installer issue. This may change in the actual release, so check the release notes and *ESP Installation Guide* before you start.

Another characteristic of ESP to be aware of: FSIS and FSIA should be the only heavy-duty application running on the server. ESP should not be run on a domain controller, a mail server, or a DNS server system; generally, the less going on besides ESP, the better.

Local Disk Drives

First a quick point: ESP wisely recommends using a separate physical disk or volume for data and for program files installation. However, this isn't the default choice during the actual install program, so you need to remember to change it.

All modern search engines are very disk intensive. For maximum performance, the ESP documentation recommends high-end disks: SCSI, high RPM, RAID, and so on. FAST understands the internal workings of ESP and wants customers to be satisfied with the product, so they do not encourage use of any but the highest performing disk drives.

However, if hardware cost is a factor in a particular project, or perhaps in some cases more of a factor than absolute performance, then slower disks may be acceptable. There are many variables: If an application truly needs to scale, then buying less capable hardware may mean that a larger number of overall machines are needed, which can actually increase cost over the long term. However, smaller applications may never need to scale and may not need the absolute fastest hardware. In those cases, our advice would be to choose quality and support over overpaying for that last notch of performance.

Keep in mind that once a system is not using vendor-suggested configurations, the quoted throughput numbers are clearly invalid as well. Organizations taking this route should plan to do their own benchmarks. Or perhaps employ a hybrid approach whereby production machines get the premium hardware, but development and staging do not.

RAID: The Type Matters

If you're reading this chapter, you probably already know that RAID is the technique of combining multiple physical hard drives in such a way that they act as a single hard drive but with one or more improved qualities over a single hard drive. The FAST ESP documentation already contains information about RAID recommendations, so we won't review all that here.

For those readers who are less familiar with RAID, however, there are a couple things that might come as a surprise:

➤ There are many different types of RAID, and those numbers after the word RAID are really important! Although some RAID setups are optimized for performance, others are really there to improve reliability or ease of recovery. Depending on the setup, RAID is not always significantly faster than other setups.

➤ The write speeds for RAID can be much slower than the read speeds. A busy ESP system does lots of writing to the hard drive, so this asymmetry in some RAID setups can be surprisingly important for search.

Network Storage

Search engines in general, and ESP in particular, are very disk intensive. In the past, network storage was slow, so most vendors would discourage the use of any network storage devices. Modern network devices are faster, and we have seen organizations successfully use network storage for search engines.

However, there are a few things to keep in mind, some of which come as a surprise to network administrators:

➤ It's not necessarily the sustained average throughput of network storage that is the bottleneck. Search engines typically make many round trips reading and writing files, so latency is actually a more critical factor. Optimizing network topology can greatly affect latency.

➤ Appropriate file locking and preserving transaction order is important. For example, some older implementations of NFS didn't handle file locking in a manner consistent with either Windows or Unix, causing the infamous "stale NFS file handle" error messages and other problems.

➤ Ensure that network file handles are configured appropriately high, in line with what the local operating system is configured for.

➤ Simultaneous system access to network storage can substantially impact performance, depending on the specific system. This needs to be factored in.

If disks are being hosted on a running server, instead of on a dedicated network appliance, there is a nontrivial load being placed on that server. Moving processes to a remote machine to increase processing throughput, while still having those remote processes access disks on the original system, is often a false economy.

Solid State Storage

Solid state hard drives (SSDs) are getting a lot of press, but the technology doesn't seem to provide much in the way of benefits for Enterprise Search. The bad news is that SSD technology includes limits on how many times a given sector can be written to, and, as we've said, search platforms do a good deal of writing to disk drives. Unlike databases, changing even one or two fields in a searchable document causes a rewrite of a fairly large amount of data on disk. ESP tries to minimize some of this, but it's still a relatively expensive transaction in terms of file I/O. We would suggest staying away from SSD.

If you want throw hardware at the problem, consider buying more RAM instead. And instead of trying to engineer an in-memory disk solution, consider letting ESP and the operating system have full use of that extra RAM. Modern operating systems are already very good at leveraging extra RAM, and ESP uses memory-caching techniques as well. We suggest a 64-bit solution for FSIS and FSIA if at all possible.

Operating System and Software

The release notes and *ESP Installation Guide* also contain information about the latest and officially supported operating systems for ESP. For Windows servers, Microsoft supports the following platforms for ESP:

➤ Windows Server 2003 (32/64 bit)

➤ Windows Server 2008 (64 bit only)

Sadly, it looks like the new FSIS and FSIA, at initial release, will not be supported on Windows Server 2008 R2, although Microsoft claims that the platform will be supported with a patch or service pack when the problem is solved. The problem was certainly detected late in the QA process, because the release notes include the release in the supported versions but with a footnote saying the platform is not supported. We've seen some organizations actually use ESP on 2008/R2, and for the most part it runs fine, but in production, it's better to follow the prescribed and supported platforms.

Before starting the ESP installation in Windows servers, the target system needs to have version 8 of the Visual C++ runtime libraries included in the "Visual C++ 2005 SP1 Redistributable Package" available from Microsoft. The URL is included in the *ESP Installation Guide.*

For the record, we understand that ESP will run on Windows 7 and possibly Vista with 8GB of memory. They may suffice for demo systems, but for production, go with the recommended server systems.

On non-Windows platforms, the supported distributions are:

➤ Red Hat Enterprise Linux 4 (x86 32-bit only)

➤ Red Hat Enterprise Linux 5 (x86 32- and 64-bit)

➤ SuSE Linux Enterprise Server 10 (x86 32-bit only)

➤ SuSE Linux Enterprise Server 10 (x86 64-bit only)

➤ Sun Solaris 10 SunOS 5.10 (x86 64-bit only)

Note that CTS and IMS are only supported on Windows platforms.

Some organizations have successfully used CentOS 5 for ESP, but there may be some packages that will need to be downloaded manually. The release notes and *ESP Installation Guide* are the final authority on the subject.

The Final Infrastructure: Java

ESP 5.3 is written in Java and Python, and the installer is no different. Before ESP can be installed on a server, Java 1.5 or 1.6 has to be installed. The *ESP Installation Guide* calls for a full Java Development Kit, the JDK, which includes the Java Runtime tools (the Java executable and libraries) as well as the developer tools (the Java compiler and its libraries).

Microsoft suggests downloading the software from java.sun.com; we strongly recommend that you stick with Sun Java rather than the other versions available, including the OpenJDK. The other versions may have their benefits, but the risk of incompatibility is just not worth it.

Once you've installed the Java JDK, make sure the proper environment variables are set. The PATH is, of course, critical, but JAVA_HOME is important once you get ESP installed and running. Many of the command line tools for ESP use JAVA_HOME in the scripts, and some fail with strange messages if it's not set.

 JAVA_HOME should be set to the path where the bin *and* lib *directories are located. The ESP scripts often attempt to execute* %JAVA_HOME%/bin/java....

After you've installed Java and set the appropriate environment variables, test both your runtime and compiler version by typing:

```
java -version
```

It should report something like this:

```
java version "1.6.0_14"
Java(TM) SE Runtime Environment (build 1.6.0_14-b08)
Java HotSpot(TM) Client VM (build 14.0-b16, mixed mode, sharing)
```

Notice HotSpot(TM), which verifies that you're using the Sun/Oracle Java version.

Test the compiler as well, by typing:

```
javac -version
```

This should return something like:

```
javac 1.6.0_14
```

Java and the JDK are standard on some Linux platforms; make sure that the type installed is the Sun/Oracle Java, not another variety, for both `java` and `javac`.

Virtual Systems

Increasingly, enterprises are looking to virtual platforms as a way to be cost efficient and more energy efficient. Until recently, FAST was quite specific about virtual machines (VMs): they were not supported. As discussed earlier in the chapter, ESP prefers exclusive access to hardware, and really performs best with high-speed SCSI drives connected on a dedicated channel.

In the real world, ESP does run on virtual environments, albeit not as optimally as it might on a dedicated system. The FAST folks inside of Microsoft have started to soften the message on VMs, not because the ESP architecture has changed, but because VMs are getting faster and enterprises demand it.

Using VMs, especially in development and staging environments, is a great way to test applications, scalability, and failover; we recommend it highly. In production, test and decide what works best.

VMWare Performance

The ESP documentation warns of up to a 40 percent degradation in performance on VMWare, although that reference is specific to VMWare, doesn't give any other technical details, and is more than a year out of date as of this writing.

VMWare comes in several different models, including the "bare metal" design, where a minimum host operating system is loaded on the physical server. Presumably this would offer the best performance.

Hyper-V Performance

In testing we did with other search technology on Microsoft's older Virtual PC platform, we saw a performance penalty in the range of between 5 to 30 percent, and we're guessing on average it would be under 10 percent. For production machines, please check with your Microsoft sales representative for official support policies.

There's also a difference between emulated and synthetic device drivers that impacts performance. We won't go into details, but for maximum performance we understand that Microsoft recommends synthetic device drivers.

HyperV and Linux

If you're running Linux under Microsoft Hyper-V you'll still want to have X-Windows access on at least one of the ESP nodes. Under Microsoft's virtualization there can be problems with, of all things, the mouse driver when running on the virtual machine console, even when accessing the console via Remote Desktop.

Microsoft has attempted to address this by providing their open source Linux Integration Components for Hyper-V client machines. Sadly, given all the versions of Linux and Microsoft components out there, the instructions you'll find online for setting this up will likely be incorrect. It can be made to work: some assembly is needed, and you'll need to allocate some time.

There are other options for accessing Linux clients remotely, which avoid these specific Hyper-V problems, such as remote X-Windows servers, VNC, or Linux RDP drivers. However each of these alternatives comes with their own technical challenges. As a starter, you'll likely need to adjust or disable firewalls on both ends of the connection, as all modern OSs are rather locked down in their default configurations.

ESP Linux installation is also discussed in Chapter 8.

Preparing to Install ESP

There are a few prerequisites for ESP that need to be addressed before beginning the actual installation, including obtaining the software and license files and installing required prerequisites. This section provides the needed information.

This book will go to press before the final release of FSIS and FSIA are available; check the release notes and documentation that ships with your final released product to ensure that installation instructions have not changed, or check with the website for this book for additional information.

The Surprisingly Important Installation and Prerequisites Guides

The *ESP Installation Guide* really is required reading before beginning the installation. FSIS also includes a lengthy *Prerequisites Guide* that spells out a number of detailed requirements for specifically for CTS and IMS. There are a number of important details, which, if missed, can lead to a good deal of wasted time and effort later in debugging mysterious problems. This caveat applies to both Windows and Linux systems: be warned that most server default server installations will likely not run ESP correctly.

Some examples of system surprises include:

➤ Some Microsoft runtime libraries are required to run ESP.

➤ ESP is very finicky about some Windows patch levels.

➤ Antivirus software and daylight savings time settings can prevent successful installation.

➤ The software is very particular about TCP/IP and DNS server settings; for example, ESP requires symmetric name and IP address resolution, and this may not be set up correctly for new servers, and changing IP addresses or names once a system is installed can cause problems.

➤ ESP is very susceptible to insufficient RAM memory, and this can also be hard for new administrators to recognize.

➤ A default Red Hat installation will probably not have all required system libraries installed. You will probably need to install additional libraries. ESP has specific SSH setup requirements for every machine that will be part of a multimode installation involving keys and cached logins. To be thorough, remote SSH scripts should be able to run from every machine to every machine, without any login or confirmation prompts.

➤ There are various options for installing on Unix systems, especially if X-Windows is not available or has its ports blocked.

ESP has other specific requirements as well, and some of these have been version specific. Save time later: read the *Installation Guide* and the release notes!

Downloading the Package

Depending on how you license ESP, you may receive media or a download address. You'll also receive a license file, likely via email, from Microsoft, or it may come from your local sales or technical contacts at Microsoft. Various components of ESP — the SDK, certain connectors, or related applications — may be bundled into separate packages, as well. FSIS will include CTS and IMS; FSIA will not.

License File

Typically, the license file will be delivered in a separate compressed file that contains a documentation file, README.TXT, and the actual license, fastsearch.lic. The license file is a text file and should not normally be edited; the README file describes what changes can be made without invalidating the license. Keep a safe copy of the original master license file to protect against system failures and for potential future reinstalls.

The documentation suggests you copy the license file into a subdirectory under the directory where ESP will be installed. That is, in fact, where it will be after installation; we suggest copying the license file onto the destination system in a temporary directory or even to the desktop. The installation program will prompt for and validate the license file, and will move it into the correct location in the directory structure.

Incremental or Roll-Up Packages

As Microsoft updates installer packages, some releases are complete, while enhancements may be incremental. The FSIS and FSIA products are identical to ESP 5.3 Service Pack 3 (SP3), which is a full ESP 5.3 release plus changes that have been made since the initial ESP 5.3 release; thus, at the initial release of FSIS (and FSIA), we anticipate that the esp5.3.sp3.slipstream will be a full standalone installer, at least on Server 2008. For other operating systems, we anticipate the base release will be on esp5.3.0 and updates will need to be added incrementally.

On the Linux platform, the installation program, SETUP, is a Java program, so the system must have at least a Java runtime in the PATH. Follow the directions in the release notes for updating the images you receive.

Differences Installing FSIS

With FSIS, installation involves two different steps: installing ESP 5.3, and installing CTS and IMS. The ESP product installs as it does in FAST ESP 5.3 and FSIA, as described here. The new CTS and IMS components have additional prerequisites and new installation methodology. Check the documentation that ships with FSIS for up-to-date information.

Some Differences Between Windows and Linux

Most of our ESP discussions in this chapter and in Chapter 8 apply to both Windows and Linux. ESP is built on an Apache Foundation Tomcat server, which is very Linux-like, and some experience with Linux (and with Tomcat) will be helpful, even on the Windows platform. As of the FSIA/FSIS release, ESP is supported on Windows, Linux, and Solaris x86. FSIS components CTS and IMS are supported only on Windows.

There are a few quick differences between the platforms to review:

➤ Path names to files on Windows include a drive letter and backslashes (\). Linux paths use just forward slashes (/), the same slash normally used in fractions.

➤ Upper and lower case don't matter on Windows, but they certainly do on Linux. To be safe, assume that case matters: it's a good habit to get into.

➤ Lists of path names are different on Windows and Linux, both for the main shell path that's used to find executables and for the Java `CLASSPATH:`. Windows separates the list with semi-colons (;), whereas on Unix you use a colon (:).

Doing the Install

Once you've reviewed the release notes, prerequisites, and ESP Installation Guide, and the platforms and supporting tools are in place, you can begin the installation. The documentation is pretty good, but we'll cover it briefly here. Remember in this chapter only a simple single-node installation is covered; more complex multi-node and non-Windows platforms installation are covered in Chapter 8.

In the first stage of the installation program, you are asked to provide some fundamental information, and offered an opportunity to view the software license terms. Next, Setup prompts for the location of the license file, `fastsearch.lic`.

On a new installation, Setup then asks for permission to download a number of required open source packages, and as the various modules are downloaded, displays a number of status screens. Setup prompts you to click Continue after all files have been successfully acquired. You aren't asked to approve downloads if the software is installed on the system.

Setup prompts for the type of installation: single node, multi-node, or advanced. In this example, choose Single Node. Multinode installations are covered in Chapter 8.

Single node is one in which all ESP processes will execute on a single system. While it is not unheard of in the real world to have a single system in production, it's not a bad idea to make your first installation of ESP a single node: a certain amount of familiarity with ESP is useful, and a single node test system will help you learn before you get to a production installation.

Multi-node installations, with various components distributed across two or more systems, are more common in production instances of ESP, and more complex. Chapter 8 covers multinode installations on both Windows and Linux platforms.

The Advanced option provides a way to install ESP from a configuration file that describes the layout of all modules and all systems. This really is an advanced option that requires in-depth understanding of both ESP and the network performance requirements and sadly is beyond the scope of the book; check with the ESP documentation and your FAST technical resources for information.

Along the way, Setup on Windows will need the username and password for the various ESP modules to run as Windows services. The account needs to have administrative privileges, and needs Run As A Service privilege. While the Administrator username and password will work, many organizations create a specific account for ESP with the appropriate rights. Note that, as ESP crawls file systems and directories, it will have the privileges associated with the account, and it is often a better security practice to assign ESP a unique username to differentiate it from standard Administrator operations.

After you have selected a single node installation, Setup prompts you for two distinct directory locations:

➤ The directory into which the ESP program and utilities should be installed

➤ The directory where the ESP data files should be created

The program directory is pretty standard in all software installations, although we'd suggest that the directory be one with no spaces in the path, that is, not the Program Files directory. Setup suggests `c:\esp`.

The data directory should be located on a different drive — technically, a different spindle, not simply a different partition from program files. This drive should be big enough to store the ESP index — anywhere from 100% to 200% the size of the text of the data to be indexed. The data disk should be the fastest drive available, and write access speed is probably more important than pure seek time or RPMs.

 When ESP indexes data, it really only extracts the text within a data file. As a worst case, you can use the sum of the size for all files to be indexed, but in reality that may be more than needed: documents with large embedded images have a much smaller text footprint than the file size.

After Setup has the directory location, it prompts for the installation language. Select the default language for ESP's advanced linguistic processing; specify the language that reflects the majority of documents to be search enabled.

Setup next prompts you for the base port, with the default specified as 13000. ESP includes a number of processes, and these communicate using system ports. ESP reserves a range of 4000 ports, and the base port defines the starting number. Thus, in a system using the default base port 13000, ESP will use many, but not all, of the ports between 13000 and 16999 for communication.

Some of the ports in the range are well defined and active; others are not always documented. Normally, use the default unless you have a specific need to use a different range.

The next information Setup needs is the default type of index profile file to be used for the installation. The index profile is the file that contains the vast majority of site-specific preferences and options, including document fields to be used, and default relevance.

The options are:

➤ **Standard Web Profile** — An index profile with standard fields and weights, without stemming (lemmas). Query-side lemmatization is still available, but search performance might not be optimal. This makes sense where index size needs to be as small as possible and where users search with exact queries or where search performance is not critical.

➤ **Web profile with lemmas** — An index profile with standard fields, but with lemmas. Lemmatization is how ESP transforms different word stems to support different forms of terms, and handling this at index time will make the index larger, but it helps maximize search-time performance.

➤ **Profile with geo-search** — This is a standard profile with additional fields for longitude and latitude, a great capability of ESP where geographic proximity is part of relevance — for example, locating a nearby branch office.

➤ **Custom** — Use this option if you've created your own custom index profile.

Select the option that makes the most sense. That said, lemmas add capabilities that users like, so we suggest using them where index size isn't critical.

Chances are the index profile file will be edited a number of times before ESP moves into production, so simply choose the profile that bests matches the options you will start with. ESP provides the capability to load a new profile in an operating instance, but be aware that some changes may force a complete re-indexing of all content, so it's best to settle on a final index profile before you have too much data loaded.

Setup will prompt for an email address or name, which is given as the user agent by the crawler as it visits sites. Thus, information is logged in a web server log and is a nice way to provide contact information for questions a web owner may have about who and why the crawler is visiting.

Setup may also prompt for an email address and server, used to email service notifications when the ESP server has issues. Enter appropriate values, if you want ESP to give notice when it has issues.

Finally, Setup offers an opportunity to review the installation options and starts the actual installation.

When setup is complete, it displays the URL for logging in to the FAST Home interface; copy it and keep it. Normally it is:

```
http://server:16000
```

At this point, Setup may prompt for a reboot; in our experience, you should reboot at this point even if not prompted. We've seen cases where Setup did not prompt for reboot, but ESP just didn't work properly until the system was rebooted.

Surprises During Installation

There are a number of common errors and problems that may occur during setup. Usually, the solution is simple and to the point — if you know what to do.

All Platforms

Here is one installation problem common to all platforms:

➤ JAVA_HOME was not set prior to starting installation. Even if Java is in your path, you still need to set JAVA_HOME, especially on a multimode installation. JAVA_HOME should point to the directory that contains the bin directory.

On Windows it's set in Control Panel. On Linux, it's usually set in the .bashrc file for the ESP account.

Windows Surprises

In Windows, the following are some examples of installation problems:

➤ The wrong version of Java was installed. Remember, ESP will run in Java 64-bit, but it has to be installed using Java 32-bit.

➤ A login that does not have correct privileges was specified.

➤ IPv4 vs. IPv6. Remember, ESP needs IPv4.

➤ The ESP account needs Run as a Service privilege

➤ ESP does not like to use shared or mounted drives, since it runs as a service, and the devices are sometimes not available early enough in the boot-up process. Test if the installation directory on the host is on a shared partition (administrative share).

The ESP Installation Guide and release notes contain additional information on troubleshooting the ESP installation.

Install Checklist

Use the following list to ensure that your install goes smoothly:

➤ Read the Release Notes.

➤ Read any prerequisite documents.

➤ Read the *ESP Installation Guide*.

➤ Confirm Java is installed, including environment variables.

➤ Set up the ESP system account with proper privileges.

➤ Disable any virus checking software, and disable Daylight Savings Time.

➤ Remember ESP likes IPv4 not IPv6.

➤ Unpack the software and license key.

➤ On Windows, confirm whether it will be a slipstream or incremental installation.

Multinode installations will have additional login and SSH requirements as discussed in Chapter 8. Finally, remember that all of this list could be overridden by the Release Notes or other Microsoft documentation!

Quick Start: Build and Search

Now that you have an idea of the core components, this section will jump into a quick start to demonstrate how to actually create an index. The collection we build here will also prove useful in examples throughout the remainder of the chapter.

The objective of this section is to walk you through creating an initial collection, performing basic searching using the Search Front End (SFE), and performing basic administration tasks with the FAST Home and Search Business Center (SBC) consoles. Our assumption here is that ESP has been installed using the default port range.

ESP URLS AND PORT NUMBERS

The processes that make up an ESP installation communicate on ports, so knowing the port numbers various processes are using is critical to using the product. By default, ESP installs at a starting port, or base port, of 13000. For purposes of this section, our assumption is a standard ESP installation; if the various URLs and port numbers do not work, determine the base port used in your installation and adjust the port numbers in the URLs that follow accordingly. If the URL here addresses port 16000, 3000 higher that the default base port, you will need to use a port 3000 higher than the base port in your installation. You will need the system name for the system on which ESP is installed; in the examples that follow, the server is `niesearch2`.

Chapter 8 includes a discussion of all the ports used by ESP.

Creating a Collection

The basic unit for nearly every search platform, including ESP, is the collection — the index of documents to be searched. Collections, sometimes called indices, are created by platform-specific tools to retrieve documents and perform a transformation of each document into the format the search platform uses to retrieve content. The collection is to documents what the index is to a book, except that the search collection indexes each and every word in all documents.

 In ESP, collections are actually logical units maintained as part of the overall index file structure. Nonetheless, collections are treated as distinct entities, so we will treat them as such throughout the chapter.

Collections are created and managed using the ESP Admin GUI. In ESP, the process of creating an index involves a Connector Crawler, a Document Processor, and the Index and Search elements described in Figure 7-1 at the beginning of the chapter.

1. Log into the FAST Home console by starting a web browser and entering the follow URL:

`http://niesearch2:16000`

2. You'll be directed to a login screen; the default username is *admin* with no password. Later in the chapter you'll learn how to assign a password for production ESP systems. Notice that the request to port 16000 has redirected you to the login process on port 16089.

3. Once you successfully log in, you'll see the FAST Home screen shown earlier, in Figure 7-2, although on a new system you may have no search profiles defined, so the screen may look more empty than the one here. Click the ESP Admin GUI link on the right of that screen to display a screen similar to the one in Figure 7-4. Since this is a new installation, no collections will be defined, so the lower portion of your screen will likely be blank here as well.

4. Click the Create Collection link to access a series of screens where ESP needs to have information to create the collection. For this Quick Start, feel free to use the following information.

At the New Collection screen, enter:

➤ **Collection Name** — Enter **CollectionOne**. Note that collection names cannot include spaces or special characters, and they cannot be renamed.

➤ **Collection Description** — Enter **First test collection with FAST ESP**. Unlike the Name, the collection description can be changed later.

5. Click Next to select the Cluster. In our Quick Start on a simple single-node system, we have only one available cluster, webcluster.

6. Click next to select the pipeline, shown in Figure 7-6.

On this form, select the pipeline from the list displayed when you click on the pull-down list arrow to the right of the Available Pipelines field. The Available Pipelines list can be a bit overwhelming; for now, scroll down to the SiteSearch pipeline, and click Add Selected. The selected pipeline will show SiteSearch (webcluster). Click Next.

7. Select the Data Source. By default, the Enterprise Crawler is the only source configured; click the pull-down list, and add the Enterprise Crawler so that it displays in the Selected Data Source field. Click OK to configure the data sources as shown in Figure 7-7.

The initial screen presents the most common options for configuring the Enterprise Crawler, which is used for web-based content. Adding a file system data source is covered later in this chapter in the section titled "Integrating the Integrating the FileTraverser into the ESP Admin GUI."

For purposes of the Quick Start, use a relatively small website simply to minimize crawling time. Verify your server has access to the website you select.

8. Fill in the Start URL field, and click the right arrow to copy it into the list box. The Start URLs and Hostname include and exclude filters work together to ensure that ESP crawls and indexes content you want. These two options together help ensure you don't inadvertently follow links to other sites, which could result in crawling much more content than expected.

Note that, in both fields, user entry is performed in the text box on the left, and clicking on the right arrow moves the site name into the right box. By default, ESP replicates the starting URL in the Hostname field, and specifies that, in order to be crawled, the hostname of any hyperlink must match the domain exactly. To exclude a part of a site, enter the URL that matches the section to be skipped in the Hostname Exclude field.

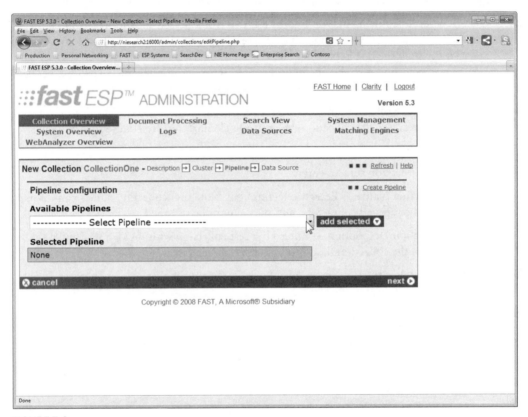

FIGURE 7-6

Use care when specifying include and exclude patterns; it's possible that a bad pairing of values could initiate an attempt to crawl virtually the entire Internet. Keep an eye on your document counts while testing combinations of patterns!

Notice that you can specify more than a single staring URL, which is one way that FAST provides the ability to consolidate multiple websites into a single collection. (The other method is by use of Search Profiles, described later in this chapter.) Refer to the *Enterprise Crawler Guide* for complete information on crawling sites.

9. Set the Request rate near the bottom of the form. ESP provides the option to set a request rate, which is really a niceness factor, specifying how long the crawler will wait between page fetches. You can specify a specific number of seconds to wait, or you can select suggested intervals from the pull-down.

If you own the site and need to index quickly, set the number low; if you want to index a production or external site, it's suggested that you use a longer delay. If site administrators notice your crawler retrieving pages at high speed, they may decide to ban your IP address from any crawling: be nice.

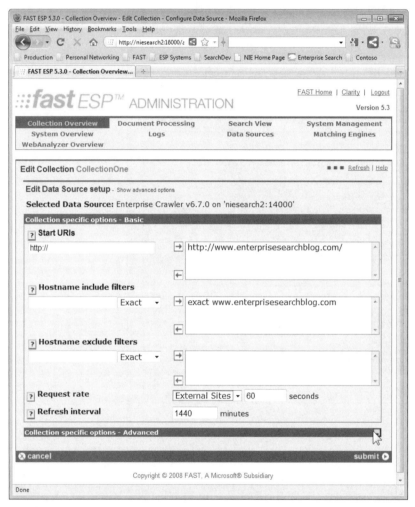

FIGURE 7-7

10. One final field on the current configuration screen is the Refresh Interval, which determines how often to revisit the site. If you need to re-index the site periodically, set this time interval accordingly. If you only need to index the site once, set the value to zero. These parameters will work for many web sites; to view additional options, click the button to the right of the Collection Specific Options — Advanced bar at the bottom of the screen.

11. Review your input and click Submit. Once you click submit, ESP will begin crawling and indexing. At one fetch every 60 seconds, the full index will take some time.

12. Click OK to see the Collection Overview summary for the new collection shown in Figure 7-8.

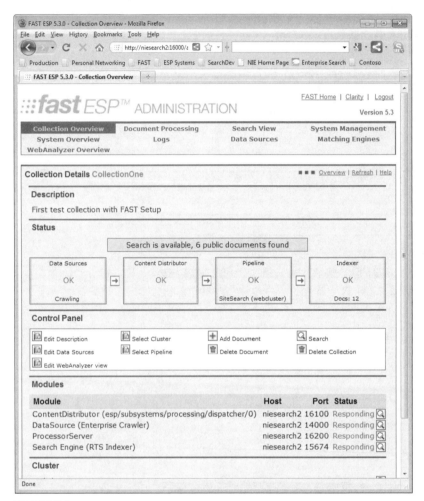

FIGURE 7-8

You access the main ESP Admin GUI screen by clicking the small document icon to the right of the collection name (between the Docs count and the trash can icon). Once the Collection Details shows the collection has documents and search is available, you can click the Search View to actually search your content, which we cover in the next section.

Searching the Collection

As soon as the collection has content, as confirmed in Figure 7-8, it is available to be searched. Depending on the Request Rate you entered, it may take several minutes before there is much content that is searchable.

From the ESP Admin GUI, click Search View on the top menu and you'll see the Search Front End (SFE) shown in Figure 7-9.

FIGURE 7-9

Make sure the Simple Search tab is highlighted and the All Words pull-down is selected, and enter a search term that you would expect to find on the site you are indexing. Click Search and you'll see your results.

A few other details to point out:

➤ In the upper right of the screen, SFE reports Searching in Webcluster. Clicking the Switch link as shown in Figure 7-9 provides a way to limit search to a specific collection or to a search view, which is managed in the SBC. We'll discuss search views later in this chapter.

➤ There are four types of search available: Simple, Contextual, Similarity, and Fielded. All of these are available in ESP through the SFE or through custom search applications.

➤ The Advanced Controls link provides a way to customize the features displayed as part of the SFE search result list. It also provides a way to output very detailed debug information about internal and external fields in result documents that is very useful for developers and IT staff.

➤ To the right of the search result are clusters that let you drill down into the results. ESP provides many of these clusters automatically, and the SFE view gives good insight into how the clustering engine works. The default, Unsupervised Clustering, and the more powerful Supervised Clustering, are beyond the scope of the book, but provide a great capability for implementing conversational search for your users.

The SFE can be customized to produce a pretty decent test front end for search. As more documents are available, we'd invite you to experiment with the SFE to learn the kinds of features and capabilities available through ESP.

We'll have more to say about SFE throughout this chapter, but refer to the *SFE User Guide* for more information on using the SFE.

Managing ESP

There are three primary interfaces to ESP: FAST Home, ESP Admin GUI, and the Search Business Center. This section introduces each of these interfaces in greater depth, although many of the features and capabilities go beyond the scope of what we can cover in this book. After all, Microsoft has hundreds of pages of documentation covering these topics. Use the documentation as the ultimate source of information.

To access the ESP console interfaces, find the name of the system where ESP is installed, launch a browser, and navigate to port 16000 on that server. Our test system is named `niesearch2`, so the URL we use is:

```
http://niesearch2:16000
```

You should see a login page like the one in Figure 7-10.

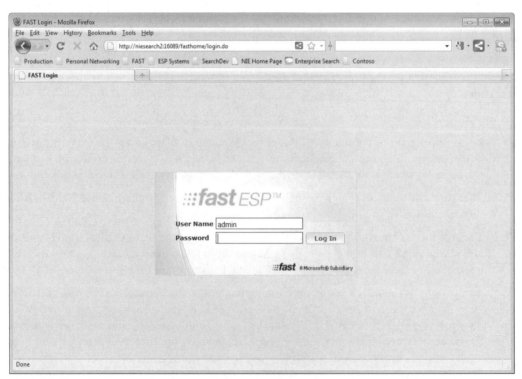

FIGURE 7-10

The ESP console listens on a port that is 3000 (decimal) higher than the base port specified during installation. Adjust the URL accordingly.

The default login for a new installation is `admin` with no password; we recommend setting the password to a non-blank value before making the site available on your corporate intranet, especially for a production system. Instructions for changing the password are included later in the chapter in the section, "Setting the Administrative Password."

After a successful login, you'll see the FAST Home screen.

FAST Home

The FAST Home screen serves as the primary login screen for anyone involved in the administration of ESP. It provides access, based on login, to the various management consoles that make up ESP. This allows different users to access the ESP system based on their responsibilities: an IT administrator may have full access to ESP services, whereas a business line manager may have access only to control the characteristics of a single collection.

When you've logged into a new system, FAST Home, as shown in Figure 7-11, is the first screen a user will see after a successful login.

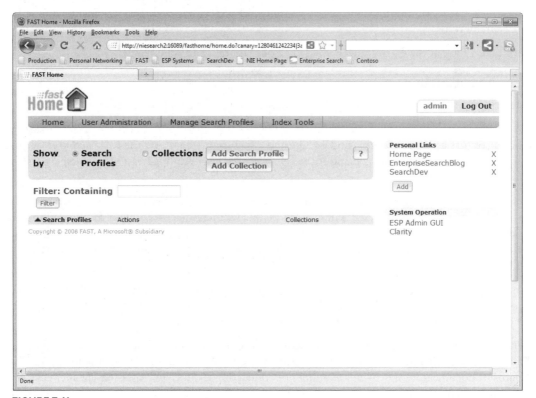

FIGURE 7-11

FAST Home is the portal for overall ESP administration. It provides access to other ESP modules via tabs and hyperlinks; and once collections and search profiles exist, FAST Home displays their status and links to them. We'll have more to say about on Search Profiles later in the chapter.

The tabs on FAST Home are:

➤ **Home:** Returns to this screen

➤ **User Administration:** Allows users with admin privileges create ESP users and assign them to groups

➤ **Manage Search Profiles:** Links into a sub-menu of the SBC for creating, modifying, and removing Search Profiles

➤ **Index Tools:** Query independent document boosting

Other tasks available from FAST Home include the ability to view search profiles and collections; on-screen help; and links to other locations including the ESP Admin GUI and an ESP tool Clarity, which we'll touch on briefly later in this chapter. If a system has several profiles or collections, the user can filter the list to make it more manageable.

The lower portion of the FAST Home screen is blank in Figure 7-11 because there are no search profiles defined yet. The connection between FAST Home and the ESP Admin GUI is a loose one, in that collections listed here will be *only* those that are included in one or more search profiles. Other collections may exist, and they will become visible in FAST Home once they are included in at least one Search Profile.

Let's take a look at the capabilities behind each of these tabs in FAST Home.

User Administration

The first step in setting up ESP is to define logins and roles for people involved in the day-to-day management of search.

Administrators create user logins and groups and assign rights based on the role each user or group will play in the ongoing management of the site. Clicking User Administration will display a screen like the one in Figure 7-12.

Enter a user name, the user password, and select the privileges the user should have. Groups are optional, but can be helpful when a number of people will have access to FAST Home and the SBC. Additional tabs under User Administration include Access Rights, which views users and groups with privileges over collections and search profiles; and Links, for creating hyperlinks to useful sites for ESP users.

It is also possible to export and import user lists, which makes it easy to move users and groups between ESP installations. The export file is in XML, and passwords, which can also be exported, are encrypted in the export file for security.

Finally, ESP users can be authenticated by external user management systems. In the current release, ESP uses Java Authentication and Authorization Servers (JAAS), but only for authentication. The Microsoft documentation provides examples of connecting to an LDAP user management system; it is possible to create others.

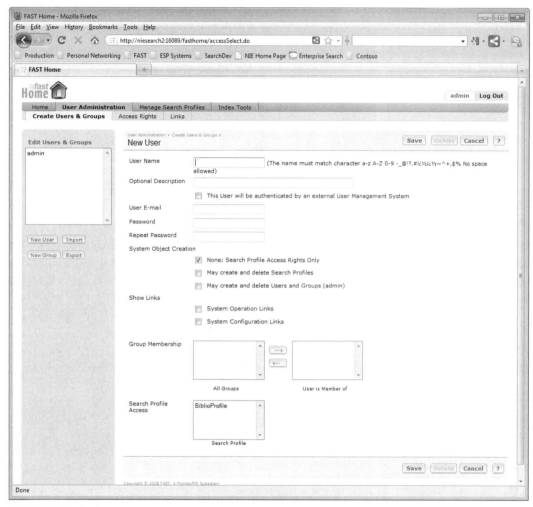

FIGURE 7-12

User rights determine what features and capabilities a user has, so the initial screen for users with different roles may look different.

Figure 7-13 shows a low privilege user login screen on the left and an administrative login on the right on the same ESP system. Each of these capabilities is based on the privilege assigned by the administrator.

Note the privileged user on the right has System Operation and System Integration links. Both users have added Personal hyperlinks that can be used to link to other frequently-visited sites. The differences between what each user sees on login is based on the roles and rights defined by their user name and group.

The *Search Business Center Guide* has an excellent discussion of user and groups and the privileges associated with each system object.

FIGURE 7-13

Manage Search Profiles

Search profiles are high-level constructs that form a logical set of business rules for one or more collections. This set of rules includes one or more collections; information defining dictionaries for language, synonyms, and spelling corrections; how relevance is calculated; the layout of the search result list; and what facets are included and how they are presented. Many of these options originate from the index profile file, illustrating how important that file is in ESP. We'll discuss the index profile file later in the chapter in a section titled "About the Index Profile File."

All of these settings are available to search applications, including the built-in Search Front End, which can function as a reasonable search interface with minimum custom software development.

Creating a Search Profile

A new ESP installation has no search profiles. Before a profile can be created, at least one collection has to exist; we'll assume here that you have at least the collection created in the Quick Start section above. If no collections exist, click the link to the ESP Admin GUI and create one before returning here to create a Search Profile.

1. Log in as a user with sufficient privilege to create collections and click Manage Search Profiles and click New. Enter a name for the Search profile, and select a collection from the Available box and move it into the To Search box with the right arrow button. Leave the Published Search profile URL blank. Your screen should look like the one in Figure 7-14.

 Like collections, search profiles cannot include special characters or spaces; names are pretty much limited to alphanumeric characters.

2. Click Create and Edit Settings to define other properties of the search profile. If you accidentally click Create, navigate to Manage Search Profiles, pull down the Actions tab, and choose Edit Settings before continuing.

There are two things worth noting here: first, editing settings has linked into the Search Business Center at the Search Profile Settings tab. Second, there are two rows of tabs in the SBC console, so use care as you click through the menu and submenu tabs.

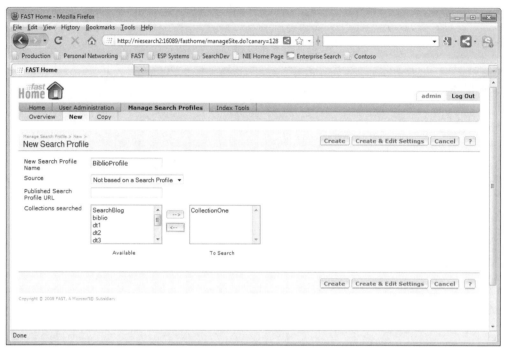

FIGURE 7-14

Editing Search Profile Settings

In the Search Profile Settings tab shown in Figure 7-15, there are six submenu tabs.

The options when editing a search profile are:

➤ **General** — The General submenu tab, selected in Figure 7-15, provides a way to customize the search profile by associating an image file with it, and the option of adding additional collections as desired. The General screen also shows the URL for this search profile once it is published, a process to be addressed shortly.

Search profiles are displayed at the main FAST Home menu; and associating an image with each profile, or each type of profile, can help FAST Home users recognize search profiles more easily.

➤ **Query Handling** — This tab provides a way to edit input parameters and spelling dictionaries. This is how the SFE is customized for specific languages, dictionaries, or suggestions. Figure 7-16 shows the kinds of capabilities that are controlled in Query Handling.

We suggest you set any language options that are required, but that you use the default dictionaries as appropriate.

The Advanced Options provides a way to define fields as name-value pairs that are passed to the search front end application at run-time. In the figure, the `annotation_class` value is set to pass a value `user` in the Static Query Parameters field; this is required to capture search activity for SBC search activity reports. This is described in the section titled "Enabling Graphics Reporting in SBC."

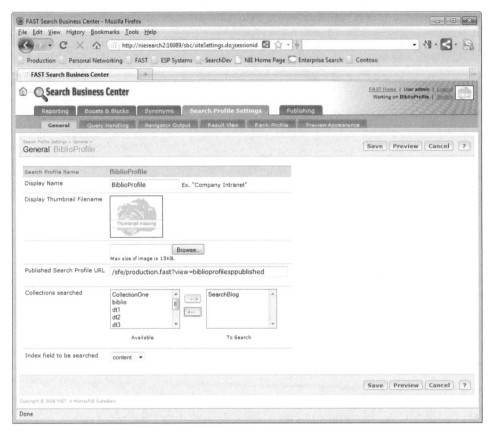

FIGURE 7-15

➤ **Navigator Output** — Often, fields in the index profile file are developer friendly but may not be appropriate — or in the correct language for — search users. This submenu provides a way to set the display names for each navigator/facet, and to define how elements of each facet should be displayed. Figure 7-17 illustrates that, in addition to Display Name, the Navigator Output tab provides a way to define default navigator positioning, as well as how elements of each facet are displayed.

The figure also has one Custom Output pull-down menu opened to illustrate the flexibility in sowing facet values. Note also that the index profile includes default behavior for navigator output.

➤ **Result View** — This tab provides a way to control which fields are eligible for display in the result list produced by the SFE; there are, by default, three options defined in the index profile file. The Result View tab, based on the index profile file, shows which fields are available for display in a result list; the fields actually displayed are selected under a submenu of the Preview Appearance tab.

➤ **Rank Profile** — This tab allows the SBC user to set how relevance will be calculated on a field and weight basis. The only options in SBC are those rank profiles defined in the index profile file; each pre-defined rank profile name appears in the pull down menu for Available Rank Profiles. Figure 7-18 shows the field weights defined in the default rank profiles in the index profile file.

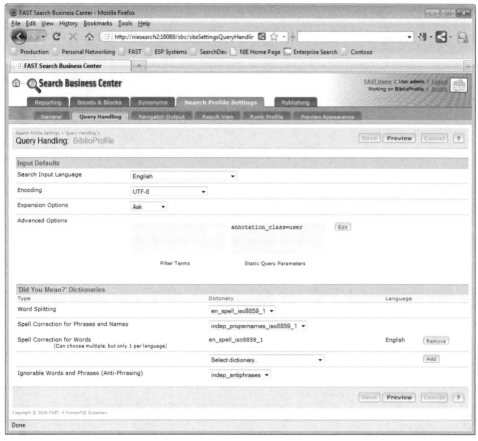

FIGURE 7-16

The rank profile defines the fields used in calculating relevance, and the relative weight assigned to each field.

➤ **Preview Appearance** — This tab, shown in Figure 7-19, enables selection of four additional elements of the result list that deal with the result layout.

The submenus on the Preview Appearance tab are used to define the following:

➤ **General Settings:** Style sheets, clustering, and similarity search

➤ **Document Summaries:** Layout of the result list entries for each document

➤ **Document Summary Templates:** The look and feel of the result list

➤ **Contextual Search:** Fields and scopes for contextual search

➤ **Navigators:** Location and settings for navigators/facets

Taken together, these search profiles provide a way for a business line manager or content owner to adjust the result list layout and facets. The settings here are available to any search application including the Search Front End; using them can reduce the complexity of search application programming, while providing business and content staff the ability to tweak interface parameters without additional application coding.

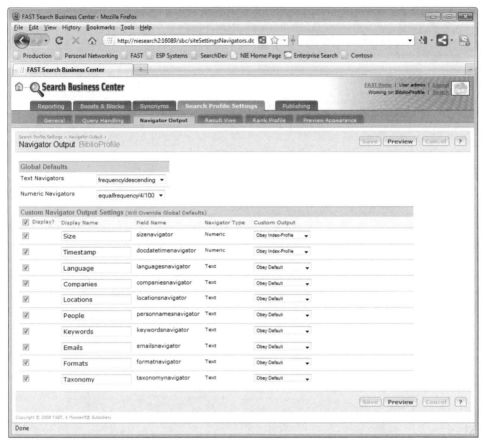

FIGURE 7-17

Refer to the *ESP Search Business Center Guide* and the SFE user and developer guides for additional information.

Publishing a Search Profile

When editing a search profile, any changes made do not reflect in the SFE until — and unless — it is published. This provides a way for changes to be made, previewed, and fine-tuned prior to making changes visible to search users. In some organizations, review is necessary as well, so the publishing step may be based on approval.

SBC provides a way to preview the effect of any changes by clicking the Preview tab and executing a search. Note that this tab is available on most of the submenus. Preview displays a generic search form, and searching will reveal the result of editing the settings.

An unpublished profile can also be viewed within the SFE. In the upper right of the SFE back in Figure 7-9, clicking the Switch link displays a pull-down list of all published and unpublished search profiles. Once the result list appearance is right, publish the search profile by clicking Publish on the top row of tabs. Notice that in the previous figures, the Publish tab has a star highlighting the tab, which indicates that the profile has changed since it was created or last published.

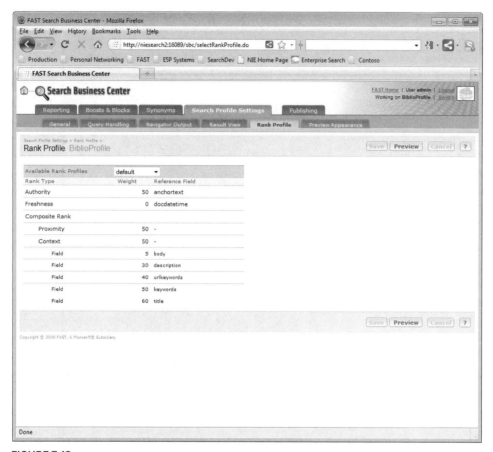

FIGURE 7-18

On the Publish screen, the SBC user can publish or undo any changes since the last published version of the search profile.

Index Tools

One last menu item on the FAST Home screen is Index Tools. Some background is in order before we dive into Index Tools, however.

When determining relevance, ESP applies weights to various fields based on the rank profile, part of the index profile file that contains so many ESP defaults. There are two ways to impact the relevance of documents in addition to straight relevancy scores: boosts and blocks, and boosts.

Both of these capabilities stem from the requirement in some organizations to promote a specific document. For example, for the query "annual report," there's a good chance the person searching wants the current year's annual report. Left to fixed relevancy models, all of the annual reports should show up, but the current report may not be at the top of the result list all of the time. By using a boost, you can increase the effective score for the current annual report, and it will tend to show up first.

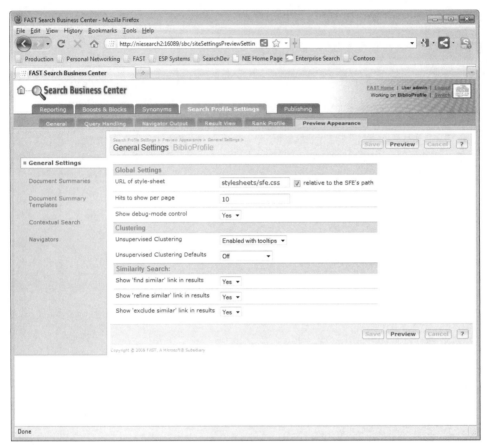

FIGURE 7-19

Boosts and blocks are managed from the Search Business Center. The term *boosts* means that the relevance score of a document is increased. *Blocks*, as used here, provides a way to remove a document from a result list. Because the SBC manages individual search profiles, boosts and blocks apply to only *specific queries in specific search profiles*. Boosts and blocks cause the current annual report to rank higher when the search is "annual report," and the user was searching against a search profile containing the collection where the document had been indexed. We'll be discussing boosts and blocks in our discussion about the Search Business Center later in this chapter.

Boosts are managed from the Index Tools menu. Boosts let a FAST Home user increase the effective relevance for a given document, *regardless of what query is used or which search profile contains the collection from which the document was retrieved*. If a boost is applied to "annual report," it will show up high in the result lost, regardless of what query was used, and regardless of which search profile contains the collection that contained the document.

To summarize: boosts and blocks, from the SBC, impact relevancy only where the search was "annual report." Boosts, from the Index Tools menu, cause the annual report to rank higher in every query that includes the document in the results.

Clicking Index Tools links to a page like that shown in Figure 7-20.

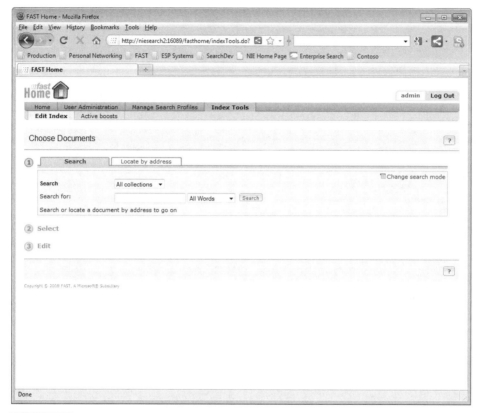

FIGURE 7-20

Notice there are two submenu tabs, Edit Index and Active Boosts.

Under Edit Index, there are two options:

➤ **Search** — If you don't know the name of the file or URL you want to boost, you can search for it, and can narrow your search to a specific collection if you know which collection includes the document. You can also change the type of search to perform using the Change Search Type link.

Figure-7-21 shows the result list for the search term "protein."

In the result list, the fields to display can be modified to help located the correct document.

If the sixth document, ADA426888, "Mutational effects…" is the document to be boosted, select the checkbox to the left of the result; click Use Selected to see a screen like the one in Figure-7-22.

Enter a boost value; 10000 is the default weight, so to insure a higher result lists placement, enter a higher value, up to 30000. Some experimentation may be necessary to obtain desired results.

➤ **Locate by Address** — If the URL for the document to be boosted is known, use the Locate by Address method. Enter the fully qualified URL, and that document is listed in a form much like Figure 7-20. Select it, enter a boost value, and save it.

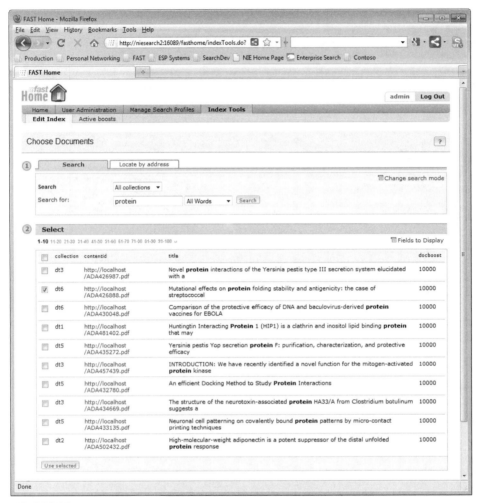

FIGURE 7-21

Active boosts

To view active boosts, click the Active boosts submenu. Figure-7-23 shows the report.

To remove an active boost, simply select the button to its right and click Delete Selected.

Revisiting FAST Home

Earlier in this section, a search profile was added and published through the SBC. Before moving on to cover the rest of the capabilities in SBC and in the ESP Admin GUI, it makes sense to illustrate the impact of these changes on both the FAST Home screen and on a search result.

Figure 7-24 shows the FAST Home after creating a search profile as described earlier in this section. Notice that BiblioProfile displays as the only search profile available. To edit the profile, simply click on Search Business Center; the next section will cover other options in SBC.

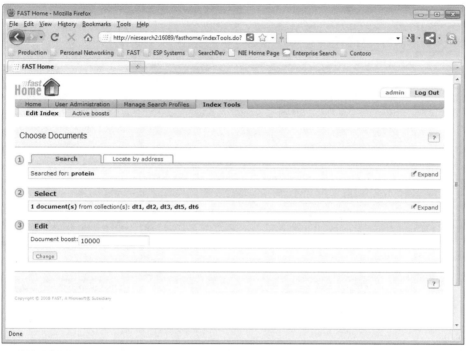

FIGURE-7-22

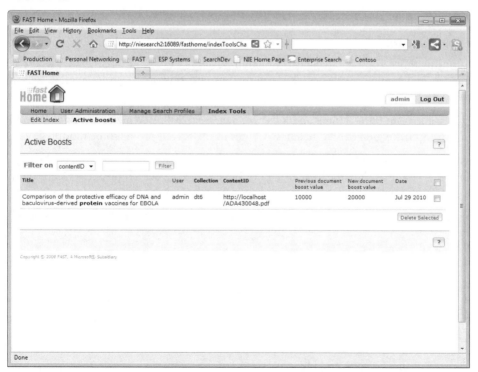

FIGURE 7-23

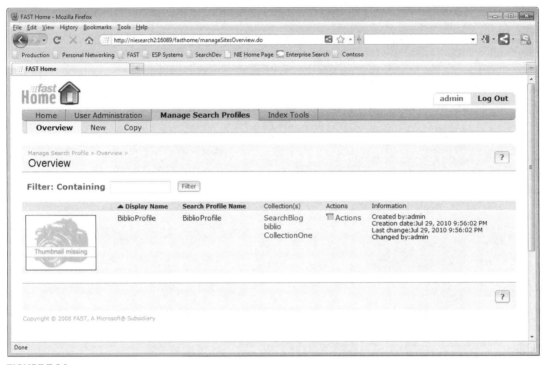

FIGURE 7-24

Search Business Center

The second administrative console in ESP is the Search Business Center, or SBC. This is where business line managers and content owners can control the business side of Enterprise Search: search activity, boosts and blocks, synonyms, and relevancy.

The SBC is accessible from FAST Home under the Manage Search Profile menu; or, once a search profile is defined, by clicking on Search Business Center in the search profile to be modified.

In a previous section, we created and edited a search profile. That search profile can be edited directly from FAST Home as shown earlier in Figure 7-2 by clicking Search Business Center in the profile to be edited. You will see a screen like the one in Figure 7-25.

The reporting screen shows the primary screen for the SBC for a specific profile. The menu items are:

➤ Reporting

➤ Boost & Blocking Terms

➤ Synonyms

➤ Search Profile Settings

➤ Publishing

Let's see what each of these menus provides.

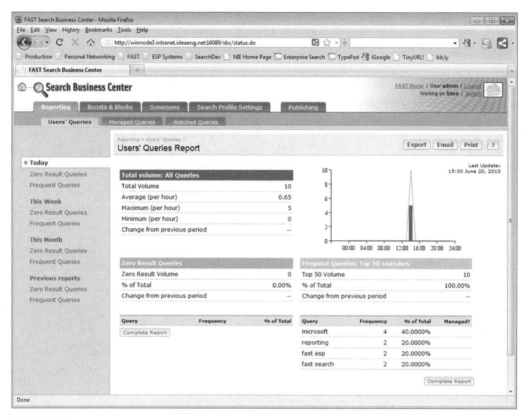

FIGURE 7-25

Reporting

The Reporting tab provides access to search activity reporting, including top queries and zero result queries, and reports on managed and watched queries.

The first submenu, Users' Queries, includes graphic reports for the most recent day, week, and month, as well as historical data.

The Reporting tab extracts data from the FAST log query. For a more in-depth analysis of query activity, refer to the *ESP Query Reporting Framework* manual.

Boost and Blocks

Boost and blocks were discussed briefly earlier in the chapter, comparing them to boosts in the FAST Home Index Tools menu. Boosts and blocks are specific to a search profile as well as to a specific query.

Boosts here provide a way to rank specific documents higher in relevance than the standard ranking profile would do; this provides a mechanism for creating best bets for particular queries. Blocks provide a way to remove a document from a result list, regardless of the score it would have under the standard rank profile relevance.

When changes are made to Boosts & Blocks, they must be published before they become active.

The boosts and blocks menu has two submenus: Overview and Manage.

Overview

The Overview submenu is used to review currently active boost and blocks, which can be viewed based on query or by documents. Boosts and Blocks can be added or deleted as well.

On a new installation of ESP, no boosts or blocks are defined, so the Overview submenu is blank. Boosts/blocks can be added either by clicking Add New, or by clicking the Manage submenu. Either action will display a screen like the one in Figure 7-26.

FIGURE 7-26

The SBC provides two choices for boosting: by assigning a document a position in the top 10 results, or by assigning the document an absolute relevance number. Blocks are defined in the same manner.

To enable a boost/block, follow these steps:

1. From the Add New menu, enter the search term to boost or block, as shown in Figure 7-27.

    When you use the Top 10 button for result list item, you can ensure that document will be included in the top 10 results. Clicking Block removes the document from the result list. Note you do need to locate the desired document in the result list to take either of these actions.

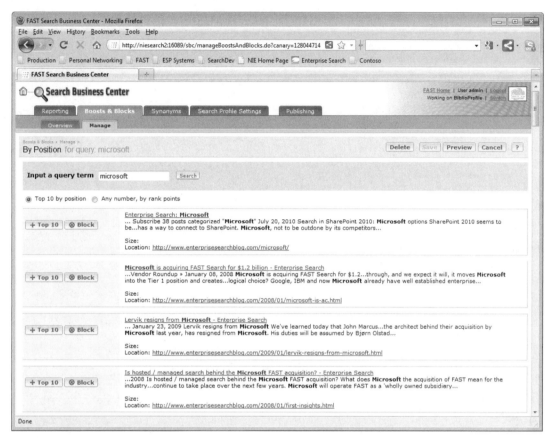

FIGURE 7-27

2. After ranking two or more documents Top 10, the result list shows buttons that allow you to move documents up or down in the result list, as shown in Figure 7-28.

By using Top 10 and the up and down arrows, you can establish the result list order for documents that match the query. Click Save to save your boosts.

3. To block a document from the result list for a query, click Block in the result list. It will not appear in the result list as long as the block is active.

Once boosts/blocks have been defined, the Overview submenu shows them, as illustrated in Figure 7-29.

Clicking on any Boost or Block brings up the Manage submenu for updating or removing the boost/block. To view which documents have active boosts/block, click the By Document link.

Note that when you save a change, a star appears in the Publish tab, indicating that changes have been made to the profile, and are available in Preview mode; but, until the changes are published, they are not visible on the site. We'll talk about publishing later in this section.

Remember to publish the changes to the search profile when boosts or blocks are updated!

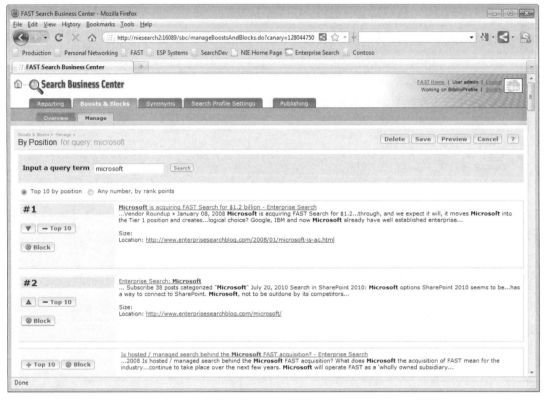

FIGURE 7-28

Manage

To manage boosts and blocks directly from the Manage submenu, a search has to be performed to find documents. Generally, once boosts/blocks have been defined, the Overview submenu is the easiest way to manage them.

Synonyms

The Synonyms menu provides the business line or content owners the ability to define synonyms for common search terms. Often, these are defined based on observed vocabulary in search reports: search users are using an unexpected vocabulary in searching for content, and a synonym can help resolve the problem without re-tagging and re-indexing documents.

The Synonyms menu has two submenus: Overview and Import and Export.

Overview

The Synonyms Overview submenu, shown in Figure 7-30, provides a mechanism to manage synonyms.

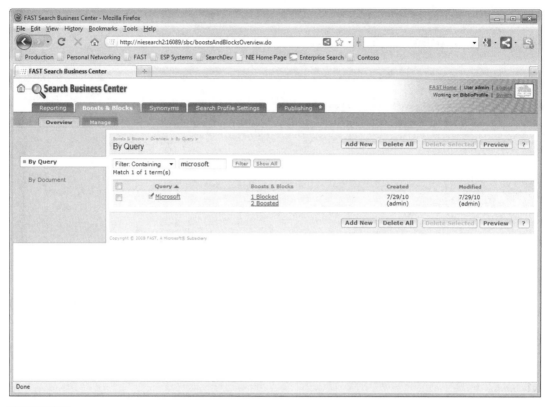

FIGURE 7-29

Business line and content owners use this submenu to define synonyms for queries. There are three different mappings available:

➤ **One-way Expansion** — When the search user enters the key term, ESP returns documents containing the key term and the provided synonyms. Searches for any of the synonym terms will not return results for the key term.

➤ **Two-way Expansion** — When the search user enters the key term, ESP searches for the key term and any synonyms defined. However, searches for any of the synonym terms also returns documents that contain the key term.

➤ **Rewrites To** — When the search user enters the key term, ESP returns results as if the search had been the terms in the synonym field.

Rewrite behaves as if the search user entered any of the synonyms rather than the key term. This can be useful if search users consistently misspell a product or if a product name has changed.

Remember to publish the changes to the search profile when boosts or blocks are updated, although you preview the results by clicking the Preview button.

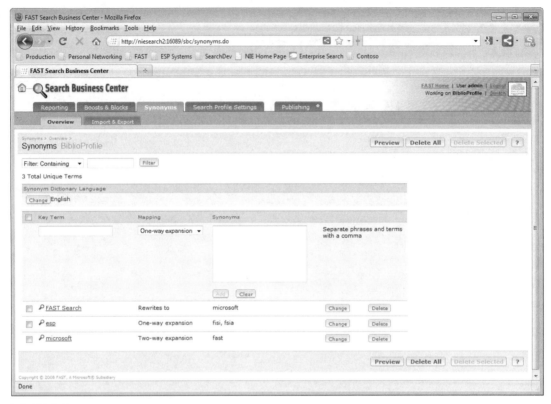

FIGURE 7-30

Import and Export

Microsoft provides the ability to import or export synonyms in a bulk fashion to save data entry time across multiple instances of ESP. The ESP Search Business Center Guide describes the format for importing; but the easiest way to learn the syntax is to create a few synonyms, using each type of mapping of single and multiple terms, and export it. Then study the format and create an import file.

Search Profile Settings

The Search Profile Settings menu is what you use to create and edit a search profile from the FAST Home Manage Search profiles link. Since that was discussed earlier in the chapter, there is no need to discuss it again here. Refer to the earlier section, "Manage Search Profiles."

Publishing

The Publishing tab on the Search Business Center Publishing screen is used to publish search profiles and synonym changes, and to publish boosts and blocks. The tab can also be used to delete any pending changes to search profiles, synonym changes, or boosts and blocks.

If a number of conflicting changes have been made to a search profile, only the most recent changes are actually published. If multiple users manage the same search profile, use care when making simultaneous changes.

ESP Admin GUI

We'll start our look at the three consoles with the ESP Admin GUI. This is the screen most likely to be used by IT, developer, and operations staff because it is where collections are managed, searches tested, and customizations made to the indexing process.

The ESP Admin GUI is made up of several different sub-screens:

- ➤ Collection Overview
- ➤ Document Processing
- ➤ Search View
- ➤ System Management
- ➤ System Overview
- ➤ Logs
- ➤ Data Sources
- ➤ Matching Engines
- ➤ Web Analyzer Overview

Let's look at these in greater depth.

Collection Overview

Earlier in this chapter, the Quick Start section introduced collection building from the Collection Overview screen. To see this screen, refer to Figure 7-4.

On this screen, ESP displays the existing collections with links to edit or remove them, and a link to create a new collection as was done earlier in the chapter. The Collection Overview is discussed in the *Configuration Guide*.

Document Processing

The Document Processing element, shown in Figure 7-31, exposes the ESP predefined document processing pipelines, as well as individual pipeline stages that can be integrated into standard or custom pipelines.

Each of the defined pipelines can be examined using the magnifying glass button; can be essentially cloned as a starting point for a new, custom pipeline using the plus sign button; or removed from the system using the trash can icon.

Individual pipeline stages, further down the same screen, feature the same capabilities (and icons), but individual stages can be edited. Chapter 8 includes a section on creating a custom pipeline stage.

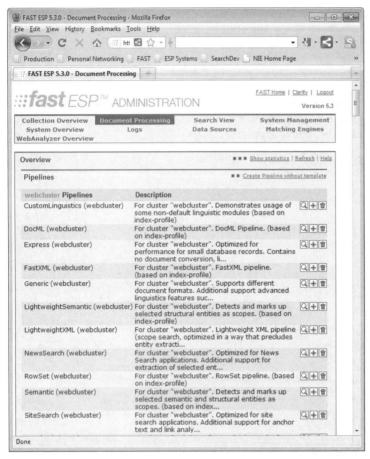

FIGURE 7-31

Pipelines and stages are discussed in the *Configuration Guide* and in the *Document Processor Integration Guide.*

Search View

The Search View links to the Search Front End (SFE), which was discussed briefly in the previous section. The SFE starts in a new window or a new tab in your browser, depending on which browser is used. Don't be surprised if clicking the link seems to have no effect: look for a new window or tab.

The SFE is discussed in the *SFE User Guide* and the *SFE Developers Guide.*

System Management

The System Management element shows the status of each component of ESP and is shown in Figure 7-32. On multinode systems, each process on each node is presented.

Individual processes can be started or stopped, and the screen reports on collection size to assist in monitoring disk capacity. System Management is discussed in the *Operations Guide.*

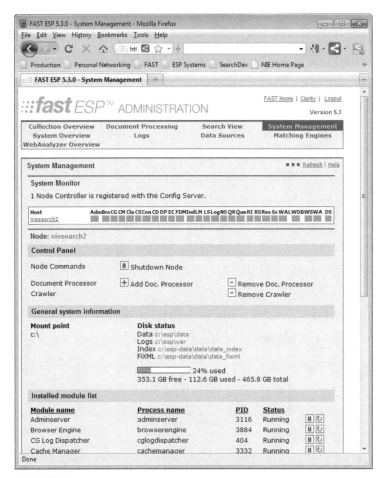

FIGURE 7-32

System Overview

The System Overview screen, shown in Figure 7-33, provides a quick overall status of an instance of ESP, including the number of nodes, search servers, and process servers.

It also reports the port number that each of the processes uses and its current status (responding or not), and a link to a detailed view of individual modules.

Logs

The Logs screen is an excellent and often underutilized source of information. Errors and warnings don't always cooperate by displaying near the top of the log as they do in Figure 7-34; ESP displays the last error or warning in its own section of the screen.

The Logs screen also provides pull-down menus to select specific areas of interest including common and uncommon errors.

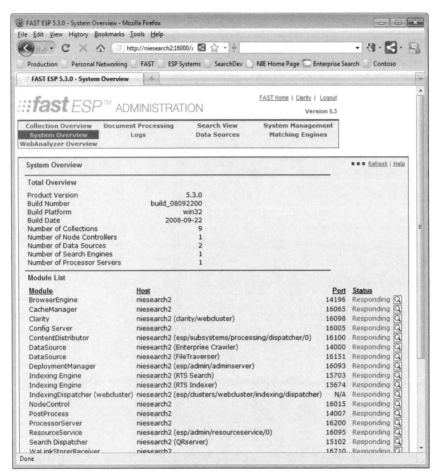

FIGURE 7-33

Log files are discussed in the *Troubleshooting Guide*.

Data Sources

The Data Sources screen shows the data sources available for feeding content into ESP. The screen shown in Figure 7-35 includes two sources: the standard Enterprise Crawler and the FileTraverser used for crawling file systems and file shares.

The file traverser is a command line tool, but ESP can be configured to include it in the ESP Admin GUI as a data source. Database/JDBC and other connectors can be configured as data sources as well.

By clicking in the List Collections link adjacent to each data source, data including detailed configuration and statistics for each collection are available.

Data sources are discussed in the *Configuration Guide*.

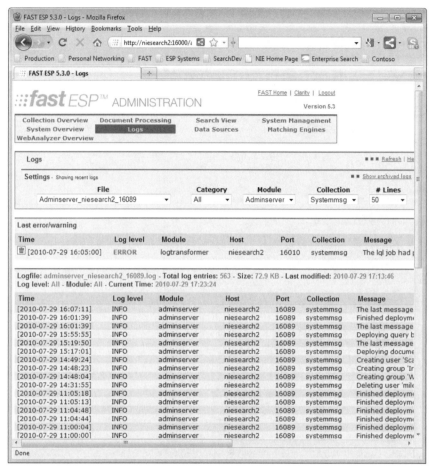

FIGURE 7-34

Matching Engines

The name Matching Engines is possibly the least useful name for what this element provides: a view into collection status and the ESP partitions, and the capability to upload an updated index profile file. (Recall the caveats to changing the index profile discussed earlier in this chapter!)

Figure 7-36 illustrates the Control Panel in the Matching Engines after clicking on the niesearch2 Search Column link.

While the page in Figure 7-36 has only a single node, a link would show for each column/node in a multinode installation. See Chapter 8 for a discussion of multi-nodes, rows, and columns.

The Control Panel within Matching Engines shows the status of the three ESP partitions. ESP uses three partitions; to maintain indices the partitions are maintained in directories in the ESP Data directory specified during installation. Partition 0 is where new content lives: Partition 0 is a smaller partition, so newly submitted documents become searchable more quickly. Things change quickly in Partition 0.

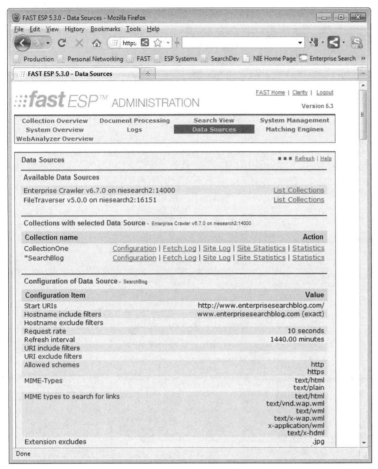

FIGURE 7-35

After some period of time, ESP will move newly indexed content into Partition 1. Content here changes less frequently, but because our new document is already searchable, moving the index into Partition 1 is not time-critical.

When indexed documents prove to be less dynamic, ESP moves the index data for those documents into Partition 2, which changes less frequently and grows larger as more documents are added.

These three partitions operate as a single search index, and ESP determines when and which documents to move to the larger partitions. Presumably more frequently changing documents will tend to remain in Partition 0, but where a document index lives doesn't affect search performance.

Microsoft doesn't support annually manipulating the index partitions outside of the supported tools, and we concur!

Matching Engines is discussed in the *ESP Operations Guide*.

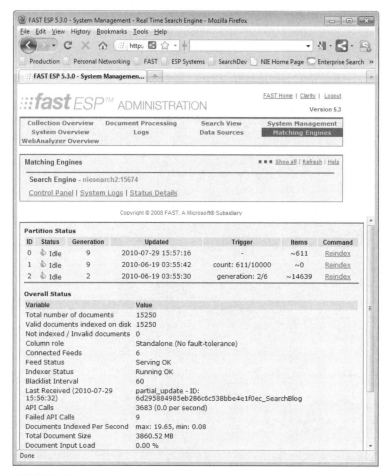

FIGURE 7-36

Web Analyzer Overview

The Web Analyzer provides a basic popularity ranking scheme for the sites that are crawled using the Enterprise Crawler data source. During indexing, it analyzes the hyperlink test and link to establish a page-popularity. Figure 7-37 shows the Web Analyzer running during a crawl of a website.

The Web Analyzer gives ESP an element similar to that used on Internet search sites that include links as an element of relevance.

Clarity Overview

ESP includes a tool called Clarity, better known as the "monitoring tool." There are links to Clarity in the System Operation links of FAST Home, and at the top of the ESP Admin GUI. Clarity provides a single view into all active ESP nodes, which makes it one of the few tools that provides overall ESP farm status. Clicking on the Clarity link from ESP Admin GUI displays a screen like the one in Figure 7-38.

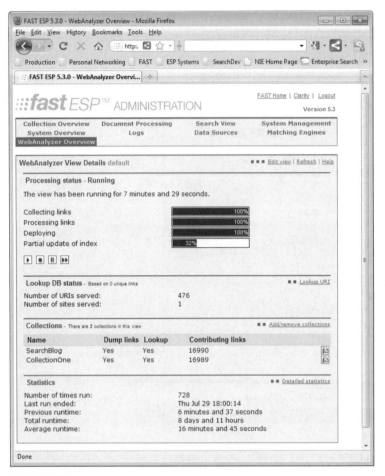

FIGURE 7-37

Until recently, FAST bundled an open-source graphic tool called RDRTool, but because of licensing issues FAST, and now Microsoft, was no longer able to bundle it with the ESP distribution. It appears that, as of this writing, the tool is available from `http://oss.oetiker.ch/rrdtool/download.en.html`, but other sites may offer versions as well. RDRTool seems to have a good following on the web.

Clicking either Clarity link brings up a screen with six menu options:

➤ **Administration** — The administration screen provides six additional menu items dealing with administration of ESP clusters, from a single node system to a large multi-node installation.

➤ **Indexing Overview** — This menu provides an overview of all indexing nodes, and provides some additional useful status reports.

➤ **Content Overview** — The Content Overview menu gives a high-level view of content processing across all ESP systems. If RDRTool is installed, some of the reports here are graphical; if not, it displays "Graph Unavailable."

➤ **Cache Overview** — This menu shows a screen with cache data from previous scheduled Clarity runs. A cache status logger has to have been scheduled before the cache status is available.

➤ **Alert Overview** — This menu gives a nice tabular chart for each node showing green/yellow/red status for each service/port running as part of ESP.

➤ **Graph Viewer** — Shows graphics reporting if the RDRTool has been installed.

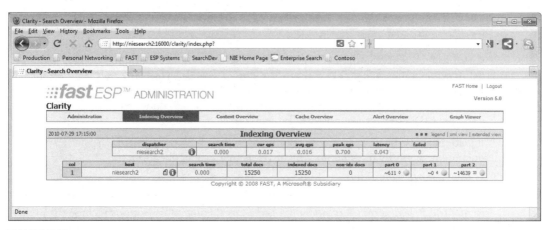

FIGURE 7-38

Clarity has only limited documentation and support, and is normally the purview of FAST consulting services. That said, the information Clarity displays can be quite useful for spotting trouble before it happens. Future releases of FSIS and FSIA will hopefully enjoy better documentation and support for Clarity and the information it provides.

Command-Line ESP Admin Tools

While much of the ESP administration and management can be accomplished from the various consoles discussed earlier in this chapter, there are a number of command-line tools that provide a more detailed look into, and control of, the processes that make up ESP.

Just about all of these command-line tools provide usage information by using the option -h; for example:

```
nctrl -h
```

The *Operations Guide* and other manuals provided with ESP provide in-depth descriptions of the command-line tools. While a full explanation of each is beyond the scope of this book, not to mention serious duplication of effort, this section provides a summary of the more useful tools and options.

The command-line tools fall into two general categories: those that are related to the ESP Admin function, and those that are related to the Search Business Center capabilities.

Tools for ESP Admin Operations

The FAST Admin GUI provides an interactive way to manage collections. Some of the command line tools that provide related functionality include:

➤ **indexerinfo** — The `indexerinfo` command tool provides information that can be useful to confirm document counts, the number of document in the index queue, and whether a given document is actually indexed. These can be quite useful in debugging problems.

One nice `indexerinfo` command shows how many documents are indexed and searchable in a collection:

```
indexerinfo doccount CollName
```

Some other useful commands include the `reportcontents` command, which will output a list of all documents in a collection or for a given indexer. Unfortunately, the output report shows the internal ID, which is sometimes difficult to translate into the file name. The advanced options of the Search Front End, while in debug mode, will display these internal document IDs, so they are potentially searchable.

It also includes the `hasdocument` command, which lets you confirm whether a specific document, again by internal document ID, is in a given collection.

➤ **indexeradmin** — The ESP documentation calls `indexeradmin` the indexer configuration and action tool. Its options provide a way for a system administrator to control just about any element of indexing on every node in a large farm. Some of its options include the ability to perform an internal consistency check on indexer process, pause and resume operations, and throttle a batch of document deletes to minimize any performance hit.

A drastic but sometimes useful task during development and testing is the command to clear all content in a collection. To erase the contents of the `CollName` collection, use the command:

```
indexeradmin cleancollection CollName
```

Note that the collection name in `indexeradmin` is case sensitive, which is not the case in SBC. Use `indexeradmin` with care.

➤ **collection-admin** — This tool gives command-line access to any of the steps that would normally be performed in the ESP Admin GUI, and it provides a quick way to look into, and control, the operation of ESP for experienced administrators. A few of the things you can do in collection-admin include:

➤ Create, modify, or delete a collection

➤ List all collections

➤ View details of specific a collection

➤ View pipeline stages

➤ List pipeline, modules, data sources, and clusters

➤ Clear contents of a collection

The command syntax is a bit unusual, partly because it has so many options. Some useful commands and their respective outputs:

➤   To see a sorted list all collections:

```
collection-admin -m list -o
```

➤   To view details of a single collection:

```
collection-admin -m list
```

➤   To create a collection:

```
collection-admin      -m addcollection \
-n mycollection \
-p "LightWeightSemanticSiteSearch(webcluster)" \
-d "Test collection using collection-admin command"
-c webcluster
```

Creating a collection is a bit more complex than many of the command-line tools; but when you break it down into its components it's not too bad. Specify:

➤   Command option `-m` with the mode command `addcollection`

➤   Collection name using `-n`

➤   Pipeline using `-p` (don't let `(webcluster)` bother you here)

➤   Collection description with the `-d` parameter

➤   The cluster where the collection is to be created using `-c`

Not so bad, was it? Note that the backslash (\) at the end of each line indicates a continuation, not an actual character to insert in the command.

➤   **nctrl** — The `nctrl` utility is for managing processes defined in the node controller file `NodeConf.XML`. This file contains information on which processes will start, with what parameters, and in which order, when ESP starts. It also provides these processes under which the ESP environment will run. Each node in a multinode setup has a copy of the file appropriate to the overall configuration for that node.

`NodeConf.XML` is not a file that should be edited in most cases, although it is the file that must be manually edited to add the FileTraverser feature into the FAST ESP GUI. Nonetheless, most of the parameters in the file are fixed during the installation and should not be changed without using extreme care.

Earlier in this chapter, the `nctrl` command was used to perform two tasks: reloading the `NodeConf.XML` file, and starting the controller connection process. The most common `nctrl` commands which were used earlier and which you'll find most useful include:

➤   **status** — Displays a listing of the currently running ESP processes along with information on the capacity of the ESP data disk. The `sysstatus` command produces the same report.

➤ **start** *[process name]* – Start the specific process. Examples include:

```
nctrl start logserver
```

Multiple process names can be included on the same `nctrl` command.

➤ **stop** *[process name]* — Stop the specified selected processes.

Running `nctrl stop` with no process name will shut down all processes including the `ncrtl` process. Use care when using the `stop` command!

➤ **reloadcfg** — reload the configuration from the `NodeConf.XML` file.

The `nctrl` program has a number of other options described in the ESP Operations Guide including add, remove, suspend, kill, and resume.

➤ **psctrl** — The processor control tool provides a way to monitor and control specific systems/nodes within an ESP farm.

As with `nctrl`, `psctrl` has a number of commands and some are more intuitive than others. The `psctrl` utility provides a way to test whether specific ports on different servers/nodes are responding using the `ping` command, and the `statistics` command provides a lengthy report on the status of pipelines and ESP processors. Other commands are described in the ESP Operations Guide.

➤ **doclog** — The document log utility `doclog` is used to obtain the status and the log of recently processed (indexed) documents. By default, the logs from all processor servers registered with the configuration server are consolidated and can be reviewed with this tool.

Output from the various command options can provide an audit trail of steps taken by ESP during indexing, for example.

SBC-Related Commands

The Search Business Center provides a number of functions including the management of search views and of boosts and blocks. The command-line tools that offer similar functionality follow.

➤ **boostbt** — The boost bulk tool provides a way to access boost and block information in a way that respects views and search profiles. It also provides a way of exporting and importing boosts and blocks which allows bulk operation on boost and blocks, as well as a mechanism of moving boosts and blocks from one instance of ESP to another.

The `boostbt` tool provides the ability to:

➤ Import and export boosts and blocks

➤ Publish and deploy boosts and blocks

➤ Administer boosts and blocks

➤ **exportsearchprofile** — This tool provides a way to export all of the information associated with a search profile in ZIP format, providing a way, along with the `importsearch profile` tool, to move search profile information between installations of ESP. The exported file is also a good way to crate backups of the active profiles on an installation. This tool does not export indexed documents.

Microsoft suggests that the tool not be used to manipulate search profiles, which should be done in the SBC GUI.

➤ **importsearchprofile** — This tool mirrors the functionality of the `exportsearchprofile` tool. It provides the ability to restore a previously saved search profile, and can be used in the process of moving search profiles to new deployments of ESP.

➤ **view-admin** — Views in the SBC map collections into groups and control how search operates. The `view-admin` tool provides a command-line method of managing search views for backup and recovery, and to replicate search views on new deployment of ESP. It does not include search profiles, which are managed using `importsearchprofile` and `exportsearchprofile`.

Using the `view-admin` tool provides a way to:

➤ Create and delete views

➤ Deploy or undeploy views

➤ Import and export views

➤ List view status and information

➤ Validate views

The QR Server Interface

ESP clusters are organized around index profiles and the query server (QR Server) that essentially processes searches and servers results for all collections and profiles within a cluster. There can be multiple QR servers; see Chapter 8 for a discussion of scaling ESP with rows and columns of systems in multinode systems.

Like the various ESP administrative interfaces you're read about earlier in this chapter, the QR Server is exposed on a port 2100 decimal numbers higher than the base port, port 15100 by default.

Figure 7-39 illustrates the QR Server page.

The QR Server features various options including:

➤ Log displays recent QR Server activity.

➤ Search includes an interface for testing search and examining raw results in the XML format they are returned in following a search.

➤ Configuration displays general configuration information about the QR Server including server and query statistics.

➤ Control provides an interface to clear the results cache, statistics, and blacklisted items.

➤ Statistics displays information about the result cache maintained by the QR Server including the recent queries per second (QPS) metric.

➤ Blacklist contains information about any documents blacklisted using various command line or SBC tools.

➤ Reference provides sample FAST Query Language command syntax (which is used to perform more than simple term searches in the Search menu fields), HTTP query parameters for search and for Geo search, and for overriding default facet/refiner behaviors.

FIGURE 7-39

The QR Server is a great interface for developers to use in testing queries at a very low level, and observing how various FQL and HTTP parameters will impact the XML returned after a search request.

Figure 7-40 shows the QR Server result following a simple query. Notice that browsers typically provide the ability to open and close XML elements by clicking, which makes it easier to browse the raw XML output from QR Servers.

We'll have more to say about the FAST Query Language shortly.

Some updates to custom dictionaries can require restarting the QR Server, so operationally these changes should be planned for relatively quiet periods.

Note that the QR Server, and requests made to port 15100 either interactively or via an HTTP request, bypass normal ESP security, so IT staff should verify it is blocked from any potential unauthorized intruders.

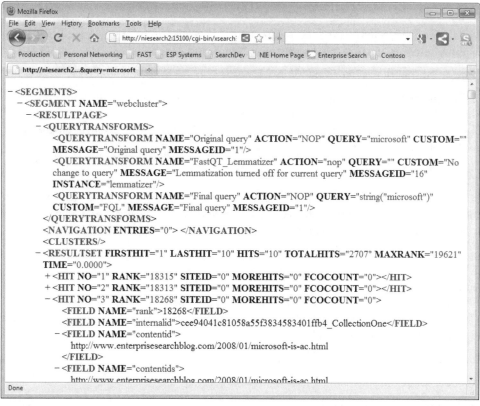

FIGURE 7-40

THE FAST QUERY LANGUAGE, FQL

Like most modern search platforms, ESP supports a query language that is used to execute searches, and the language, called FQL, is powerful and complex. Here, we will only provide a brief teaser of some of the capabilities of FQL. Some of the types of searches that can be executed in FQL, by typing them directly into the QR Server screen, include:

➤ **Simple** — A simple phrase is, in fact, a single term, for example: `Microsoft`.

➤ **Phrase** — A query for a phrase if two or more terms: `and(fast,search)`

➤ **AND** — Two or more terms that must all be present:
`and(title:Microsoft,fast)`

➤ **Fielded AND** of a field value and at least one of two terms — `and(title:acquisition,or(microsoft,fast))`

➤ **XRANK** — A powerful ESP operator that allows boosting based on one or more of the search terms: `xrank(or(esp, fast), microsoft, boost=500, boostall=yes)`

continues

continued

> This last operator, **XRANK** will boost document scopes for content that contains the terms "esp" or "fast" as well as the term "Microsoft".
>
> For more information, refer to the *Query Language and Parameters Guide*.
>
> Finally, from any web browser, the proper URL can perform queries with unblocked access to port 15100. A simple query URL is
>
> ```
> http://niesearch2:15100/cgi-bin/xsearch?   \  offset=0&hits=10&query
> =and%28fast%2Csearch%29%0A
> ```

While ESP has many ways to tune search, a long term business objective should be to develop and rank profiles default weights that work for your content, and provide business and content owners access through the Search Business Center.

Other ESP Goodies

Up until now, we've looked at the major components of the ESP administrative environment: FAST Home, the Search Business Center, and the ESP Admin GUI. There are other bits of information that help facilitate the management of ESP without diving into the more advanced topics covered in Chapter 8. The more useful ones include:

➤ Integrating the FileTraverser into the ESP Admin GUI

➤ About the Index profile file

➤ Setting up the administrative password

➤ Enabling graphics reporting in SBC

Let's take a look at them now before you move on to Chapter 8.

Integrating the FileTraverser into the ESP Admin GUI

By default, the Enterprise Crawler is the only data source available in the ESP Admin GUI. ESP includes a command line utility to index files, documented in the ESP File Traverser Guide. Nonetheless, the sheer number and complexity of the options can be daunting.

To improve the ease of file indexing, ESP provides a way to add FileTraverser as a data source in the ESP Admin GUI. The ESP documentation calls this the ConnectionController.

We recommend that any site that will be indexing file-system content use this capability. The process to accomplish this is to manually edit the `Nodeconf.XML` file, and then restart two ESP processes.

1. Start by making a backup copy of the node controller file `$FASTSEARCH\etc\Nodeconf.XML` file.

2. Next, open `Nodeconf.XML` in a text editor; one that understands XML structure helps. Towards the end of the `<startorder>` section, add a line that reads:

```
<proc>connectorcontroller</proc>
```

3. Next, a few lines below, within the `<!-- Connector Controller -->` section, add the following lines:

```
<process name="connectorcontroller" description="Connector Controller">
    <start>
        <executable>connectorcontroller</executable>
        <parameters>-P $PORT</parameters>
        <port base="3150"/>
    </start>
<outfile>connectorcontroller.scrap</outfile>
</process>
```

Spacing and alignment isn't critical, but confirm the tags are properly nested.

4. Save and reload the `NodeConf.XML` file.

Because the node configuration file has changed, ESP needs to reload the updated file, and the new connector needs to be started. Execute the following two commands:

```
$FASTSEARCH/bin/nctrl reloadcfg.
$FASTSEARCH/bin/nctrl start connectorcontroller.
```

Once the connector controller has started, the FileTraverser will be an option as a data source in addition to the Enterprise Crawler.

About the Index Profile File

The index profile file is to ESP what a schema is to a relational database — and more. It exists as an XML-format file in the ESP directory structure and contains a number of components:

➤ Standard fields contains field names and data types, as well as other properties including whether the field should be indexed, included in a result list, and whether the field can be used for sorting.

➤ Scope fields are typically those that contain an internal structure, and are often used for search of XML format documents. This allows searches within a specific scope, for example within an XML element.

➤ Composite fields are similar to scope fields except they are conceptual regions of similar data. For example, with HTML documents, it may be useful to search for terms in the TITLE, DESCRIPTION, and KEYWORD tags as well as in the entire BODY. By including these fields in a composite field, searches can be easily be performed across all of these different fields at once.

➤ Rank profiles define relevance profiles for various type of search; these rank profiles are visible in the Search Business Console to a business line manager who may need to apply one relevance model to one search profile, and a different relevance model to a different search profile.

➤ Result list layouts define the properties related to entity extraction, and facets in default result list design. These, too, are exposed in the SBC when manipulating search profiles.

➤ Document clustering is related to, and included within, the result list section of the index profile file, and defines parameters related to supervised and unsupervised clustering.

Together, these describe the fields that will be potentially extracted and used during indexing and searching; the various relevance ranking options that can be set in the SBC (and via programmatic calls to ESP); the layout of the result list; and the files that will be used for clustering and facets (refiners).

During installation, Setup prompts for the default index profile, as discussed briefly earlier in this chapter and in depth in the *ESP Operations Guide*. Each of the default index profile files contains a number of common field definitions that might be expected: title, description, teaser (document summary), document date, and others. Many organizations have field names unique to their business — perhaps client name, part numbers, or something else — so the index profile can be modified to meet custom requirements.

However, partly because the index profile file contains such fundamental information regarding the structure of data and collections, there are restrictions on what can and cannot be changed in a live, fully populated collection. ESP characterizes these changes into three categories, based on the level of restart required. The *ESP Operations Guide* describes these well, but basically they are:

➤ **Hot changes** — Changes that can be made to a fully populated, potentially live collection

➤ **Cool changes** — Changes that can be applied to a populated collection but which require a restart of the ESP services

➤ **Cold changes** — Changes that can only be applied to an offline collection, and which require all content to be re-indexed

Because of the impact of cold changes — potentially days of re-indexing — best practices suggest thorough planning prior to production roll-out. This means identifying all fields and profiles likely to be important during the production life of the ESP instance. It also means that in early development, collections should include only subsets of full content so fields, profiles, and clustering options can be tested and thoroughly understood prior to that initial complete index of all content. Proper planning up front can prevent a good deal of frustration and dissatisfaction later on.

Setting the Administrative Password

A fresh installation of ESP sets the FAST Home login to `admin` with no password. Security best practices suggest that the password should be set to a non-blank value; in ESP this is accomplished by editing the file that contains many of the parameters for ESP, `$FASTHOME/etc/esp4j.properties`.

Edit that file and find the section that contains username and password:

```
# Configurable authentication data for logging into adminserver.
#
esp.adminserver.username=admin
esp.adminserver.password=
```

Add a username of your choosing. Microsoft doesn't provide guidance on what special characters are supported, so some experimentation might be in order if unusual characters are part of a password.

Once the change is made, restart the ESP log transformer processor:

```
nctrl restart logtransformer
```

The documentation points out the potential vulnerability of ESP if this configuration file is available for access by users, so the recommendation is to set permissions on this file for read access only by the ESP login account.

Enabling Graphics Reporting in SBC

Reporting doesn't work out of the box in the Search Business Center, and while the *ESP Search Business Center Guide* explains the necessary steps to enable the reporting, many developers and IT professionals may not read that manual.

Search activity is maintained in a MySQL database created as part of the setup process. Nonetheless, there are two steps required to enable SBC reporting:

➤ Set up a hidden field in all queries to be logged

➤ Manually run specific scripts to harvest search activity

Here are the details.

Setup Up a Hidden Field

While the search activity database is created during setup, logging the activity requires a specific parameter be set either in the search form or by the calling program.

In the SBC, logging requires a hidden field be defined that will be passed with every search. To do this:

1. From FAST Home, click the Search Business Center link for the search profile you want to enable for logging.

2. Click the Search Profile Settings tab.

3. Click Query Handling.

4. In Advanced Options, click Edit to allow input into both the Filter terms and Static Query Parameters boxes.

5. In the Static Query Parameter field, enter

```
annotation_class=user
```

6. Click Save.

At this point, that hidden field will be passed to ESP with every query from SFE, which will cause search activity to be captured.

In custom search applications, `annotation_class` needs to be set in the search code. Refer to the API documentation for details. Remember, the reporting activity is presented as part of the SBC, so even custom code needs to set the parameter in order for the activity to be properly logged.

Harvest Search Activity from the Logging Database into SBC

Once search activity is enabled and information is being logged, additional steps are needed to display the activity in the SBC. These steps, which provide the logged database activity to SBC, require two programs be run.

First, confirm that the environment JAVA_HOME is set properly. Then execute the following script:

```
@echo off
echo Running logtransformer downloader
call c:\esp\components\logtransformer\bin\launch downloader
echo Running logtransformer log merger
call c:\esp\components\logtransformer\bin\launch logmerger
echo Running Query report Generator
call c:\esp\esp4j\bin\queryreportgenerator
```

Note that because these ESP tools are themselves batch files, the must be *called* rather than simply run. Results will show up in SBC within a few minutes, depending on system load.

The script should be scheduled to execute periodically, depending on the business use case.

Documentation by Role

To help you get a feel for what documentation is important, we've organized a suggested reading list based on your role and the tasks for which you are responsible.

System Preparation and Setup/Technical Administration

If your role involves planning, installing, maintaining, and troubleshooting ESP, you need to read the following documentation:

➤ *Installation Guide* — Preparing for installation. Read this guide, the release notes, and the prerequisite documents carefully!

➤ *Product Overview Guide* — ESP has many subsystems and optional components. If you're new to ESP, you'll benefit from reviewing this.

➤ *Configuration Guide* — A summary of ESP concepts, particularly the index profile file that defines much of the functionality of ESP.

➤ *Deployment Planning Guide* — Planning, implementing, and deploying ESP.

➤ *Troubleshooting Guide* — Identifying problems and working with Microsoft support.

➤ *Operations Guide* — Setting up and running an ESP site or farm.

➤ *Migration Guide* — Information regarding upgrading from earlier versions of ESP.

➤ *FAST Home Guide* — Managing users who access FAST Home for creating and editing search profiles and the Search Business Center.

➤ *SBC Guide* — This provides information on search profiles, high level result list format/layout, adding boosts and blocks, and accessing activity reports.

➤ *Query Reporting Framework Guide* — How to access search activity statistics, beyond the simple reporting in the SBC, from log files.

➤ *Security Access Module* — Understanding security and how ESP integrates with external security infrastructure.

➤ *Feeding Proxy Guide* — Indexing content in multi-node and multi-site environments that require replication.

Business Administration/Boosts and Blocks

If your role involves managing the user experience and search analytics, read the following documentation:

➤ *FAST Home Guide* — Managing users who access FAST Home for creating and editing search profiles and the Search Business Center.

➤ *SBC Guide* — This provides information on search profiles, high level result list format/layout, adding boosts and blocks, and accessing activity reports.

➤ *Query Reporting Framework Guide* — How to access search activity statistics, beyond the simple reporting in the SBC, from log files.

Submitting Content into to ESP

If your role involves fetching data from the web, databases, files, and so forth, and injecting it into ESP for indexing, rely on the documentation listed here:

➤ Basic Fetching and Feeding

    ➤ *Enterprise Crawler Guide* — Spidering from Web Servers

    ➤ *File Traverser Guide* — Spidering File Servers

    ➤ *Indexing Database and XML Guide* — Spidering Databases and XML

    ➤ *Document Processor Integration Guide* — Defines document handling after injection

➤ Advanced Fetching and Feeding

    ➤ *Content Integration Guide* — Creating custom indexing applications in C++, Java, or .NET languages

    ➤ *Browser Engine Guide* — Indexing content with JavaScript and Flash in the spider

    ➤ *CCTK Guide* — Developing a custom connector, a newer approach than using the direct content integration APIs

    ➤ *Feeding Proxy Guide* — Remote Data Feed Replication which happens prior to indexing

    ➤ *Security Access Module* — Understanding security and how ESP integrates with external security infrastructure

Customizing the Indexing Process

If your role involves advanced content indexing or display, review the following documentation:

➤ *Configuration Guide* — A summary of ESP concepts, particularly the index profile file that defines much of the functionality of ESP. Especially:

    ➤ Chapter 2, "Configuring Document Processing"

    ➤ Chapters 3–5, which cover more advanced processing

    ➤ Chapters 6 and 8, which cover the index profile, which defines the document schema and many indexing options

➤ *Document Hit Highlighting Guide* — Highlighting search terms when viewing a complete document requires index-time changes.

➤ *Document Processor Integration Guide* — Parsing documents during indexing, custom metadata, creating a custom taxonomy, and using the document processing pipeline.

➤ *Advanced Linguistics Guide* — Using advanced linguistics features in ESP.

➤ *Classifier Guide* — Automatically assigning documents to categories, supervised clustering.

➤ *Web Analyzer Guide* — Store, analyze, and re-rank documents based on internal site links.

➤ *Security Access Module* — Understanding security and how ESP integrates with external security infrastructure.

Developers

ESP features one of the richest APIs available in a commercial search product. This makes it very powerful and flexible, but it also means lots of documentation. If your role involves developing applications using ESP:

➤ *Product Overview* — ESP has many subsystems and optional components. If you're new to ESP, you'll benefit from reviewing this.

➤ *Configuration* — A summary of ESP concepts, particularly the index profile file that defines much of the functionality of ESP.

➤ *Enterprise Crawler Guide* — Spidering from Web Servers.

➤ *FileTraverser Guide* — Spidering File Servers.

➤ *Document Processor Integration Guide* — Parsing documents during indexing, custom metadata, creating a custom taxonomy, and using the document processing pipeline.

➤ *SFE User and Development Guides* — Using the Search Front End application.

In addition to the previous developer documentation, the ESP developer may also benefit from the following manuals, depending on his or her requirements:

➤ *Classifier Guide* — Automatically assigning documents to categories, supervised clustering

➤ *Web Analyzer Guide* — Store, analyze, and re-rank documents based on internal site links

For advanced application coding, integrating content sources, and architecting the ESP installation, use the following:

➤ *Application Integration Guide* — Creating and running ESP applications

➤ *Content Integration Guide* — Creating custom indexing applications in C++, Java, or .NET languages

➤ *Browser Engine Guide* — Indexing content with JavaScript and Flash in the spider

➤ *CCTK Guide* — Custom Connector Toolkit for developing custom indexing applications using the content integration APIs

➤ *Feeding Proxy Guide* — Remote data feed replication prior to indexing

➤ *Security Access Module* — Understanding security and how ESP integrates with external security infrastructure

➤ *Advanced Linguistics Guide* — Using advanced linguistics features in ESP

Technical Assistance

As with most complex software packages, very few people become fully versed from only reading. It may be helpful at first, and revisiting documentation can help as well, but formal training and hands-on real-world experience will help get past the basics.

Most organizations find it helpful to have at least some staff participate in formal training. Microsoft's FAST University offers classroom, online, and self-paced classes among other resources.

Microsoft maintains a web page on the Microsoft Support website at `http://support.microsoft.com/`. Searching the site for your FAST ESP problem may be a good first step in locating an answer before you call for support.

Microsoft also has the FAST Solution Center at `http://support.microsoft.com/ph/15080`. There, Microsoft maintains links to the FAST Extranet, a FAST Technical Community Newsgroup, and links to FAST University. We've found some of the links may not work as expected as the transition of support responsibility transfers from FAST to Microsoft; nonetheless, these two sites are good starting points.

There are a small number of community support organizations where FAST ESP is well known and actively discussed. While they are not supported by Microsoft, many of the participants work in organizations implementing FAST ESP and who are happy to share what they have learned. The groups we are familiar with are listed in the Resources section of the book.

CTS AND IMS

We would be remiss if we didn't talk about the two newest Microsoft search components: the Content Transformation Services, or CTS, and the Interaction Management Services, IMS. While initially planned to integrate only within FSIS, it will be available with FAST Search for SharePoint and FAST Search for SharePoint Internet Sites, and will, no doubt, find their way into other future Microsoft products.

Early versions of this technology were demonstrated at FAST Forward even before the acquisition by Microsoft, and they have been in use at selected customer sites for more than a year. Sadly, general release is scheduled to occur after this book goes to press, so we will not have the opportunity to describe it in the technical detail we would like. Visit the book website at `wrox.com`, and some of the blogs and websites mentioned in Appendix A for updates.

Introducing CTS and IMS

Microsoft has been working for a number of years on breakthrough architectural innovations in search, through a nextgen development program within FAST. This program includes technology framework development and a modular approach resulting in innovation and product capabilities in three areas:

➤ **Content Analytics** — Technology that enables the sophisticated capture and enhancement of information across diverse content sources. These tools perform the following functions:

  ➤ Collect data from all sources — inside and outside the organization: structured data, unstructured data, and rich media

  ➤ Enhance the meaning and structure of information to improve its quality and its value to end users

  ➤ Unify content into a single index

➤ **Contextual Matching** — Technology that matches user intent with potential results, delivering relevance and expressiveness. The tools help with the following:

  ➤ Decide what is most relevant to the end user

  ➤ Structure the query to the index and enable advanced query processing

  ➤ Control the speed with which results are delivered

➤ **Interaction Management** — Technology that facilitates a conversation between people and systems. These tools enable companies to build algorithmic, intent-driven user experiences and deliver a personalized search experience that:

  ➤ Defines the way that users access and consume information and controls the end-to-end user experience.

  ➤ Orchestrates the business process and provides business users with control over what is presented and how.

  ➤ Enables developers to create search-enabled experiences.

CTS is a giant step forward in back-end technology. Imagine a document content pipeline on steroids! IMS is a jump forward in the front-end development of conversational, interactive user interface design.

Content Transformation Services

Content Transformation Services (CTS) is a graphical, intuitive environment for content capture, refinement, fusion, and feeding. Through CTS, developers and business managers will be able to create and manage process flow for content and queries and realize the full potential of search-driven applications. What makes CTS so interesting? It helps businesses:

➤ **Acquire and deliver content through advanced connectivity** — CTS can connect to, combine, and transform any content type. Structured, unstructured, and rich media content are all treated in a uniform, transparent way. The processed content may be written to a range of target systems, including databases, files, streams, and Microsoft search products and SharePoint repositories.

➤ **Enrich content and improve data quality** — Search applications can now: combine structured and unstructured content using fuzzy algorithms or exact matches; enrich content using linguistic analysis and entity extraction; and consolidate and cleanse data using search technology. The full power of FAST's content processing technology is available for content enrichments.

➤ **Create new content entities for search-driven services** — By aggregating and enriching content sources on the fly, new content entities can be created for use in search and other applications. This content can draw customers, drive revenue, and create unique insight in many ways.

The Content Transformation Services provides for rapid deployment of processes and work flows as new sources, use cases, or features are added. Then, a corresponding content analytics runtime engine handles the content processing according to the flows defined in CTS. The runtime engine includes capabilities to combine different flows of analyzed/mined data, and to perform advanced operations for filtering, joining, or grouping of diverse data before feeding it into the search index or other sources (like data warehouses).

The Content Transformation Services boasts of the following:

➤ It lets you easily integrate different data sources including text, semi-structured and structured data, and rich media.

➤ It provides full flexibility in processing with 1:1, multiple source, and multiple destinations.

➤ It performs with native performance for textual content, sources with many small data records, and large rich media blobs.

➤ It includes libraries with more than 300 operations available for text, media, and data refinement.

With all of the technology it provides, CTS provides ease of use and extensible architecture. Administrators and developers can quickly develop content flows in a graphical environment based on the familiar Visual Studio. Wizards help you navigate sources, and preview functionality makes it easy to visualize the content as flows are being created. Interactive debugging and multiple levels of abstraction (nested flows) provide development efficiency. In addition, a high-level expression language and editors simplify content transformation.

CTS lets the advanced user incorporate custom operators, extend the expression language, and pause execution flow for interactive debugging, so content can be inspected and even manually edited before the execution is resumed.

Finally, CTS is extensible: developers and Microsoft partners can extend content by modifying existing operators, or by supplying new operators that plug into the CTS framework. For example, specialized entity extraction, classification, and statistical software can be integrated as operators. The following are just a few of the areas that can be utilized or extended:

➤ Workflow

➤ Document readers and writers

➤ Operators

➤ Content conversion and enrichment

➤ Data mining and structures (ETL-like)

➤ Linguistic operators

➤ Mining

CTS benefits from its integration into Visual Studio by leveraging the development environment and presentation framework. Visual Studio 2010 also extends to teams and to nondeveloper roles including project manager, architects, QA, and content owners.

Finally, CTS operates independently from search; for example, it's possible to create applications that use statistical and pattern analysis in SQL Server to create applications that provide insight across structured and unstructured information. CTS will enhance creation of applications for fraud detection, compliance monitoring, trend analysis, and many other areas not easily accomplished with today's technology.

Interaction Management Services

Interaction Management Services (IMS) is a capability that will allow organizations to deploy a new generation of intent-driven and conversational user experiences. Through IMS, developers will be able to rapidly create search-enabled applications and business managers will be able to set rules for what information is presented and how. IMS deliver capabilities and benefits that provide the following:

➤ **Ability to create search-driven user interfaces with ease** — Developers will be able to easily create search-driven front-ends by embedding search components into pages. Common controls such as hit lists, navigators, tag clouds, refinement sliders, and zero-term-search elements will be available out-of-the-box. Developers will be able to add custom components to support their unique user interface needs. The framework will allow for easy wiring and interoperation of controls on a page. Pages will be able to be modified without radical redesign.

➤ **Advanced control over query and results processing** — Logic for handling queries and results will be separated from the index and brought closer to the end-user experience to allow for greater flexibility. Query and result management will be handled algorithmically and through business rules. Federation will happen at the time of query, supporting greater control and freshness in information delivered. Relevancy and facets will be calculated on-the-fly.

➤ **Ability to deliver personalization based on user intent** — The IMS engine will capture user information through defined profiles, behavior, and social collaboration like tagging and rating. The user is presented with an individually tailored interface through personalized relevancy models and recommendations. Algorithmic models will monitor and tune the user experience.

➤ **Control over user experience through GUIs** — Through the familiar Visual Studio interface, IMS allows developers to access the design and manage analysis engine, workflows, and query- and results-side processing. Business users will be able to manage content spotlighting, facets, federation, and relevancy through a graphical console. IMS provides tools to integrate with outside analytics and reporting capabilities.

Interaction Management Services does for query processing what the Content Transformation Services does for content processing. In fact much of the underlying technology (the studio and the runtime engine) are common, which means that developers can work in a familiar paradigm and IT pros have a common set of deployment and administrative tools.

Summary of the CTS and IMS

As we mention in Chapter 12, ownership of Enterprise Search in corporations has slowly moved from IT and operations to business line and content managers. These two new technologies certainly seem to indicate a further shift, with content and business staff setting things up so that user behaviors are running the show. It sounds promising; we're excited to see how it works out!

SUMMARY

This concludes the first of two chapters on ESP. There is much more we could have added; after all, Microsoft provides more than 2000 pages of documentation for ESP 5.3. But we've provided a quick start for ESP, a detailed description of the FAST consoles, highlighted some of the more useful commands, and provided some goodies that were never really very clear in the original documentation.

In Chapter 8 we will look at more complex installations, including multinode installs on Linux, details about the ports used by ESP, and a description of the architecture and why it is the way it is.

8

Customization and Deployment of FAST ESP 5.X

WHAT'S IN THIS CHAPTER?

➤ Looking at how ESP scales up across multiple machines to handle more content and searches

➤ Understanding ESP subsystems and how they scale

➤ Understanding the effects of networked storage

➤ Managing virtualization and ESP

➤ Working with multinode installations

➤ Working with Linux and Solaris installations

➤ Using the Document Processing Pipeline

This chapter defines the basic components of Microsoft FAST Enterprise Search Platform 5.x. FAST ESP. The main focus is understanding multinode installations. Why and how are extra machines added to an ESP installation, and how are processes allocated? Multinode setup is the cornerstone of most ESP production installations. Additional configuration for Unix and Linux systems are considered.

FAST ESP is a highly scalable, robust search platform that can be customized. In addition to scalability, ESP can be configured to handle virtually any type of data, given enough customization effort. On the front end ESP offers virtually every results list navigator in the industry, although those can also take some effort to fully utilize, and very few search applications would ever use all of them.

THE BIG PICTURE: WHY IT'S BUILT THIS WAY

Virtually all production FAST systems are multinode, for both scalability and reliability. Even for a small number of documents and light search traffic, production search systems are usually deployed on a minimum of three nodes to allow for failover.

In the early days of search engines the core indexing and search all took place on the same computer. If you wanted to handle more data or searches you bought a bigger or faster computer. We refer to this as monolithic architecture. The problem with this approach is that, eventually, you have the largest and fastest computer available, and you can't scale any further. Although computers have steadily improved over the years — the Moore's Law effect — so have the demands of users. So just waiting for the next fastest computer to become available wasn't a solution.

When computer networks became ubiquitous inside institutions and corporations there were attempts to distribute the work across multiple computers. For example, one computer did the indexing, another computer the searching, and the search engine index was shared or transferred across the network. This was an improvement, but some key components still had to fit entirely within one physical machine.

As time went by these remaining monolithic processes have been refactored and broken down into smaller subprocesses that can be put onto multiple machines. This meant that, when more processing power is needed, additional computers could be added, and some processes could be relocated, and possibly even run in parallel. This rearchitecting of code, which is still evolving today, ushered in the age of search engines that routinely run on large clusters of cooperating computers, the age of the multinode search engine.

The distribution of the various processes across the ESP machines can seem a bit bewildering and arbitrary at first, but there are a few underlying principles that dictate most of these decisions.

The typical ESP server farm can be thought of as having two classes of machines:

➤ **The main *grid* of *core search nodes*:** They run some of the RTS processes, which are discussed later in this chapter.

➤ **All of the other supporting machines:** These also do quite a bit of work, such as spidering and document processing.

Scaling up a server farm means adding additional machines from each category, and then configuring them in a few specific patterns.

The Core Nodes

The core search nodes are the fundamental building blocks of the overall system. They contain and manage the actual bits and bytes of the binary search index files.

As you may recall, in previous chapters we talked about the all-important search engine index, the set of highly optimized binary files that reference all of the words in all of the documents that the system has indexed. In ESP the RTS Indexer creates the actual bits and bytes stored in a FAST ESP search index, and RTS Search consults those bits and bytes when it's running a low-level search.

The binary index files normally reside on the local hard drives inside these core machines, although network storage is sometimes used. In larger systems, the RTS Indexer can be placed on a separate system and then the index files are replicated over to the RTS Search nodes. Both ESP and the underlying operating system use in-memory caching of various forms, but *conceptually* we're talking about binary index *files*.

> *The FAST abbreviation RTS nominally stands for Real-Time System, which in this context refers their highly optimized nature. In this section, on core nodes, we're referring only to the RTS Search and RTS Indexer components. We are not including ESP's RTS Dispatcher in this core-node building blocks definition. Also, note that RTS isn't used consistently in the FAST guides, but don't worry, it's the function of these core nodes that matters, not what they're called.*

Sounds simple, right? The RTS Indexer creates the search indices, and RTS Search consults them to look up the words in your query. Well, there are a *few* more details, such as where the RTS Indexer gets all that data to shove into the index, how the search terms get to RTS Search process, and how the low-level matches get funneled back to the users. For input and output tasks, the core nodes are just one end of a relatively long chain of events. As you've probably already guessed, that's where all those other supporting machines come in.

Everything else fans out from RTS Index and RTS Search! These primary RTS nodes are replicated into logical columns and rows, to scale up the number of documents and number of searches, respectively. Other machines are added for various supporting tasks.

Getting Data into and out of the Core

Search engines can be viewed as data-processing blocks at different levels of detail. A FAST server farm can be viewed as a system that ingests documents and queries, and then outputs search results. Here, we zoom in just a bit to explain the input and output halves of the picture.

Inbound Documents

Since we're considering all this in terms of data flow, let's look at the approximate flow of data on the way into ESP. The process of getting data into the system can be subdivided into fetching documents, filtering and processing documents, indexing documents, and so on. The process involves information moving from the Internet to a disk cache, then being converted and transformed into XML files, and finally arriving on disk as a highly optimized set of binary index files.

Although the following list seems more detailed than some of this book's other high-level overviews, it still doesn't show every intermediate component:

1. The crawler or spider reads instructions from its database of links to traverse.
2. The crawler fetches data from the Internet.
3. Results are written to a cache and sent to the link extractor.

4. Links are sent to the link analyzer, and page data is sent to the document processor pipeline.

5. Each node in the pipeline operates on an evolving intermediate representation of the document as it's filtered and parsed. Metadata is added and normalized. Documents are converted from their binary format into text. The document's text is analyzed and possibly expanded, sometimes using an external dictionary. Entries are extracted. The links database is consulted to evaluate relevancy.

6. Output is written to ESP's internal intermediate FIXML XML format in a compressed disk library, and indexing information is routed through the content distributor.

7. The document is then assigned and passed to one of the "columns" in the grid of RTS nodes.

8. At least one of the nodes in the selected column is running the RTS Indexer. It converts the FIXML data into the bits and bytes for the binary search index. Those bits and bytes are written to disk.

9. In most systems that index data is also replicated to other nodes in the column.

Notice most steps that take place before the document is actually indexed by the RTS Indexer. In particular, notice that spidering and document processing happen *before* indexing, and often on completely different machines.

This often comes as a surprise to people who have worked only on smaller search engines. On older single-box search engines, or on search appliances, it's often said that you need to spider your web pages or index your documents before you can search, and the terms *spider* and *index* are used almost as synonyms. Behind the scenes, these smaller systems are performing many of the same functions as ESP, but all those separate activities are normally hidden from the administrator. On larger systems these terms do not mean the same thing at all — and are treated as vastly different tasks.

In ESP, when handling web-based content, a document is spidered, then processed, then indexed, in that order. These tasks take place on different nodes and, when scaled up, have very different resource consumption profiles. For example, fetching documents requires lots of network bandwidth, whereas indexing consumes memory and CPU. And of course most of these processes use lots of disk bandwidth.

If content were coming from another source, such as a database of custom-built feeds, then the first few steps dealing with links and fetching Web pages would be replaced with other tools, but would align with the preceding list at Step 5 after content enters the document-processing pipeline.

Searches and Outbound Search Results

Considering user interaction also from a data-flow perspective, the process is as follows:

1. An application server receives a search submitted by a user via an HTTP socket.

2. It calls a Java server process.

3. That process contacts ESP over another socket.

4. FAST uses the Query & Results (QR) server process to coordinate the high-level processing of the query.

The query is sent through the query pipeline, where it is expanded. Synonyms are added. For secure collections, the Security Access Module (SAM) adds security filters to the query.

5. The query is then routed through several more layers to be distributed among the various rows and columns for the low-level RTS Search processes.

6. RTS Search consults its binary indices to find matches, and collects the associated metadata that will need to be displayed.

7. It passes the results back up the process stack until they arrive back at the QR server.

8. If last-minute security checks are enabled for secure content, the SAM system is again consulted for each document.

9. Additional queries may be issued to the search system to populate some advanced search features.

10. Various other transforms are applied to get the data ready for display.

11. This output is fed back through the web application stack and returned to the user.

Although the names and details are different, this process is similar to the way that many other search engines work.

QR Server Versus RTS Search

The QR Server and RTS Search process accept submitted searches and return matching documents, but the difference is when this happens, and what work actually gets done.

The QR Server is a relatively high level subsystem that accepts searches from ESP's embedded web-based search application or from API calls made by another search application. QR can also modify the search that users type in, to add synonyms for example. More importantly, the QR Server knows how to contact all required subprocesses to get search results from the entire search grid.

In contrast, the RTS Search process is very low level. It knows only about its immediate search indices on its own search node. And it expects the query to be in its final form. RTS is the process that actually does the searching, whereas the QR process is only coordinating search activities, and not doing any actual searching itself!

Here are some of the higher level functions QR adds on top of RTS's basic search results:

➤ Lemmatization (consult the ESP doc for details)

➤ Adds Synonyms to search terms

➤ Other types of query transformations

➤ Distributes the search request through the core search grid

➤ Merges results

➤ Removes duplicate documents that are accidently returned by more than one RTS

➤ Adjusts search engine rankings and relevancy scores, for example preferring more recent documents in some search profiles.

➤ Applies boosts and blocks for specific searches (see Chapter 7)

➤ Provides logic for sorting and paging through results

Scaling in General

Primary scaling is done by adding more core search nodes. Additional nodes can be tasked to either handle more documents, or to run additional searches against the same set of documents. In larger systems, you can add nodes to perform both tasks, and this is where the concept of a "grid" comes in. When nodes are added to handle more content, FAST refers to adding columns to the grid. When more searches need to be handled, more search rows are added.

The designation of "row" and "column" is somewhat arbitrary; it has no physical bearing on how machines are placed in server racks, but FAST has been using this particular terminology for a long time. So, each column handles one slice of the content to be indexed.

Outside of the main search grid, other tasks often require scaling up. Although primary search nodes are scaled up in a grid of rows and columns, these other nodes are not organized in such a regular pattern. For example, spidering and document processing are both resource intensive tasks that frequently need to be scaled up. However, one search system may need to scale spidering capabilities, whereas another system may need more document-processing resources.

Scaling Core RTS Search Nodes for Content

In a search grid, each column is responsible for the same set of documents, the same content. So, any RTS search process on any of the machines in that column should give approximately the same matches for the same search. An ESP search column operates as a small team, especially in terms of indexing. In one of the common configurations, only one column is used, so it is responsible for all the content.

Supporting a lot more documents in a system means adding columns that will index different sets of documents.

For each inbound document an indexing task divides up into three subtasks:

1. Select a column.

2. Convert the document from FIXML into index-format binary data — this is the RTS Index process.

3. Ensure that all nodes in the column, one node for each "row," keep their binary indexes in sync.

Scaling Non-Core Nodes for Content

In our discussion of the core search nodes, we've talked about the RTS index and search processes, and the grid these nodes are configured into. Prior to being indexed, however, a document will need to be fetched, from a database or File Traverser or from the web spider, and then sent through the document-processing pipeline for filtering and processing. When scaling up a system to handle more content it's not sufficient to just add more columns to the core grid. Spidering and processing documents can be very resource intensive, so additional machines may need to be added, beyond just the additional RTS columns. For example, if many websites will be spidered, then additional ESP crawler nodes will be needed. Similarly, if each document requires a lot of parsing or metadata normalization, then more Document Processing pipeline nodes may be needed. These aren't "core" in terms of our grid, but certainly critical in terms of "feeding" the grid.

Scaling Cores for Search Traffic

If a system needs to handle more searches, then more search rows are added to the grid. Using multiple rows also provides failover. Each row should be able to handle the same searches, and produce virtually identical results.

Scaling in Both Directions

A system that needs to handle large amounts of content and heavy search traffic will scale by adding both columns (for content) and rows (for search traffic). A large system like that would also have a large number of supporting machines for administration functions, spidering, document processing, and ancillary services.

OVERVIEW: HOW A MULTINODE INSTALLATION WORKS

This is a very simple summary; we'll revisit some of these steps later. First of all is the design, which covers how many machines you'll need, which processes will be assigned to each machine, and so on. Next, for the actual machines, there's *lots* of prep work. Your default server configuration will likely *not* work, especially not for a multinode installation.

Then, you've got two choices for the actual ESP installation:

➤ The easier way, what we call the über-install, carries out the entire installation from just one machine! After interactively defining the grid of all the machines, automation kicks in and ESP actually connects to the other grids, downloads the files, and fires off the remote installations and configurations as well. This is pretty darn cool, and it's ESP's default method.

➤ Then there's the not-quite-as-easy per-machine installation, what ESP calls an "Advanced Installation." The installer is run on each individual machine and reads its configuration from a shared `InstallProfile.xml` file.

Why would *anybody* choose the second method, if the first method is so much easier? There are several common reasons:

➤ If part of the über-installation fails for one or two of the remote nodes, the installation can be rerun on just the failed nodes, to just install themselves. This allows an otherwise successful multinode installation to be "patched" for a couple of servers that might have failed.

➤ If the server farm needs additional machines, you can edit the shared install profile XML file to add those new machines to the model, then run installations on those individual nodes, using the new configuration.

➤ Linux clusters that can't run X-Windows cannot perform the normal multinode über-installation. However, they *can* run from the install profile for a particular node, using the console-based character-only command line installer. This would be needed only if *none* of the nodes could run X-Windows; you only need *one* X-Windows machine to run the über-installation on all other machines. We talk more about this later in the chapter. The good news is the ESP installer provides a convenient multinode installer process, and then offers several other options as workarounds.

After the installations are complete, then comes the system testing, data indexing, and search front-end creation.

MULTINODE INSTALLATION PREP WORK

ESP's scalability is one of the industrial-strength capabilities that make it a high-end tool. As we said earlier almost all production ESP systems are multinode, even for small data sets and low search traffic.

As with other multinode engines, setups are a complex topic, and we cannot make anybody an expert in a single chapter. Also, since opinions vary, even two FAST experts might come up with slightly different designs to meet the same specs.

High-Level Checklist

There are some general tasks to consider when doing a multinode setup:

➤ **Overall capacity planning** — How many machines are going to be required?

➤ **System Design** — Which processes will reside on which servers?

➤ **Acquiring the proper license** — This will be a .zip or .lic file given to you by your salesperson or during the Microsoft order fulfillment process.

➤ **Acquiring and setting up the machines and operating systems** — Virtualization can be used for development and test systems.

➤ **Network setup** — Most of the requirements for this are in the ESP documentation, and we provide some step by step guides for enabling SSL on Unix.

The good news is that the *ESP Deployment Planning Guide* walks through many of these concepts in great detail, so here we're going to review a few points we really want to highlight. This assumes a basic understanding of the subject, access to the primary ESP doc, and general technical common sense.

TCP/IP Configuration Should Not Be Changed After Installation

Allocate your TCP/IP addresses and network configurations only once. Do not plan to change network addresses or names after installation. This would include a fixed IP address, of course, and also a fully qualified domain name.

There's a seemingly reasonable idea that occurs to a number of administrators: they will do a preliminary installation of ESP on their machines on one network, and then move them into their final home at deployment time. This plan is further bolstered by ESP configuration files that appear to contain all the settings that would need to be changed. Don't believe it!

During an ESP installation, the software tucks away lots of references to both the system's DNS name and its IP addresses in numerous nooks and crannies. You are *very unlikely* to ever find them all. What's worse, there's a tendency to iterate over the initial failed attempts, to assume that there's just "one more place that I must have missed." The nearly hopeless process is further slowed down by the sometimes less visible ways the now partially misconfigured system manifests its symptoms, and the time it takes for endless reboots.

Although some FAST employees have managed it, just performing a complete reinstall from scratch in the new data center may actually take much less time and aggravation. You have been warned! If a FAST or Microsoft consultant does propose doing this, and they seem very confident about it, then you might inquire about their actual experiences in doing it successfully.

Check Your Firewall against ESP Ports

ESP makes heavy use of TCP/IP networking, and uses lots of TCP/IP ports. Security administrations in high security environments are often not comfortable with requests like "can you just open all the ports between these machines and our Intranet?" Table 8-1 shows most of the ports used by ESP, including the general scope and direction of those ports. For example, when one ESP node sends a document to another ESP node, those ports don't need to be opened to machines outside of the ESP cluster. If all of the ESP nodes are kept on their own physical subnet, then these inside ports don't need to be open externally. Sockets opened on other ports do need talk to outside machines. For example, if a system is indexing web content, then the crawler would need to fetch unencrypted web pages via http, which is normally on port 80, so the spider will need to make requests over port 80 to the outside world.

During installation ESP asks for a base port to use, with a default of 13,000. It then adds an offset to that base for its various internal services. Many of the ports an administrator will use are around base port plus 3,000, so that on a default installation most of the ports you'd see would be around 16,000.

In addition to ports unique to ESP, there are number of standard ports that a systems administrator will need to allow. These assume standard ports, and we're using the standard service names for those ports.

Additional access often needed:

➤ SSH (or Telnet): Much of the coding and some administration is done via the command line

➤ SCP (copy via ssh) or FTP

➤ (On Windows) Remote Desktop / RDP or VNC for the console admin GUI and checking web pages

➤ (On Unix, if possible) X-Windows or VNC for the console admin GUI and checking web pages

➤ Any SSH tunnels that are needed

➤ Ports for crawling/spidering (standard HTTP and HTTPS)

➤ Port(s) for database access, such as JDBC, or accessing data from a Content Management System (CMS). JDBC and CMS ports vary by vendor; there are no universal standard ports.

There is no official table from Microsoft/FAST listing these details, and they are likely to change slightly depending on the version.

In the following table a + indicates an offset from a BASE PORT which defaults to 13,000. For example the ESP Alert Engine is +0101, so default would be 130101. Inside means that the traffic is between nodes within this ESP cluster and is internal to the operation of ESP.

TABLE 8-1: ESP Ports and Network Boundary Direction

Port(s)	Component	Service	Protocol	Direction
+0100	Alert Engine Dispatcher	Add Alert Listener	HTTP	inside
+0101	Alert Engine Dispatcher	Middleware Servants	IIOP	inside
+0110+10*n	Alert Engine	Alert Retrieval	HTTP	inside
+0111+10*n	Alert Engine	Middleware Servants	IIOP	inside
+1000	Single Node Enterprise Crawler Master	XML-RPC	N/A	
+1002	Single Node Enterprise Crawler Master	Post Process Communication		N/A
+1003	Single Node Enterprise Crawler Master	Slave Communication		N/A
+1004	Single Node Enterprise Crawler File Server	HTTP	N/A	
+1005	Single Node Enterprise Crawler Post Process	Slave Communication		N/A
+1006	Single Node Enterprise Crawler Post Process	XML-RPC	N/A	
+1007-1198	Single Node Enterprise Crawler Überslave	XML-RPC	N/A	
+1199	Single Node Enterprise Crawler GUI Log Dispatcher	XML-RPC	N/A	

+1000	Multi Node Enterprise Crawler Übermaster	XML-RPC		sometimes outbound
+1001	Multi Node Enterprise Crawler Übermaster	Master Communication		sometimes outbound
+1100	Multi Node Enterprise Crawler Master	XML-RPC		sometimes outbound
+1102	Multi Node Enterprise Crawler Master	Post Process Communication		sometimes outbound
+1103	Multi Node Enterprise Crawler Master	Slave Communication		sometimes outbound
+1104	Multi Node Enterprise Crawler File Server	HTTP		sometimes outbound
+1105	Multi Node Enterprise Crawler Post Process	Slave Communication		sometimes outbound
+1106	Multi Node Enterprise Crawler Post Process	XML-RPC		sometimes outbound
+1107-1198	Multi Node Enterprise Crawler Überslave	XML-RPC		sometimes outbound
+1199	Multi Node Enterprise Crawler GUI Log Dispatcher	XML-RPC		sometimes outbound
+1200	Multi Node Enterprise Crawler Duplicate Server	Post Process Communication		sometimes outbound
+1201-1298	Multi Node Enterprise Crawler Duplicate Server	Duplicate Replication		sometimes outbound
+2000-2999	Real Time Search	Multiple processes		Inside
+2100	QRserver		HTTP	Inbound
+2101	QRserver	Privileged search	HTTP	Inbound
+2103	QRserver	Administration	IIOP	inside
+2150 - +2151	fdispatch	Top-level dispatcher		inside
+2160 - +2161	fdispatch	Search dispatch for live index		inside

continues

TABLE 8-1 *(continued)*

+2170 - +2171	fdispatch	Search dispatch for online silos		inside
+2180 - +2181	fdispatch	Search dispatch for offline silos		inside
+2200	Completion Server		HTTP	inside
+2300+(n-1)	Unity	Search HTTP n <= 10	HTTP	inside
+2800+p	Real Time Search	Fixmlindex, p is partition number	inside	
+3000	Admin GUI		HTTP	inbound
+3005	Config Server		XML-RPC	inside
+3006	Config Server		IIOP	inside
+3010	Log Server			inside
+3015	Node Controller		XML-RPC	inside
+3055	License Server	FLEXlm Manager		inside
+3056	License Server	FLEXlm Vendor Daemon		inside
+3065	Cache Manager		XML-RPC	inside
+3066	Cache Manager		IIOP	inside
+3070	Storageserver		MySQL?	inside
+3075	SAM	SAM Core	SSL	inside
+3076	SAM	SAM Core	XML-RPC	inside
+3079	SAM	AD Monitor	SSL	inside
+3081	SAM	NTFS Monitor	SSL	inside
+3088	Adminserver		Tomcat Shutdown	inside
+3089	Adminserver		HTTP	Inbound
+3091	Adminserver	JMX	HTTP	inside

+3093	Adminserver	Deployment Manager	IIOP	inside
+3094	Adminserver	Deployment Manager	IIOP/SSL	inside
+3095	Resource Service		IIOP	inside
+3096	Resource Service		IIOP/SSL	inside
+3097	Logtransformer	JMX		sometimes outbound
+3098	Clarity			inside
+3099	Name Service		IIOP	inside
+3100	Content Distributor		HTTP/ HTTPS	inside
+3101	Content Distributor		IIOP	inside
+3200-3299	Processor Servers			inside
+3200+5* (n-1)	Processor Servers		XML-RPC	inside
+3201+5* (n-1)	Processor Servers		IIOP	inside
+3400-3499	Anchor Server			inside
+3400+3*(n-1)	Anchor Server	Ping		inside
+3401+3*(n-1)	Anchor Server			inside
+3402	Anchor Server		IIOP	inside
+3500	Rel Bench			inside
+3501	Rel Benc		IIOP	inside
+4000	SAM	SAM Generic User Monitor	SSL	sometimes outbound
+4001	SAM	SAM Generic User Monitor	SSL	sometimes outbound
27000-27009	License Server (default)		N/A	inside

Symmetric DNS

ESP places a specific additional requirement on its network configuration: it requires forward-confirmed reverse DNS (FCrDNS). This simply means that the machine's name should resolve to an address, which can then be reverse-resolved back to the exact same name. Checking this on each machine is a simple step process:

1. Verify the TCP/IP address of that machine.

On Unix this is typically done with `ifconfig`, for example:

```
ifconfig eth0
```

On Windows use the `ipconfig` command via command-line prompt, or the Network Control Panel.

2. Reverse-resolve that IP address to its name.

Assuming the address was *1.2.3.4* one of these commands can be used:

```
host 1.2.3.4
nslookup 1.2.3.4
dig -x 1.2.3.4
```

3. Using the machine name returned in the previous step, forward-resolve that name back into an IP address and verify that it matches. This would usually be done with the `host` command, using the returned address in the previous step.

This check should be done on each machine, for itself, and all other machines in the cluster. Note that some processes can use SSH to talk to other processes that happen be on the same server, so test that the machine can reach itself.

UNIX-SPECIFIC CONSIDERATIONS

There are a few considerations specific to Linux and Unix, and let's take care of the one nontechnical item first.

Input Mode for Various Admin Tasks

On both Windows and Unix, ESP uses a mix of control methods to install, configure, and control the system. Some tasks can be performed multiple ways, but other tasks require a certain operational mode to use.

The following are tasks you perform from a web browser:

➤ Common business administration tasks

➤ Common technical administration tasks, including the Spider

The following tasks you perform from the command line:

➤ Common and advanced technical administration tasks

➤ *Single-node* installation

➤ Advanced installations

The following is a task you perform from the native/graphical interface (Windows/X-Windows):

➤ Full *multinode* installation

 Multinode installs on Linux usually require X-Windows, or some rather detailed workarounds.

You Probably Need X-Windows

Doing a complete multinode installation is the one task that really benefits from a full graphical user interface (GUI), and since most ESP production installations are multinode, this is bound to come up! If all goes well, the installation only needs to be done once, and usually only from one of the nodes. Although many Linux shops have X-Windows running on desktop machines, in the form of KDE, Gnome, or twm, the servers acquired for ESP are possibly located elsewhere, and may not have X-Windows installed or available.

For some sites, this presents a challenge for one or more reasons:

➤ You are unable to access the physical console of a remote server.

➤ You are unable to run graphical logins to a remote server, for technical or policy reasons.

➤ You lack familiarity with remote graphical logins and/or port tunneling.

There are other options for accessing Linux clients remotely, which avoid these specific Hyper-V problems, such as using remote X-Windows servers, VNC, or Linux RDP drivers. However, each of these alternatives presents its own technical challenges. As a start, you'll likely need to adjust or disable firewalls on both ends of the connection, as all modern OSs are rather locked down in their default configurations.

In the rare case where doing even one X-Windows installation is not feasible, where not even one machine can run X-Windows, then the InstallProfile.xml file would need to be created by some other means. There are several options for creating the master InstallProfile.xml file, although probably none is officially supported by FAST, so this should be considered a last resort technique.

These options are covered in more detail in the next section.

Minimum X-Windows Resolution

One final note on X-Windows: you need a minimum resolution of 1024x768. If you run at 800x600 or lower you can't access some of the buttons in the installer dialog boxes.

Figure 8-1 and 8-2 show examples of the same ESP installation being started on an 800x600 screen, and then 1024x768. Notice in Figure 8-1 that you cannot see the buttons on the bottom of the dialog box.

FIGURE 8-1

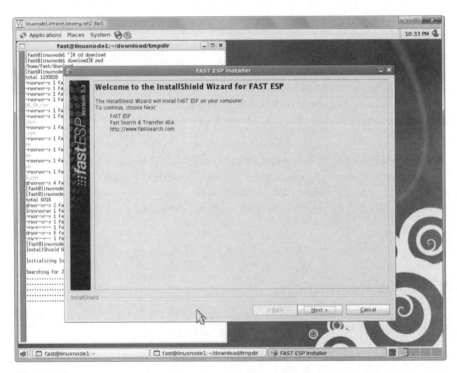

FIGURE 8-2

Unix Multinode Non-GUI Installs

Doing multinode installs of any software isn't trivial. It may come as no surprise that a Unix/Linux multinode install has a few extra hurdles. Of course, if you're on those operating systems all the time, maybe you like this sort of thing!

On both Windows and Unix, a multinode installation begins with an initial installation on one of the nodes. During this initial install, an interactive wizard walks the administrator through the task of assigning different processes to different physical nodes. When the installation is complete, ESP writes out an installation configuration file called `InstallProfile.xml` that contains the process assignments for all server nodes in the ESP cluster.

The good news is that ESP has both a graphical installer and a command line/console installer. The graphical installer uses Java's Swing/AWT components and should work on any X-Windows systems that can run other graphical applications. For nongraphical command line installation, you start the same installer as for a graphical installation, but you pass in the `-console` command line option.

Here's the catch, though: although the GUI version supports full multinode configuration and installation on all machines, the character-based console version is not quite as capable. The limitation of this command line installation mode is that it lacks the interactive Process Assignment Wizard. So, when performing the installation via SSH, you can't use the installer to allocate different processes to different physical machines. Instead, you *must* read in these settings from a previously created `InstallProfile.xml` file. ESP assumes that at least *one* of your Unix machines will have X-Windows available, so at least one machine can run the graphical Process Assignment Wizard.

This is an issue for some sites because, although an administrator may be able to run X-Windows on some machines, firewalls or other system configuration issues may prevent them from running X-Windows on all the nodes in an ESP installation.

The Two Normal Scenarios

For a multinode Unix installation, there are two normal scenarios:

➤ **The GUI über-install** — Use ESP's default graphical installer for what we called the über-install. You interactively define the various nodes, and then ESP installs to *all* of the machines from that one running installation. This is by far the preferred scenario.

➤ **GUI install and backfill** — In this variant, you still run the main GUI installer on one machine, and it creates an `InstallProfile.xml` file. You then run the installer on remote nodes, in ESP Advanced Mode, and point it to the central `InstallProfile.xml` configuration. You can use either the graphical or the command line text-only installer on the remote nodes.

Other GUI Choices for Unix Installations

As a last ditch effort to follow the supported ESP installation route, we'd like to review a few other ways to access X-Windows. You may have already thought of some these, but many new Unix administrators come from a Windows background and some of these choices are certainly not as obvious.

Casual Linux administrators are usually accustomed to using the mouse and keyboard attached to the server they're using, forgetting that a remote machine running X-Windows can also be used. It's actually pretty rare to have an environment where X-Windows can't be run at all, not even once, not even with some odd temporary arrangement.

➤ **Remote X "server"** — First, consider that the X-Windows server needn't be running on the same machine as the application that requires X-Windows, which is the ESP installer in this case. An X-Windows "server" (which is actually what most people would think of as the graphical terminal "client") can even be run on Windows or a Mac. So an X-*Server* is actually the X-Windows *terminal* that the administrator sits at.

➤ **Microsoft Windows machines used as X-terminals** — X-Windows can also be run on Microsoft Windows machines or Apple Macs to connect to a remote Unix machines. Using Windows as a graphical terminal would require an open source or commercial X-Windows server; for example, the popular open-source *Cygwin* package includes X-Server in some configurations.

➤ **VNC** — VNC is a popular open-source standard for remotely accessing graphical machines. It has the advantage of being multi-platform, so that Windows, Mac, and Unix machines can all interconnect with each other, bringing the complete mouse supported GUI desktop with them. Linux distributions often support VNC, either preinstalled or as an add-on.

For this to work, a VNC server process needs to be running on Linux, and a VNC Viewer needs to be installed on the Windows or Mac being used as a terminal.

VNC has various firewall and secure tunneling options, so this is also a bit advanced.

➤ **Windows Remote Desktop (RDP)** — Another choice is to run software on the Unix machine that supports Windows Remote Desktop/RDP clients. Essentially, it gets the Unix box to emulate a Windows server, in terms of viewing the remote desktop. Instead of seeing a Windows server when you connect, however, you see the X-Windows desktop. Many Windows machines already have Remote Desktop installed.

Can You Tunnel?

Regardless of what machine is used as a graphical terminal, connecting to the ESP server may need to cross a number of network boundaries. As a reminder, consider using SSH tunneling to one of the machines to an external X-Server. Although somewhat advanced to set up, even in sites with tighter security it's often possible to tunnel X-Windows over SSH and still use the GUI installer on one node.

The two machines in this connection would be:

➤ The machine being used as the X-Windows terminal, oddly named the X-Windows. This could be a Microsoft Windows machine running X-Windows software.

➤ The machine running ESP Linux installer, which is the X-Windows client.

To summarize, the machine running the ESP software, which we would normally talk about as one of the ESP servers, is referred to as the client in the context of this X-Windows connection. If you're new to Unix, we assure you this isn't a typo.

Tunneling X-Windows is a moderately advanced technique, but remember you'd normally only need to get X-Windows running once, or perhaps only a handful of times.

Network Settings

For all of these techniques, you might encounter firewall issues on both ends of the connection and in the middle.

➤ On the Windows side, check the Security settings in the Control Panel.

➤ On Linux, check the `iptables` command.

➤ On any intermediate network switches, hubs, and routers, you may need to open a port or set up port forwarding.

➤ You may need to look up the `xhost` command on Google (or Bing) to allow remote connections; this is another aspect of nonconsole access that admins sometimes forget. We can't walk you through all that here, but hopefully having some keywords will give you a head start.

You might need the temporary X setup only once! All of the options mentioned so far revolve around trying to run the ESP graphical installer. If you can do this even once, it can be used to interactively assign processes to nodes and create a master `InstallProfile.xml`*.*

Other Choices for Bootstrapping InstallProfile.xml

To do an install, you need to access an `InstallProfile.xml` file from somewhere. Assuming that you don't want to create one entirely from scratch, here are a few other ways to either get one that you can use directly, or get one that's pretty close that you can manually edit.

Once you have the `.xml` file, you can use it with the character-based console installer on each machine.

Using a Temporary Virtual Linux Box

A virtual Linux machine could be temporarily created that has the same network configuration as one of the eventual physical machines. This virtual machine could presumably exist on a convenient network segment. For convenience, you might even be able to run X-Windows on the same virtual machine's console, so that no remote X-Windows sessions would be needed. This would feel more comfortable to a Windows administrator.

This machine wouldn't necessarily even need to run the exact same Linux distribution. For example, instead of RedHat, this machine could run CentOS, which is a distribution very similar to RedHat. This can allow you to work around problems trying to access an "official" CD or DVD installation, by using a more convenient network-based distribution.

Linux can even be run under Microsoft's Hyper-V virtual machine framework.

Using Microsoft Hyper-V and Linux Client Machines

If you're running Linux under Microsoft Hyper-V, you'll still want to have X-Windows access on at least one of the ESP nodes. It is also highly recommended you install Microsoft Linux Integration Components for Hyper V.

There are other options for accessing Linux clients remotely, which avoid these specific Hyper-V problems, such as using remote X-Windows servers, VNC, or Linux RDP drivers. However, each of these alternatives presents its own technical challenges. As a starter, you'll likely need to adjust or disable firewalls on both ends of the connection, as all modern OSs are rather locked down in their default configurations.

ESP Linux installation is also discussed in the multinode section in this chapter. You might also check this book's website for updated information.

Using a Temporary Windows Microsoft Machine!

In theory, a dummy initial install could be done on a Windows machine, with it pretending to be the main node of the Unix environment. You'd want it to have a network configuration identical to that of one of the Unix machines. You would configure the nodes, but then abort the install; ESP would still output an `InstallProfile.xml` file.

Edit that file and change the Windows-specific entries into their Unix equivalents. Use that configuration with the command-line console installer on each node, pointing to that configuration.

As you recall, the install profile for Windows and Unix were very similar, with the only differences being some attributes in the definition of the nodes at the top of the file.

The path names in the file would be in Windows' syntax and would need to be manually edited. You may need a different or temporary license from Microsoft/FAST for this, although as of this writing we didn't need to do that.

Also, since the temporary Windows machine will have the same network configuration as one of the Unix machines, make sure those two systems are never on at the same time!

Custom Install Profiles

In the event that you didn't have any Unix machines with X-Windows, you could in theory create an install profile from scratch, and then use the character-mode Advanced Install option on each node. In the part of this chapter where we review a three-node installation, we do provide the install profile listing for the three-node system. You could use this as a template.

Or, as we suggested earlier, you could start a fictitious installation on a Windows machine that temporarily has the same network name and TCP/IP configuration. When you exit the installation, just swap out the Windows-specific settings for Unix-specific settings. In Listings 8-1 and 8-2, we show the same node declaration from a Windows and a Unix installation profile. This is toward the top of the install profile, and you'd have one of these for each node.

Available for download on Wrox.com

LISTING 8-1: Windows Install Profile Node Definition

```
...
<host id="node0">
    <property name="hostname" value="espnode1.intranet.ideaeng.net"/>
    <property name="platform" value="Windows"/>
    <property name="username" value="INTRANET\fast"/>
    <property name="install-dir" value="c:\esp\"/>
    <property name="index-dir" value=""/>
    <property name="fixml-dir" value=""/>
    <property name="temp-dir" value="C:\Temp\"/>
    <property name="remote-cmd" value="SSH2"/>
    <property name="baseport" value="13000"/>
</host>
...
```

Available for download on Wrox.com

LISTING 8-2: Unix Install Profile Node Definition

```
...
<host id="node0">
    <property name="hostname" value="linuxnodde1.intranet.ideaeng.net"/>
    <property name="platform" value="Linux"/>
    <property name="username" value="fast"/>
    <property name="install-dir" value="/home/fast/esp/"/>
    <property name="index-dir" value=""/>
    <property name="fixml-dir" value=""/>
    <property name="temp-dir" value="/tmp/"/>
    <property name="remote-cmd" value="SSH2"/>
    <property name="baseport" value="13000"/>
</host>
...
```

Differences between Microsoft Windows and Unix Node Definition

Note the following differences between Windows and Unix node definitions:

➤ The `platform` attribute (Windows vs. Linux)

➤ The `username` attribute on Windows should include domain name and backslash (`INTRANET\fast` vs. just `fast`)

➤ The `install-dir` and `temp-dir` attributes have operating-system specific syntax, including backslashes (`\`) instead of forward slashes (`/`). This would also be the case for any of the `*-dir` attributes that you chose to fill out, such as `index-dir` or `fixml-dir`.

The only other issue is that, when doing an interactive installation, ESP checks that all of these accounts and directories exist on all the machines. If you decide to hot wire a custom install profile, you take on this responsibility.

As a reminder, we do present a complete install profile later in this chapter, and you may find other install profiles to use as templates as well. Knowing the few tweaks for the Windows and Unix node definitions should let you repurpose any example you come across!

Hand-Created Install Profile

An `InstallProfile.xml` could be created by hand in a text editor. You'd need to find a good template to base it on.

Create a Custom OEM Profile

For very advanced sites, it should be possible to create a custom OEM installation profile for a silent install across all systems. This is covered in Chapter 6 of the *FAST ESP Installation Guide*. Although rather advanced, it is careful and performs many system checks, and tries to roll back changes if it finds problems.

Custom Automation

If an ESP installation will be dealing with dozens or possibly hundreds of nodes, it might make sense to invest in some type of additional automated scriptable deployment system. Such a system might go further in terms of automated installation and use stock machine images and Java installations. This might also be a good option for sites that use lots of virtual machines for testing or automated machine provisioning. Since it's not supported, we don't recommend using ESPDeploy. However, sites that routinely deal with large deployments probably already have tools for automated deployment. ESP can be scripted with XML configuration files and SSH. It's a very Unix-friendly piece of software.

Specific Unix SSH Requirements

For multinode installations ESP must be able to talk to all nodes on the system via `ssh` commands without *any* interactive prompts. This means SSH must be configured so that it doesn't require passwords, and not prompt to confirm the connection to the remote host. These are the two usual sources of SSH prompts. If ESP encounters any of these prompts the commands will fail.

If you're a Unix guru you may know all this already, but we're going to walk through it here because we've found that not *everybody* knows this!

Summary of SSH Setup Procedure

We're going to set up a subdirectory of SSH credentials on one server, and then replicate that to all the other servers in the farm. Here's a summary of the general steps required:

1. Ensure the same logins and directories on all machines

2. Create credentials to replace passwords

3. Publish the public key

4. Authorize all hosts

5. Copy and distribute the SSH credentials

The examples assume that you have created the user "*fast*" on all of your systems and are currently logged in as that user. Of course, you would substitute the name of one of your servers into these commands.

The host authorization prompt comes before the password prompt, but we're going to take care of the password prompt first.

Replace Passwords with SSH Credentials and Keys

SSH keys can be used to remove the password prompt. This is done on one of the Linux nodes, and then the output will be copied to the others. Remember that, in this example, you are logged in as the user *fast* and that we're assuming this is a new system, or at least that the FAST account is new.

To make sure that you don't already have SSH keys set up, enter the command:

```
ls  -la  ~/.ssh
```

We're assuming that you'll see the message "No such file or directory". If you do see files, then there might already be keys in place, and you might want to talk to the systems administrator. You may not need to generate new keys, although you'll still need to distribute them to all the nodes.

1. Assuming that you have a new system and FAST account, enter the command:

```
ssh-keygen  -t  rsa
```

2. Press Enter for all of the prompts. The conversation looks like this:

```
Generating public/private rsa key pair.
Enter file in which to save the key (/home/fast/.ssh/id_rsa): (press Enter)
Created directory '/home/fast/.ssh'.
Enter passphrase (empty for no passphrase): (Enter)
Enter same passphrase again: (Enter)
Your identification has been saved in /home/fast/.ssh/id_rsa.
Your public key has been saved in /home/fast/.ssh/id_rsa.pub.
The key fingerprint is:
a7:76:8c:71:50:ee:8f:c2:d5:13:03:f3:26:a9:5e:a4
fast@linuxnode1.intranet.ideaeng.net
```

The important part of the output to notice is the directory structure that *ssh-keygen* has created for you in /home/fast/.ssh

Notice that this directory starts with a dot, so it would not normally be visible to the ls command. So, if you go to FAST's home directory and enter ls, you wouldn't see .ssh. You'd need to use ls -a to see it, with the -a meaning approximately "show all, including hidden files." However, you can just cd directly to it if you know the path.

3. To explore that directory, enter the following command:

```
cd  /home/fast/.ssh
ls  -1
```

You will get the following results:

```
total 16
-rw-------  1 fast fast 1675 Jun 27 16:47 id_rsa
-rw-r--r--  1 fast fast  418 Jun 27 16:47 id_rsa.pub
```

It created two files for you. If this is not a new system, it's very important to notice if there are any other files there; this will affect one of your later steps, so if there are make a note of them!

4. Enter the following command, and take a look at the first file:

cat   id_rsa

You will see the following:

```
-----BEGIN RSA PRIVATE KEY-----
MIIEogIBAAKCAQEAyEyLjHEIaOKtbQnQYBeU6ECd+fi+fESfIIvtH+VpFv80LpQd
Q7jTlzSMtlovKGTVszydGriG7VkZSR8keumlewiRWa7UW4KPLyh0cwAL7/FyGesp
My4n6HXSIwNx5DQuyE3AWnFb1FKuQQpWI5c7NFVDpybkcbObgO/mMBTsFvUPJYHB
        ...
        (20 lines of gibberish omitted!)
        ...
PBJ9mPopbkvLntgnbyiu43pCdHYQ5bYhtjOIsdfJsANnPamC31fi3ApTPV9SEbbH
K6GkyuJmgBsdYONYzqiyTLo2jvCYATgd+t1RCtArt6RkSnN2HyA=
-----END RSA PRIVATE KEY-----
```

Now view the second file:

cat   id_rsa.pub

You will see the following:

```
ssh-rsa AAAAB3NzaC1yc2EAAAABIwAAAQEAyEyLjHEIaOKtbQnQYBeU6ECd+fi+fESfIIvtH+VpFv80
LpQdQ7jTlzSMtlovKGTVszydGriG7VkZSR8keumlewiRWa7UW4KPLyh0cwAL7/FyGespMy4n6HXSIwNx
5DQuyE3AWnFb1FKuQQpWI5c7NFVDpybkcbObgO/mMBTsFvUPJYHBZ/rFSL/degrQC0Ws1iDLpYKDtkS1
/F4MUhX/gTnu3j6YlqyHeCgYQBhoDGj7es9dHIIjldXjArUpB4fGRzME6+gcByVazXy8iczWTEzY1nkN
nnQjhr7bNdwtv9d59zErghwb9guDPeZ4TkIxjmPVb9Eb1+8fdCaXdGXAyw== fast@linuxnode1.int
ranet.ideaeng.net
```

5. You now need to publish the public key. In the .ssh directory make sure you do *not* already have a file called authorized_keys2.

cp   id_rsa.pub   authorized_keys2

If you do already have an authorized_keys2 file, then it's OK to append these contents to the end. You may want to consult your administrator, but the command would be something like:

```
cp  authorized_keys2  authorized_keys2.bak
cat  id_rsa.pub  >>  authorized_keys2
```

6. Later you need to distribute this information to all of the other machines that will be running FAST ESP.

Removing SSH Host Authorization Prompts

The first SSH prompt happens when a user connects to a new host for the first time from the host they normally use. They're prompted to confirm connection to that new machine:

1. You use the command (for example, inserting your network info):

```
ssh  linuxnode3.intranet.ideaeng.net
```

The local system replies with:

```
The authenticity of host 'linuxnode3.intranet.ideaeng.net (192.168.15.62)' can't
be established.
RSA key fingerprint is 4c:ab:df:32:3f:8c:12:2f:c9:ea:51:c8:f1:23:12:71.
Are you sure you want to continue connecting (yes/no)?
```

2. If you answer yes, then an entry for the new machine will be added to ~/.ssh/known_hosts file on the machine you're connecting *from*. Although it seems trivial to just type in *yes* and press Return this one time, ESP fail if you don't. ESP is playing it safe.

For small to medium search farms, you can start on each machine and SSH once to every other machine, and also to yourself, and manually type in yes. This is also a quick fix if new machines are added to an existing ESP server farm. If you use this manual procedure, keep these things in mind:

➤ For each unique pair of machines, the connection should be initiated twice, once in each direction.

➤ Make sure to use the fully qualified machine name. If you forget and just use the short name, the wrong fingerprint will be saved, so the process won't work.

➤ It's a good idea to ssh into the node you're on. For example, if you're on node2.mydomain. com, then you should remember to ssh node2.mydomain.com, in addition to nodes 1 and 3.

➤ We sometimes take the extra step of sshing with the short name in addition to the long name, and also by IP address. That way, no matter how a machine is referenced, perhaps by a busy administrator, it will have a saved fingerprint.

In reality, not every machine in a FAST cluster (or farm) needs to talk to every other machine, so in theory you could experiment and eliminate some of those combinations.

For really large server farms, this gets tedious, and at least on the initial server farm setup, there's an easier way. You've already started creating a template .ssh directory on your initial machine, and the file that all of these *yes* authorizations are stored in is inside this directory.

Assuming that you're on node1, you will ssh into all the other nodes and to node1 itself. In addition to ESP possibly needing to ssh to another process on the same physical machine, we also want to have all nodes in this master copy. At this point, you'll still need to also type in the password for each login.

From the ~/.ssh directory do another **ls -l** and confirm that there's a file called known_hosts and cat that file out to check it:

```
cat  known_hosts
```

You get back the following response:

```
linuxnode1.intranet.ideaeng.net,192.168.15.60 ssh-rsa AAAAB3NzaC1yc2EAAAABIwAAAQ
EA1YyBH6j01b+cai9u+V7PFwwQUUiexDudSrsxa6d9GR6Y4bOmu8SIjlWAPpVwwn3v3AaAKFvYlekJvX
gLDH+s7HbfjU7dNp4KcCH9+F6K54z1MAxJJVVRbi6RK+ybIh0+EogE03dVlKw8vSKrRMpcTrvAFecj3Z
0aKFkUTEzXRatkj5K+t/lHELCg3Qf0urLSn5WCjFHuIlI7Vgex97EWFj2RoyZlfAnQIpGFmYrrHDapjz
kczYrSkMAIqD9SlCXnNsaPI+AZ+77ikC9FK9vDOMmjhbriKkQ5pye7g4ZMrvMZksk0CVKt+nJP5G3oqs
7QERZfPCkeliniuWqfAZR82Q==
linuxnode2.intranet.ideaeng.net,192.168.15.61 ssh-rsa AAAAB3NzaC1yc2EAAAABIwAAAQ
EA1YyBH6j01b+cai9u+V7PFwwQUUiexDudSrsxa6d9GR6Y4bOmu8SIjlWAPpVwwn3v3AaAKFvYlekJvX
gLDH+s7HbfjU7dNp4KcCH9+F6K54z1MAxJJVVRbi6RK+ybIh0+EogE03dVlKw8vSKrRMpcTrvAFecj3Z
0aKFkUTEzXRatkj5K+t/lHELCg3Qf0urLSn5WCjFHuIlI7Vgex97EWFj2RoyZlfAnQIpGFmYrrHDapjz
kczYrSkMAIqD9SlCXnNsaPI+AZ+77ikC9FK9vDOMmjhbriKkQ5pye7g4ZMrvMZksk0CVKt+nJP5G3oqs
7QERZfPCkeliniuWqfAZR82Q==
linuxnode3.intranet.ideaeng.net,192.168.15.62 ssh-rsa AAAAB3NzaC1yc2EAAAABIwAAAQ
EA1YyBH6j01b+cai9u+V7PFwwQUUiexDudSrsxa6d9GR6Y4bOmu8SIjlWAPpVwwn3v3AaAKFvYlekJvX
gLDH+s7HbfjU7dNp4KcCH9+F6K54z1MAxJJVVRbi6RK+ybIh0+EogE03dVlKw8vSKrRMpcTrvAFecj3Z
0aKFkUTEzXRatkj5K+t/lHELCg3Qf0urLSn5WCjFHuIlI7Vgex97EWFj2RoyZlfAnQIpGFmYrrHDapjz
kczYrSkMAIqD9SlCXnNsaPI+AZ+77ikC9FK9vDOMmjhbriKkQ5pye7g4ZMrvMZksk0CVKt+nJP5G3oqs
7QERZfPCkeliniuWqfAZR82Q==
```

Not very exciting, but notice the three lines starting with the names of the nodes, so we see that linuxnode1, 2, and 3 are all listed; the order isn't important.

Distributing the SSH Credentials

For this next step, you need to be one level *above* the .ssh directory. If you're still in the .ssh directory you can just do a cd   .. (or just a cd by itself, which will also take you home):

1. Now create a tar file with contents of the .ssh directory.

    ```
    cd
    tar  cf  fast-ssh-keys.tar  .ssh
    ```

    This is a really small file, so you don't need to worry about using compression or zip.

2. Now you ensure that the new tar file is there:

    ```
    ls  -l  *.tar
    ```

    You get the following results:

    ```
    -rw-rw-r-- 1 fast fast 10240 Jun 27 17:41 fast-ssh-keys.tar
    ```

    Now you want to get this tar file to each of the other nodes. Assuming that you're on node1 of a three-node system, copy the file to node2 and node3. This tar file has very sensitive data in it, so it's best not to use FTP to transfer it. The ssh command has company, the scp command, which does a secure copy. You use that to transfer the tar file. Ironically, you will have to answer yes and enter passwords for the scp command too, just as for ssh, but not for much longer!

    You'll also notice that we add the account name and an at sign (@) in front of the remote machine name (notice the fast@ prefix). This could also be done with a command line option, but this is quicker.

Here are the transactions for getting the `tar` file to the two other machines:

```
scp  fast-ssh-keys.tar  fast@linuxnode2.intranet.ideaeng.net:
```

You get the following returned:

```
The authenticity of host 'linuxnode2.intranet.ideaeng.net (192.168.15.61)' can't
 be established.
RSA key fingerprint is 4c:ab:df:32:3f:8c:12:2f:c9:ea:51:c8:f1:23:12:71.
Are you sure you want to continue connecting (yes/no)? yes (Enter)
Warning: Permanently added 'linuxnode2.intranet.ideaeng.net,192.168.15.61' (RSA)
 to the list of known hosts.
fast@linuxnode2.intranet.ideaeng.net's password: (enter password and press Enter)
fast-ssh-keys.tar                         100%   10KB  10.0KB/s   00:00
```

Then enter:

```
scp  fast-ssh-keys.tar  fast@linuxnode3.intranet.ideaeng.net:
```

You get the following:

```
The authenticity of host 'linuxnode3.intranet.ideaeng.net (192.168.15.62)' can't
 be established.
RSA key fingerprint is 4c:ab:df:32:3f:8c:12:2f:c9:ea:51:c8:f1:23:12:71.
Are you sure you want to continue connecting (yes/no)? yes (Enter)
Warning: Permanently added 'linuxnode3.intranet.ideaeng.net,192.168.15.62' (RSA)
 to the list of known hosts.
fast@linuxnode3.intranet.ideaeng.net's password: (enter password and press Enter)
fast-ssh-keys.tar                         100%   10KB  10.0KB/s   00:00
```

Now you need to unpack these credentials onto the other machines. You can open a separate terminal window for each of them, or hop on over from your existing SSH session; we'll assume the latter.

1. Starting on `linuxnode1` enter:

```
ssh  fast@linuxnode2.intranet.ideaeng.net
(enter password)
```

2. You're now on the new machine, and by default `ssh` puts you in the home directory, which is exactly where you want to be. Let's check that the `tar` file is here, and that there is not an existing `.ssh` directory.

```
ls  -la
```

You should see `tar` file, but *not* an existing .ssh directory. If there's one there, you'll need to manually combine them, or get some help.

3. Now you unpack the file:

```
tar  xf  fast-ssh-keys.tar
```

4. You do another **`ls -la`** to confirm that the *.ssh* directory is now there, and then, for extra credit, an **`ls -la .ssh`** to see the contents of the directory.

In theory, you could have done a recursive copy of the `.ssh` directory from the master node to the other nodes without creating the intermediate `tar` file. Checking and coping with hidden directories is a bit unusual, however, and it's nice to check that isn't one already there. If you do this a lot, however, that might be an option to consider.

REVIEWING A THREE-NODE LINUX INSTALLATION

Even ESP gurus will disagree on the best installation approach; put five experts in a room and you'll get 10 or 12 best setups. Three-node setups are a common baseline installation: they exhibit multi-node processing, but are not overwhelming. This might be a good setup for a developer using virtual machines, for example. A three-node setup could also power a very small production search application with failover.

In three-node ESP setups, it's very common to have a one column by two row set of main search machines, what ESP would call a "one-column" setup, and a third machine for administration and support functions. A one column by two nodes setup is actually a two-row setup, so each row can handle the same searches and should produce the same results. Heavy query traffic can be load balanced between the two rows, which also provide failover for each other.

In the classic three-node setup, the two search nodes are almost identical, except that the top node also does indexing. This leaves the third node, the support node, to run almost everything else, however, including spidering and document processing. This example shifts that around a bit; we've moved the spidering and document processing from the third node to the bottom node in the two-node column. The idea being that the top node in the column will perform most of the searches, so the bottom node can afford to pick up some of the work from the poor overworked admin/support node. We're not claiming this is the perfect setup, just a bit of an interesting tilt on the setups that are already in the ESP documentation.

For example, although we've shifted the processing load around, we'll incur some extra network traffic when the document processor passes content to the content distributor. If this were a big concern, additional network cards could be used to add extra network capacity. Busy production systems are likely to have way more than three nodes. As systems grow, monitoring will show the various bottlenecks. Ironically, as you fix each bottleneck, another bottleneck will move to the top of your list! Fortunately the software doesn't require perfection in order to run, and it's common to make adjustments over time in large systems.

This setup is also rather specific to feeding in Web-based content via the web crawler/spider. If content were coming from a database, or perhaps being injected with a custom feed using one of the feed APIs, a different layout might be in order. Chapter 7 has an outline of the ESP documentation, with a section for developers, which includes references to these other data feeding options.

Allocation of Processes

Machine naming is a bit odd with ESP. When human IT folks allocate machines, they tend to start with 1, 2, and 3, and so on. However, computers love base-0 numbers, as does ESP, so it internally names nodes starting at 0. We have the three Linux nodes listed here:

➤ `linuxnode1 = ESP node0`

➤ `linuxnode2 = ESP node1`

➤ `linuxnode3 = ESP node2`

ESP uses the following names in its installation profile:

➤ **node0**

   ➤ `administration-set1`

      ➤ `configserver1`

      ➤ `logserver1`

      ➤ `clarity` (monitoring)

      ➤ `httpd1` (for admin web UI)

      ➤ `resourceserivde1`

      ➤ `adminserver1`

      ➤ `storageservice1`

   ➤ `logtransformer1`

   ➤ `contentdistributor1` (divide content between columns)

   ➤ `webanalyzer1` (cross-page hyperlink statistics)

   ➤ `indexingdispatcher1`

   ➤ `nameserver1`

   ➤ `lmgrd1` (license server)

➤ **node1**

   ➤ `search1` (RTS Search)

   ➤ `qrserver1` (high-level search handling)

➤ **node2**

   ➤ `search2` (RTS Search)

   ➤ `crawler1` (web spider)

   ➤ `procserver1` (document pipeline)

   ➤ `procserver2` (2nd pipeline)

The no processes appear in italics under `node0`, the seven items directly under `administration-set1`, are configured as a single group in the installation UI, although they appear as separate entries in the installation profile.

Under the third machine, node2, notice that there are no processes appear in italics, the crawler and the two document processors. In a "classic" three-node installation, these would reside on node0, our small tilt on the three-node theme.

Installation Profile

Listing 8-3 showing the installation profile used for our little Unix three-node-tilt node setup.

LISTING 8-3: Installation Profile for Three-Node Linux Setup

```xml
<?xml version="1.0"?>
<system-configuration name="FAST ESP Installer generated configuration"
version="5.1.5">
  <host-set>
    <host id="node0">
      <property name="hostname" value="linuxnode1.intranet.ideaeng.net"/>
      <property name="platform" value="Linux"/>
      <property name="username" value="fast"/>
      <property name="install-dir" value="/home/fast/esp/"/>
      <property name="index-dir" value=""/>
      <property name="fixml-dir" value=""/>
      <property name="temp-dir" value="/tmp/"/>
      <property name="remote-cmd" value="SSH2"/>
      <property name="baseport" value="13000"/>
    </host>
    <host id="node1">
      <property name="hostname" value="linuxnode2.intranet.ideaeng.net"/>
      <property name="platform" value="Linux"/>
      <property name="username" value="fast"/>
      <property name="install-dir" value="/home/fast/esp/"/>
      <property name="index-dir" value=""/>
      <property name="fixml-dir" value=""/>
      <property name="temp-dir" value="/tmp/"/>
      <property name="remote-cmd" value="SSH2"/>
      <property name="baseport" value="13000"/>
    </host>
    <host id="node2">
      <property name="hostname" value="linuxnode3.intranet.ideaeng.net"/>
      <property name="platform" value="Linux"/>
      <property name="username" value="fast"/>
      <property name="install-dir" value="/home/fast/esp/"/>
      <property name="index-dir" value=""/>
      <property name="fixml-dir" value=""/>
      <property name="temp-dir" value="/tmp/"/>
      <property name="remote-cmd" value="SSH2"/>
      <property name="baseport" value="13000"/>
    </host>
  </host-set>

  <administration-set>
    <configuration-service id="configserver1" host-ref="node0"/>
```

```
   <log-service id="logserver1" host-ref="node0"/>
   <clarity id="clarity1" host-ref="node0"/>
   <administration-gui id="httpd1" host-ref="node0"/>
   <resource-service id="resourceservice1" host-ref="node0"/>
   <admin-service id="adminserver1" host-ref="node0" smtp-server-host=""
smtp-server-port="25"/>
   <storage-service id="storageservice1" host-ref="node0" admin="root"
adminpassword="d4tAs34rch" user="fast" userpassword="fast"/>
 </administration-set>

 <log-transformer-set>
   <log-transformer id="logtransformer1" host-ref="node0"/>
 </log-transformer-set>

 <data-source-set>
   <crawler id="crawler1" host-ref="node2">
     <property name="organization" value="NIE"/>
     <property name="admin-email" value="support@ideaeng.com"/>
   </crawler>
 </data-source-set>

 <content-distributor-set>
   <content-distributor id="contentdistributor1" host-ref="node0">
     <property name="master" value="true"/>
   </content-distributor>
 </content-distributor-set>

 <search-engine-set>
   <search-engine id="search1" host-ref="node1">
     <property name="search" value="true"/>
     <property name="index" value="true"/>
   </search-engine>
   <search-engine id="search2" host-ref="node2">
     <property name="search" value="true"/>
     <property name="index" value="false"/>
   </search-engine>
 </search-engine-set>

 <document-processor-set>
   <document-processor id="procserver1" host-ref="node2"/>
   <document-processor id="procserver2" host-ref="node2"/>
 </document-processor-set>

 <query-result-processor-set>
   <query-result-processor id="qrserver1" host-ref="node1">
     <property name="default-language" value="en"/>
     <property name="languages" value="en"/>
   </query-result-processor>
 </query-result-processor-set>

 <webanalyzer>
   <webanalyzer-node id="webanalyzer1" host-ref="node0" server="true" max-
```

```
   targets="1" link-processing="true" lookup-db="true"/>
     </webanalyzer>

   <subsystem-dispatcher-set>
   </subsystem-dispatcher-set>

   <indexing-dispatchers>
     <indexing-dispatcher id="indexingdispatcher1" host-ref="node0"/>
   </indexing-dispatchers>

   <name-service>
     <name-server id="nameserver1" host-ref="node0"/>
   </name-service>

   <license-service>
     <license-server id="lmgrd1" host-ref="node0"/>
   </license-service>

   <search-engine-cluster-set>
     <search-engine-cluster id="webcluster">
       <property name="index-profile-type" value="standard"/>
       <property name="copy-index" value="true"/>
       <search-engine-column id="col0">
         <search-engine id-ref="search1"/>
         <search-engine id-ref="search2"/>
       </search-engine-column>
       <query-result-processors>
         <query-result-processor id-ref="qrserver1"/>
       </query-result-processors>
       <indexing-dispatchers>
         <indexing-dispatcher id-ref="indexingdispatcher1"/>
       </indexing-dispatchers>
     </search-engine-cluster>
   </search-engine-cluster-set>

 </system-configuration>
```

Starting the Installation

Since this chapter has already talked about Unix, and the rest of the previous chapters are all about Windows, we decided to lead you through a sample installation in CentOS using ESP's Linux distribution. Although this is the FAST 32-bit distribution, we were running with 64-bit CentOS and Sun/Oracle Java 1.6 JDK, aka "Java 6."

1. You start by downloading the ESP license file and binary installer into your *fast* account's download directory. Then you create a temp directory underneath and unpack the ESP installer into it with these commands:

```
mkdir  tmpdir
cd  tmpdir
tar  xfz  ../setup_Linux.tar.gz
```

Which gives you the following files:

```
drwxr-xr-x 2 fast fast    4096 Jul  8 2008 data
lrwxrwxrwx 1 fast fast       6 Jun 27 21:50 lmhostid -> lmutil
-rwxr-xr-x 1 fast fast  740492 Jul  8 2008 lmutil
-rwxr-xr-x 1 fast fast  651110 Jun 17 2008 setup_Linux.bin
-rw-r--r-- 1 fast fast 4703135 Jun 17 2008 setup_Linux.jar
drwxr-xr-x 6 fast fast    4096 Jul  8 2008 updates
-rw-r--r-- 1 fast fast     269 Jul  8 2008 VERSION.xml
```

Figure 8-3 shows the two startup directories and the startup sequence of the ESP installer.

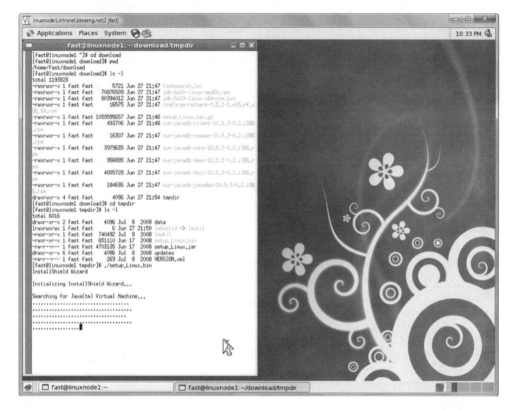

FIGURE 8-3

2. As with the single-node installation in the previous chapter, you'll see a startup logo, then be asked to accept the license agreement. On this multinode install, you still have to allow ESP to download the third-party libraries. The nice thing here is that it will only download them once and then do local copies to the other nodes. (See Figure 8-4.)

3. Use the file browser to point ESP at your license file, which you should have unzipped already. (See Figure 8-5.)

4. In the next screen choose, Multi Node as shown in Figure 8-6 to tell ESP that you'll be doing a multinode installation.

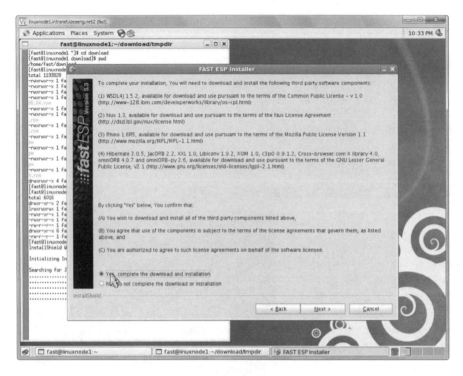

FIGURE 8-4

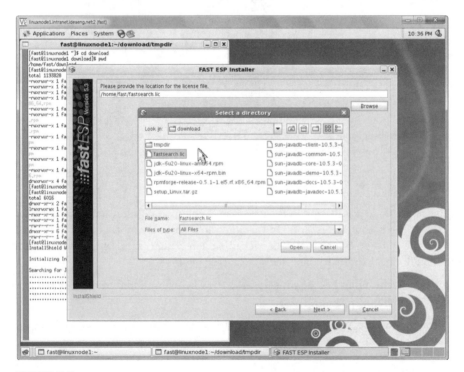

FIGURE 8-5

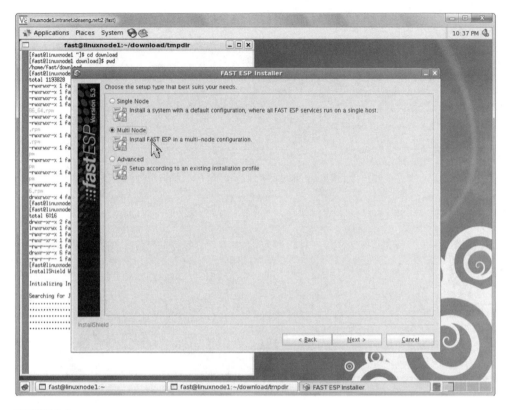

FIGURE 8-6

Defining Nodes

The next step is to define the host names of the machines on your network that will run the ESP software. We won't bore you with all of the intermediate screens, but Figure 8-7 is what you end up with.

The process for defining hosts/nodes is as follows:

1. Click the Add Host button in the bottom left.

2. Type in the TCP/IP name of the new machine.

3. Review the guesses and default values the wizard automatically puts in.

4. Optional: Click the Test Connection To Host button. These tests will also be performed later by the installer.

Once all the hosts have been defined, it's time for the next step, assigning processing roles to each host.

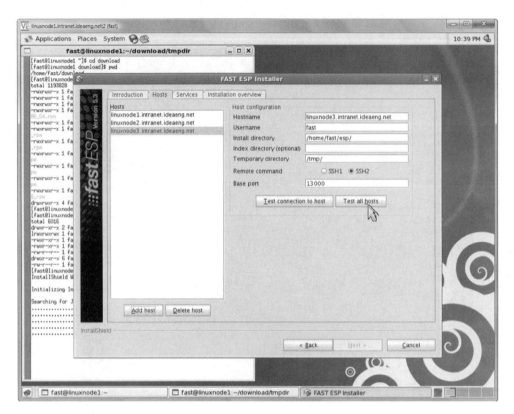

FIGURE 8-7

System Tests

ESP then goes out to test. As you progress through the tests, ESP flags any machine it finds fault with. You can then expand the log file and see the error. Figure 8-8 shows an example of an error caused by the JAVA_HOME environment variable *not* being defined on one of the remote nodes.

It's important to remember that, even if all of these initial tests do pass, it doesn't mean you're all set. Other errors can still occur later in the process, so consider this just a preliminary milestone.

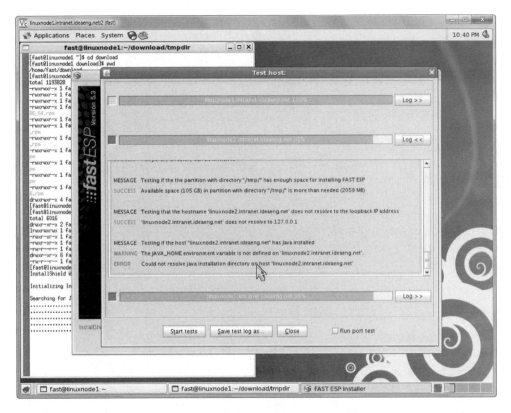

FIGURE 8-8

Assigning Processes

ESP then guides you through the allocation of different processes and services to each of the previously defined nodes. The initial screen shows all of the required services in red, since they have not been assigned yet. (See Figure 8-9.)

You assign services to each node. Most are pretty straightforward, if you've already decided where processes will go. We've omitted many of these interim screenshots. Some of the services have a more involved configuration. For example, the Web Analyzer is the subsystem that tracks links between web pages. This can be process-intensive, so an entire subcluster of processes can be devoted to just that task. The dialog box, thus, has more choices, although we've gone with a relatively simple 3-node setup for this example installation. (See Figure 8-10.)

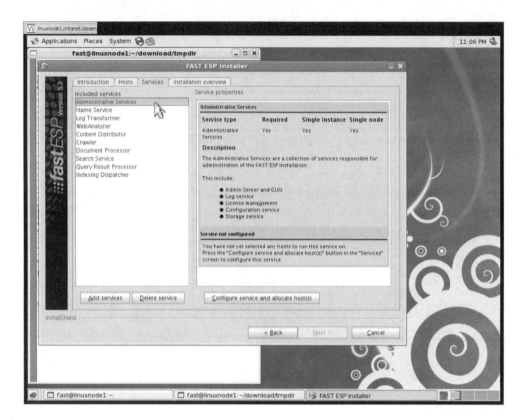

FIGURE 8-9

Similarly, you have great flexibility when setting up the Enterprise Crawler, ESP's web spider. For some search applications, the spider/web crawler can consume the most resources. Again, the dialog box in Figure 8-11 allows for flexible configuration.

Document processing is also different in that you define each processor as a separate service. Figures 8-12 and 8-13 show how you define a second document processor and then assign it to the same node as the first. The rule of thumb is a maximum of two document processors per unallocated CPU core, but we're only defining two in total here.

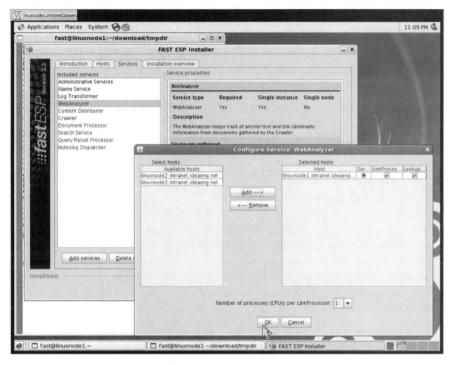

FIGURE 8-10

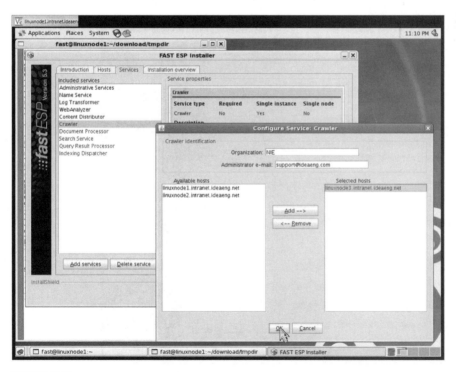

FIGURE 8-11

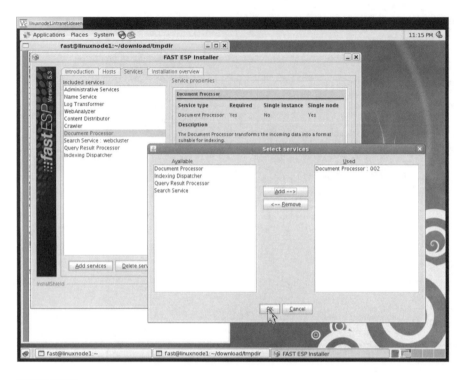

FIGURE 8-12

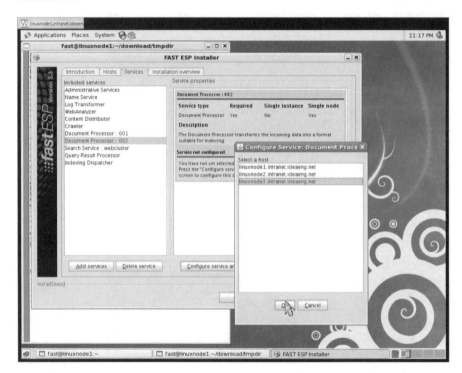

FIGURE 8-13

Figure 8-12 shows the first part of these steps, creating a new instance of a Document Processor, with the following steps:

1. Click the Add Process button.

2. Select that process type in the left Available column.

3. Click the Add button, which moves it to the Used column on the right.

4. Then click OK.

Figure 8-13 show the steps for assigning the new document processor instance to a host machine, with the following steps:

5. Click the Document Processor: 002 to select it.

6. Click the Configure Service and Allocate Hosts button.

7. Select linuxnode03.

8. Click OK.

For Search Services, you define a cluster and then assign processes to it. In Figure 8-14 we've clicked Configure Service for the Service Service button, and then ESP asks us to name the new service.

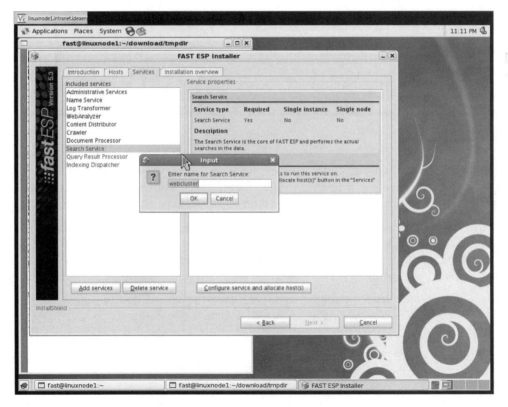

FIGURE 8-14

We create the service for the search cluster. In Figure 8-15 we've opted to assign the search service we just created, called `webcluster`, to linuxnode2 and linuxnode3, thus defining our single column (column 0) as having two nodes (technically ESP would say "2 nodes high").

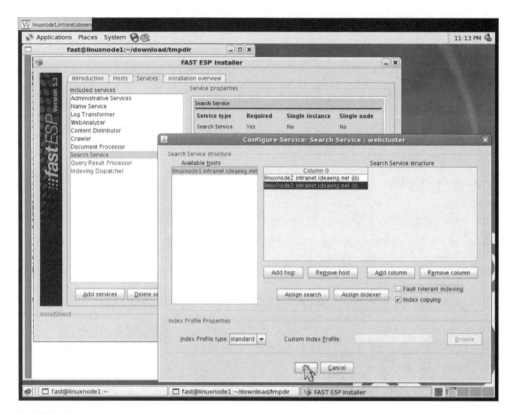

FIGURE 8-15

In Figure 8-16, when it's initially defined, it's missing additional information that hasn't been entered yet and is shown in red. Keep in mind we just created it a second ago, but it's just giving us an immediate reminder. These messages will disappear as we progress through the rest of the wizard.

Query and result processing, what ESP calls the QR process, is the higher-level search director. The dialog offers many language options, although you should really check only the ones you'll be using. More is not better, because of the extra memory consumption. Figure 8-17 shows that we put QR on column 0, row 0, our host named linuxnode2.

When you've initially completed the configuration, ESP checks it out and may provide warnings or errors. In Figure 8-18, ESP is suggesting an additional document-processing service.

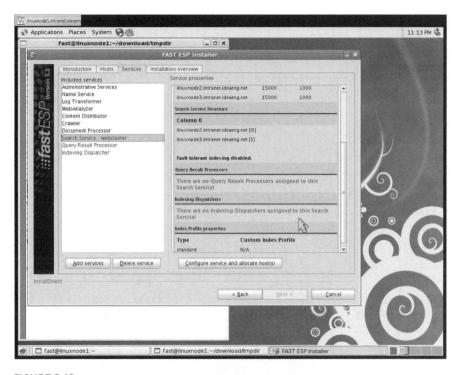

FIGURE 8-16

FIGURE 8-17

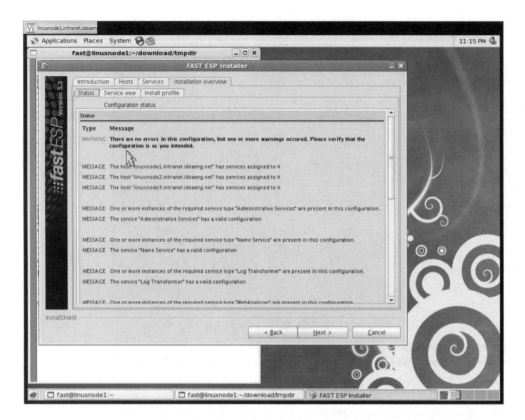

FIGURE 8-18

After you have finished all of the assignments and ESP has checked the assignments, you can save all this information to disk with a copy of your Install Profile. Although ESP should leave one behind by default, it's nice to copy this to somewhere safe and give it a more distinctive name. If you're using a temporary machine to bootstrap an `InstallProfile.xml`, this is particularly important! (See Figure 8-19.)

ESP then runs another set of tests, as shown in Figure 8-20.

If everything goes well, it then presents a confirmation screen, as shown in Figure 8-21.

Copying Node Files

In the GUI-based über-installation model, ESP then copies over all of the files it will need to all of the nodes. This can take quite a while, perhaps more than an hour. Also, when copying particularly large files, the progress bar can stall and not move for many minutes, but be patient, it's working! (See Figure 8-22.)

FIGURE 8-19

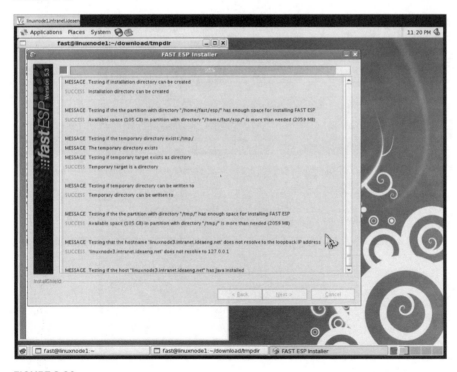

FIGURE 8-20

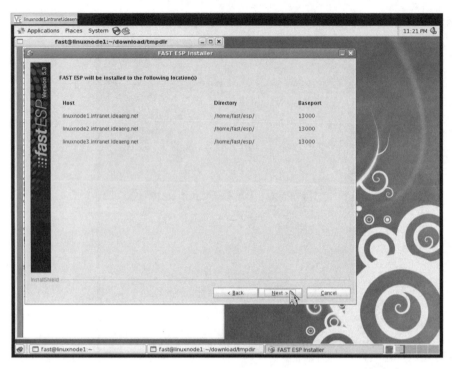

FIGURE 8-21

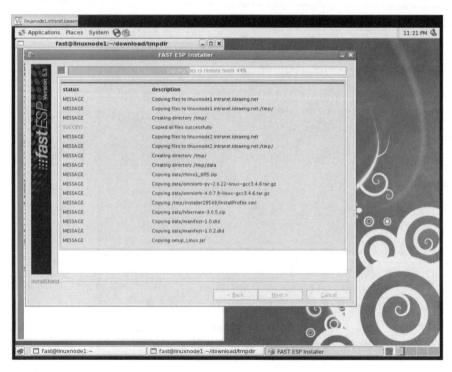

FIGURE 8-22

Installing

ESP then runs a remote installation on all of its nodes, including itself! This is also a very lengthy process that can make it appear that the system has hung. (See Figure 8-23.)

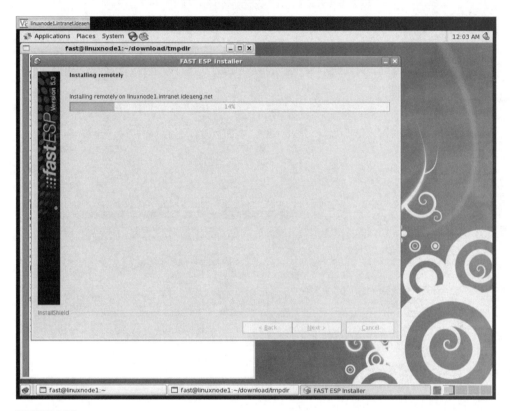

FIGURE 8-23

The rest of the installation is about what you'd expect, more slow bar graphs, and then eventually it's finished. Remember, however, we said that, just because the initial tests pass, it doesn't mean you're home free. Figure 8-24 shows an example of an error that occurred late into a Windows installation. In this case, even though a Windows domain login was used, the installation was started while logged in as a local Administrator. This is an easy mistake to make, and it doesn't show up until very late in the process.

A three-node installation is a good practice run, and something we'd suggest for even an ESP developer to try.

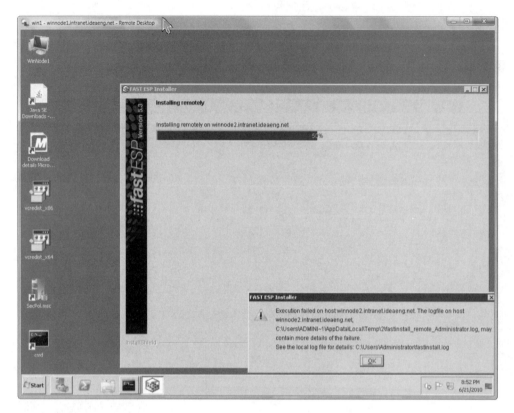

FIGURE 8-24

BACKING UP QUIESCENT STATES

Systems administrators should not expect to back up running ESP installations and be able to restore them reliably. There are similar problems with most other search engines.

Search engines maintain a very complex and delicate operational state that is, in part, file system based. The easiest way to back up and restore systems is to do so when they are shut down, across the entire ESP instance.

One approach is to think in terms of doing periodic backups when the system is down and then bootstrapping in additional data.

ESP 5.3 also supports archival static partitions. This allows you to pull out parts of the index. It's likely these could be part of a more elaborate backup and restore plan.

Another option, if you're using virtual machines, is to take a snapshot of the machines when the services are stopped. The *ESP Operations Guide* has more information on backup and restore procedures.

A FEW ESP TERMS YOU MIGHT COME ACROSS

The FAST product has been renamed in the past, and has a lot of subsystems that are normally hidden from casual administrators and developers. However, these systems are mentioned by name at times, either in current documentation or perhaps when talking to an ESP consultant. Here are a few terms that are good to know.

About Python and FAST Cobra

Python is a general programming language and is used with a number of search engines, including ESP. It is the primary language of the FAST Document Processing Pipeline, so many of the document-handling and metadata operations are accomplished with Python.

Like other interpreted languages, Python needs an executable to run Python scripts. FAST ESP's Cobra is a specially compiled Python interpreter that includes linkage to the other ESP subsystems. If you were to run ESP `.py` scripts with the standard Python interpreter you'd get errors about libraries not being found. Simple Python scripts would run under either environment.

So, Cobra is just ESP's version of a Python interpreter that includes special ESP libraries.

References to FDS

As you dig into the FAST documentation you'll see a few references to FDS; this stands for FAST Data Search and is simply the older name of the ESP product line. FDS refers to the 4.x product, whereas ESP refers to the 5.x product. Some things haven't changed since FDS 4.x and are still applicable.

The Mythical ESPDeploy Application

ESPDeploy is an internal software synchronization tool used for configuring multinode ESP instances. Like many other software companies FAST's consultants created various tools to make customer setups faster. However, ESPDeploy was never intended for direct customer use and is hence "unsupported" software. It may also be referred to as ESP Deploy.

You should know that it does exist, but we don't recommend you use it for the following reasons:

➤ It has never been officially supported by FAST, and the internal documentation is not generally available.

➤ Even if you acquire the internal documentation, it isn't particularly thorough. Although it does provide some reference material, some fundamental parts of the overall usage model are missing.

➤ Some of the functions it performs might be easier to handle with other tools. Its real payback is in larger deployments.

➤ In practice, wholesale changes to large farms are somewhat less common than might be expected.

➤ Shielding new ESP administrators from the details of these tasks might hinder their deep understanding of the ESP system, knowledge that could come in handy in the future.

➤ We don't expect Microsoft be any more enthusiastic than FAST was about supporting this, and newer releases will clearly use other tools.

So, given all these reasons not to use it, why mention it at all?

➤ Administrators of existing ESP systems that were set up by FAST employees may use ESPDeploy, so it's good to at least know what it is.

We also mention it here to give it proper perspective. When people hear about something interesting and are then told they can't have it, there's a tendency to want it even more. Over time, without real information to go on, the presumed usefulness and functionality of such a tool might grow and grow. We want to nip that in the bud. It's a somewhat useful tool if you know how to use it, but is not generally magical or awesome. Generally, you'll have better luck with tools you already use and understand.

➤ If you have a really large installation and will be doing lots of patches and reconfiguring, and don't already have tools for this, then it's something you might consider.

Should you forbid the use of ESP Deploy in your installation? We'd generally advise not using it in new systems. However, if you have a working system that uses it, then it's probably best to leave it be. If you have a new system and the consultants you bring in insist on using it, perhaps you should allow it. However, have a long discussion about it. At a minimum, you'll want to be left with full documentation, plus complete instructions on its usage in your particular setup, and specific training/walkthrough for your staff. Having a chat with your salesperson about tech support's policy would also be a good idea. The rule of thumb should be that, if ESPDeploy is used, your staff should understand exactly which tasks it is performing and have some idea how to perform those tasks by other means should that ever become necessary.

CUSTOMIZING THE DOCUMENT PROCESSING PIPELINE

The secret to great search relevance is great indexing. The problem is, with many enterprise search engines, it takes a good deal of effort to intercept and improve the document-indexing process. Sometimes you want to add extra metadata from an external source, or you want to clean up the field values that will be populated automatically during indexing. Some technologies require entire custom low-level code in C or Java, but this is complex and time consuming.

ESP solves some of these problems with its document pipeline architecture, which was introduced in Chapter 7. The ESP document processing pipeline uses a series of small Python programs, known as *processing stages*, to transform raw documents into data ready for indexing.

Figure 8-25 shows the overall architecture of ESP's indexing and searching, and how the document pipeline fits into this overall architecture. The figure presents a simplified overview of how ESP works as opposed to the more modular architecture shown in Figure 7-1, but it illustrates where the document pipeline fits in the overall system.

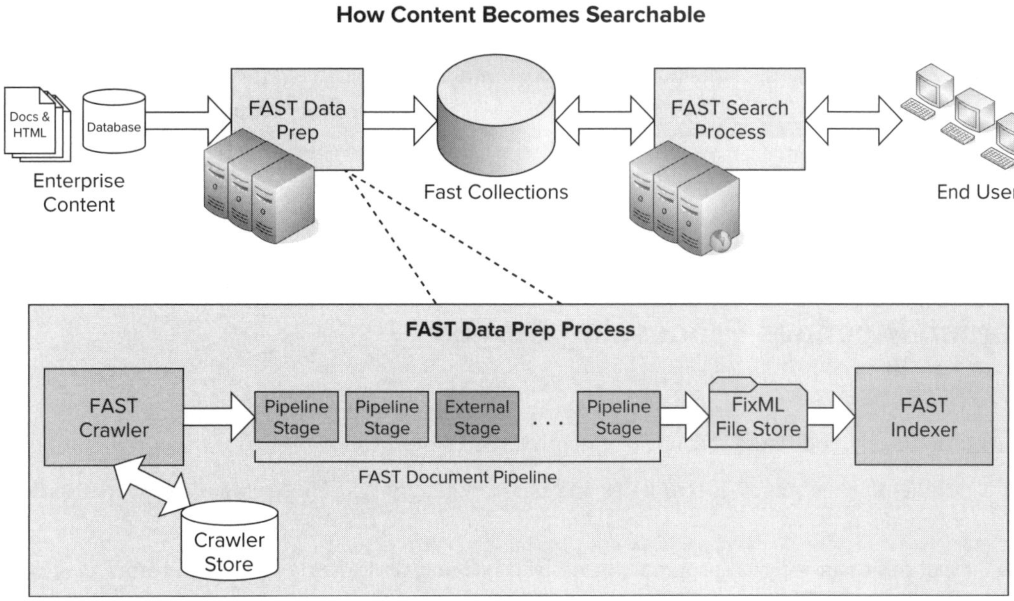

How Content Becomes Searchable

FIGURE 8-25

Although there's still occasionally some code to modify, it's broken up into smaller more manageable pieces, and it's in a scripting language, Python, which makes small quick changes easier, assuming you know Python. But even better, there are a number of reusable template stages for some common tasks, so you might not need to write any code at all!

About ESP's Internal Data Representations

Diving in a bit deeper, document pipelines transform raw documents into ESP's normalized internal document representation; that information is then written XML files on disk in an XML format called FIXML. For some advanced pipeline modifications it's useful to know about this and the related formats, and you'll see the term FIXML mentioned in the ESP doc.

When an ESP administrator talks about reindexing documents, or running the *postprocess* command, they're actually referring to sending the FIXML files through the system again to the RTS Indexer. Postprocess may seem a bit odd for something that happens just before indexing, but it's after the document processing pipeline has run, so that's why it has that name. A related term, *refeeding* the documents, is further back in the chain of events, and refers to resending all of the raw documents back through the document processing pipeline.

Although FIXML files are written to disk, they aren't usually stored as individual files. Instead ESP uses a *FIXML Store*, which is an on a disk repository of compressed binary files. It's these

FIXML files that you send to the indexer. See the ESP doc for the `getfixml` command for more details.

A related ESP XML format is *FastXML* — a subset of FIXML. It is the officially supported form of XML for data heading into ESP. If an external program wishes to feed data into ESP, one option is to simply send it to ESP in the FastXML format. Although FastXML still has to go through a document processing pipeline, it's much shorter. There's only a small amount of work to do, as only a few extra fields have to be added to go from FastXML to FIXML. For example, one extra internal ESP field that gets added is the index time lemmatization of the document's terms. See the ESP documentation for a definition of that lemmatization.

You may want to consider using FastXML if you need to import a lot of data from another source into ESP quickly.

Managing Pipelines Processing Stages

After cloning or creating a pipeline there are four general ways to customize it:

1. Modify the order and settings of existing processing stages.

2. Clone pipeline stages or templates and change the settings. Those stages can then also be rearranged.

3. Call out to an external program, either by a system call or over a socket, and store the results.

4. Create entire custom stages in the Python programming language, using Python to directly manipulate the document.

We'll be showing method 3 in this chapter, and methods 1 and 2 are just subsets of method 3. Example code for method 4 is shown in Chapter 9.

When a new collection is created, it's assigned a processing pipeline. If a new type of data is to be indexed, a custom pipeline is created. The easiest way to create a new pipeline is to clone an existing pipeline that's similar to what you want to build. You can then clone and modify the stages within that new pipeline. You clone and manage pipelines and stages in the technical administrator GUI, which is shown in the next section. You need to leave the comfort of the admin GUI only if you need to modify Python code or set up external systems.

Simple Pipeline Modification Example

With a basic understanding of the pipeline architecture, and the ability to call external processes, it's possible to write a pipeline stage in just about any language you choose.

One of the stages Microsoft provides is called `ExternalDataFilterTimeout`. It lets you launch your own program via a standard system call. This little-known document pipeline stage lets you write custom stages in just about any executable language — C, C++, Java, and even shell scripts and batch files. It provides the ESP Document Pipeline with external system call capability right off the shelf! The only drawback is the overhead of the systems calls, which are generally less efficient than code running in the current process. This is particularly true if the external program takes a long time to start up each time it's called. In a high throughput environment it would be better to have a persistent external program listen on a port, and have a custom Python stage that would open a socket and connect. For this example we're sticking with plain old system calls.

Now back to the issue at hand: creating a pipeline stage that doesn't need to be written in Python, by using the standard `ExternalDataFilterTimeout` stage template. That stage does a system call based on attributes that are set in the GUI, which also includes an on-screen description of the parameters. The `Input` attribute tells it what data to send to the program via `stdin` (standard in), and the `Output` parameter tells it where to store the results captured from `stdout` (standard out). The system call is done using a timeout, so that a hung external process will not entirely hang the overall document processor instance. The system logs timeouts and any other non-zero return codes as errors in the ESP logs along with any corresponding `stderr` (standard error) output. The logs are available in the admin GUI. Any error causes the pipeline to be aborted for that document.

The ESP doc provides information about the `%(input)s` and `%(output)s` variables that need to be set in the `Command` configuration parameter. They will be substituted with the names of the input and output temporary files. You can also tell the external program where there is a temporary working directory with the `%(tmpdir)s` formatting the `Command` configuration parameter.

Configuring the Pipeline

In this Windows server–based example, we're going to perform a simple task: use a standard Windows batch file to insert the value of an environment variable into one of the unused generic fields defined in the default index profile. You can pick any environment variable — PATH, USERNAME — but for this simple example, we use the name of the server we are indexing on: COMPUTERNAME.

To do the job, we will follow these steps:

1. Create the batch file

2. Create a document pipeline stage

3. Create a document pipeline using the new stage

4. Create a collection that uses the new pipeline and submit a single document

5. Verify that our stage works by using the SFE

It may sound complicated, but it's not rocket science.

Step 1: Create the Batch File

The first step is to create a simple batch file that echoes the value of the environment variable. This is a trivial batch program. Call it **SYSNAME.BAT** and save it in the BIN directory within the FAST home directory; check the environment variable FASTSEARCH if you're not sure.

```
@echo off
echo %COMPUTERNAME%
```

You could leave the first line off; the real meat is the second line. As you will see, however, if you omit the @echo off line, you populate the field with the Windows CMD prompt as well as the system name.

In the CMD program, test your new batch file to verify it displays something like the test result shown here:

```
C:\esp\bin>SYSNAME
FIREBOLT
C:\esp\bin>
```

Step 2: Create a Document Pipeline Stage

Start the FAST Administrative Console and click Document Pipeline. If you see an Advanced Mode link to the right of the Overview label, click it so you can see all of the stages in the document pipeline you will create.

Scroll down the list of pipelines and stages until you see one named `ExternalDataFilterTimeout` in the Default Stages section. Click the plus-sign (+) to the right of the row, and you will see a screen like the one in Figure 8-26. If you are using other versions of FAST, you may see a slightly different screen.

FIGURE 8-26

Fill out the form as follows:

➤   Name: **myExternalStage**

➤   Input: **size**

➤   Command: **c:\esp\bin\sysname.bat <%(input)s >%(putput)s**

➤   Output: **generic1**

The name is easy, and it makes sense that you want to put the output from the script into the generic1 field. We've found that you need to provide a non-null field name to make the stage work, and in almost any data source, you should find that size is defined and populated. By the way, we've found that URL, COLLNAME, and even CONTENTID are not available at this stage of the pipeline.

The syntax for the command looks odd, but you need to match it exactly. What happens when you execute this stage is that FAST puts the input field value in a temporary file and will expect the output field to be stored in a different temporary file. FAST passes you the names of the input and output files, and the syntax the FAST Python code is looking for matches that shown above.

When you have created your new stage, click the Submit button at the lower right of the form, then click OK to return to the Document Pipeline screen.

Step 3: Create a Document Pipeline Using the New Stage

Now that you have a stage defined, you need to create a document pipeline to experiment with.

At the top of the Document Pipeline screen you'll see the Generic pipeline. Click the plus-sign (+) at the right to display a screen like the one shown in Figure 8-27. Depending on whether you are using FDS, InStream, or ESP, you may see a slightly different screen, likely with a pull-down list of stages.

FIGURE 8-27

Name your new document pipeline — perhaps **myExternalDP**. Select the stage you created in step 2, and click the right arrow to move it into the list of stages in the current pipeline. Use the up and down arrows on the right to move your stage between the FastHTMLParser and the

`TeaserGenerator`. (Hint: If you do not see a long list of stages, you are not in Advanced mode. Click Cancel, then, at the top of the Document Pipeline screen, click the Advanced Mode link and start at the beginning of this step.) When you have named your document pipeline and inserted your customer stage in the right place, click Submit and then OK. Time for the next step.

Step 4: Create a Collection and Submit a Single Document

Now you have created a custom stage and added that stage to a new document pipeline. It's time to create a collection using your new document pipeline.

Click Create Collection, then enter a name and brief description for your new collection. Click Next.

You may need to select a cluster if you have more than one, but generally you will see a prompt saying that webcluster is your only option; click Next.

At the Pipeline Configuration screen, pull down the list to see the list of available document pipelines; yours should be visible. Select it, click Add Selected, and Click Next. If your document pipeline is not in the pull-down list, go back to step 3 to make sure you created the pipeline properly. When you view the Document Pipeline screen, you should see your pipeline in the list.

Now you have the option to select data sources — do not! Rather than select one, click OK and return to the collection Details screen. Click the Add Document link, and enter a URL for a web page you have access to: your company home page or a public site you know. Click Next, and FAST will spider your URL and attempt to parse it. If you did everything right, you will see a status indicating the document was submitted. Return to the Collection menu and wait until it shows that the collection is searchable; you may need to refresh the screen every now and then. Once you see that collection is searchable, go on to the final step.

Step 5: Verify That Your Stage Works

Once you see that the collection is searchable, click the Search View link at the top of the screen. Select the collection, press the Advanced bar, and select All Fields. Click Submit Query, and you should see a page like the one shown in Figure 8-28.

Scroll down if necessary and confirm that the system name is displayed in the generic1 field — success!

Some Caveats

While adding an external program to a pipeline stage is relatively easy, remember that the pipeline stage runs for each document during indexing. Calling an external program takes a bit longer than executing native Python code, and executing a batch or command file takes even longer. If your application needs to index millions of documents, and it takes 1/10th of a second for the custom pipeline stage to execute, it may add over 25 hours to the indexing process. It would be much better to look into a Python, C, or C# stage rather than rely on the otherwise easy-to-use `ExternalDataFilterTimeout` stage. On the other hand, for prototyping a new application, it may be just what you need.

FIGURE 8-28

Here you've seen how you can use something as simple as a Windows batch file to customize your FAST document pipeline. You can accomplish the same thing in just about any command-line-enabled language: C, Perl, or WSH, or any of the popular shells on Unix or Linux. When you want to use Python, you don't need to execute an external program; you can integrate that right into the pipeline natively.

ESP Template Pipelines and Stages

As we said earlier, the easiest way to create a custom pipeline is to start with a clone/copy of a similar pipeline. Or if you're trying to create a custom stage, it's easier to at least start with another one as a template.

ESP ships with quite a few pipeline and process stage templates, and the Web GUI shows a short description next to many of them. Here's our take on the set of pipelines shipped in ESP. We simply divide them into what we'd consider "basic" and "more advanced" pipelines. Generally the basic ones are good for importing mostly processed data from another source, such as a database or XML repository. The advanced ones have more stages and do a lot more parsing. Some of the more advanced linguistic pipelines can actually be rather CPU intensive, so might require more machines to keep up.

Here is a list of simpler/lightweight ESP pipelines:

➤ Express

➤ FastXML

➤ DocML

- ➤ LightweightXML
- ➤ XML
- ➤ RowSet

Here are some more advanced/complex ESP pipelines:

- ➤ Generic
- ➤ CustomLinguistics
- ➤ SiteSearch
- ➤ NewsSearch
- ➤ LightweightSemantic
- ➤ Semantic

You'll find a bit of information in the pipeline *Web GUI* and *ESP Guides*; however some are not documented very well and you may need to experiment a bit.

If you happen to have been in the Web GUI before reading this chapter, you'll know that there are way more template stages than pipelines. Some are essentially undocumented, and FAST simply lists them alphabetically. The following list sorts them by their normal order of appearance and general functional category. You'll notice a general, logical progression of functions from one set to the next, and that later sets of stages build on the work accomplished by the previous stages. None of the ESP pipelines use all of these stages, and the order of use is different in a couple of places.

Following is a list of ESP template stages, arranged by usage order, and functional category.

- ➤ System Group 1:
  - ➤ DocInit
- ➤ Data Centric:
  - ➤ DocumentRetriever
  - ➤ MergeDocML
  - ➤ CopyUri
  - ➤ RowSetXSLT
  - ➤ FastXMLReaderData
  - ➤ FastXMLReader
  - ➤ XMLParser
  - ➤ XMLExtract
  - ➤ XMLLanguageDetector
  - ➤ XMLScopifier*

- ➤ XMLScopifier2*
- ➤ GeoScaler*

➤ Document Processing and Converting, Set 1:

- ➤ URLProcessor
- ➤ URIEquivalence
- ➤ Decompressor
- ➤ FormatDetector
- ➤ SimpleConverter
- ➤ FlashConverter
- ➤ PDFConverter

➤ Language Group 1 and Parsing:

- ➤ SearchExportConverter
- ➤ LanguageAndEncodingDetector
- ➤ EncodingNormalizer
- ➤ FastHTMLParser

➤ Your Custom Stages: This is usually where your stages will go, though it is not a requirement.

- ➤ Entities Group 1 / CPU Intensive:
- ➤ Stan3Address
- ➤ Stan3News
- ➤ Stan3NewsAttributeCopy
- ➤ PersonExtractor0
- ➤ PersonExtractor1
- ➤ CompanyExtractor0
- ➤ CompanyExtractor1
- ➤ LocationExtractor0
- ➤ LocationExtractor1
- ➤ UppercaseExtractor

➤ Document Processing Group 2:

- ➤ TeaserGenerator
- ➤ LinkNormalizer
- ➤ CrawlerLinkFilter

- ➤ LinkFilter
- ➤ AnchorTextRetriever
- ➤ AnchorTextFormatter
- ➤ Tokenizer*
- ➤ Language Group 2:
  - ➤ OffensiveContentFilter
  - ➤ SynonymExpander
  - ➤ ScopeTokenizer*
  - ➤ Lemmatizer*
  - ➤ SentenceBoundaryDetector
  - ➤ npTagger
  - ➤ npStopWordsExtractor
  - ➤ npStopPhrasesExtractor
  - ➤ npExtractor
- ➤ Entities Group 2:
  - ➤ EmailExtractor
  - ➤ DateExtractor
  - ➤ TimeExtractor
  - ➤ URLExtractor
  - ➤ JobTitleExtractor
  - ➤ UniversityExtractor
  - ➤ PersonExtractor0
  - ➤ PersonExtractor1
  - ➤ PersonExtractor2
  - ➤ PhoneticNormalizer
  - ➤ AirlineExtractor
  - ➤ CompanyExtractor0
  - ➤ CompanyExtractor1
  - ➤ CompanyExtractor2
  - ➤ LocationExtractor0
  - ➤ LocationExtractor1
  - ➤ QuotationExtractor

- ➤ AcronymExtractor1
- ➤ AcronymExtractor2
- ➤ TickerExtractor1
- ➤ TickerExtractor2
- ➤ TickerExtractor3
- ➤ PriceExtractor
- ➤ PhoneNumberExtractor
- ➤ USZipCodeExtractor
- ➤ USNewspaperExtractor
- ➤ FilenameExtractor
- ➤ ISBNExtractor
- ➤ MeasurementExtractor
- ➤ TeamExtractor1
- ➤ TeamExtractor2
- ➤ DegreeExtractor
- ➤ OSExtractor
- ➤ StreetExtractor
- ➤ UppercaseExtractor
- ➤ Language Group 3:
  - ➤ NounPhraseExtractor1
  - ➤ NounPhraseExtractor2
  - ➤ EntityVectorizer
  - ➤ XMLifier*
  - ➤ Vectorizer*
  - ➤ Scopifier
  - ➤ Lemmatizer*
  - ➤ XMLifier*
  - ➤ ConceptSuppressor
- ➤ Entities / Data Tweaking Group 3:
  - ➤ DateTimeNormalizer*
  - ➤ DateTimeSelector*

> ➤ MapperTransformer
>
> ➤ RankTuner

➤ System Group 2:

> ➤ FIXMLGenerator
>
> ➤ DictServiceOutput
>
> ➤ RTSOutput
>
> ➤ LinkOutput

 An asterisk indicates somewhat inconsistent ordering.

This list will at least get you started in the right direction.

SUMMARY

If there's only one thing you take away from this chapter it should be the mindset of multiple node systems. Ideally your developers and QA staff will be using a minimum of three-node systems to do their work, even if they just use virtual machines. The age of monolithic search engines, where the only way to scale up your search was to buy a bigger box, is thankfully gone. All modern search engines that scale up are multinode. You'll also see this with the open source Lucene/Solr/Nutch codebase, and with other commercial offerings like Endeca and Autonomy. Even the venerable Google Search Appliance for Enterprise scales up by adding multiple nodes, although in that case it's still considered a closed system, so you don't get as much of a feel for managing a cluster.

With the rise of virtualization and "clouds," these are good skills to have, regardless of which software you're working with. If you set up a really large ESP server farm, or have very complex data to index, then you've still got some reading to do! Some of the info you'll need is buried in the many ESP Guides, and other information can be found online. You can even email questions to newsgroups like ours at `http://fast.searchdev.org`.

A close second in importance is the document pipeline, and how it translates from raw documents into FIXML through a series of small pipeline stages that you control. And if you can't find the stage you need, you can write your own in Python, or call out other programs via system calls or sockets. These are the types of "secrets" that the consultants have in their tool chest.

9

Advanced Topics

WHAT'S IN THIS CHAPTER?

➤ Using FAST search scalability, for indexing more documents and handling more searches

➤ Reviewing the various types of taxonomies, typical taxonomy workflow, and taxonomy rule sets

➤ Performing entity extraction and the FAST Structural Analysis Toolkit

➤ Tweaking relevancy in FAST

➤ Implementing unsupervised clustering and noun phrase extraction

➤ Reviewing the requirements for Enterprise class Federated Search

Many applications don't need industrial strength search, but when you've got highly specialized requirements or gigabytes of data, you'll be glad to have access to ESP!

Some people assume that "Advanced Search" means jamming a results list chock full of every search widget under the sun; this is often a bad idea! Remember that contemporary users start out having used an Internet search portal like Yahoo! or Google, so anything on the screen that doesn't fit with that mental model has to be easily understood and safe to ignore.

In the early days of search, there was a high-end search company geared to intelligence analysts. Over the years, their flagship search product evolved to include most of the enhancements requested by these advanced knowledge workers. When "normal users" opened up the search application, however, they experienced "shock and awe." There were way too many things on the screen to digest. Other early engines were heavily influenced by librarians, and by very smart groups of "power users." These products often featured quite complex user interfaces.

Were these vendors wrong to respond to their advanced user base? No, but modern engines have the ability to be packaged in multiple ways, with the same search engine powering the back end. If we had the power to control space-time at our fingertips, we would have counseled vendors to offer multiple interfaces to their engines.

"Advanced" doesn't always mean search interface bells and whistles. Sometimes it has more to do with the amount of raw data the engine must handle, the data that must be extracted and combined, or the relevancy algorithms employed behind the scenes. Sometimes the best advanced applications are the ones that make it look easy!

SCALABILITY

Scalability generally refers to either how much content a system can search, or how many searches it can handle at a time. More demanding applications may need to accommodate both of these requirements. In Chapter 8, we talk at length about customization and deployment of ESP, which includes the planning server allocation and configuration, but we also cover it here briefly because scalability is one of reasons to invest in high-end search engines.

We can't give you lots of specific numbers in this section. Everybody's data is different, requirements are different, machines and software change quickly over time relative to published books, and there are plenty of potential legal concerns. If scalability is a concern, you need to be discussing this with your ESP sales team and/or search engine consultants. You may also want to consider a performance-related trial project.

ESP Rows and Columns

A single ESP installation is distributed among multiple server computers, with each box taking on one or more logical roles. Although some of these machines have ancillary roles like administration, datafeeds, and licensing, a core set of machines performs the primary role of actually searching.

When the ESP documentation talks about "rows" and "columns," it is talking about a grid of these primary search servers logically arranged in rows and columns. Handling more content means adding more columns; handling more searches means adding more rows. It is possible to have a one row by one column grid, for a small low-traffic system, or perhaps a development system, although generally we'd consider a one column by two row grid as the minimum.

Scaling the Amount of Data

To scale up the amount of content that can be searched, additional "columns" are added. To remember this, it may be helpful to envision additional grain silos or piles of poker chips, "more stuff." Depending on your machines, the content being indexed, and probably dozens of other factors, a nominal load is 5 to 10 million documents per column. If there's a requirement to handle a particularly large amount of data, say 100 million documents, and the prospect of 10 to 20 columns is daunting, there may be ways to optimize for fewer columns. This would be a good topic to discuss with the ESP sales team or consultants.

Other search engines sometimes refer to this as adding "shards" or "sharding," essentially slicing up large amounts of indexing work among multiple systems.

Latency and Updates

When a source document is modified, it takes a finite amount of time before a full-text search sees that change. Although changes to documents may not be quite as costly as a complete re-index, it's still a nontrivial operation. If a search system requires particularly low latency, or there are an above average number of updates being performed, this also increases the number of columns required. Designing a system for handling rapid indexing requirements and lots of changes is very similar to designing a system to handle more content.

Metadata and Pipelines

Outside of the primary rows and columns grid are supporting machines. Generally, as more content is handled, systems also need more document-processing pipeline machines, although this may not scale linearly. If documents have a lot of fields, or if document pipelines are particularly complex, then substantially more document-processing machines may be needed. These resources can be particularly critical in low-latency systems.

Licensing and Content

Search licenses are often tied to the amount of content. Make sure that you understand your data in terms of document size and count, and understand whether your license is based on content or document index size.

Scaling the Number of Searches

To scale up the number of searches that can be handled, additional "rows" are added. To remember this, it may be helpful to envision slippery plastic lunch trays in a busy cafeteria being pulled out by students, or more tracks going back and forth at a really big train station, "more customers."

Average and Peak QPS

Estimating how many queries run per second can be difficult, since search activity often fluctuates throughout the day, often much more than document updates.

Most webmasters know their query volume in terms queries per day or per month or, in the best case, possibly down to the queries during peak hours. However, a consistently responsive search application needs to handle peak loads, not just the average load. If your ESP license has a QPS (queries per second) cap, it will be rated for peak QPS, not average. Converting from average QPS to peak QPS is tricky without actual data at that scale. Different sites have different activity profiles, so the ratio of peak to average is very site-specific. It is generally not safe to assume that it's just double the traffic or five times the traffic; we've seen ratios of over 20 to 1. What makes this even more critical is that end users are directly exposed to search slowdowns, and will notice even a half-second delay, whereas few users would notice if a document has 1 vs. 2 minutes of index latency.

Our advice is to base this on actual data at the second-by-second scale, when available. The only mitigating factor for doing this seemingly large QPS inflation is that many sites overestimate their traffic, based on very optimistic growth projections. Even if the site is a huge success, most applications don't see all that traffic show up on day 1. Since rows can be added over time, instead of implementing needlessly large buildups, the buildups can instead be spread out over time. The only issue here is that provisioning new systems can take months in some organizations, so a phased buildup has to be more proactive than reactive to staying ahead of the growth curve.

Like estimating ESP column indexing capacity, calculating how many queries per second a row of servers can handle has many variables. We generally think of ESP rows as handling twenty-five to possibly hundreds of queries per second, although it's impossible for us to give exact numbers. Some of the variables to keep in mind include how large typical searches are, the type of search operators and matches being done, options that were selected in the index profile, amount of metadata being retrieved, and what advanced results list options have been enabled. Sorting and facets can consume more resources and lower QPS capacity.

Other search engines usually handle heavy query loads through the use of replication; the same search index is available from multiple servers, and searches are distributed among these resources. This is conceptually very similar to what ESP rows accomplish, although there can be differences in the implementation details.

Failover Rows

ESP can automatically route searches to other active rows if a particular search row goes down. So, in addition to providing higher overall QPS, additional rows also provide higher reliability through redundancy. We said earlier that, although you can have a 1x1 grid of search servers, the minimum is usually 1 column by 2 rows in order to maintain failover capability.

Don't Bet Entirely on Caching

Some architects believe that many of their searches will be similar and, therefore, if search results can be cached, they could save on equipment and even possible licensing costs.

Pure caching of results, where the search engine is not even contacted, tends to not be the panacea that some envision. The reality is that, in most search applications, the number of identical searches that occur within a given cache time is not sufficient to result in a substantial savings. The occurrence of duplicate searches goes even further as query length increases or the system is used by full-time knowledge workers.

So, if you're serving popular DVD rental titles, you might have a fair amount of query overlap, but if you've got engineers pasting error logs into your search box, that overlap goes way down.

INTEGRATING WITH A TAXONOMY

The good news is that ESP supports taxonomies; in terms of the infrastructure, it's part of the base functionality. If taxonomy data is available in an index, ESP can be configured to display it.

The not-so-great news is that "supporting" a taxonomy and actually "having" a taxonomy are two different things. Where does the taxonomy itself come from? And how do documents get put into the tree? These questions are not so easy to answer.

But before diving into that, we need to review a few things.

Background and Definitions

"Taxonomy" is such a broadly used term that we need to talk about what we mean by it, in terms of the base ESP engine.

A *taxonomy* is a set of concepts or labels that are organized in a hierarchal manner, often called a "tree."

Unlike some search engines, the base ESP taxonomy doesn't include the rules or searches that put the documents into this tree.

Types of Taxonomies

We generally divide taxonomies into three broad categories:

➤ **Subject-based taxonomy** — This is the traditional organization by subject. Subject-based taxonomies are created by domain experts. Some classic examples would include the Dewey Decimal System and the categorization of life on Earth into kingdom, phylum, class, order, family, genus and species — you do remember the Linnaean system from high school biology class, right? A more modern example is how Yahoo! and DMOZ.org organize subjects from broad to specific as you go down the tree.

Figure 9-1 shows several subject based abbreviated taxonomies. The taxonomy on the left is the results of a search for "bush" and the search engine is showing the subject categories for documents containing that word. As a proper name, the U.S. has had two presidents with that surname. Several musical acts have also had that name. "bush" also applies to plants and several types of beer, and in the latter case then engine has also matched the alternate sound-alike spelling "Busch." By clicking one of these hyperlinks the person searching can quickly drill down to that subject area.

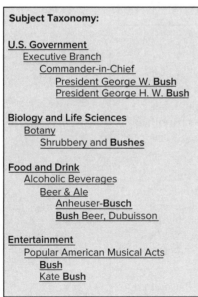

Example: public Internet search

Example: Enterprise portal

FIGURE 9-1

➤ **Content-based taxonomy** — Organizing the specific data you already have into categories and subcategories. For example, a company might organize website content at the top level by department, or research material might be sorted by source. This type of organization is sometimes amenable to automation.

Figure 9-2 shows several content-based taxonomies. The first one is organized by department and subdepartment. The second is organized by the type of data, Press Releases vs. Documentation, and then different rules underneath; press releases are then organized by year, but documentation is organized by subtype and then by document format.

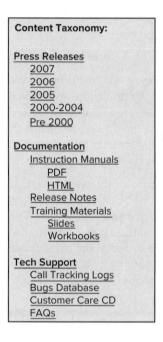

FIGURE 9-2

➤ **Behavior-based taxonomy** — Organized by what users are actually searching for, or around other user activities. For example, a behavior-based taxonomy could focus on popular searches derived from search analytics. Another example is sites that are driven by user tagging of content.

Figure 9-3 shows a taxonomy that highlights the topics users have been searching for the most. Most users seem to be looking for automobiles, real estate, and professional services. And within autos, there are particular brands of luxury and used cars that are being searched for. The property and service search activity indicate similar preferences.

Figure 9-4 shows a different type of behavior-based taxonomy of sorts. On this site users are allowed to tag certain products with keywords, and those keywords are displayed in alphabetical order, with their font size indicating how many times each tag has been used. Some products could be associated with more than one tag on this page, for example a TV set could be tagged with

FIGURE 9-3

both its type (LCD or Plasma), and its brand. This type of tag cloud is not considered by some to be a real taxonomy because it doesn't have any hierarchy to it. All tags are equal, aside from their frequency of occurrence, so this taxonomy is essentially "flat." And product attributes, types and brands are all mixed in together, whereas a traditional taxonomy would break them out separately. But there's no *requirement* for a taxonomy to be tightly segregated or tree-like, it was just the traditional way. These tag clouds are a very popular style of organizing documents,

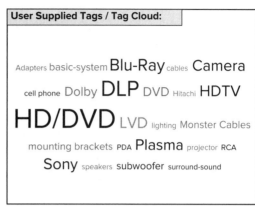

FIGURE 9-4

enough so that it's been given a special name of "Folksonomy," essentially a taxonomy created by people ("folks" like you and I!)

Many taxonomies are a blend of the first two. Modern taxonomies tend to be very pragmatic and evolve over time.

Taxonomies Versus Ontologies

For casual users, these are very similar concepts, but there are differences. Ontologies are often broader in scope. In some cases a taxonomy could be considered a subset of a larger ontology, a taxonomy "tree" in an ontological "forest." Ontologies can organize topics from multiple perspectives. Golf can appear as both a human activity and also a type of sporting apparel, for example.

Ontologies have a more controlled vocabulary, more specific definitions of conceptual relationships, and more rigorous methodologies than taxonomies. Taxonomies vary by how much additional information they contain. A taxonomy can be just a logical grouping of a subject, possibly with or without supporting terms, and whether or not data and actions have been associated with each node.

The preference for one term over another can depend on the group that's discussing it. *Ontology* seems to be preferred by academics and deep researchers, while *taxonomy* is almost universally used in the commercial space.

Other Terms Associated with Taxonomies

Topics and *Topic Trees* have been used by at least two companies to refer to taxonomies.

A *knowledge base*, or *KBase*, may also refer to a taxonomy or ontology. In addition to the base taxonomy, there may be a set of documents that have been matched up, in which each document has been assigned to one or more taxonomy nodes. In this usage a "taxonomy" = "just structure," whereas "knowledge base" = "structure" + "data."

Other terms that are sometimes associated with taxonomies are agents, profiles, saved searches, and rule sets. Depending on the vendor, there may be an action associated with the taxonomy. In some systems, you can flag a particular node or branch in a taxonomy and tell the software to perform some action whenever a new matching document is found. For example, whenever an intelligence communiqué matches the Terrorism topic notify Colonel Frye immediately. In this case a "taxonomy"

= "just structure," whereas "agents" = "structure" + "action." Saved searches and rule sets can be much simpler than a typical taxonomy. Agents, on the other hand, were a heavily used and hyped software industry and computer science term. Of course "agents" also have broader definitions well beyond the scope of this book.

A *folksonomy* is a newer type of taxonomy where users tag content. The photo and video tagging on sites like Flickr and YouTube are a type of folksonomy. In our classification of taxonomies we'd refer to that as a *behavior-based taxonomy*, since it is driven by users' actions. In addition to being community driven, folksonomies are often not hierarchal; there is typically no tree structure to tags.

Another set of related terms include *Concepts, NLP (Natural Language Processing), Semantic Analysis, LSA (Latent Semantic Analysis)*, and the *Semantic Web*. These terms are used by many of the same companies that talk about taxonomies and ontologies. Although the terms have broader definitions, in this context, the vendors are referring to their technology that assists in creating taxonomies and/or processing documents.

Although you may not want to memorize all these terms, having this list around may help in translating vendor jargon.

Faceted Navigation and Taxonomies

Taxonomies and facets are both examples of a broader class of results list navigators, which includes all of those clickable things presented to a user along with their matching documents. Results list navigators also include tag clouds, document clusters, clickable timelines of matches, sorting, related searches, and any other action a user can take to drill down into their results. Microsoft calls facets *refiners*.

Taxonomies deal with overall groups of documents. Faceted navigation tends to deal more with structured data within a document and field level. They can represent document metadata, database fields, or entities that have been extracted in the FAST document pipeline.

Of course, ESP supports facets and taxonomies. Although both can be used in the same application, this might lead to a complex search interface and, therefore, can be confusing to casual users.

We generally prefer faceted navigation if there is enough high-quality data present to support it. eCommerce sites tend to make heavy use of product attributes in facets, giving users many options for drilling down into results. In some cases, a very limited taxonomy is added to represent product categories.

Taxonomies are certainly better in domains where very detailed taxonomies are available and the user community is familiar with the concept. From a user interface standpoint, there's overlap between complex facets and taxonomies, which is not surprising since they are both results list navigators.

Taxonomies as a Symptom?

This is where the really interesting conversation begins! Do you really need a taxonomy?

If this were just a technical book we would commence with the bits and bytes of how to jam taxonomy data into ESP, but the ESP documentation already covers those low-level details. What you should really ask is whether or not taxonomies are even applicable for your specific application, or the best choice. Although this section is all about taxonomies, surprisingly the answer to the question of whether you even need a taxonomy is sometimes a resounding "No!"

Some application designers consider using taxonomies in the vague hope that this will somehow "fix" search, without being exactly sure how or why. They may not even be aware of the other techniques out there. They've heard the term "taxonomy" and thought it sounded promising. We call this "taxonomies as a symptom," but we're not talking about *you* of course!

A simple fix for this situation is to consider the other technologies and enumerate why taxonomies are a better fit. These other types of navigators were listed in the previous section. The type of navigator you choose will have a lot to do with the specific data being used and the business requirements to be met. If the business requirements include leveraging existing industry-specific taxonomies that are key to R&D or library sciences projects, then ESP has got you covered!

Taxonomy Workflow

At a very high level, the project workflow would be:

1. Design or acquire the taxonomy.
2. Create taxonomy rules, in the language of the engine you're using.
3. Apply the rules to new documents as they arrive.
4. Display and use taxonomies in the search interface.
5. Test, tweak, and maintain.

For projects that are a good fit for taxonomies, Step 1 has probably already been anticipated and possibly started. Step 5 is equally apparent. So, it's likely that you need to design or acquire a taxonomy and, of course, it will need to be maintained over time.

And although Step 4 might sound like the most difficult, ESP has actually got that built in! If taxonomy data is present, ESP can easily use it.

This leaves us with Steps 2 and 3, creating taxonomy rules, and applying them to new documents as they arrive. Of these, Step 3 is normally the easier task. Applying rules to new documents is normally handled in the document-processing pipeline. After a pipeline stage is installed, or written, it should either work or fail; it's an automated process either way.

Step 2, creating or translating rules, is the task that's most wide open. There are countless ways it could be done, and this is where a taxonomy vendor's value-add really comes into play. If you acquire a taxonomy from a vendor that specifically supports ESP, then both of these should be covered. We do suggest a very thorough review of how the vendor will integrate with ESP and the taxonomy administrators.

Taxonomy Rule Sets

The quickest way to build a custom taxonomy is to license a base taxonomy for your industry from a third party, and then overlay your organization's internal vocabulary on top of that.

FAST Partner Teragram

Previously FAST had partnered with a company called Teragram to provide a rule creation environment. That old partnership is a bit cloudy these days because FAST was acquired by Microsoft and Teragram was acquired by SAS, both of which are very large companies. We believe this product is still available, although perhaps not through Microsoft. For the latest information, please ask your Microsoft search sales representative or drop us a line.

The way this package works is rather interesting:

1. A human operator runs the Teragram taxonomy interface.

2. The operator shows Teragram different sets of training documents and tells the system which category/taxonomy branch each document belongs in.

3. Teragram then analyzes the words in the various documents, to figure out which words are common to documents in a category and which words are different between categories.

4. Teragram uses these statistics to create a set of rules based on the words that are best suited for distinguishing between the various taxonomy categories.

5. These Teragram rules are then imported or saved into the Teragram categorization server.

6. The ESP document processing pipeline is configured to send specified fields during document processing to the Teragram categorization server. Teragram will return taxonomy categories for the document if the preconfigured rules and thresholds are met.

The marketplace around Microsoft's search products is rapidly evolving and other products for various FAST/Microsoft engines will likely be available when you read this.

Rolling Your Own

If you are creating your own taxonomy, you need to create some type of ruleset and then call upon it from the document-processing pipeline.

Although the fancier Teragram engine makes use of the full text of the documents and advanced statistical algorithms, we've found you can do quite a bit of useful work just looking at metadata fields, such as the document's URL. Once you get that working, you can get fancier by looking at other fields or the text of the documents as well.

For a simple example, you can even combine two of the steps into one. Repeating a portion of our previous task list:

2. Create taxonomy rules, in the language of the engine you're using.

3. Apply the rules to new documents as they arrive.

Steps 2 and 3 can put into a single pipeline stage written in the Python programming language. Python is a popular language in the search engine industry and is also popular with some statisticians, and AI and machine learning programmers, so learning it can certainly come in handy! Although it's not mentioned much in the Microsoft documentation, Python is still the primary pipeline language in ESP, although you can call out to processes written in other languages if you need to.

Outline of the Procedure

Here is an overview of the process of creating a custom document pipeline:

1. Create Python code and put it into the correct directory. For rules-based stages, you could design a Python stage that reads in external text files, such as a site map.

2. Create an XML configuration for that stage in another directory. This will include parameters for accessing the external data file.

3. Restart document processing nodes so that it sees the new stage.

4. Clone a pipeline to contain the new stage.

5. Decide where in the pipeline the new stage will go.

6. Instantiate and configure the new stage in that pipeline. This includes setting the parameters to access any external data files your stage needs.

7. Create a new collection or modify an existing one to use the new pipeline.

8. Feed documents through the pipeline.

9. Test and debug.

Most of these topics are covered in detail in the *ESP Document Processor Integration Guide*. You might also want to check out the guides for Content Integration, ESP Classifier, CCTK, Configuration, Query Integration, Security, Enterprise Crawler, File Traverser, and DB/XML Indexing. We realize that's a lot to cover, but it's better to have too much documentation than not enough.

Sample Stage Python Code

This example assumes the FASTSEARCH environment variable is set, for example to `C:\esp`, or a similar directory on Linux/Unix.

On a Windows system this file would go in `%FASTSEARCH%\lib\python2.3\processors\`. On a Unix or Linux system it would go in `$FASTSEARCH/lib/python2.3/processors/`.

A really simple example would just look at literal URL prefixes and map them to different taxonomy trees. So, the example pipeline stage code shown below in Listing 9-1 is slightly more interesting. We'll map documents based on CGI parameters. This is a very common form of URL for sites driven by a content management system (CMS). In such sites, all of the URLs have a very similar URL structure, but logically they belong to different parts of the site. This Python stage adds that category structure back into to the documents.

Available for download on Wrox.com

LISTING 9-1: MyMapper.py

```
"""
Map URLs into a Taxonomy based on a CGI field
Read from file:
C:\esp\etc\processors\MyMapper\my-cgi-codes.txt
Format:
code(tab)category


Reprinted with permission from New Idea Engineering, Inc.
```

```
http://www.ideaeng.com
"""
from docproc import Processor
from docproc import ProcessorStatus
from string import split
import urllib
import re
import os
import sys
from pylib import Logger

class MyMapper(Processor.Processor):
    # Specific to this pipeline
    def setupRegex( self, parameters ):
        cgiField = self.GetParameter( 'cgi_field' )
        patternStr = '[\?&]' + cgiField + '=([^\?&#]+)'
        self.myPattern = re.compile( patternStr, re.DOTALL|re.MULTILINE
|re.IGNORECASE)
        filterStr = self.GetParameter( 'uri_filter_opt' ).strip()
        if filterStr != "":
            self.myFilter = re.compile( filterStr, re.DOTALL|re.MULTILINE|
re.IGNORECASE)
        else:
            self.myFilter = None


    # Specific to this pipeline
    def setupMappings( self, parameters ):
        debug = False
        mapFileName = self.GetParameter('mapping_file')
        # Build a path, relative to where other stages' config data is
        fullFilePath = os.path.join( os.environ['FASTSEARCH'], "etc",
"config_data", self.GetName(), mapFileName )
        if( debug ):
            log( log.FLOG_STATUS, self.GetName() + ': opening file ' +
fullFilePath )
        # Read in the file
        data = open(fullFilePath, 'r').read().split("\n")
        # Initialize our hash/dictionary
        self.myMap = {}
        # Parse each line
        lineno = 0
        for line in data:
            lineno += 1
            if( debug ):
                log( log.FLOG_STATUS, self.GetName() + ': ' + fullFilePath + ':' +
str(lineno) + ": '" + line + "'" )
            # Ignore blank and commented out lines
            if line == "" or line.startswith( "#" ):
                if( debug ):
                    log( log.FLOG_STATUS, self.GetName() + ': skipping
blank/comment
line' )
                continue
            parts = line.split("\t")
            if( debug ):
                log( log.FLOG_STATUS, self.GetName() + ': ' + fullFilePath + ':' +
```

```
str(lineno) + ": " + str( parts ) )
            code = parts[0].lower().strip()
            taxo = parts[1].strip()
            if( debug ):
                log( log.FLOG_STATUS, self.GetName() + ': ' + fullFilePath + ':' +
str(lineno) + ": code='" + code + "', taxo='" + taxo + "'" )
            self.myMap[ code ] = taxo
        # end for each line
        # Sanity check
        if len(self.myMap) < 1:
            log( log.FLOG_WARNING, self.GetName() + ': No valid entries found in '
+
 fullFilePath )
        else:
            log( log.FLOG_STATUS, self.GetName() + ': Loaded ' +
str(len(self.myMap)) + '
entries from ' + fullFilePath )

    # Called when module is loaded
    def __init__(self, name):
        Processor.Processor.__init__(self, name)
        log( log.FLOG_STATUS, self.GetName() + ' loaded, in Python '
+ sys.version )

    # Called by FAST ESP at start, and when config has changed
    def ConfigurationChanged(self, parameters):
        self.setupRegex( parameters )
        self.setupMappings( parameters )
        self.defaultValue = self.GetParameter('default_value')
        self.optSourceAttr = self.GetParameter('source_attribute_opt').strip()
        # self.srcSeparator = self.GetParameter( 'source_separator' )
        log( log.FLOG_STATUS, self.GetName() + ' started.' )


    # Called by FAST ESP for each document
    def Process(self, uri, document):
        taxo = self.defaultValue
        finished = False

        if self.myFilter:
            try:
                test = self.myFilter.findall(uri)[0]
                log(log.FLOG_STATUS, "Filter: Allow '" + uri + "'" )
            except:
                log(log.FLOG_STATUS, "Filter: DISallow '" + uri + "'" )
                finished = True
        else:
            log(log.FLOG_STATUS, "No filter")

        # Do we still want to look at it?
        # We have a default from above
        if not finished:

            # Which attribute do we want to look at?
            attr = uri
            if self.optSourceAttr != "":
```

```
                    attrName = self.optSourceAttr
                    log(log.FLOG_STATUS, "Using field '" + attrName + "'" )
                    if document.Has( attrName ):
                        attr = document.Get( attrName )
                        # attr = attr.split( self.srcSeparator )
                    else:
                        log( log.FLOG_WARNING, self.GetName() + ': No attribute ' +
attrName
+ ' in doc ' + uri + '; will use use uri' )
                else:
                    log(log.FLOG_STATUS, "Using default uri" )

                # We can consider multiple values
                # So promote everything to a list
                attrValues = attr
                if not type(attrValues) in (tuple, list):
                    attrValues = list( [attrValues] )

                # Try each value
                foundOne = False
                for value in attrValues:
                    code = None
                    # Parse the URL, look for our CGI field and value
                    try:
                        log(log.FLOG_STATUS, "checking '" + value + "'" )
                        code = self.myPattern.findall(value)[0]
                    except:
                        log(log.FLOG_STATUS, "Did not find a code")
                        code = None

                    # If OK so far, now lookup the code
                    if code:
                        # We always normalize for dictionary lookups
                        norm = code.lower().strip()
                        log(log.FLOG_STATUS,"Looking up normalized code '"+norm+"'")
                        if self.myMap.has_key( norm ):
                            taxo = self.myMap[norm]
                            foundOne = True
                            log(log.FLOG_STATUS,"Found taxo '"+taxo+"'")
                            break
                        else:
                            log(log.FLOG_STATUS, "No taxo for " + norm )
                    # end for each value
                # end if the URL matched our optional filter

                # Save our answer (which may still be the DEFAULT)
                log(log.FLOG_STATUS, "Final: Setting taxo='" + taxo + "'" )
                document.Set( "taxonomy", taxo )
                # And we're done!
                return ProcessorStatus.OK

# Only used if trying to test from the command line
if __name__=='__main__':
    from docproc import Document     # needed only for standalone mode vs.
in content processing pipelines
```

```
        from docproc import DocumentLogging      # needed for document level logging,
    i.e.: document.GetLogger().Info('message')

        stage = MyMapper('MyMapper')     # instantiate stage
        stage.RegisterParameters({\
            'HostName': 'localhost',
            'Port': 16089,
            'mapping_file': r'C:\esp\etc\config_data\MyMapper\my-cgi-codes-codes.txt',
            'cgi_field': 'topic',
            'default_value': 'General',
            'source_attribute_opt': '',
            'uri_filter_opt': r'^http://www\.mysite\.com/articles\.cgi\?id=[0-9]+'
            })

        stage.ConfigurationChanged( stage.GetParameters() )
        # build a test document to run your stage on
        docid = "doc1"    # every doc must have a docid
        url = ""http://www.mysite.com/articles.cgi?id=1234&topic=5"
        testdoc = Document.Document( docid ) # create document to send to stage
        # set logging so stage logging can be captured
        testdoc.SetLogger( DocumentLogging.Logger() ) # captures doc logging
        # set attributes on the document needed by this stage
        testdoc.Set( 'url', url )
        testdoc.Set( 'data','my test data' )
        # run the test document through the stage
        stage.Process(url, testdoc)
```

Sample Stage Configuration File

Now we need to tell ESP about the new pipeline code.

The example configuration file shown in Listing 9-2 assumes the FASTSEARCH environment variable is set to `C:\esp`, or a similar directory on Linux/Unix.

On a Windows system this file would go in `%FASTSEARCH%\etc\ processors\`. On a Unix or Linux system it would go in `$FASTSEARCH/etc/processors/`.

LISTING 9-2: MyMapper.xml

```
<processors>
<processor>
  <load module="processors.MyMapper" class="MyMapper"/>
  <desc>
    <brief>
        Will read in a list of codes and taxonomy names
        to match them against
    </brief>
  </desc>
  <config>
     <param name="mapping_file" value="codes.txt" type="string" />
     <param name="cgi_field" value="topic" type="string" />
     <param name="default_value" value="General" type="string" />
     <!-- A field to use ONLY if you can NOT get info from the main URL -->
```

```
        <param name="source_attribute_opt" value="" type="string" />
        <param name="uri_filter_opt" value="http://optional-inclusive-prefix-filter"
type="string" />
      </config>
      <ops>
        <add/><mod/>
      </ops>
    </processor>
    </processors>
```

Sample Mapping File

The sample file shown in Listing 9-3 maps certain section codes to areas of the website. The file can be anywhere as long as the path matches up with the configuration.

LISTING 9-3: my-cgi-codes.txt

```
5       Marketing
6       Marketing/Press Releases
7       Support
8       Support/Downloads
9       Support/Documentation
```

In Listing 9-3 the various topic IDs present in the URLs will be mapped back into the site hierarchy. If the taxonomy field is displayed in the results, visitors will be able to drill down into their search results. Chapter 8 has a thorough discussion of, and a sample of, ESP pipeline stages

A BRIEF OVERVIEW OF OTHER ADVANCED ESP FEATURES

ESP has a lot more features! As Microsoft integrates the FAST product line they are working to improve documentation and examples, or reengineering other components. The point here is that some advanced features are not thoroughly documented, and we can't make up for that here. What we can do is to make you aware that these features exist, why they're useful, and where you might go for more information.

Structural Analysis Toolkit

Structural Analysis Toolkit (STAN) is a very advanced entity extraction framework in ESP. It has a number of built-in rules that are used in some of the default document pipelines. For example, the News pipeline automatically extracts the names of people, places, and companies, using the STAN subsystem.

How Entities and Fields Relate to Navigators, Refiners, and Facets

It's helpful to provide clickable drill-down links in search results, to allow users to narrow down the scope of their search. For example, on a real estate search application a search for "colonial" might match thousands of listings. But if the results list includes hyperlinks for various cities and states, price ranges, and types of listings, users can quickly filter through the matches. These types of links are called facets, and they are a subset of overall results list navigators.

Figure 9-5 summarizes the evolution of facets. In the early days of search, companies put advanced search forms in their search applications, so that users could filter their search results against specific fields. This was a nice idea, but rarely used. Programmers realized that the exact same filtering logic could be applied **after** an initial search was done, so that instead of displaying a form before a search was run, those same fields could be displayed as clickable hyperlinks in the results list. Clicking a link would re-run the search, but this time with the filter active. Although this results in the user performing two searches instead of one, it saves time because it saves on typing, and perhaps requires a bit less up-front thought. The figure also shows parametric search, which is very similar to facets, and was an intermediate step in this evolution. Parametric search was essentially facets, but without document counts and without zero-results checks.

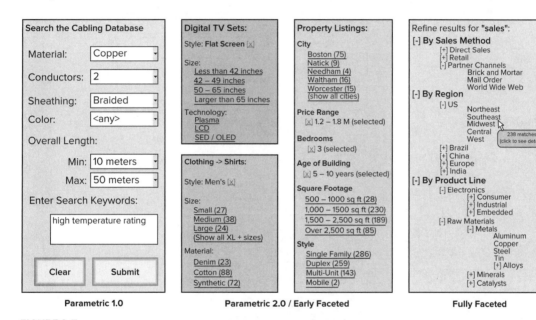

FIGURE 9-5

This all sounds great if the real estate data is coming from a database that has fields for city, state, price, and type of listing — the point being you need field data if you want to present facets, or do you?

Imagine a competing real estate search engine that actually has more listings, but where all of the listings are just blobs of text taken from various classified ad sources. The attributes of the properties are still usually there, in the text of the listings, but not in a structured way that can be displayed in facets.

Figures 9-6 and 9-7 illustrate this difference. In Figure 9-6 the first search application's data comes from well defined sources like databases or structured XML and documents, where the metadata is well defined. So it's very easy to map that metadata into clickable facets.

But Figure 9-7 represents data coming from many sources and is unlikely to have any consistent metadata.

This is where entity extraction and the STAN toolkit come into play. Using STAN, you can bridge the gap between unstructured text and structured navigators. You can recognize and tag city names, amounts of money, zip codes and area codes, and other helpful information. Once extracted, the information is stored in ESP fields, just as if it had come from a database, so it is available for faceted searches. But be aware of the fine virtual fine print, "some assembly required."

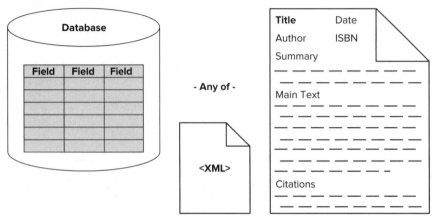

FIGURE 9-6

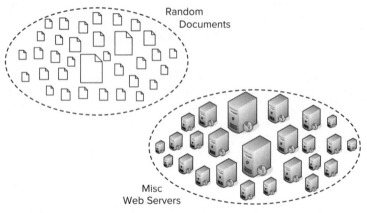

FIGURE 9-7

Figure 9-8 conceptually illustrates entity extraction. Even with the text of a document, certain text patterns are relatively easy to recognize as a person, place, or other specific type of asset. Phone numbers, addresses, social security numbers, and dates have some patterns that can be recognized with rules. Of course phone numbers and addresses have some variation, even within a specific country, so the rules need to be flexible, or be expressed in a number of ways. Recognizing peoples' names, or other proper nouns representing cities and states, is often accomplished with the help of dictionar-

Entity Extraction

Martin Luther King, Jr.
(408) 555-1212

1600 Pennsylvania Ave.
Washington, DC 20500

001-01-0001
July 4th, 1776

$4,725,000.000

FIGURE 9-8

ies. A simple rule might notice a run of words with initial capital letters, and suspect that it's a proper noun, but determining whether it names a person, place, or company name often requires a dictionary. Even this can be inexact, since cities and companies are sometimes named in honor of a person.

Figure 9-9 shows some examples of facets that could be displayed after entities have been extracted. This is a bit different than the previous facets in that we may not know the relationship of the person or place to the document in question. For example, is a listed person the author of the document, or the subject of the document? Perhaps that person appeared in the CC field (Carbon Copy) of an email message. But if you click one of the people or places, the documents will be narrowed down to only those in which that name appears, and hence it's still very useful.

People:
Bob Walsh
Mary Ng
Satish Murtha
Dave Morgan
Anne Chen
Deborah Shea

Places:
Charlotte, NC
Chicago, IL
Dallas, TX
Denver, CO
Jacksonville, FL
Seattle, WA
San Jose, CA

FIGURE 9-9

Various Methods for Entity Extraction

There are three main techniques for entity extraction, and STAN supports all of them:

➤ **Dictionary-based** — You list the names of people, places, and companies in large dictionaries, and the system spots them in the text.

➤ **Rule-based** — You look for sets of digits, numbers, or other combinations of punctuation text, such as phone numbers and zip codes.

➤ **Hybrid** — Combing various rules and dictionary matches; this is something STAN really excels at!

STAN goes well beyond many other entity extraction systems in that, as matches are found, they can be used as conditions in larger matches.

For example, a U.S. zip code has two primary forms: five digits or five digits followed by a hyphen followed by four more digits. This is easy to spot with a pattern rule. A large percentage of cities, states, and street names can generally be identified by dictionaries. STAN can then notice that it has a number, street, city, state, and zip code and decide it has a valid U.S. postal address. Other systems can do this as well.

STAN can go further, however; it can have other rules for itemized product listings, and then a page with two addresses, a block of line items, and amounts of money are likely to be product orders, invoices, or shipping manifests. This higher-level ability to recognize broader attributes of a document can be extended all the way to page recognition — for example, sorting out press releases from product collateral from resumes and order forms.

This all sounds great, but in its current form adding complex STAN systems is a fair amount of work. It gets more complicated if you're dealing with content from different languages and countries, which requires additional dictionaries and many more formats of entities. STAN does accommodate applying different sets of rules, such as recognizing the U.S. vs. German format postal addresses, depending on the content. Extracting entities for different countries means creating additional STAN files.

STAN Workflow

At a very high level, the tasks for STAN include the following:

1. Create custom dictionaries to spot different terms. You'll have different dictionaries for different tasks.

2. Create and refine XML rule files, which include dictionary lookups, simple pattern matching, and rules based on other rules having matched.

3. Configure a custom document-processing stage to use the STAN rules and dictionaries.

4. Create a custom document pipeline to use the custom STAN stage.

5. Create or modify a collection to use that pipeline.

6. Test, debug, and refine.

If you've read this chapter from the beginning, you'll notice this is similar to the taxonomy example. Many of the fancy things users like in their search results actually operate with data that originates in the document pipeline.

Getting all this just right can be time-consuming. Although we suspect that Microsoft will eventually release a nicer graphical tool for doing these types of things, at the moment you need the following:

➤ Knowledge of XML.

➤ Knowledge of regular expressions, AKA "Regex."

➤ Knowledge of the content, entities rules, and data sets (most organizations learn lots of things about their data that they never knew during this highly iterative process).

➤ Knowledge of command-line tools for compiling and managing dictionaries and the ESP dictman tool.

➤ General experience with web administration, scripting, and debugging skills.

In addition to understanding the previous technologies, keep these limitations in mind:

➤ Though it would be nice to add terms to some of ESP's entity dictionaries, some of them are digitally protected and cannot be exported. Although you can query most of them with dictman utility, you can't get a global view of all them and merge them with your own lists.

➤ If the application is multilingual, then knowledge of the various languages and the regional differences in how entities are formatted, such as phone numbers and addresses. A healthy understanding of character sets and character encoding is also helpful.

➤ ESP's documentation is less than thorough on some of the steps. Even within FAST/ Microsoft, advanced knowledge of this tool isn't widespread.

These aren't criticisms; this is a very powerful tool, and if you really need it, it's there. This is the type of tool that simply isn't available in most other engines and is one of things that makes ESP "industrial strength."

Relevancy Tweaking

Search engine relevancy has been written about many times. FAST ESP has more ways to adjust and tune relevancy than almost any other commercial engine on the market. If your business lives and dies by search, then you may want to micromanage every aspect of relevancy. This is in contrast to engines that promise to do everything automatically, and wonderfully, but may limit how much you can adjust them, which is more of the "appliance" mindset.

Most engines have passable default relevancy rules and, despite vendor hype, most of them can benefit from tuning of some sort. Like most other items involving software, with extreme flexibility comes increased complexity. With FAST, the controls are there, should you decide you need them, or you can leave them alone. At the extreme end of flexibility and complexity are the open source search engines. Lucene and Solr fully disclose their entire relevancy algorithms, down to the bit-by-bit level, in the form of wiki documentation and actual Java source code. If you're reading this book, you've probably decided to go with a commercial engine for various business or technical reasons, and ESP is probably the most flexible engine in the mainstream commercial space.

Default Relevancy

Most engines, including ESP, include some variant of the TF/IDF algorithm, which can be summarized in two deceptively simple points:

➤ **TF (term frequency)** — If a term appears more times in document A than in document B, then document A is more likely to be related to that term than document B is. There's usually some scaling involved to compensate for short vs. long documents.

➤ **IDF (inverse document frequency)** — If term X appears in many documents, but term Y appears in only a few, then term X is *less* valuable in distinguishing between documents than term Y.

The engines combine these two factors in some fancy way.

Don't let the X and Y in the second part distract you. Suppose that your company's name appears on darn near every page on your website (say "Acme" for example), whereas the word "support" appears on only a fraction of your overall pages. If somebody goes to your site and searches for "Acme support," the word "support" is more valuable when sorting because Acme appears on all the pages. Yes, both words are important; it's just a question of which one is better for relevancy. If one page has the word "Acme" on it five times and "support" only once, and another page of similar size has "support" five times and "Acme" only once, that second page is more likely to be about "Acme support." Acme is less useful because it appears on every page; it's very easy for Acme to appear five times. But if the word "support" appears five times on a page, that page is very likely to be about "Acme support."

The general TF/IDF algorithms worked well for a long time, when the number of documents was limited. As document counts grew and grew, however, a very large number of documents could have many instances of two or three words on a page, so sorting them by the TF/IDF rankings started to give somewhat random results. The key point, however, is that TF/IDF is only looking at the content of the actual documents and the terms in the user's query. It is a self-contained set of calculations.

Google's improved relevancy included folding in external link popularity data, and this helped launch them during the .com days of the late 1990s. Endeca also went beyond the TF/IDF model; they allowed companies to fold external business data into relevancy calculations. Web 2.0 sites allow users to flag documents with 1 to 5 stars or give them a thumbs up, and then these ratings are folded in. All of these techniques leverage external information, data that was not directly part of the documents' text.

ESP can do this too, if you have the external data to overlay. FAST offers many ways to tune relevancy — another one of its industrial-strength capabilities. It's there if you need it!

Relevancy Tuning Options in ESP

There are some ESP concepts to be aware of when tuning FAST search. Some of these apply to other search engines as well, although FAST/Microsoft employees and ESP documentation tend to use specific words to refer to them.

➤ A *static boost* is something that is applied to a document at index time and affects the relative score of that document for all searches.

➤ A *dynamic boost* is an adjustment made on a per-query basis. So when a user does a specific search, this boosts a particular document.

➤ Popular searches — the searches that many users type in — can be individually tuned.

➤ The *long tail* is the opposite of popular searches. It refers to many unique searches that visitors do. Each particular search is only run once or twice, but the large number of these varied searches can actually represent a large percentage of overall search traffic. Since there are so many different searches, it's not practical to tune all of them individually, so a different strategy is needed.

➤ *Organic ranking* is the order of documents that the engine would normally give back, without being specifically told to bring certain documents to the top individual searches. In other words, for your top 100 searches, you might want to create specific rules that force certain pages to the top of the results. For all of those other searches in the long tail, however, you have to rely on the automatic organic ranking that search engine will provide. A good search engine doesn't rely exclusively on manually tuning every possible search.

➤ Many interesting relevancy-tuning tricks actually require special data to be indexed ahead of time. Because of this, many relevancy tweaks involve the ESP index profile and custom document pipeline stages. Earlier we discussed how Google and Endeca fold external data into the document index with custom data overlays. Using the index profile and document pipeline is the way you'd implement these types of tricks in ESP.

➤ ESP allows you to use different rank profiles for different searches. So, for example, somebody searching your intranet for marketing information might prefer more recent documents, whereas a researcher in the same company might value the source of the data. ESP can simultaneously support both of these use cases by having predefined rank profiles associated with the search application. Typically, these choices are made automatically for the user by the developers and administrators for each search application, although this could be exposed as an HTML form control for advanced users. Keep in mind that each rank profile might require different data to have been stored in the search index ahead of time, in different fields.

FAST ESP overall relevancy tuning includes:

➤ **Boosting proximity matches** — For example, if the words "white" and "house" appear next to each other in a document, give that document a higher score than if those two words were on separate pages. Even if the number of word occurrences and size of two documents were the same, the document with "white house" would score higher for the search "White House." This type of search is a very good candidate for adjustment in the index profile.

➤ **Adjusting the relevancy of documents from certain data sources** — This is the "quality" factor in the index profile.

➤ **Preferring documents that are more recent, what FAST calls "freshness"** — This assumes that you have accurate document dates!

➤ **Adjusting relevancy based on the text links pointing to a web page** — ESP calls this *authority*.

➤ **Increasing the importance of text in specific fields or zones in the document** — For example, the words in the title of a book or chapter are usually more important than the text.

➤ **Preferring documents that are geographically closer to a particular point, specified by longitude and latitude** — This can be a bit complex to implement.

➤ **Using the Search Business Center web interface** — You can boost certain documents against specific searches by using the Search Business Center web interface.

There are no built-in boosting parameters for elements like user ratings or user tags, or favoring documents that are clicked on more often. However, these can all be added by, you guessed it, injecting custom data in the document pipeline and the appropriate declarations in the index profile. Additionally, user queries can be augmented to use these fields at search time. The infrastructure is there for advanced developers to use.

FAST's Hybrid Security Model

ESP can store user credentials in the search index so that access to certain documents can be checked efficiently during a search, instead of filtering out lots of inaccessible documents later on. This type of query-based security is called *early binding*.

Figure 9-10 shows how the search index actually stores Access Control List (ACL) authorization information along with the regular document metadata.

Although it's generally more efficient, early binding security has one flaw in that a document's security might change just before the user does a search, and the ESP index would not reflect that updated access level yet. The worst case scenario is that an employee's access to a document is revoked the split second before they run a search, and they are still able to see the title and summary.

Figure 9-11 shows the older style of security filtering, in which the engine brings back all matching documents, and then checks each of them one at a time. This technique is called *late binding*, and while it is much less efficient, it does give the engine the most up-to-date information about access levels, as the document's access is checked with the external security system just before it's sent to the user. This is the one advantage of late binding security.

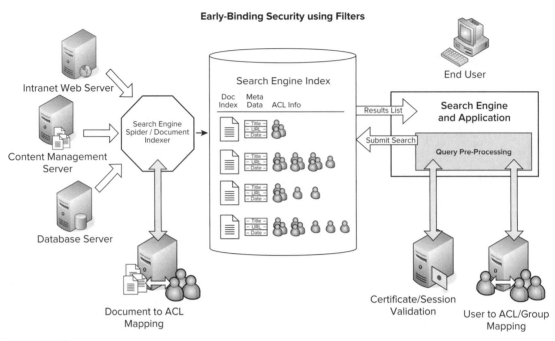

FIGURE 9-10

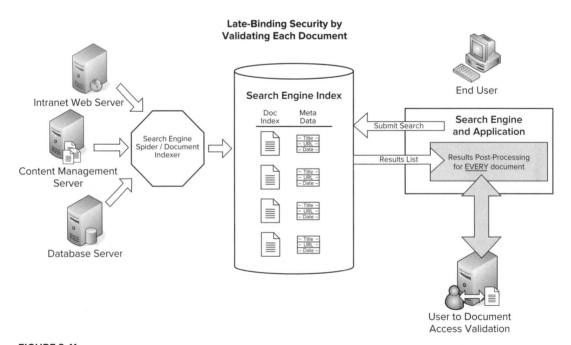

FIGURE 9-11

This is incredibly inefficient, however. If a new user only had access to about 1 percent of the company's content, then on average the system would need to check 1,000 documents with the external system just to display 10 results!

Fortunately, FAST ESP offers the benefits of both techniques by using a hybrid approach that employs both! ESP does an early binding search to prefilter all inaccessible documents. Then, as it's about to include each one to be formatted for display, it does the last minute check and actually contacts the external security system one last time. If access was recently revoked, the document is removed. This is way more efficient than just using late binding, because there are a relatively small number of documents to check, usually only 10.

There's a very unlikely edge case that this hybrid system doesn't handle perfectly. If, instead of being recently denied access, a user was actually granted access at the last minute, the early binding wouldn't see that and would not return the document. It would never have had a chance to be double-checked at the last moment. So, a user who was just granted access to a document a few seconds earlier might miss it. If the user searched again a little while later so that enough elapsed for the ESP index to be updated, he or she would see it. Having somebody not see something in an edge case, however, is generally much more acceptable than letting somebody glimpse classified stuff. Again, the odds of this happening are pretty small, and if the user just runs the search again a few seconds or minutes later he or she will see it. Most organizations consider this acceptable.

The *Security Access Module (SAM) Guide for ESP* is your gateway to this rather involved subject. Be warned that it gets a bit more complicated if users have completely different logins for different repositories that FAST is searching. It can map from one security domain to another, but it does take additional setup. It's there, however, if you need it!

Unsupervised Clustering and Noun Phrase Extraction

As mentioned before, there are many types of results list navigators. Most engines have links to go the next page of results or sort results by relevancy or date. More sophisticated engines like ESP also support facets and taxonomies. If you don't have enough structure in your data to drive facets, you can even use STAN to do sophisticated entity extraction, so that you can effectively "upgrade" your unstructured data.

Suppose, however, that *none* of those techniques is an option for you. You don't have structured data, you're not going after any of the standard entities that ESP can parse, and writing your own entity extraction rules is just completely out of the question. Suppose that you've even ruled out letting users tag your documents and photos, or there are just not enough users to arrive at a critical mass of tags. What then?

Unsupervised clustering is an attempt to add results list navigators to completely unstructured data, based solely on the words and phrases found in the text. This magic is accomplished by a set of basic Natural Language Processing (NLP) rules that know how to break apart sentences in various languages and then feed these fragments into various statistical algorithms to try to make some sense of it. The sentence-parsing rules and mathematical algorithms vary from vendor to vendor, and we think FAST produces some of the better results in this category as well.

The ability to extract metadata and use it as facets or refiners is unique to FSIS/FSIA/ESP 5.3 in the Microsoft/FAST search product line.

Figure 9-12 shows a number of noun phrases of the style produced by FAST. A noun phrase, as its name implies, consists of a primary noun, and then any qualifying words around it, typically adjectives. FAST Linguistics Guide states that nouns convey the majority of relevancy in comparison to other parts of speech.

ESP already includes quite a few dictionaries for various languages, so it is able to recognize nouns and their associated adjectives in most mainstream languages. Unlike some of the other advanced features, this one is mostly preconfigured.

Because of all the NLP and statistical ruminations, unsupervised clustering sounds "sexy" in a geeky sort of way. Some vendors have even pushed their clustering techniques as a primary selling point.

Clusters:
White House
State of the Union
Air Force One
binding resolution
U.S. Senate
2009 budget
bipartisan support
exit strategy
California budget
Campaign finance reform

FIGURE 9-12

However, the authors of this book have been around the software industry long enough that we actually want things to be useful, not just "cool." Although having the option of using unsupervised clustering is nice, we consider it a fallback position behind other more predictable navigator techniques. If you have high-quality structured data, use facets, or consider using entity extraction to populate facets. Or, if your content has a natural overall structure, consider using taxonomies. Unsupervised clustering is generally a last resort. An application needs navigators, and there's just no other option. In that case, ESP still has you covered, and it's a pretty nice implementation. It also makes for a cool demo, but beware of overpromising to your users.

And finally, beware of any unsupervised clustering demo that uses a limited set of subject matter, such as only medical texts, which are limited in scope and have a rather tightly controlled vocabulary. In the real world, enterprise search needs to deal with HR, engineering, support, and marketing documents, all in one big index. Clustering demos or proof-of-concept projects (POCs) would ideally use a similarly wide variety of content.

Federated Search

We end with what is potentially a cost saver for some applications but also something that can represent a fairly complex integration, federated search.

Figure 9-13 shows the traditional search engine model, where a central search engine indexes content and serves up search results across organizational boundaries. The same engine can provide results for different applications and groups of users. Note that, although conceptually this is one search instance, it would likely be installed on a number of cooperating servers, each handling different processing roles.

As shown in Figure 9-14, the idea behind Federated Search is that, instead of indexing all of your content into one giant search engine index, you can send a user's search to multiple engines that are already in place, and then just combine the results.

The potential cost savings here include:

➤ You avoid licensing fees that are tied to per-document or per-gigabyte metrics.

➤ It is more efficient to use the search that's already embedded into each repository.

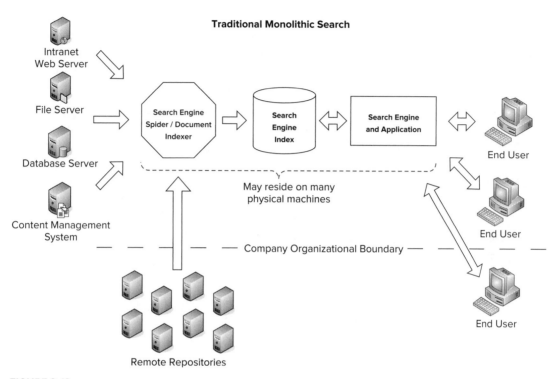

FIGURE 9-13

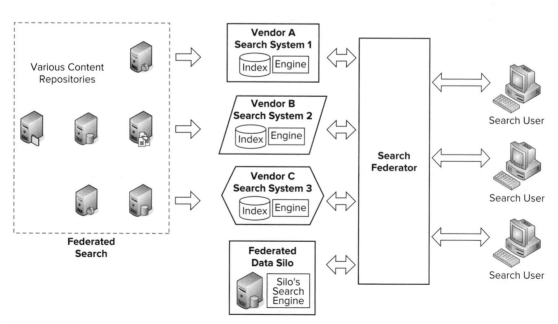

FIGURE 9-14

If your content management system (CMS), bug tracking, and tech support databases all have a search function built in, why not just use it? Why schlep all that data over the network to be indexed by a second search engine and have to pay extra for the privilege? Also, presumably each vendor is more familiar with their repository's structure, so they ought to be even better at searching their own data then some third-party engine.

This can be true in some cases, and ESP does have an optional federated search toolkit called Unity. So here again, if you need it, ESP has you covered. Microsoft is also pushing other forms of federated search, including SharePoint federation, IMS, and support for the OpenSearch standard.

The biggest issue with most low-end federated search platforms is that they only handle the simple case of combing results from various public sources. So they can combine results from Yahoo!, Google, and Bing, or perhaps they can search both Flickr and YouTube at the same time. This is very far away from what an Enterprise Class federated search needs to handle.

Issues that high-end federated search often need to handle include the following:

➤ Maintaining security credentials across disparate systems; this is similar to the SAM issues mentioned in the earlier section.

➤ Combing results from different engines in a meaningful and useful way even though they use complete different relevancy algorithms and scales.

➤ Interfacing with a large number of systems with different APIs, some of which may be internally developed. Some enterprise systems may not even have a formal API, so "screen scraping" of some form may be required.

➤ Mapping advanced search syntax between engines.

➤ Combing even simple navigation elements like Next Page and Sort By.

➤ Combing complex results list navigators like facets or taxonomies. It's very unlikely that the different systems will have the same sets of fields and values, so quite a bit of mapping needs to be done both at display time and then when processing a merged facet click.

At this time, no federated search tool on the market handles this complete feature set in a conveniently packaged, easy-to-configure way. Most advanced federated search projects require custom code at this point in time, regardless of any vendor's hype.

Therefore, ESP's Unity product takes the very reasonable strategy of offering a toolkit as well as some packaged repository connectors. The Unity toolkit is Python-based, and the Software Developer Kit (SDK) may be an extra charge, though check with your sales rep on any such licensing issues. Unity does include some hooks for managing and mapping users' security credentials, which is also a huge benefit. There are a handful of other high-end federated search toolkits on the market, if none of the FAST/Microsoft options suffice.

Vendors don't seem to talk much about federated search beyond saying that they do have it. This might be because of the complexity of high-end federated search. Or, perhaps it's at odds with the potential revenue for direct license fees for per-document or per-gigabyte line items. Or, perhaps most customers want to know that it's an option, but don't actually get around to using it.

SUMMARY

In this chapter you learned that FAST search can be scaled onto multiple servers to accommodate more documents and more searches. FAST can also search other sources via federated search.

You've also seen why taxonomies are often not just a drop-in solution. You need to think about the type of taxonomy that best matches your application, then come up with a workflow that will accomplish this. We showed you a simple document-processing pipeline stage written in Python that maps web pages into a simple taxonomy based on URL parameters.

FAST also provides entity extraction in the form of their STAN toolkit. FAST offers a number of ways to adjust search engine relevancy. FAST also provides another type of results list navigator in the form of unsupervised clustering based on its automatic noun-phrase extraction.

PART IV
Enterprise Search 2.0

10

Enterprise Search Is Social Search

WHAT'S IN THIS CHAPTER?

➤ Understanding social computing

➤ Defining social search

➤ Examining social activities that affect search

➤ Exploring social search in SharePoint 2010

➤ Implementing social search in SharePoint 2010

➤ Extending social search

This chapter defines *social search*, and explains how it can be applied within the business context and how it can improve relevancy and add value to the user search experience. After reading this chapter, you will be able to take the customization knowledge gained in the previous chapters and apply it to implementing a customized social search solution as well as recognize the potential for a search solution leveraging social features of the platform. Specific solutions will be demonstrated for tagging search results by users and finding subject matter experts. You will witness the dynamic effects of user tagging on search results and understand more about collaborative searching. At the end of this chapter, you will know how social search features in SharePoint 2010 work and be able to configure and manage people and expertise search.

 Parts of this chapter are attributed to John T. Kane, with appreciation.

SOCIAL COMPUTING

From birth, human beings are extremely social and have an urge to interact with one another through gestures, body language, and spoken language. Social interaction is an important part of our lives and helps shape human character, behavior, and decisions. The communication channels we choose vary in form and sometimes are not explicit or direct. They provide a basis for inference, the decision-making process, and activity coordination.

The premise of social computing is that computer-generated systems support functionality by making socially produced information available to their users. This information may be provided directly (for example, in a form of user review or rating) or indirectly in the form of analyzed statistics and user behavioral patterns to imply or explicitly suggest actions or items (for example, the order in which items are displayed on a shopping site).

Social computing refers to systems that support the gathering, representation, processing, use, and dissemination of information that is distributed across social collectivities, such as teams, communities, organizations, and markets. Moreover, the information is not anonymous, which is significant precisely because it is linked to people, who are in turn linked to other people.

SharePoint 2010 provides a full-featured platform to support social communities within the enterprise by means of blogs and wikis. It supports the grouping of similar users or content. It allows users to provide their feedback on the content by means of tags, ratings, and comments. SharePoint's authentication model provides system access transparency yet has strong built-in user recognition and stores user information within its user profiles store, thus supporting the diversity of the community members.

An imperative part of the social computing concept is a search that allows people to find other people or information and allows the search results to be mined in different ways either to zero in on a specific item or person, or to discover other information that leverages the collective wisdom of the community.

SOCIAL SEARCH

We all have had the experience of helping our relatives or friends find things on the Internet. Usually, this takes the form of making either emailed or verbal suggestions for terms to enter into their search engine. These suggestions can take the form of help in finding a good skiing resort or vacation destination. However, what if the search process took into account your friend's suggestions, much like today's social networks such as Facebook or Twitter? This process is often called social search, which is defined as "any system that enables people to help others filter and find information on the web. It's simply an extension of the natural patterns of how humans interact with each other and with information in the real world." (Source: http://www.sla.org/pdfs/sla2007/richmansocialsearch.pdf)

These patterns can be explicit or implied, meaning that the searcher will be asked to select suggestions or that previous search history can be utilized to assist the search results in the background. Google's page rank is a form of social search because it utilizes the backward pointers between web pages in its ranking algorithm. What is driving the need for social information to be included in the search process? What and how social information can be incorporated in the search processes is the subject of this chapter.

Social information on the web is relatively new and mostly started with sharing of bookmarks through such sites as Del.icio.us, Furl.net, and Flickr. After more interactive Web 2.0 sites became popular, more social information was available for use. Still later, social networks such as MySpace and Facebook emerged.

In addition, social bookmarking sites are valuable because human beings are in charge of defining what appeals to them independently. Their tags also get shared and help contribute to *folksonomies*, which are user-generated taxonomies that aid future searching.

 The word folksonomy is a combination of folk *and* taxonomy; *it describes a collaborative method of adding metadata and classifications to data that provides an organic system for content organization.*

Unlike formal taxonomies that are created by dedicated professionals which is a high quality, but costly of time and effort process that is required to produce taxonomy, folksonomy comes at a lower cost by allowing people just tag the content, distributing the workload amongst a large number of people. Thus, a valuable page that ranks poorly with the search engines may become findable because a group of users has identified and shared it. This technique has spread to blogs and other websites and is often implemented through tag clouds. Search interactions between the searcher and search engine can be either explicit, implicit, or some combination of the two. Explicit interactions depend upon people who actively share their opinions via tags, comments, or other methods. Implicit interactions happen when searchers use what others have contributed via tags and comments. The underlying search engine utilizes these tags and comments to improve the relevancy of the search results when keywords do not exist in the original web page or document. Some examples of this are "did you mean" and "see related" suggestions that are often displayed by Internet search engines.

In the search engine relevance calculations, implicit sharing can provide for excellent and highly relevant content as a feedback mechanism. Searchers are not asked to do any extra work such as tagging or bookmarking content, even though tagging remains useful. Search engines that utilize implicit feedback take advantage of internal content such as metadata, or clicks (number of people selecting that content for certain keywords) rather than requiring the searcher to tag or provide additional feedback.

Today, with the advent of Web 2.0, blogs, and wikis, people are more used to providing comments, feedback, and tags. This interactive feedback can be utilized by the search engine to provide advanced relevancy for content that does not contain the explicit keyword. While explicit feedback does not provide the best search results, a combination of implicit and explicit tagging that is inherent in SharePoint 2010 can increase search accuracy. Enterprise Search is different than Internet search, and the ultimate beneficiaries of the technologies developed for Internet search are, in fact, those in the organizations that have users who actively tag and search for content, and those who can benefit from improved search engine relevancy.

In April 2007, Forrester Research reported that 48% of U.S. adults participated in some form of social computing. Some 13% have uploaded content, 19% posted comments, 15% bookmark and tag, and 19% participate in social communities. Forrester found that 33% are spectators or the audience for user-generated content such as blogs, podcasts, and videos. Pew/Internet American Life Project (May 2007) looked at online and cell phone users. Nearly 19% of U.S. adults have uploaded or shared content online, including artwork, photos, videos, or stories. About 18% post comments, too. Overall, 31% of adults are elite tech users who are heavy and frequent Internet users who are also engaged with user-generated content (Source: sla.org/pdfs/sla2007/richmansocialsearch.pdf).

Understanding how users search today and how this social interaction works is the basis of what we will discuss in more detail.

Types of Social Activities That Affect Search

Search is a social activity, and there have been efforts to apply the various types of technologies to improving search relevancy. Some of these methods can be summarized as personalization, cooperation, and collaboration. Additionally, the type of search — informational, navigational, or transitional — interacts with what you are searching for and your level of expertise in the content domain. For example, if you are a product manager for a car manufacturer, then you are an expert on cars and are very productive and effective in searching for car-related content. However, if you are looking for the best HDTV, you would be considered a novice and could benefit from product reviews and the knowledge of others who are experts in the HDTV domain. These factors can be incorporated into the search process.

Search personalization is a process whereby past search history is utilized to customize your search results. This is can be effective if your search history is consistent over time and your typical searches are almost always the same. It is less effective when you are searching across a number of different and unrelated topics, For example, if "relational databases" and "skiing" are contained in your search history, neither contributes to improving the search results of the other.

Collaboration (or cooperation) is an activity that often starts as asking questions of coworkers on what are the best keywords to search for a database topics or the best ski resort. You may share these keywords or search links via email, IM, or other social websites with your colleagues or friends to help find the best results. One lesser known search technology from Microsoft that helps in online search collaboration is SearchTogether (`http://research.microsoft.com/en-us/downloads/fa64a85d-3443-481c-aadf-dccf30c24824/default.aspx`).

SearchTogether provides for easy and secured search collaboration between you and your friends to help you get better search results. However, while this technology is limited to a small network of friends and family members, similar technologies can be utilized to extend this to the corporate world. SharePoint 2010 utilizes profiles of people and their interests and fields of expertise and incorporates this knowledge to achieve better search results (see Figure 10-1).

What you are searching for and your level of expertise for that topic are also factors for improving search relevancy via social search technologies. This is often referred to as search roles and modes. You can be a Novice, Intermediate, or Expert in one or more topics you can be information gathering, looking for a known-item search, doing research, or discovering new information (serendipity) as you search for content within your organization or via an Internet search engine. The matrix can be diverse and challenging as you initialize your search with some basic keywords (usually one or two words) and then change and adapt to the search results and your satisfaction as to how relevant the content is to what you are truly seeking. (This process is more formally called *information seeking*.)

Before you start your actual search for content related to your work or research, you will already be formulating in your mind what keywords or phrases to utilize in your search of internal and/or external content. You may have already discussed the issues and topics with your boss, coworkers, or customers to generate ideas and gather requirements for your search. Additionally, you may already know of some internal or external websites that could be useful as a starting point in your search and these websites, blogs, or wikis can also be input as search keywords. Without realizing it, you have already participated in a social search activity. During the actual search process, and depending upon the search mode (informational, navigational, or transactional), you may have foraged for content from other sites as well as asked, emailed, or IMed colleagues to provide help with the actual keyword selections, if you are not getting the results you expected. Your experience level (novice, intermediate, or expert) in the topic area you are searching impacts the amount of interaction you have with others who can help you. SharePoint 2010 provides for People Expert help by incorporating online profiles and indexing these profiles to provide you with experts who may be helpful to your search. Additionally, after the first search session has completed, you may take a break or leave the search and network with other colleagues, who may know others who could be helpful and provide better search keywords. Finally, if you find the results you are looking for, you can distribute your results via email, IM, or other means. This enables you to get more feedback to refine your initial search efforts. Search is often thought of as a solitary effort, but in reality it is a very interactive social activity.

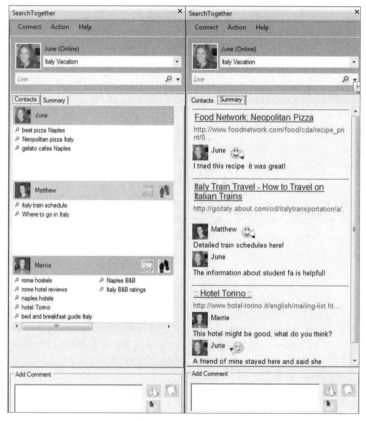

FIGURE 10-1

SharePoint 2010 has social search incorporated in several key components that allow for administrators, contributors, and searchers to utilize effectively all these aspects of social search. Some of the key areas we will discuss in the next section are:

➤ People, profiles, and behavior

➤ My Sites

➤ Emailed topics and their effect on your Expertise ranking

➤ Relevancy tuning and on-the-fly changes for weighting of results

➤ People search by phonetic name search, by expertise, focus, and recently authored documents

➤ Customizing search results to include tagging (boosting) of search results.

SOCIAL SEARCH IN SHAREPOINT 2010

Social search plays a significant part in SharePoint 2010 and will provide improved search results. In this section you will gain specific knowledge of how to use these new social search features in SharePoint 2010. Administrators and developers will learn how to incorporate and customize social search into any SharePoint 2010 installation.

We often have our own internal and external personal networks, something akin to mentors and colleagues, to lean on when we need help and answers. However, at times when we need them they are not around, in meetings, busy, or out of town, and we need help now. In this case, we do need to find the right person at the right time (to paraphrase, "for want of a nail, the war was lost") with the right knowledge to help us. And quite often people do not even know who to ask; this is especially true in larger and/or globally dispersed companies. When a company has more than one office, it is virtually impossible for people to constantly stay updated on what the other office is doing and know the field of expertise and expertise level of people who work there. Corporations and their employees often spend hours looking for something or redoing work that has already been done by other people in the past or other groups within the company. This time and effort can cost the company millions of dollars in lost time that can never be recovered.

SharePoint 2010 has been designed to provide the right information to the right person at the right time. Enterprise social search is not only about connecting people to people but also about providing assistance during the search process and adapting dynamically based on usage patterns and available metadata. SharePoint 2010 also provides search for people names that support phonetic and common nickname matching.

Outlook 2010

The newly released Office 2010 family includes Outlook 2010, which provides additional levels of support for social functionality and integrates with SharePoint 2010. This integration has been made possible through the Outlook Social Connector, which connects people to social and business networks, including Microsoft SharePoint, Windows Live, and other popular third-party sites, so people get more information and stay in touch with others without leaving Outlook.

The Social Connector allows people to stay up-to-the-minute with the people in their networks by accessing everything from email threads to status updates in one single, familiar, centralized view. End users can synchronize their contact data right into Outlook 2010 and obtain information about colleagues such as newly posted or tagged documents, site activity, and more. By connecting to SharePoint Server 2010 social data, they can receive updates at their workplace, and easily track the communication history such as recent email conversations, meetings, and shared documents. Social Connector works with Exchange — so if you click a colleague's name in the From line, it can show a picture and profile, as well as SharePoint-hosted blogs and activity feeds tagged for sharing.

The Social Connector is an add-in client tool for Outlook 2010, and you download it and add it to your Outlook. While not directly related or shipped with SharePoint 2010, it is one more tool for staying connected online for users who prefer to remain in Outlook.

Developers can connect to and feed social streams from line-of-business applications or integrate their solutions directly into Outlook. This means that anyone can build a provider to connect the OSC to a social network, their company's line-of-business applications, or literally any system that can produce streams of activity about its users, through a publicly available SDK.

Implementing Social Search in SharePoint 2010

Let's take a closer look at the services that comprise the social features and support social search within SharePoint 2010. There are three service applications that are critical to the SharePoint 2010 farm setup for social search.

➤ **User profile** — The user profile application is a data source that can be automatically populated from Active Directory/Lightweight Directory Access Protocol (AD/LDAP) or other line of business (LOB) repositories storing data about employees, such as a Human Resources (HR) database.

➤ **Managed metadata** — The managed metadata application provides a way to store relationships between metadata values and allows administrators to provide some control over the health of the data in the profile store and metadata.

➤ **Search service** — The search service application features tunes results, refinement, and ranking to take advantage of the data coming from the user profile application and the managed metadata application.

All of these applications are specific to SharePoint 2010 and not FAST Search for SharePoint 2010. People search is being served and managed by SharePoint 2010; while FAST search adds value to social search, people search is the core competency of SharePoint.

User Profile Service Application

The User Profile Service application is a shared service in Microsoft SharePoint Server 2010 that enables the creation and management of user profiles that can be accessed from multiple sites and farms. Administration of the User Profile Service application can be delegated to a service application administrator by the farm administrator. Refer to Chapter 4 for more information on setting up the User Profile service.

User Profile Synchronization

When the User Profile Service application is created to populate the user profile store with information automatically, you have to start the User Profile Synchronization service and configure synchronization connection from the Manage Services On Server administrative interface within the Central Administration site.

You can connect to a directory service and configure settings to synchronize user profile information between the directory service and SharePoint User Profile Store. To connect to the Active Directory Domain Services (AD DS) the account that is used must have at least Replicate Directory Changes permission on the AD DS domain(s) from which you wish to import data. Additionally, this account must be a member of the Farm Administrators group or must be a designated account to administer User Profile Service Application. Synchronizing profile information is useful, for example, for importing bulk user profile information from external sources into the user profile store in SharePoint Server 2010. The directory services for which synchronization is supported in SharePoint Server 2010 include the following:

➤ **Active Directory Domain Services (AD DS)** — To export properties, such as profile pictures, from SharePoint Server 2010 to AD DS you need to grant the farm administrator account Replicate Directory Changes permission on the object and all child objects for the AD DS domains to which you want to export data from SharePoint Server 2010.

Read/Write permissions are also needed on the container that stores the user picture attribute, for example, the ThumbnailPhoto *attribute. Additional permissions can be granted using Access Control Lists (ACLs) in AD DS. SharePoint Server 2010 will not write profile data back to AD DS unless the Write permission is explicitly set on the account that has Replicate Directory Changes permissions.*

➤ **Business Data Connectivity (BDC) service** — The information imported from BDC is used to supplement user profile information imported from AD DS. Standalone Business Data Connectivity Service imports are not supported.

➤ **Novell eDirectory version 8.7.3 (LDAP)** — Full synchronization for users is supported and not incremental.

➤ **SunOne version 5.2 (LDAP)** — Both full and incremental synchronization are supported. You must set up a change log to use incremental synchronization.

➤ **IBM Tivoli 5.2 (LDAP)** — Both full and incremental synchronization are supported.

Profile synchronization occurs when profile information has changed in the SharePoint Server 2010 profile store or when profile information has changed in the directory service. When the Profile Synchronization is configured, changes to either store are detected. Importation or exportation occurs, depending on the import/export settings for a particular user profile property.

Some user profile properties, such as first name, last name, and account informa-tion are automatically mapped to their corresponding properties in the external directory service. No user profile property is set to Export by default. You must explicitly define the user profile properties that you want to export back to the directory service from the user profile store.

To start the User Profile Synchronization service, go to the Central Administration website, and make sure that you are logged in to the server under the Farm Administrator account:

1. Click Manage Services on Server under System Settings.

2. Click Start next to the User Profile Synchronization Service (See Figure 10-2).

User Profile Service	Started	Stop
User Profile Synchronization Service	Starting	
Visio Graphics Service	Started	Stop

FIGURE 10-2

Once started, the Synchronization Service configures the Forefront Identity Manager to manage the synchronization.

My Site

My Site is a personal site in Microsoft SharePoint Server 2010 that provides users in an organization with a rich set of social networking and collaboration features. These features give users a way to discover areas of expertise, projects, and business relationships from one central location. My Site allows users to share information about themselves and the work they are performing. Sharing this information within the enterprise encourages collaboration, builds and promotes expertise, creates social communities, and directs relevant content to the people who search for it. The information that is shared on My Sites can be protected to ensure different privacy levels. Each user can view his or her My Site website by clicking his or her user name in the top, right corner of any page and then clicking My Site (see Figure 10-3).

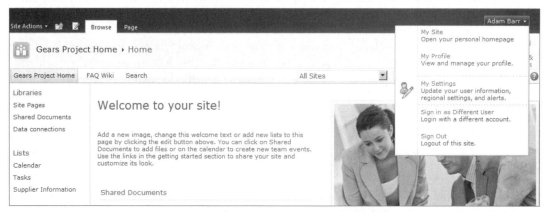

FIGURE 10-3

My Site Web sites in SharePoint Server 2010 include the following (see Figure 10-4):

➤ **A profile for each user, where users can share their expertise, profile pictures, and so on** — We are people and are naturally curious about the colleagues who are providing us valuable help. SharePoint 2010 provides the means for uploading and maintaining photographs of colleagues, as this makes a big difference in encouraging collaboration. Research has shown that people are less likely to engage with someone who doesn't have a profile photo.

➤ **Newsfeed page** — For tracking activities such as social tags, status updates, and comments by colleagues.

➤ **A tag and note tool that helps people conveniently tag or post notes on sites directly from a web browser** — Social tagging lets people add metadata to profiles to describe their expertise, or content to describe a document's topic and meaning.

➤ **A shared picture library, shared document library, and personal document library** — My Site libraries let people store their documents and pictures in one central location that can be accessed from any computer in the network and make those files searchable.

➤ **The ability to add custom web parts, such as a Really Simple Syndication (RSS) viewer for viewing RSS feeds from blogs, news sources, and so on** — Adding web parts and modifying pages on My Site allows people to customize and personalize their SharePoint 2010 experience.

➤ **An organizational browser that uses Microsoft Silverlight 3 to provide a dynamic organizational browsing experience** — Combine all My Site features with SharePoint 2010's new Organizational Browser (showing who reports to whom) and Note Board web parts (for adding comments or questions to My Sites, profiles, tags, or pages), and you have a solid foundation for finding experts and relevant content.

➤ **The ability to manage colleagues and membership connections from one location** — The Colleagues web part is a presentation of other organizational members that the person works closely with in the organizational structure and memberships. It also allows users to add and remove colleagues manually. The Colleague Tracker web part enables the presentation of recommended colleagues and allows the user to modify colleague tracking by profile information. For example, a person can modify the Colleague Tracker to present updated colleagues when profile properties, authored documents, and blogs change. SharePoint's Sites, Links, and Membership web parts aid users in viewing their own SharePoint 2010 sites, group and mail list memberships, and links, as well as those that they have in common with others. The In Common With web part provides a summary view of information relating to the memberships, organizational managers, and colleagues that a visitor has in common with the owner of a My Site.

➤ **Presence information** — When integrated with Office Communications Server and Exchange Server, presence information indicates online instant messaging status, out of office messages, and contact information whenever user information is presented.

SharePoint Server uses this information to personalize the data presented on a user's My Site website. To provision My Site websites and enable social computing features, such as social tagging and newsfeeds, you must enable the User Profile service.

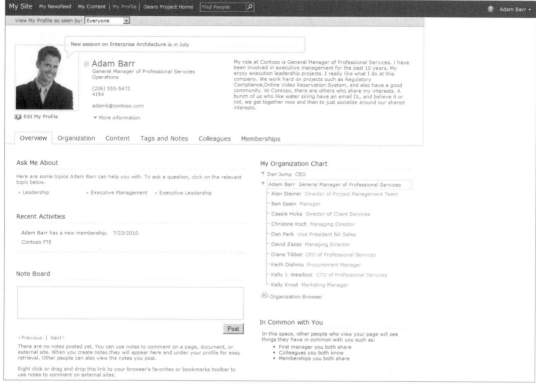

FIGURE 10-4

If your organization includes multiple farms or multiple User Profile service applications that host My Site websites, you can prevent users from creating multiple My Site websites by using the Trusted My Site Host Locations feature. This feature enables you to specify trusted My Site locations. When trusted My Site locations are specified, users are redirected to the My Site that is intended for their user accounts, regardless of where they are browsing when they click the link to create a My Site website. This feature ensures that each user can create only one My Site website in the organization, which makes search results more relevant.

User Profiles

Building information-rich people profiles is imperative for accuracy and usefulness in people search. Microsoft has made it easy for administrators to add custom properties to the profiles to extend the features for future social search interactions. To optimize people search, you can encourage users to include their photos and update their profile information. Turn on Outlook Knowledge Mining and encourage users to publish suggested keywords from Outlook. Keyword and Colleague Mining extracts information from the email people send in Microsoft Outlook. The extracted keywords and colleagues are incorporated into people's My Sites as suggestions that easily can be added to their profiles, leading to better search results for people and expertise and providing an easier way of supplementing people profiles with information that is relevant and searchable. This is a two-step process that requires the end user to provide consent for email analysis in Outlook and at the SharePoint server side.

To enable knowledge mining from Outlook, go to the File menu and select Options. From the Options menu select Advanced and place a checkmark beside the option Allow Analysis of Sent E-mails To Identify People You Commonly E-mail And Subjects You Commonly Discuss, And Upload This Information To The Default SharePoint Server. (See Figure 10-5.) The next step is for the user to update their Ask Me About profile property from the My Profile page of their respective My Site with suggested keywords mined from Outlook e-mails. Suggested keywords are visible only to the profile owner, but once those keywords are added they will be indexed as part of the user profile.

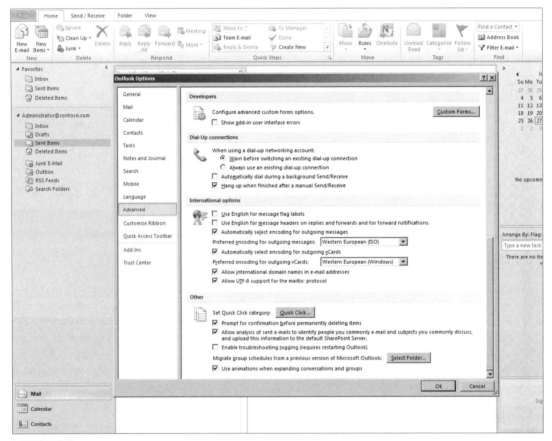

FIGURE 10-5

As administrator you can add custom profile properties and customize personal profile attributes.

To add custom profile properties, follow these steps:

1. Open the Central Administration web page.

2. Click the Manage Service Application link in the Application Management section.

3. Click User Profile Service Application.

4. Go to Manage User Properties.

5. From the Manage User Properties page, click Add User Property.

6. Fill out the required information and click OK. (See Figure 10-6.)

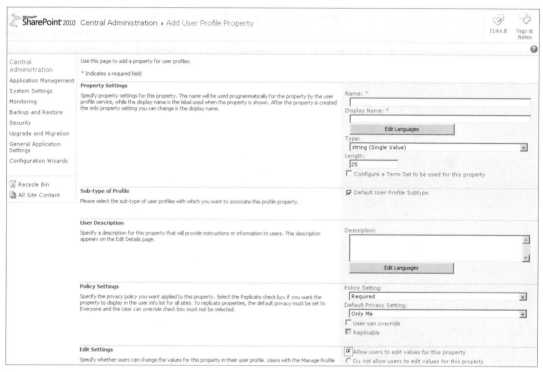

FIGURE 10-6

End users can add information into this new profile property, if you enable end users to edit this profile property by selecting the Allow Users To Edit This Property radio button at the profile property creation time, or at the Edit Profile Property page. New and existing profile properties can be mapped and automatically populated with external information sources such as AD or LOB systems through synchronization with those systems. End users can be somewhat reluctant to manually populate their information. This is especially true when people are presented with empty fields; filling them requires more effort than adding information from a list of suggestions does. Providing choices from which the users can choose can be achieved by creating a term set and mapping a new user profile property to it. For example, in a manufacturing company, it might be beneficial to add a "My Product Expertise" profile property and map it to the Products term set. Follow these steps to create a custom term set and map it to the user profile property:

1. Open the Central Administration web page.

2. Click the Manage Service Application link in the Application Management section.

3. Click Managed Metadata Service.

4. From the Taxonomy term store Managed Metadata, select New Group and provide this new group with a name.

The term sets can also be populated by importing a CSV file to it after the term set is created. (See Figure 10-7.) Create a new user profile property and map it to the term store by selecting the Configure a Term Set To Be Used For This Property check box. From the drop-down list of term sets, select the term set name. To enable end users to select terms from this term set to populate the new profile property and display this information to others, ensure that the options Allow Users To Edit Values For This Property, and Show In The Profile Properties Section Of The User's Profile Page are selected. Once the property is created, it becomes accessible to end users from the Edit My Profile page, shown in Figure 10-8. After the people profiles are recrawled, the information stored within the new property becomes available within people search.

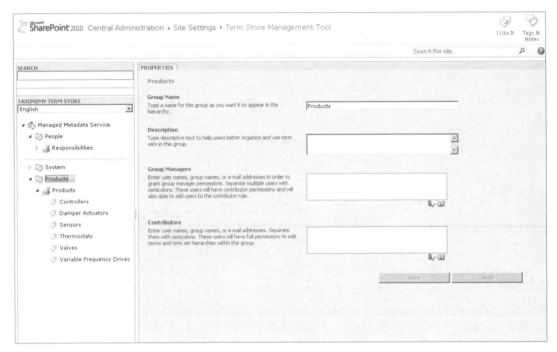

FIGURE 10-7

People Search

SharePoint Server 2010 provides an address book–style name lookup experience with improved name matching that makes it easier than ever to find people by name, title, and organizational structure. This includes phonetic name matching that returns names that sound similar to what the user has typed in a query. It also returns all variations of common names, including nick-names. For example: searching for "Bob" returns name matches for "Rob" and "Robert" as well. (See Figure 10-9.)

Getting your job done means working with the right people, and search leverages this notion by ranking people search results according to social distance. A person who is in your designated circle of colleagues and acquaintances appears higher in your search results than someone who is not in your circle. People search comes with its own rank model, which is designed specifically for finding people and expertise within the enterprise.

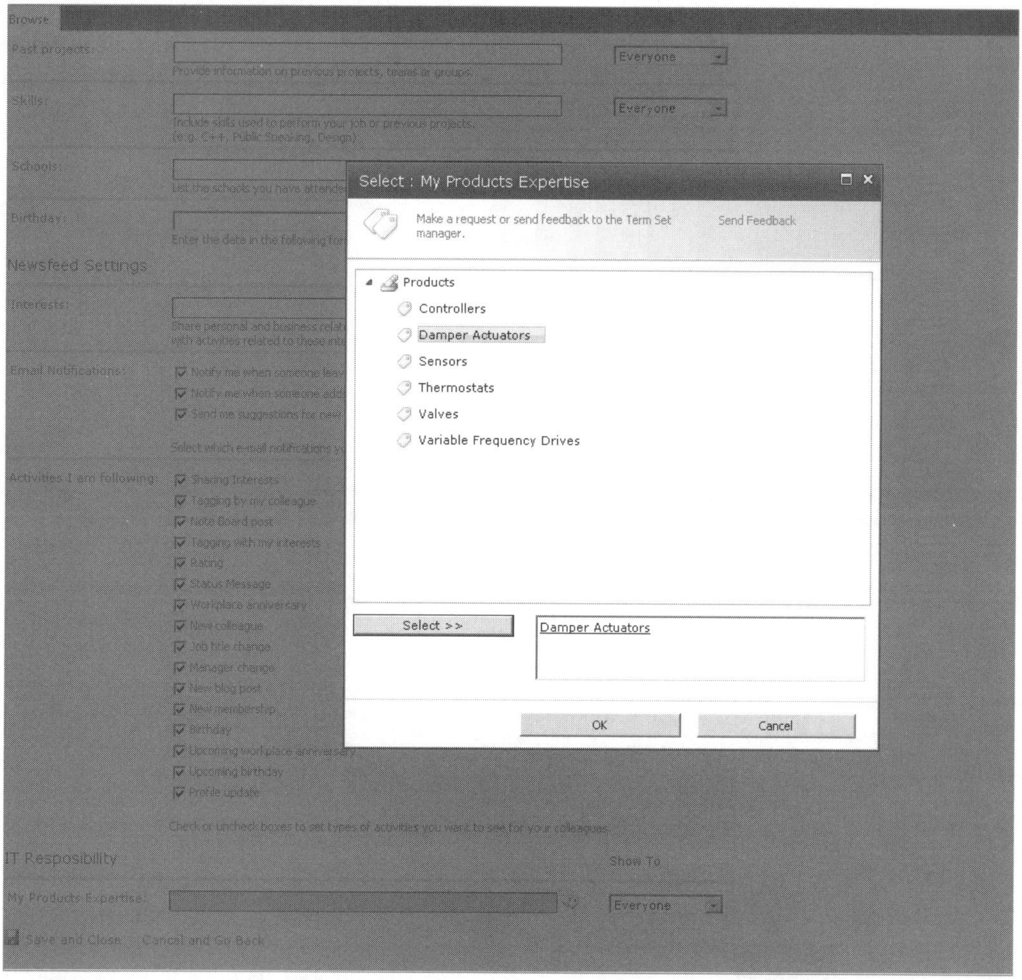

FIGURE 10-8

On My Site, the My Profile page displays personal profile information and allows people to fill out profile fields manually, thus building richer profile information through expertise tagging. The importance of populating the user profiles within people search and social search cannot be understated. The User Profile page lets users list the areas in which they have experience as part of their profile. This information can be helpful to other users in the organization when trying to locate subject matter experts for a particular area.

The default relevancy rank profile on the People Search page is designed for people performing an expertise search, but can be changed from the Search Results page view to social distance information (distance from your colleague) to apply the social distance sorting instead of sorting by relevancy.

Refiners

Refiners are an important part of improving the search experience, as they provide additional methods of filtering the result set beyond just including search terms in a query. Refiners also aid people in discovering information that they do not necessarily have knowledge about. SharePoint 2010 Search Center provides a number of out-of-the-box (OOTB) refiners for people search. You can add custom properties to the people search results page as refiners by creating managed properties and mapping them to this new crawled property. Adding profile properties as refiners will aid end users in discovering expertise within the company in a multidimensional way. SharePoint people search offers a number of refiners out of the box, such as:

➤ Job Title

➤ Responsibilities

➤ Schools

➤ Skills

➤ Past Projects

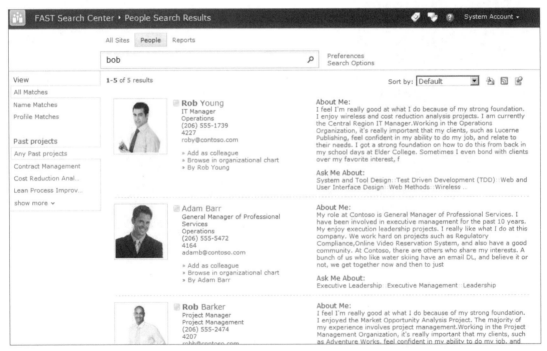

FIGURE 10-9

These refiners allow automatic refinement on relevant pivots. Adding additional refiners, such as tags, can allow people to see the information not just about others, but by what others are tagging content with, by their social feedback.

Self-Search

When people are presented with the people search option, the first thing that many search is their name. To search for yourself has been officially described by the compound verb "vanity search." Enterprise Search also allows people to search for themselves and others to determine what is happening now in their area of expertise as well as to keep up with colleagues. An additional benefit to this is that it helps you build your profile and create and maintain search terms so that other people can find you in a search (see Figure 10-10).

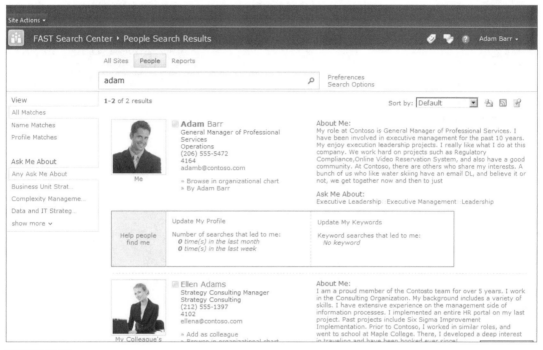

FIGURE 10-10

Social Search Experience

Social search can add significantly to the quality of search results, as all search relevancy is, by its nature, subjective and based upon personal judgment. If search quality is good, searchers will have more confidence. This leads to increased usage, which further increases search quality, and this leads to improved productivity, faster results, and less time spent searching for existing content. (See Figure 10-11.)

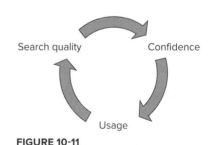

FIGURE 10-11

Suggestive Search

SharePoint 2010 incorporates the FAST pre-query suggestions that are also a form of social search. These pre-query suggestions are mined from previously executed queries and are dynamically generated before the search button is clicked. They are typically displayed in a drop-down list in the Search box. This feature allows people to get some insight into how others are searching for content and provide suggestions based on collective query patterns.

Additionally, Related Searches are post-query suggestions that can appear on the right side of the search result page as Related Searches (See Figure 10-12).

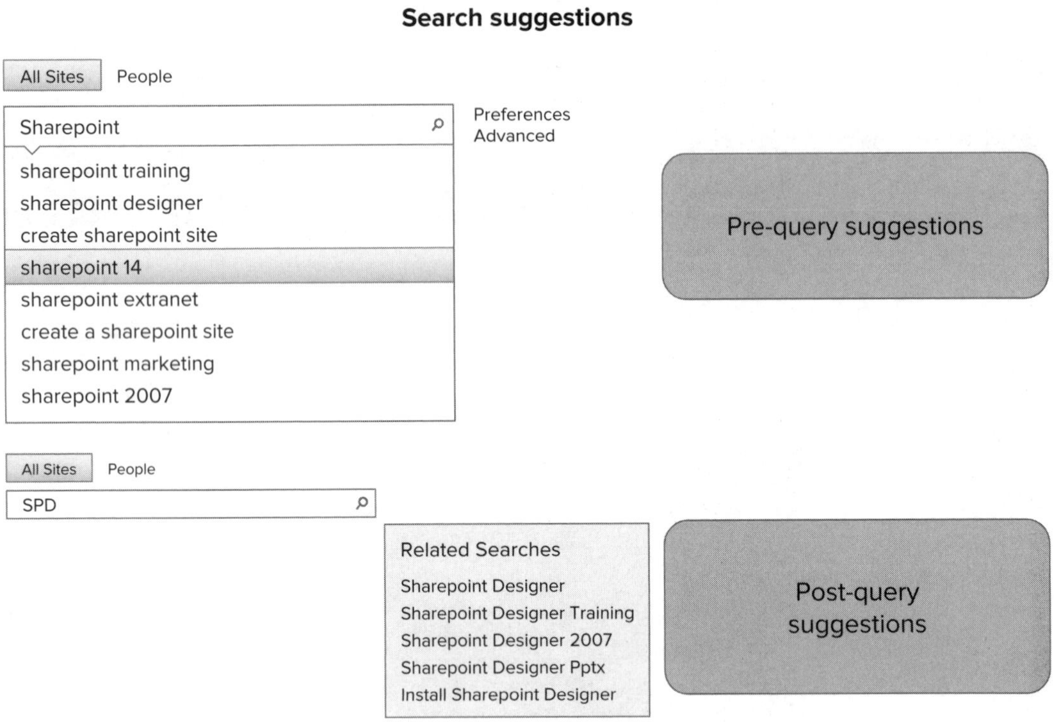

Search suggestions

FIGURE 10-12

Contextual Search

FAST Search for SharePoint 2010 allows site collection administrators to associate best bets, visual best bets, document promotions, document demotions, site promotions, and site demotions with defined user contexts in order to personalize the search experience and increase the level of relevancy. These features allow the right content to be displayed within the right context on top of the search results, thus improving the end user search experience. Search results ranked by popularity is rarely helpful from an enterprise context. More so, what is highly relevant to one user or business unit may not be as relevant to another.

Let's take a look at real-life example where you can use best bets within the user context, a company that has global offices and different branches within various countries, and employee benefits policies that vary depending on the country the office is in:

1. To create the user context from the site collection administration FAST Search User Context, click Add User Context and give it the name **USA Employees**.

2. Associate it with the USA office location user property (see Figure 10-13).

By creating another user context for employees located in Canada, called Canadian Employees, you can use the best bets or visual best bets features to display benefits information.

To achieve this, follow these steps:

1. From the Site Collection Administration page, click Visual Best Bets and click Add New.

2. Provide the title for the visual best bet and the URL to the Image of HTML code snippet.

3. Select the user context, for example, USA Employees, and fill out the link to the USA Benefits.

4. Click OK.

   Repeat the same steps for creating the visual best bets to the Canadian employees benefits page and select the Canadian Employees user context.

Now when people from the USA and Canada are searching for their benefits information, they will receive relevant links at the top of their search results. You can use a similar technique to promote the relevancy of sites and documents.

FIGURE 10-13

User contexts can be created by associating them with multiple office locations and the Ask Me About property values from within the user profiles. SharePoint Server 2010 enables you to identify varying levels of authoritative pages that help you tune relevancy ranking by site, where information from sites for local teams can be promoted and ranked higher within search results if the person executing the search is associated with the local office. FAST Search for SharePoint 2010 allows you to promote individual documents, increasing the granularity level of the ranking and, furthermore, enabling you to associate each promotion with user contexts.

Click-Through Relevancy

Click-through behavior is another powerful way people interact with search. Their behavior influences the search experience and evolution of the relevancy within the search engine. When people execute queries, they click on items that might be the answers for their search. Without even realizing it, people are actually teaching the engine to optimize the relevance of search items. By analyzing the logs for items that were clicked from within search results, Search adds ranking weight to those items. The next time the same query is executed, documents or items previously clicked will be ranked higher and displayed higher in the search results. The relevancy in this approach can get a little bit skewed as people often click on the wrong document, but this is why this document can be demoted by site collection administrator.

Social Tags

Social tags are indexed as part of the people content source. The tag is stored with the person — not the item — until it gets to the search system. This is important because it means that end users can tag external content: anything that can be referenced through the URL. Search results with social tags are boosted within the relevancy model and improve the search experience because other users found this content worth providing some feedback about.

Social tags are also provided within the Refiners panel, where users can filter search results by specific tag.

Social tagging is the way of building folksonomies, and while a folksonomy is not a replacement for a formal taxonomy, it is used to augment it. Folksonomies are useful as a source for candidate terms or new term harvesting, and for content that is less structured and might be tougher to organize (such as discussions, wikis, or blogs) or material that does not justify structured tagging (such as obscure web pages). In some cases, use of user generated tags makes a lot of sense, for example, if a group of scientists working on a chemical compound come up with a new term that has not yet been officially recorded in the formal taxonomy and start tagging their data with it.

Here are the some of the advantages of a folksonomy (or social tagging) approach:

➤ **Adaptability** — New terms can evolve quickly and be applied right away to new concepts.

➤ **Low cost** — By distributing the workload among a large number of people, there is not a lot of burden on a central group.

➤ **Flexibility** — Anyone can tag, so there are no rigid constructs.

➤ **Takes into account multiple perspectives** — Different people use different words and terminology to describe the same thing. If everyone tags according to their understanding and the terminology they are used to, all points of view are taken into consideration.

Here are the some of the disadvantages of the folksonomy approach:

➤ **Over-tagging** — Too many tags on content can make search and retrieval meaningless; recall is high, but precision is low, producing irrelevant results.

➤ **Inconsistency** — Misspellings, different punctuations, capitalization, variations in spelling all show up as different tags and cannot be used for filtering and navigation.

➤ **Skewed perspective** — Few people tend to actually apply tags, and tags from active individuals can be over-represented, thus providing a skewed perspective.

With social tagging, users could conceivably tag company content with negative terms. A corporate incarnation of this would not have the same risks. SharePoint 2010 allows administrators to have control over social tags; taxonomy by its nature is a controlled vocabulary, but folksonomies are uncontrolled vocabularies. The hybrid method (freedom of social tagging with some control and vetting processes) is actually something that social search greatly benefits from. Administrators can easily manage tags and notes provided by end users through the Manage Social Tags and Notes page, which is accessible from the User Profile Service Application Management page. They can find users' social items and delete them, but removing social tags does not remove the terms from the term store (see Figure 10-14). The Term Store Manager should be used to add or remove terms.

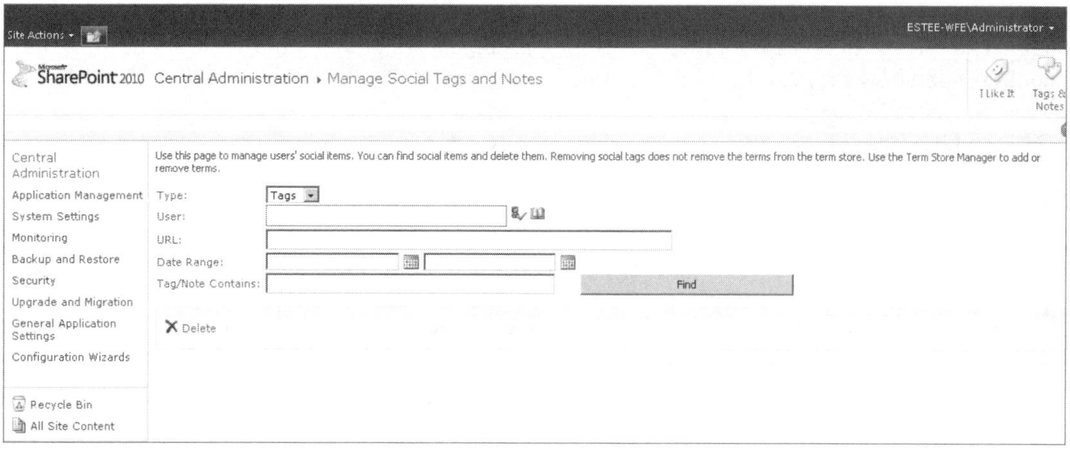

FIGURE 10-14

Social tags and recording of other social behavior can help with another ongoing problem that corporations are facing, which is loss of intellectual property as employees leave the company. People are the most valuable assets that companies have. To hire and train an employee is a costly process and can be viewed as an investment. Answers aren't all in documents. The most important resources in your organization are your people. Taking advantage of the information that they provide is one of the ways for retaining intellectual property when people leave the company and boosting the collective wisdom of personnel.

Implicit User Profile Data

Implicit profile data is the information captured by tracking user behaviors and/or content they produce. This sophisticated approach removes the burden from the end user by capturing information about user behavior, such as:

➤ What queries the person has issued

➤ What documents the person has downloaded and which ones this person has authored

➤ What groups this person has joined

➤ What links this person has followed

➤ What tags the person has created

The downside is that this implicit information is not always visible on the user profile and in some organizations transparency might be an issue. Plain people search in SharePoint 2010 is not the true social search. Personalized search adds to the user's query profile information and this is what influences the query and the matching process. For example, a user who has indicated, by his or her behavior, an interest in marketing-related information, will have marketing-related information "boosted" in the search results.

EXTENDING SOCIAL SEARCH

The concept of social search can be extended by building search applications that provide better search relevancy and uncover synergies between people that otherwise would not be discovered in large enterprises. In this section, we take a look at some examples of what these applications might look like and how they can benefit companies.

Enhancing Search Through Content-Processing

FAST Search for SharePoint 2010 provides a content-processing pipeline that analyses and processes content, and then prepares it for indexing. Refer to Chapter 5 for more detailed information on the content-processing capabilities of FAST. As part of the analysis and content preparation, content processing extracts concepts from documents and items. The content-processing pipeline can be extended to include additional stages that write those concepts into a Custom User Profile property and store it as part of the current user activity or expertise of the person who authored the document. By enhancing and supplementing the user profile information with extracted concepts, you can provide some visibility into a user's activity through a web part that can display those concepts in the form of a tag cloud.

Leveraging Social Distance Information

Working with the right people is important, and within companies that have multiple office locations, it is challenging to connect people from different offices. Search does provide relevancy based on social distance, but if the social distance information does not exist, this feature is not leveraged.

Say, for example, that Jane from marketing starts working on a marketing campaign in the New York office and decides to do a search on the portal to find previous projects similar to this that could provide her with a good start. Mark in London just finished working on similar initiative, but his content or profile will not surface as highly relevant and most likely will be overlooked in the search results by Jane. Jane will end up recreating a lot of the content that already exists and going through extensive research on creating a marketing campaign process. If Mark and Jane were connected, she would spend significantly less time working on this initiative, which is so similar to Mark's.

When concepts are extracted from content and used to populate user profiles, similar concepts can be matched to other's profile information and those people can be suggested to each other through a search-driven application. Applications can be created to suggest recommended reading and other such helpful information to end users.

Content Rating and Reviews

Another useful customization to the search results is displaying the rating of a document or a page; this is easily achieved by creating the rating managed property and modifying the XSL of the Core Results web part to display the rating. This provides additional insight into the quality of the content as it was provided by others. When you couple it with functionality that allows people to provide written reviews about the content, and display those reviews alongside the ratings (for example, top 5 reviews), from reviewers that are closer to the person searching for the content by social distance first, it even further enhances the search results and lets the person get a better view into what people in his or her social community think about the content.

SUMMARY

People's everyday usage and creation of information in SharePoint Server 2010 and Microsoft Office can have a measurable impact on search relevance, thereby helping the organization harness the collective wisdom of its people. For many organizations, SharePoint 2010 is becoming gathering place, where people create, share, and interact with information and each other. This platform creates a basis for social behavior to be taken into account in order to provide high-quality search results in many ways. It provides a solid foundation for administering the social features of search and developing search-driven applications.

11

Search and Business Intelligence

WHAT'S IN THIS CHAPTER?

➤ Exploring the merging of Search and BI

➤ Exploring ways to use Search and BI together

➤ Overviewing Microsoft BI and SharePoint

➤ Understanding the Microsoft BI Indexing Connector

➤ Looking at the Future of Search and BI

What is the difference between business intelligence (BI) and enterprise search? Both are technologies dedicated to the discovery and analysis of data. However, each tends to look at different types of information, and they have radically different approaches to finding that information.

Business intelligence and data warehousing were designed to process, manage, and explore structured data, often data from essential production systems all over the enterprise. Search tools have, for the most part, been designed to index and query unstructured data, such as websites and document repositories.

A typical search engine is something that even a novice can use to find information quickly. BI tools, on the other hand, are based on complex and refined queries that result in exact and complete data results and reports. BI applications, thus, tend to have a high level of complexity, which has meant that only business analysts or those specifically trained on BI systems could effectively use them.

Despite their differences, both BI and search are ultimately in the business of discovering information, and when effectively combined, they can provide a broad and insightful information discovery system. For example, a search system can lower the usage barrier for BI, providing access to business intelligence data from the type of search interface that anyone can use. A BI tool can also make it possible for search results to include structured strategic data, such as sales information. The combination of the two has the potential to help users find all of the potential answers to vital business questions.

This chapter gives you an overview of how search and BI are converging, why traditional BI needs search technology in order to be more widely used, and how to use search and BI together in different ways. It gives a tour of the Microsoft BI stack and SharePoint BI in particular, since that is where search and BI come together. It covers the new BI Indexing Connector available for FAST Search for SharePoint, and gives you information about how to apply it effectively. After reading this chapter you should have both an appreciation for the trends bringing search and BI together and also concrete information you can apply immediately.

SEARCH AND BI ARE CONVERGING

Over the last decade, Search and BI have been steadily growing together. Figure 11-1 shows how this has been happening. The horizontal axis shows the degree of structure in the content, from unstructured data (like documents found on fileshares, email, etc.) through semi-structured content (like XML structures or highly annotated documents) to structured content (like fully normalized databases). The vertical access shows the degree of structure or repetition in the access, from the ad hoc queries found on intranets through the saved searches typical of information monitoring applications to the scheduled and optimized queries used for operational reports.

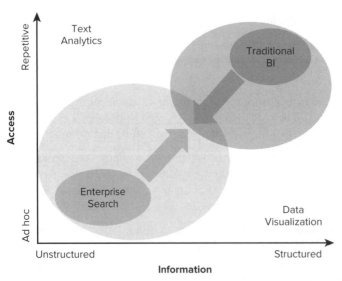

FIGURE 11-1

Enterprise Search comes from a heritage in the lower-left corner — serving users seeking ad hoc access to unstructured information. Traditional BI grew up on the upper-right, providing repetitive production reports using structured data. Year by year, the technologies have been growing along the diagonal. Search has been finding more and more applications against semi-structured or structured content, and scheduled searches or alerting has become essential for applications, such as information surveillance. BI has grown towards a more accessible, open paradigm, and the growth of data warehousing. "BI for the masses" means a wider range of queries across more types of information.

The convergence of Search and BI has been on the radar of analysts for five or six years now. For example, Forrester Research has published pieces on search/BI convergence regularly; Figure 11-2 shows an overview of how search and BI are learning from each other (courtesy of Forrester).

Search learns from BI, and BI learns from Search

Search		BI
UI User-friendly, simple interface; new query does not require IT involvement.	BI interface is getting simpler.	Complex interface with many parameters; only developers or power users can run new queries.
Source Can understand unstructured text, and even understand meaning or emotion	Content is structured for BI; search engines index databases.	Can leverage structured information to uncover trends in data.
Analysis Can surface content or data, but can't help you decide what to do about it.	Search is beginning to answer questions users didn't know to ask.	Analytics and visualization capabilities; deep dive into data to discover new knowledge.
Output Output is a relatively simple results list, and charts are the exception, not the rule.	Charts and dashboards are entering the search UI.	Output is complex, with various elements (including graphics or formatting) positioned perfectly.

FIGURE 11-2

Several Enterprise Search vendors have this convergence as a primary theme in their marketing material. There have also been a number of acquisitions in this area: Oracle, Informatica, Business Objects, and Cognos all acquired search or text analytics companies. There is a general understanding that search and BI are coming together, but there is no general understanding of what that really means. The convergence is highly hyped, but there is confusion over how to combine search and BI and what value the combination brings.

Search and BI Combine in Different Ways

There are many ways to use Enterprise Search and BI together, and quite a few inventive approaches to building systems that combine aspects of both. These fall into three main patterns:

➤ **Text Analytics** — Where "search technology" serves as a content preprocessor for BI technology. This includes text mining, semantic analysis, sentiment detection, and much more.

➤ **Search Analytics** — Applying BI to outputs of search. This includes analysis of search behavior and performance, search results visualization, and search engine optimization.

➤ **Unified Information Access** — Combining search and BI elements into one system, including report finders, query preprocessors, unified view systems, hybrid databases, and search-based datamarts.

We will describe all three of these areas next, but focus on unified information access for the rest of this chapter.

Text Analytics

Text analytics is a whole field in its own right. From a search perspective, text analytics essentially use a range of search technologies to add structure to unstructured content, thus making it amenable to structured data analysis techniques. These technologies include entity extraction, relationship extraction, classification, clustering, vector-space techniques, and sentiment detection. They uncover the meaning of words so that they can be interpreted by computers. They identify and extract the building blocks of meaning — people, places, and things and their relationships to each other. Like the data used in traditional business intelligence applications, these extracted elements can then be sorted, compared, or plotted over time to spot trends or report on the status of recurring business processes or topics of interest.

Whether text analytics techniques are "search technologies" or not is debatable. However, they are certainly natural language processing (NLP) techniques common to search and text analytics.

Unlike traditional BI, text analytics monitors predictable and unpredictable actions and interactions of people to alert businesses to the unexpected. Text analytics can be used to spot emerging trends, new markets, or trouble spots in customer relationships.

We are usually clear as to where our structured content resides, but unstructured content exists everywhere: email, documents, content management systems, intranet sites, the Web, and media (image, audio, video). Unstructured information is also found within structured content, embedded in the database fields themselves. For example, text fields such as product description, customer request, or other information are frequently found in nearly all database tables. This information is worthy of all the capabilities of the search text-mining process, and is perhaps as important as content we recognize as unstructured.

Voice of the Customer Applications

Consider the sources of information that are involved with understanding what your customers need, how they are interacting with you, and what their environment is like. This information is vital in what is sometimes called "voice of the customer" projects and applications. This information includes the following:

- ➤ News and public information
    - ➤ Over 20 thousand online mainstream news sites
    - ➤ Over 450 rich media sites; video/photo
    - ➤ Over 110 million blogs
    - ➤ Tens of thousands of forums
- ➤ Social information
    - ➤ LinkedIn, Facebook, and the like
    - ➤ Microblogs (Twitter, etc.)
- ➤ Enterprise information
    - ➤ Surveys
    - ➤ Emails

➤ CRM records

➤ Claims reports

Health care, insurance, and finance are among the industries that are adopting text analytics and linking the analysis of structured BI databases to mining unstructured, text-based email, document management, and blogs and Web sites for information. Horizontal applications include buzzmetrics (monitoring your reputation or advertising effectiveness), customer or competitive intelligence, and homeland security.

Microsoft LookingGlass

Microsoft has an offering in this area codenamed LookingGlass, which uses text analytics to collect and analyze social media. LookingGlass is a proof-of-concept business tool based on the Microsoft platform that allows you to listen to, participate in, and analyze social media. It is built to allow partners build on top of it, and allow businesses to overlay sales and support data and other key business information. The net result is the ability to keep track of what's being talked about, to take targeted actions, and to enhance the ROI of participating in social media.

LookingGlass incorporates 20 popular social media sites and full client functionality for YouTube, Twitter, and Flickr, and has even added Facebook integration. This client functionality includes the capability of posting content to multiple accounts and uses SharePoint workflows to specify posts occur at a certain time in the future, allowing you to configure a social media campaign well in advance of the actual launch. For compliance purposes, all calls in the system are audited, and copies of all social media are stored within LookingGlass.

LookingGlass also provides a robust set of analytics and visualizations out of the box, which can be extended using LookingGlass collected data, in-house data and/or a combination of the two. Figure 11-3 shows one of LookingGlass's dashboard screens.

FIGURE 11-3

LookingGlass is a platform designed to be extended, and targeted at advertising agencies. It encourages agencies to include new data streams and/or visualizations. Examples include incorporating campaign and/or POS sales data, developing new data products from LookingGlass data, gaining additional insight for counseling customers, and incorporating LookingGlass content into internal workflows. LookingGlass will also end up integrated into CRM systems such as Microsoft

Dynamics as "Social CRM" takes root in mainstream Customer Relationship Management solutions.

Summary of Text Analytics

Text analytics use elements of language understanding to enhance and extend business intelligence applications, improving productivity and presenting a clearer view of the business. Applications such as voice of the customer and social media monitoring (such as Microsoft LookingGlass) are classic examples of text analytics. Search technology is used to collect information and process it, while BI technology is used to provide analysis and visualization.

Search Analytics

Search analytics are essentially the application of BI technology to outputs of search: search query logs, search result sets, search index contents, and the like. "Search analytics" is a broad term that is interpreted in diverse ways, and is less well defined than text analytics.

Search data is a BI gold mine. Search analytics can be used to:

➤ Analyze how well your search platform is performing

➤ Gain insight into what your users are looking for, how they search, and how they navigate

➤ Identify how to fine-tune your search engine to optimize your users' search experience

➤ Identify where you need to add new content or modify existing content

BI on Search and Web Logs

The most common form of search analytics is search reports such as those included with Microsoft Enterprise Search products. They provide insight into the top queries, the queries that return no results, and so forth in order to improve the search experience. Search reports are based on the search query and result logs. The Search products that are integrated with SharePoint allow you to extend these reports using Excel Services.

Search performance reports are part of this genre, too. They are aimed at system administrators rather than search administrators, but they similarly use BI to give insight into system behavior. These reports are based on more detailed performance logs, which show where time is being spent in the system. They are invaluable for troubleshooting, but they also require a level of logging that can use a lot of disk space. Figure 11-4 shows an example of query performance reports from SharePoint Server 2010.

Mixing search logs with web logs provides the next level of search analytics. By correlating where users spent time, where they clicked through, what content was used, and the like, you can improve both search relevance and content quality. This ranges from the mundane (noticing that people are searching for a topic and finding nothing because there is no content can trigger organizations to create documents about that topic), through the sublime (automatically improving search relevance based on click-through statistics), to the extreme (creating topic pages on the fly, based on the most popular content). Some of this is built into the Microsoft Enterprise Search products that are integrated with SharePoint, as shown in Figure 11-5.

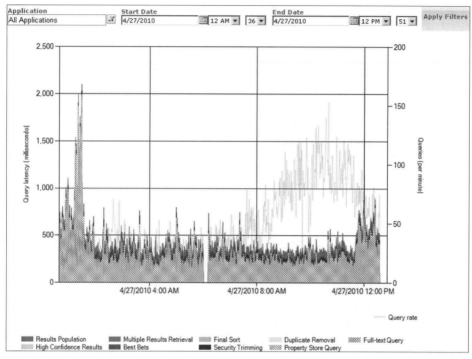

FIGURE 11-4

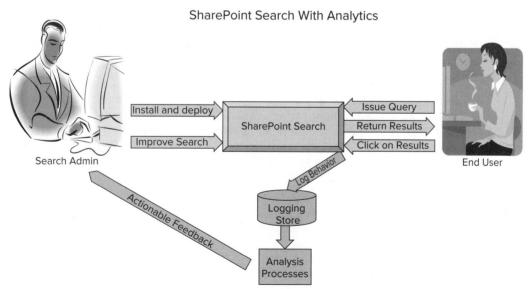

FIGURE 11-5

Figure 11-6 shows an example of search analytics from SharePoint Server 2010 based on search and web log information. There are a number of standard reports available, as well as the ability to produce custom reports.

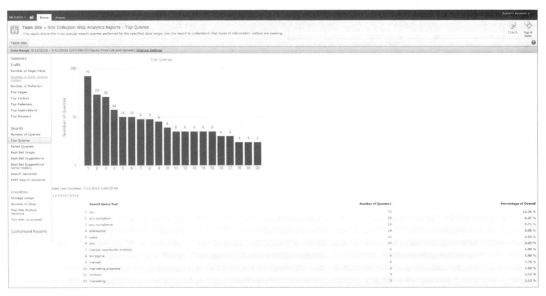

FIGURE 11-6

Adding in business context and information brings you to yet another level of insight. This kind of approach is routine for online retail search (looking at the profitability and inventory of items in an online product catalog versus their query popularity and browse/click/buy behavior.) It can, however, be very useful even for intranet applications. Simply by analyzing which groups of people are looking for what information, and what they do with it, you can identify trends and information needs within an organization. This gives you the insight needed to publish new high-impact information, tag or promote existing content to improve its findability, connect search keywords with relevant content, and optimize search relevance for the most important topics. Figure 11-7 shows an example of advanced query analytics, combining information from search logs, web logs, and business information.

Search engine optimization (SEO) is a form of search analytics that works on exactly this principle. SEO is a field on its own, with conferences, forums, newsletters, and a large industry. Generally, SEO is focused on how to get the best placement on the major web search engines (Google, Bing, Yahoo!, etc.) and how to get the most return for online advertising spending. With SEO, your control over search relevance is limited to your bids on keywords, but you do control your content and how it's tagged. Increasingly, the techniques used in SEO are becoming relevant inside the organization as well. For example, if there is a new program or policy that management wants employees to know about, ensuring that it is found on intranet searches can be more effective than creating a news bulletin to all employees.

BI on Search Result Sets

Another realm of search analytics is applying BI to search result sets. Using reporting, analysis, and visualization techniques, a whole range of new insight can be offered. As with text analytics, this is a very active area of research. Unlike text analytics, there isn't an identified industry with specialized companies focused just on this (yet).

FIGURE 11-7

One of the most common applications for using BI on search result sets is e-Discovery. Once Enterprise Search is used to find a candidate set of information for retention and analysis, a range of reporting, analysis, and selection techniques can be applied.

Unified Information Access

The dream of unified information access is to have one place to go for all information. If we can meld the open access and unstructured content indexing of search with the precision and structured content querying of business intelligence, this promises a much more complete picture of companies' information. There are many ways to combine these approaches, including report finders, search-based datamarts, guided content navigation, query preprocessors, and integrated information access platforms.

Finding and Reusing BI Artifacts

Perhaps the simplest approach for unified information access is the report finder. This uses search to find existing BI artifacts like reports, cubes, dashboards, and the like. The end user can go to one place (the Search Center) and find both unstructured content (such as internal Word documents), structured content (database and line-of-business data), and BI artifacts.

Business intelligence is a key tool for supporting performance management. Providing quick access to needed information is critical for responding quickly to events, which in turn can improve performance. But reports, dashboards, Excel workbooks, and analyses proliferate in most organizations until they become impossible to find. The report finder solves this problem.

This approach is now well accepted in the industry. Most high-end BI systems have embedded search or interfaces designed for Enterprise Search to index. Microsoft has just introduced a BI indexing connector specifically for use with FAST Search for SharePoint, which we will describe in detail in this chapter.

Search as an Alternative Datamart

Data warehouses and datamarts are found in most large organizations. A data warehouse function is to contain a wide range of data from everywhere in the organization and offer it to many different applications (some unforeseen), so it isn't optimized for any application. A datamart is usually more focused, offering a subset of data and optimized for a small set of applications. The data warehouse is probably the most expensive IT project and asset within most corporations, but most data warehouses and datamarts still fail to provide easy, fast access to enterprise data.

Enterprise Search technology has always been able to index and search structured and unstructured data. (Some platforms are better than others; we will discuss why FAST Search offerings are good at searching structured data later in this chapter). Because search is optimized for retrieval, it can provide a faster, more uniform response time than a datamart can. A search engine is also not bound to a single schema, so it is more flexible than a datamart. Some applications shine by providing unified information access by using a search engine in lieu of a datamart.

Faceted Navigation as Analytics

The faceted navigation provided by high-end search systems is proven to be easy to use and very effective. This approach goes by many different labels, from "guided navigation" to "results refinement." Whatever the name, it provides a zero-training interface to ensure that applications incorporating it can be quickly learned and adopted by everyone who needs to leverage enterprise information.

Faceted navigation helps users find what they're looking for more easily than the traditional ad hoc data access methods provided by BI. With traditional methods, users have to be familiar with the contents of the data and even the model of its underlying tables, and they have to know how to structure questions to get useful results. With faceted navigation, users can drill into any dimension of indexed information, whether it is structured (such as database content), semi-structured (such as XML), or unstructured. Faceted navigation helps users ask relevant questions by showing the valid paths to refine and explore further.

Ad Hoc Queries for Structured Data

A more ambitious form of Unified Information Access creates new reports based on key words in a search. If a user types "Sales in the fourth quarter in North America," the system would be able to tie that to the metadata to automatically generate a query and render a report, based on the query string — knowing that sales is a measure, fourth quarter is the time dimension, and North America is the geography dimension.

This is a very different model from the traditional BI deployment where users pick and choose dimensions and measures from a semantic layer, and the SQL code is auto-generated for them. This approach combines the ease of use of a search interface with the precision of BI. Appropriate dimensions can be displayed on the fly as query suggestions to guide users through their search, or can be provided as faceted navigation.

Although providing ad hoc queries on structured data seems natural, it is difficult to implement robustly. An early attempt at this, called English Query, was shipped with SQL Server 7.0 and 2000.

It was later dropped from SQL 2005 and above, primarily due to lack of use and problems expanding it beyond the English language. Microsoft showed a new project recently called the Semantic Engine that had these capabilities plus much more.

Integrated Information Access Platforms

A category of integrated information access platforms is starting to emerge, designed for handling all types of information. Some of these are hybrid architectures that combine search and database structures to support unified access to both content and data in multiple formats and repositories.

These integrated information access platforms are search technologies that are no longer limited to free or unstructured text. They provide core indexing services that focus on extreme performance and scalability for retrieval and analysis of both structured and unstructured content. The binary notion of "either in or out," which forms the basis of the relational model, is replaced with advanced frameworks that provide fuzzy matching and ranking schemes to separate value from noise, and advanced analytics to compute contextual concept relationships across billions of records, all on the fly.

There is active academic work on integrated information access platforms, as well as several vendors that market products with this position. Most current products claiming to be integrated information access platforms actually use a combination of a database core and a search core under the hood. Technology that is truly a new breed of information access is rare, though it is on the rise. Techniques for bridging between search engines, databases, and XML search are also emerging. For example, Interaction Management Services can be used to solve many integrated information access problems by combining result sets and doing on-the-fly deep federation that does fuzzy joins across multiple engines of different types.

Business Intelligence Needs Search

Business Intelligence is actually a larger industry than Enterprise Search is, but it suffers from lack of adoption. Specifically, survey after survey shows that BI tools are used by only an elite few within the enterprise. To overcome this and make BI information available to everyone, new approaches are needed. Enterprise search brings a lot to the party since it is a technology widely used by everyone in every organizations. BI needs to incorporate the ease of use of search to become truly widespread.

In this section we examine the state of traditional BI, and survey the challenges with it. The following section covers the business benefits of combining search and BI.

The State of Traditional BI

Business intelligence has become the information lifeline businesses use to assess their performance and garner vital insights from data across the enterprise. BI software incorporates the ability to mine data, analyze, and report. Modern BI software allows users to cross-analyze and perform deep data research rapidly for better analysis of sales or performance on an individual, department, or company level. In effective applications of business intelligence software, managers are able to quickly compile reports from data for forecasting, analysis, and business decision making.

In most businesses, increasing standards, automation, and technologies have led to vast amounts of data becoming available. Data warehouse technologies have set up repositories to store this data. Improved extract, transform, load (ETL) and enterprise application integration tools have increased the speedy collecting of data. OLAP reporting technologies have allowed faster generation of new reports that analyze the data. Business intelligence has now become the art of sifting through large amounts of data, extracting pertinent information, and turning that information into knowledge upon which actions can be taken.

Originally, BI was the province only of technically astute business analysts, but now many organizations are deploying it to less specialized workers in functions such as sales, marketing, the contact center, the supply chain, and other aspects of operations. This broad deployment, however, carries with it expectations about the ease of use and responsiveness of current technology and processes in providing the information needed to make timely decisions or take relevant action. These new users of BI already are accustomed to searching on the Internet and getting results rapidly by using technologies from Google, Yahoo!, or others. It's natural for them to want to use search as the interface to BI and to locate what they need promptly, wherever it resides in the organization.

Challenges with Traditional BI

For years, the primary examples of BI have been identifying trends such as which products are selling best in which markets or where in a production process prices are spiking. BI tools — including reporting, ad hoc analysis, and online analytical processing (OLAP) — serve only a small fraction of users. As measured by licenses, just 10 to 20 percent of users have access to analytics, according to most studies, although actual use is probably even lower.

Although BI tools generally require no programming and the basics can be taught in a couple of days, BI still demands a level of understanding about the data, data models, and data-manipulation processes beyond the skills or patience of most knowledge workers. Consequently, the level of IT involvement in BI remains high. Typically only a few highly motivated power users invest the time and effort to develop proficiency in traditional BI tools. IT generally has to get involved when new analysis or combinations of data are needed. This leads to less benefit and higher costs for BI, reduced ROI, and an overall lack of agility and timeliness. Surveys conducted by The Data Warehousing Institute (TDWI) reported:

➤ 83% of respondents reported that their organizations have suffered problems due to poor data quality.[1]

➤ 64% stated that it would be very important to relatively important to have an information management tool that enabled ad-hoc BI query and reporting.[2]

➤ 25% said BI is used by 5 or fewer people, while 47% said it's used by fewer than 10[2]

Another challenge for traditional BI tools is the growth of unstructured data. While structured data remains the backbone of most organizations, the amount and proportion of unstructured data is growing rapidly. A recent IDC study projected that structured data would grow at a compound annual growth rate of 21.8%, but be far outpaced by a 61.7% CAGR predicted for unstructured data in traditional data centers.

As the breadth of intelligence applications grows, the percentage of unstructured data also grows. Figure 11-8, courtesy of Gartner Research, shows the mix of unstructured data kept in data warehouses and how it varies with the scope of the application.

---

[1] TDWI, "Master Data Management: Consensus Driven Data Definitions for Cross-Application Consistency," Phillip Russom, November 2006.

[2] Ark Group Business Intelligence Survey, January 2007.

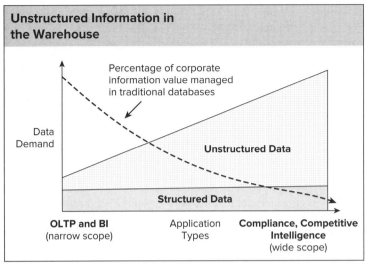

FIGURE 11-8

(Courtesy of Gartner Research)

Benefits of BI Search Combinations

The business benefits of combining BI and search include:

➤ Better business decisions with accurate, enriched data

➤ Increased productivity with real-time ad hoc querying across very large data sets

➤ Increased adoption with easy and intuitive access to intelligence

➤ Broader range of insight through correlation of structured and unstructured information

Strategic decisions are often made using unstructured and semi-structured data from a wide variety of sources. Reliable and flexible access to high-quality information can drive the success of a business. These general benefits are illustrated by two particular themes: BI for the masses, and Search as the UI paradigm for BI.

BI for the Masses

How much time does a professional spend waiting for information in a typical day? Financial analysts, for example, can spend up to hours waiting to retrieve a single query. While it is true that analysts can work on other things while waiting for information, doing so requires division of focus and multitasking; this is not the most efficient mode of work when doing intricate analyses. Ultimately, an analyst's productivity is bounded by the speed of access to the data he/she needs.

One of the shortcomings of traditional BI is that it is limited to a small number of users. Only a very few people in an organization know how to use their BI tools and how to access the company's reports.

IT departments and users have traditionally been at odds with each other over self-service analytics. IT departments seek to maintain IT governance and control; end users want to generate and manage their own content and reporting.

Microsoft has been focused on BI for the masses for over a decade now. Since the most common BI tool is Microsoft Office Excel, it is natural for them to provide some self-service capabilities for BI.

Managed self-service business intelligence is a theme for SQL Server 2008 R2. It aims to provide both end users and IT with cutting-edge tools to create, analyze and model, and share and manage business intelligence data in a secure and streamlined way.

Self-service analysis tools allow end users to quickly create solutions from disparate data sources within a familiar user interface. By publishing these solutions, users can easily share them with others. IT retains management and oversight, so they can help ensure the reliability, performance, and security of data-driven assets across the enterprise, while also gaining better visibility into how people are using their data.

Search as the UI Paradigm for BI

We've seen that many fewer people interact with BI tools than they might (or than really need to). The demand for the value of business intelligence clearly outstrips the supply of qualified business intelligence specialists who can assemble, test, and demonstrate the merit of business intelligence reports. Traditional BI tools are just too difficult and specialized for most users. The necessary solution is less strict but still useful business intelligence.

What can search teach BI in this regard? Ease of use and interactivity. However, along with this comes more ambiguity.

Search offers the broader audience a way to explore data. The results are surely more ambiguous and less precise than traditional BI. Users, however, quickly become skilled at filtering through the ambiguity and come up with answers that they trust enough to use. This works just as with information access to unstructured data, so it's a very familiar paradigm. Figure 11-9 shows an example screenshot of search used to explore structured data.

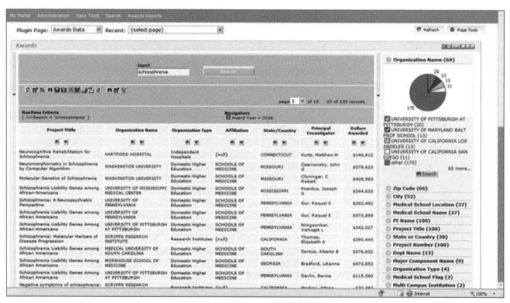

FIGURE 11-9

Searching for information when it is not readily available is, in some ways, a bigger problem than slow access to available information. While an individual can do other work while waiting for information, searching is an active activity. Time spent searching is time wasted. Analysts in strategy roles spend a lot of time looking for the datapoints that are pertinent for formulating a business strategy. They often are surprisingly difficult to find among the many research services a typical organization subscribes to.

Culture and convention, and the need for controlled, modeled, and qualified information — associated with conventional business intelligence — demanded the elimination of ambiguity. With the relaxation of such requirements to satisfy the need for exploratory and more ad hoc business intelligence comes an opportunity for information access to expand its capabilities in structured data.

ADOPTION OF SEARCH/BI INTEGRATION

We've discussed the ways in which BI and search combine, and covered the benefits of using search and BI together. But how much is this happening in the real world? Search/BI convergence is still new to most companies, but it is not unknown. There are many analyst and vendor write-ups about it, and most professionals deep in either search or BI technology have some ideas about how search and BI can complement each other. We find that the most common ideas about how companies might adopt Search/BI integration fall into the following categories:

➤ Unifying internal and external information sources

➤ Acceleration of ad-hoc BI queries

➤ Query-based retrieval of common facts, reports, and dashboards

➤ Structuring unstructured information

➤ Combining predetermined models with serendipitous discovery

Some in the industry have wondered whether search tools will eventually gain enough capabilities that they will eliminate the need for business intelligence tools altogether. This is not going to happen. However, there are varying opinions about how far search might encroach on BI's territory.

Survey on Adoption

A research study by Ventana Research[1] about level of adoption and reasons for adoption revealed that most companies see a strategic element to the integration of search and BI. Though only 30 percent of companies had already integrated BI and Search, 87 percent indicated that unstructured and semistructured data was "somewhat important" or "very important" to decision making. The value of BI-Search integration varied by function, as shown in Figure 11-10.

The majority of respondents indicated that they plan first to deploy it to executive management and analysts so that they can make more informed and more timely decisions. The survey also reveals the integration of BI with search will be the new interface to ad hoc query data; better querying was one of the top requirements participants cited. As well, 83 percent deemed it important to integrate, as part of the results delivered to business users, other forms of semi-structured data, such as XML and RSS feeds, and unstructured data, such as free-form text that can be found in documents.

---

[1] Ventana Research, "Business Intelligence and Search: Combining technologies to foster better business decisions," 2007.

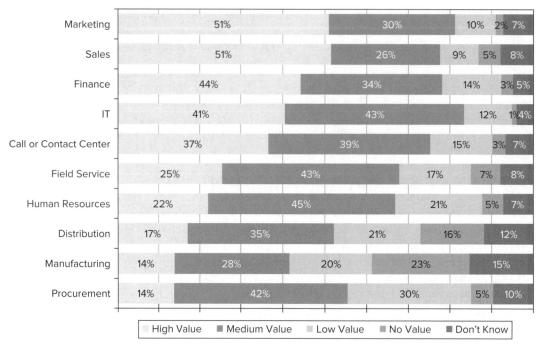

Source: Ventana Research

FIGURE 11-10

The survey uncovered a strong emphasis, expressed by more than half of all participants, on information about customers and a desire that integrated BI and search technology contribute to boosting revenue. The research found that the integration of customer-related content and documents with BI is critical to deployments, as is gaining a better understanding of the customer and activities. While search and text analytics are generic in focus and can be applied across the organization, here again survey respondents placed priority on customer information in determining the business case for adopting new BI and search technology.

While standardization is always an issue for technologists, particularly in large organizations, our study showed it is not a high priority for respondents, except those who identified themselves as CIOs.

Areas of Adoption

Business intelligence and information access products can work together effectively in many ways, as described earlier in this chapter. The survey we just discussed showed that adoption is happening but that we are in the relatively early stages. Where will this go? IDC predicts that Search/BI integration will be adopted first in the following areas:

➤   Search in business intelligence products for specific reports will improve. Titles, metadata, KPIs, data elements such as fields, and, ultimately, cells, will all become searchable.

➤   Information access will rationalize unstructured data elements within disciplined data sets (that is, text fields) so that analytical tools may act on them as though they were structured.

➤ Information access technologies will provide metadata about structured data by revealing how users examine the data (such as which products different shoppers compare in an online retail environment).

➤ Information access technologies will overlay structured data, such as call records generated by customer service representatives about a specific product, with a nuanced interpretation of the customers' sentiments about that product.

➤ Information access technologies will analyze data from outside the enterprise (such as customer sentiment revealed in blogs and social networking facilities) to augment enterprise data.

➤ Business intelligence platforms will drive processes into information access, which will prompt users to consider particular queries and results that they would not normally address.

➤ Information access products will be used to perform ad hoc queries on data sets that have not been optimized before to allow that.

Applications at the Intersection of Search and BI

We showed how search and BI combine at the start of this chapter, by discussing the patterns of text analytics, search analytics, and unified information access. These translate into real-world applications, which are found in many industries. Some of the most common ones include:

➤ Risk management

➤ Fraud detection

➤ Anti–money laundering

➤ IP (intellectual property) protection

➤ Communications

➤ Competitive intelligence and market intelligence

➤ Customer intelligence

➤ Voice of the customer

These applications fall into three main categories: customer-centric applications, information consolidation, and operational intelligence.

Customer-Centric Applications

Applications that focus on customers and on correlating many different sources of information about them are some of the strongest early applications for Search/BI Integration. There are several dimensions of this:

➤ Production and management of quality information about your customers (know your customer)

➤ Easy access for your employees to customer information (serve your customer)

➤ Easy access for your customers to information that helps them help themselves

Information Consolidation

Another class of applications for Search/BI integration focuses on consolidating information from many sources. These applications strive to deliver several key capabilities:

➤ Bridge across silos of information — unify large quantities of data across a hodgepodge of systems and information types.

➤ Unlock difficult-to-access data including SAP, Siebel, mainframe applications; structured and unstructured data combined.

➤ Provide high-performance flexible access for large numbers of users.

Operational Intelligence

A third class of applications for Search/BI integration is found in operations of all types, often characterized by regular, ongoing streams of data. This type of application is often provided as a dashboard, delivering intuitive, ad hoc access to structured operational data. However, applications in this class have much more depth than meets the eye, because they are tapping into unstructured information within operational systems as well.

MICROSOFT BI OVERVIEW

Before we get to the specifics of the new BI/Search capabilities from Microsoft, let's look briefly at the overall Microsoft BI stack, as of June 2010. Microsoft has steadily worked at BI and today is a leader in the field. It has several BI tools and applications that have BI features, aimed at different scenarios. Which BI tools that you should use depends on the specific problems that you are trying to solve. The three main product groups where there are BI capabilities are SQL Server, SharePoint, and Office. These three groups are interoperable and are used together in many scenarios.

Figure 11-11 shows an overview of the BI products and capabilities available from Microsoft.

BI in Microsoft SharePoint 2010

Daily business activities have associated information and insights that emerge in three main areas of business intelligence: personal, team, and organizational. There will be overlap across these areas. For example, a company's employees may use Microsoft Excel 2010 and Excel Services in Microsoft SharePoint Server 2010 to make relevant business decisions at the corporate level. PerformancePoint Services uses Excel, Visio Services, and Excel Services to complement its BI tools to deliver a corporate dashboard that may reflect elements of personal and team BI. By design, all Microsoft BI products interoperate so that teams and individuals inside an organization can move across the continuum of personal, team, and organizational information. The products are designed to work together across this continuum.

Figure 11-12 shows the BI services in Microsoft SharePoint Server 2010 and provides an idea of how they relate to each area.

Business User Experience

Familiar User Experience
Self-service Access and Insight
Data Exploration and Analysis
Predictive Analysis
Data Visualization
Contextual Visualization

Business Collaboration Platform

Integrated Content and Collaboration
Thin Clients
Dashboards
BI Search
Content Management
Compositions

Information Platform

Information Platform
Analysis Services
Reporting Services
Integration Services
Master Data
Data Mining Services
Data Warehousing

FIGURE 11-11

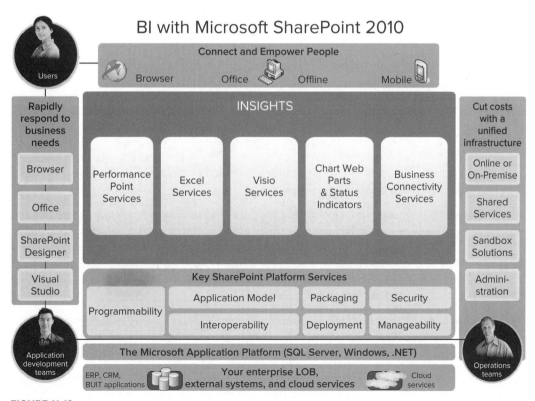

FIGURE 11-12

The key elements of BI with SharePoint 2010 include:

➤ **Excel 2010** — The end user's analysis tool of choice for viewing, manipulating, performing analysis on, generating intelligence from, and creating reports about an organization's data.

➤ **Excel Services** — A SharePoint Server 2010 application service that provides server-side calculation and browser-based rendering of Excel workbooks. Excel Services can be used for:

➤ Real-time, interactive reporting to include parameterized what-if analysis.

➤ Distribution of all or part of a workbook for analysis by multiple users.

➤ A platform for building business applications.

➤ **Visio Graphics Service** — A service on the SharePoint Server 2010 platform that lets users share and view Microsoft Visio diagrams. The service also enables data-connected Microsoft Visio 2010 diagrams to be refreshed and updated from various data sources.

➤ **PerformancePoint Services** — A performance management service that uses tools to monitor and analyze business. It provides tools for building dashboards, scorecards, and key performance indicators (KPIs). PerformancePoint Services can help people across an organization make informed business decisions that align with company-wide objectives and strategy. You can bring together data from multiple data sources (including SQL Server Analysis Services, Microsoft SQL Server, SharePoint lists, and Excel Services) to track and monitor your data.

Table 11-1 shows scenarios that are appropriate for each tool within the SharePoint Server 2010 BI suite.

TABLE 11-1: Summary of Tools in the SharePoint Server 2010 BI Suite

TOOL	SCENARIO
Excel 2010	Giving users browser-based access to a server-calculated version of an Excel worksheet. Use Excel 2010 and Excel Services to view, refresh, and interact with analytic models connected to data sources. Also use them for analysis, filtering, and presentation of locally stored data.
Excel Services	Sharing content with multiple persons across an organization. Excel Services lets you take authored content in Excel 2010 and make it available in a web browser. Excel Services is also used with a model that can be widely distributed (for example, a mortgage calculator). In both scenarios, Excel Services enables the author to publish targeted content without making the underlying intellectual property available to consumers.
PerformancePoint Services	Creating dashboards, scorecards, and key performance indicators (KPIs) that deliver a summarized view of business a performance. PerformancePoint Services gives users integrated analytics for monitoring, analyzing, and reporting.
Visio Services	Building a visual representation of business structures that are bound to data. Examples include processes, systems, and resources. An engineer can use the visualization to create data-bound objects to represent a process.

PowerPivot for Excel 2010

Microsoft SQL Server 2008 R2 PowerPivot for Microsoft Excel 2010 extends Excel to add support for large-scale data. It has an in-memory data store as an option for SQL Server Analysis Services. Microsoft views this as a way to provide BI to the masses. According to the PowerPivot site (http://www.powerpivot.com/) PowerPivot is "empowering a new class of business users to build and share powerful BI solutions with little or no IT support, while still enabling IT to monitor and manage user-generated BI solutions."

Figure 11-13 shows a screenshot of PowerPivot. The UI is very familiar since it is Microsoft Excel, but the amount of data that can be manipulated is amazing. Hundreds of millions of rows can be kept in one workbook and manipulated rapidly.

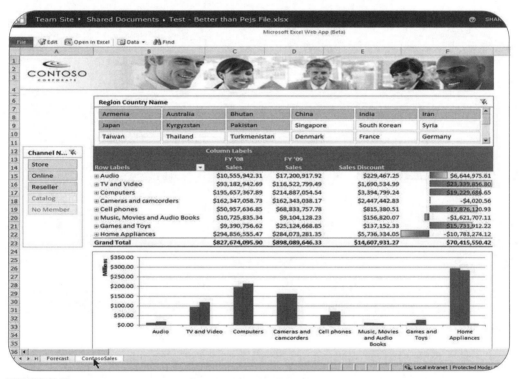

FIGURE 11-13

By using PowerPivot for Excel, you can merge multiple data sources to include corporate databases, worksheets, reports, and data feeds. There are client and server components for PowerPivot. The client is an extension to Excel workbooks that contain PowerPivot data that can be published to SharePoint Server 2010. Microsoft SQL Server 2008 R2 PowerPivot for Microsoft SharePoint 2010 is the server-side component that supports PowerPivot access in Microsoft SharePoint 2010 products, similarly to Excel workbooks, which can be published to Excel Services.

Use PowerPivot for Excel when you want to combine native Excel functionality with the in-memory engine to let users interactively explore and perform calculations on large data sets and quickly manipulate millions of rows of data in a single Excel workbook for ad hoc reports.

SQL Server

SQL Server 2008 R2, the latest version, includes enhanced XML support, integration of .NET Framework objects in databases, and improved integration with Microsoft Visual Studio and the Microsoft Office System, as well as improved analysis, reporting, and data integration services. Figure 11-14 shows the main components of SQL 2008 R2.

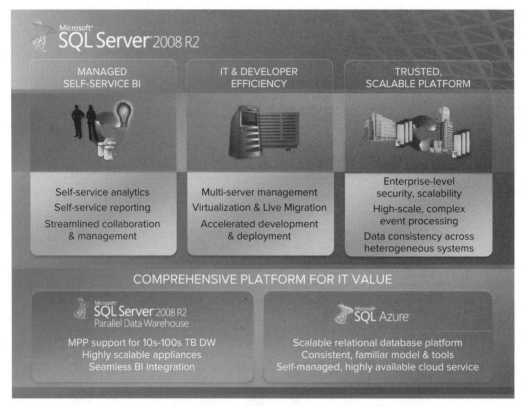

FIGURE 11-14

These include a set of elements for self-service BI including analytics and reporting (including PowerPivot), a set of capabilities for deployment and management (including full virtualization support), and large-scale platform features (including StreamInsight).

SSRS

Microsoft SQL Server 2008 Reporting Services (SSRS) is a server-based reporting platform that provides a full range of ready-to-use tools and services to help you create, deploy, and manage Reporting Services reports for your organization. After you install the Reporting Services add-in for Microsoft SharePoint Server and configure the two servers for integration, you can upload or publish report server content types to a SharePoint library and then view and manage those documents from a SharePoint site.

Reporting Services can be deployed in two modes:

➤ Native mode means a report server that runs as an application server alone, without sharing the content database with SharePoint Server. Reports can be managed and viewed through the Report Manager Web application. SharePoint web parts can be enabled so that you can select and view reports from a report server.

➤ SharePoint integrated mode means that a report server is integrated with a SharePoint Server farm and requires you to configure the report server in integrated mode and that you download and configure an add-in component on each of your SharePoint front-end webs. Integrated mode allows the user to manage and view reports from SharePoint document libraries.

SSRS with SharePoint

SQL Server Reporting Services provides tools and services to help you create, deploy, and manage reports for your organization in your own website or in SharePoint Server. It also provides programming features that enable you to extend and customize reports. The report authoring tools work with an Office-type application and are fully integrated with SQL Server tools and components, and also the SharePoint Server environment. You can build reports on SharePoint lists, publish reports to SharePoint Server 2007 or 2010, incorporate reports inside your portal by using a Web Part for reports, and fully manage your reports published in SharePoint document libraries.

When you use SQL Server Reporting Services (SSRS) with SharePoint Server, there are two modes to choose from. The standard mode is referred to as Connected mode. It requires SharePoint Server, the SSRS add-in, and the SQL Server 2008 R2 Report Server. The new mode is Local mode. It is a lightweight setup for integrating Reporting Services with SharePoint Server. It requires only SharePoint Server and the SSRS add-in.

Use SQL Server Reporting Services when you want to deliver reports that are published at set intervals and on demand. It's also suitable where report requirements are well established and customers are not always familiar with the underlying data set.

Microsoft StreamInsight and Complex Event Processing

Microsoft StreamInsight is new with SQL Server 2008 R2. It is a powerful platform that you can use to develop and deploy complex event processing (CEP) applications. Its high-throughput stream-processing architecture and the Microsoft .NET Framework–based development platform enable you to quickly implement robust and highly efficient event processing applications.

Event stream sources typically include data from manufacturing applications, financial trading applications, web analytics, and operational analytics. By using StreamInsight, you can develop CEP applications that derive immediate business value from this raw data by reducing the cost of extracting, analyzing, and correlating the data; and by allowing you to monitor, manage, and mine the data for conditions, opportunities, and defects almost instantly.

StreamInsight is the successor to a defunct capability called SQL Server Event Services (SSES). It is much more effective than the old SSES and includes a stronger architecture, better performance, and better control. Figure 11-15 shows the architecture of a StreamInsight application.

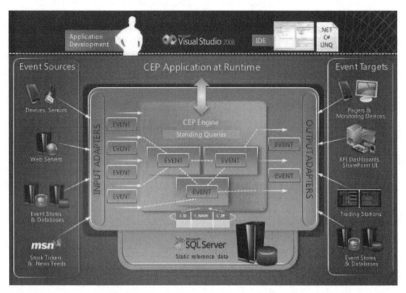

FIGURE 11-15

By using StreamInsight to develop CEP applications, you can achieve the following tactical and strategic goals for your business:

➤ Monitor your data from multiple sources for meaningful patterns, trends, exceptions, and opportunities.

➤ Analyze and correlate data incrementally, while the data is in-flight — that is, without first storing it — yielding very low latency.

➤ Aggregate seemingly unrelated events from multiple sources and perform highly complex analyses over time.

➤ Manage your business by performing low-latency analytics on the events and triggering response actions that are defined on your business KPIs.

➤ Respond quickly to areas of opportunity or threat by incorporating your KPI definitions into the logic of the CEP application, thereby improving operational efficiency and your ability to respond quickly to business opportunities.

➤ Mine events for new business KPIs.

➤ Move toward a predictive business model by mining historical data to continuously refine and improve your KPI definitions.

At first glance, StreamInsight may not seem to have anything to do with Enterprise Search. However, one of the classic areas of search is real-time profiling or alerting. This is the equivalent of content event processing, but it works with less structured events (such as newswires or intelligence wires). This functionality is included with FAST ESP, FSIS, and FSIA, and is called Real-Time Alerting or RTA. There is no direct connection between StreamInsight and Real-Time Alerting, but it is another area in which BI and search have similar functions done in different ways.

FAST for Search on Structured Data

Using Enterprise Search on structured data has benefits in many scenarios, such as:

➤ e-Commerce search (product catalogs)

➤ Insurance investigations (claims forms, medical records, etc.)

➤ Customer support (bug tracking, customer records, product bulletins)

➤ Mineral and oil exploration (geological surveys, seismic records, etc.)

➤ Logistics and operations support (inventory, shipping records, operations reports)

Search can open up line-of-business information for rapid, intuitive exploration and findability. Most organizations have enormous amounts of information in myriad forms (customer records, insurance claims, purchase orders, inventory records, sales pipeline data, patient records, geo-exploration data, product quality surveys, etc.). Applying search to any of these can open it up for consistent, efficient access by many users.

Combining multiple sources of structured data in one search index provides data fusion — simultaneous access and exploration in dynamic ways. Search is not hard-bound to the schema of any source, making it a natural way to work with information of many forms. If the schema of the information changes, or more sources are added, this doesn't require retrofitting the system; it handles these on the fly and keeps working.

FAST Search for SharePoint has many capabilities that make particularly well suited for searching structured data. Following are the top 10:

➤ **Easy access to structured data repositories** — FAST includes out-of-box connectors for many systems, has a high-performance JDBC connector suited for indexing databases, and uses SharePoint's Business Connectivity Services (BCS) for line-of-business data access. New connectors can be made easily for structured data, without code, using the SharePoint Designer's built-in tooling. The connector framework has many features that ease structured data access, such as data association (you can express foreign key relationships between data tables, so they are crawled together, searched as a single unit, and updated when either table changes).

➤ **Security models suitable for structured data** — BCS maintains security across systems, often using claims-based authorization. Search maintains this security so that users see only the information they are entitled to, even though the data source security model may be very different from Active Directory or NTFS.

➤ **Scales to extreme numbers of records** — Search systems scale in terms of the number of documents in a system. With structured data, the natural unit may be a form of a database record; there are often hundreds of millions or billions of records to be searched. FAST's extreme scale capabilities allow searching across these huge repositories (which are often the ones that need findability the most).

➤ **Deep refiners with counts over the entire result set** — These refiners give the demographics of the data and provide intuitive exploration and drill-down. Structured data has fields with well-enumerated values, fields with free-form values, and typed fields (dates, values, codes), which lend themselves to parametric search and exploration with refiners. Numeric and data refiners can use sliders, ranges, and so on for exploration, and numeric refiners can display sums or averages as well as counts.

➤ **Fast searches with many fields** — FAST has great performance even with hundreds of fields in a schema (even thousands with careful engineering). Structured data sources tend to have many fields which might be specified in a search, or might be found in an any field search. Most search systems slow down dramatically (or crash) when the number of fields gets large; FAST's technology is remarkable in this dimension.

➤ **Performance with complex queries** — Structured data exploration may require complex queries with dozens or even hundreds of terms combined (with AND, OR, NOT, etc.). FAST's technology maintains strong performance even with very complex queries. Query latency for FAST is much lower than database technology, and query processing is much more robust than competing search engines (which may fail to process complex queries). FAST implementations return results in seconds, even with extremely complex queries.

➤ **Sophisticated query capabilities with FQL** — The FAST Query Language (FQL) provides incredible searching power. This includes a rich set of operators (Boolean, proximity, numeric, range, string, phrase, anchoring, metadata, and so on) well beyond most search engines, and a full set of wildcard capabilities across fields and composite fields. It also includes sorting capabilities, such as SORTFORMULA(), which can combine terms in formulas — useful in location-based searches (find what's near) and expression-based searches (find data sets that look like this). Ranking capabilities allow dynamic changes in the ordering of results, including RANK, XRANK, and explicit term weighting. FQL is not something a human user would use, but it lets developers create unique and powerful search that is particularly useful with complex structured data sets.

➤ **Advanced linguistic processing** — FAST excels in linguistics — not just handling the widest set of languages but also in processing that enhances the findability of information. Capabilities such as lemmatization and similarity search apply to structured data as well as unstructured data, which help users find information quickly and easily.

➤ **Powerful symbol and pattern matching** — Structured data often contains codes, symbols, and patterns (part numbers like CX-65N-433-2T, diagnostic codes like Y333.44, Social Security numbers, phone numbers, zip codes, etc.). While exact matches on these can be done with any search technology, users struggle to enter them accurately and both data and queries are prone to error. FAST supports fuzzy matches, which support "find parts in stock like CX-65M433-2y."

➤ **Property extraction improves your content** — FAST includes technology to recognize entities in text: names of people, places, companies, products, and so on. This can also include patterns such as zip codes, phone numbers, and the like. This can add additional structure to the text fields found in most line-of-business data. For example, investigation reports (insurance claims, police reports, call center notes) have important information in narratives. Many systems have a fixed number of fields, forcing users to put key information in unstructured fields. Using FAST, users can find these records, not overlook them.

Details of the features and capabilities described above can be found in the product documentation (listed in Appendix A). The documentation doesn't specifically talk about search on structured data, so you have to make this connection yourself using the top 10 list above or (even better) with your particular application in mind.

THE MICROSOFT BI INDEXING CONNECTOR

The Microsoft Business Intelligence Indexing Connector was introduced in May 2010, and requires FAST Search for SharePoint. It improves search capabilities for Microsoft Excel and for Microsoft SQL Server Reporting Services (SSRS) reports and the underlying data sources that are part of the report. Users see improved results, descriptions, thumbnails, and previews, and they are able to refine search results.

The BI Indexing Connector is an example of a report finder application.

Tour of the Reports Center

When the Business Intelligence Indexing Connector feature is installed on SharePoint Server 2010, a Reports tab is added to the All Sites and People tabs, and possibly other customized search tabs. Figure 11-16 shows the Reports Tab. The Reports tab helps you narrow search results to Excel and SQL Server Reporting Services files, and it takes advantage of the additional search features described here.

FIGURE 11-16

The BI Indexing Connector offers rich result descriptions. These descriptions are broken down into categories to give users a better understanding of the search results. If the category PivotTables, Tables, Charts, or Gauges is found in a search, the keywords are highlighted and included within the context of the category where they are located. In the result shown in Figure 11-17, the keywords "Australia" and "Sales" are found in charts and tables.

FIGURE 11-17

Administrators can deploy the Microsoft Business Intelligence Indexing Connector to improve search capabilities for Microsoft Excel and Microsoft SQL Server Reporting Services (SSRS) reports and the underlying data sources that are part of the report. When the Microsoft Business Intelligence Indexing Connector is installed, an additional search tab, *Reports,* appears on the search page. By using the Reports search tab, users can see improved results, descriptions, thumbnails, and previews, and they are able to refine search results.

Searchable business intelligence assets include `.xlsx` and `.xlsm` documents, which are natively created by Microsoft Office Excel 2007 and Excel 2010. PowerPivot and SQL Server Reporting Services files are also searchable files.

Features of the BI Indexing Connector

The Business Intelligence Indexing Connector lets you increase the relevance of search queries in the following ways: After you search in the Reports tab, refinement categories enable you to limit the results of your search by selecting available filters underneath the categories. Three additional categories are included that are not part of the FAST Search Server 2010 for SharePoint list of standard refiners. They are Report Format, Data Sources, and Data Category.

As an example, if you select Table as a format underneath the Report Format category, the results of your search are limited to files that contain tables. Likewise, if you select Chart, the results of your search are limited to files that have charts in them.

When you perform a search on the Reports tab, the resulting file description for each file provides description headers that help you locate the file that you want. Additionally, thumbnail images of files in PowerPivot Gallery and a preview option are available. The following list contains descriptions of the headers.

➤ **In PivotTable** — Displays the keywords from your search that are located in a PivotTable.

➤ **In Tables** — Displays the keywords from your search that are located in a table.

➤ **Charts** — Displays the keywords from your search that are located in a chart.

> ➤ **Data Sources** — Displays the name of the data source, if one exists.

> ➤ **Sheets** — Displays the name of the Excel 2010 worksheet, if an Excel file exists.

> ➤ **Other Key words** — Displays other keywords from your search.

Refinement categories are located to the left of the search page to help you filter the results.

Even if a keyword is not found in a report, the report will be returned if that keyword is found in the datasource it uses. It will be ranked lower than reports with the term in them.

Architecture of the BI Indexing Connector

Figure 11-18 shows the architecture of the BI Indexing Connector. It is a straightforward integration of FAST Search for SharePoint with Excel Services and SQL. The primary integration points are:

> ➤ A custom iFilter that understands the format of SRSS, Excel, and PowerPivot.

> ➤ An additional tab in the Search Center, labeled Reports

> ➤ An identified location where reports are stored and available for crawling.

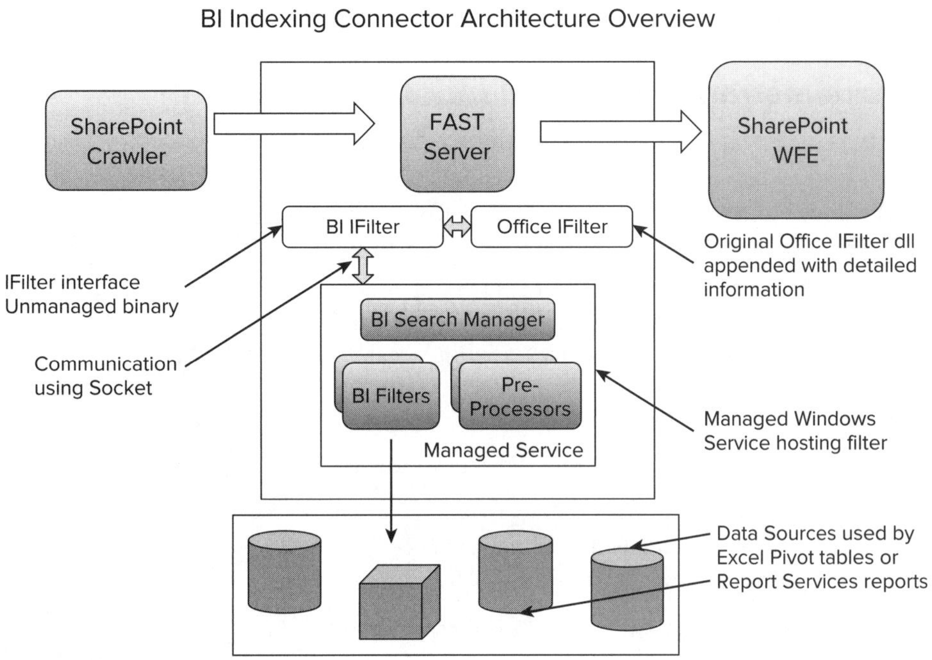

BI Indexing Connector Architecture Overview

FIGURE 11-18

The BI Indexing Connector can work with any size FS4SP installation. Figure 11-19 shows a sample topology, including FAST Search for SharePoint with Excel Service and SQL. Note that the BI Indexing Connector only works with FAST Search for SharePoint, not with ESP, FSIS, or FSIA.

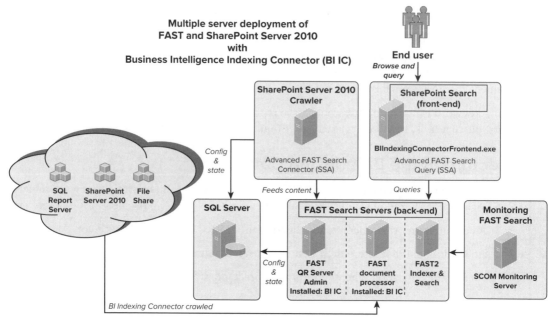

FIGURE 11-19

Setup and Administration of the BI Indexing Connector

For BIIC to work, the FAST Search Server 2010 for SharePoint admin and document-processor servers must have Business Intelligence Indexing Connector installed. In the BI Indexing Connector Configuration Wizard, you have the option to enable crawling functionality for external data sources. By default, the feature is disabled.

For a detailed description of the setup you can read the documentation (referenced in the suggested reading), but the installation itself is quite straightforward and includes a Setup Wizard. The Setup wizard program is shown in Figure 11-20 as it appears on the Start menu.

Starting the Setup Wizard takes you to the first screen, as shown in Figure 11-21.

Setup requires a service account that has the entitlements needed to crawl the desired BI reports, as shown in Figure 11-22.

It also allows you to specify the settings for the BI IFilter, as shown in Figure 11-23.

The BI Indexing Connector extends the existing IFilter interface for Office on the FAST Search Server 2010 for SharePoint crawl servers. It is installed as a feature, as shown in Figure 11-24. The following kinds of files are crawled and processed by the Business Intelligence Indexing Connector.

FIGURE 11-20

➤ Microsoft Office Excel 2007 and Microsoft Excel 2010 workbooks (.xlsx)

➤ Microsoft Macro-Enabled workbooks (.xlsm)

➤ SQL Server Reporting Services and Report Builder 3.0 reports (.rdl)

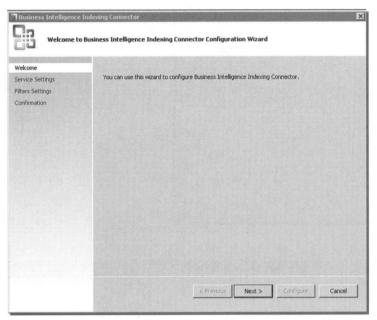

FIGURE 11-21

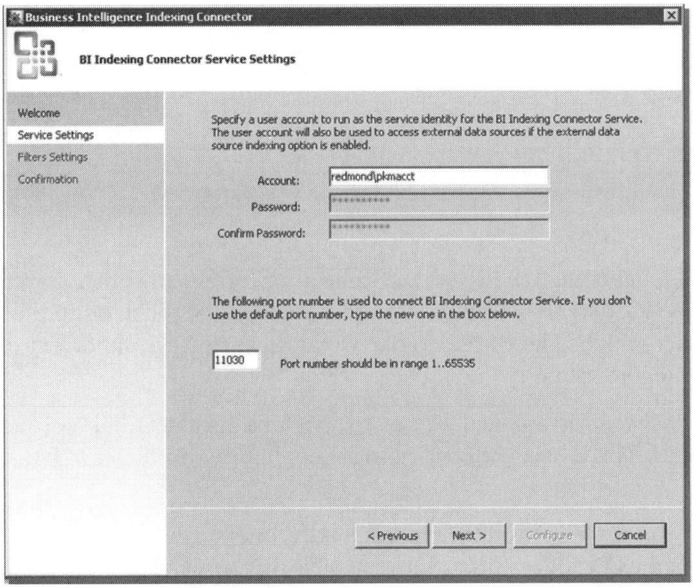

FIGURE 11-22

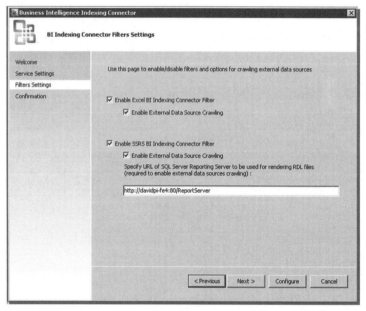

FIGURE 11-23

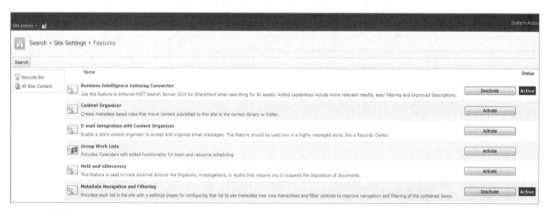

FIGURE 11-24

Once you are installed and running, operating the BIIC is the same as operating any other search. The crawls will be visible in the FAST Content SSA, and query analytics will be visible from the FAST Query SSA, like with all other search. There are two particular areas that are important to remember as you operate with the reports center:

➤ All reports that you want indexed need to be delivered to a specific document library (the one you configure at installation). This is straightforward to set up, but easy to forget as you add reports of different types.

➤ The security entitlements used are the ones on the reports, *not* the ones on the data sources. Depending on how complex the BI entitlements are, it is possible that a user will be able to find a report but not be able to read some of the data in it. Since search indexes not just the reports but the value of the data sources that feed them, it is even possible that a user could find a report based on a keyword search which matches a value in a data source, but then not be able to read it. This is likely to be a rare occurrence but will be confusing to users if it happens.

THE FUTURE OF SEARCH AND BI

The BI Indexing Connector seems to be only a starting point for Microsoft. There have been recent announcements about integrated semantic search with SQL server, the use of search technology in data quality and Master Data Management (MDM), and much more. The convergence of search and BI is not just about searching for reports that BI platforms are able to produce; there is a more fundamental convergence going on, resulting in the ability to mine unstructured information by doing extraction and categorization.

Ultimately, search and BI together will deliver pervasive business intelligence. This means the use of relatively powerful but easy-to-use tools that empower individual decision makers across the enterprise to interact with information, make effective decisions, and share the results of their work on demand.

Business Analytics will become as easy as search.

SUMMARY

The convergence of search and BI is a fascinating topic. Although analysts have been talking about it for about 8 years now, only recently have practical applications emerged that are really ready for the mainstream.

The three main patterns we discussed in this chapter: text analytics, search analytics, and unified information access, are all vibrant fields in their own right. We showed only a few examples of these using Microsoft technology. LookingGlass is a good example of text analytics; it collects and analyzes social media around a set of topics, applying techniques such as sentiment analysis. The search and web reporting built into SharePoint 2010 are examples of search analytics; they also allow custom reporting via Excel Services. The log-mining techniques included with SharePoint 2010 to improve relevance with use, present query suggestions, and perform other functions are another example of search analytics. Finally, the BI Indexing Connector available for FAST Search for SharePoint is an example of a tool for unified information access.

The competitive advantage that enterprises gain from fact-based insights into their customers, suppliers, and internal operations makes a compelling argument for extending analytics applications directly to the desk of every decision maker in the company. Search technology can make this possible.

12

The Future of Search

WHAT'S IN THIS CHAPTER?

➤ Working with a flawed business model

➤ Examining trends in Enterprise Search

➤ Looking at future directions of search

➤ Learning what you can do today

Now that you've had a chance to look at the exciting new search technologies from Microsoft and learned how to use them to best advantage, let's take some time as we close to look at where we've been in search, where we are now, and where we are going. As Yogi Berra said, "prediction is very hard, especially about the future." That said, let's get started.

THE SORRY STATE OF SEARCH

Search has been used in enterprises for more than 30 years. In the earliest days, simple keyword search offered power that was previously unheard of, and it seemed like living in the future. As the volume of digital data increased, search technology evolved to include a number of statistical algorithms and more advanced linguistics and taxonomies to deliver even better results.

The problem is that organizational digital assets continued to grow to the point that many companies and agencies now have more digital content than was available on the entire Internet in 1995. As this mass of digital content grows, it has become increasingly difficult to imagine how clever algorithms alone can deliver the high-quality results users have come to expect. Where do we go from here?

The Flawed HAL9000 Usage Model

"Find me the proposal I sent to NASA last month, HAL."

"I'm sorry, Dave, I'm afraid I can't do that."

In 1968, science fiction writer Arthur C. Clark collaborated with filmmaker Stanley Kubrick in the movie production of his landmark book, *2001: A Space Odyssey*. One of the central characters was an intelligent computer, HAL9000, who was responsible for just about every aspect of the ship and its crew. The human beings could interact with HAL just as they might to any other human crew member, and the computer understood and would give intelligent answers. This interaction seemed so natural, and advances in artificial intelligence seemed so rapid, that it was not hard to imagine a time when human beings and computers could interact easily, using natural language. HAL was "born" (according to the book, not the movie) on January 12 1997, only 29 years after the movie was released. The idea of HAL-like computers — not to mention having hotels in space — seemed reasonable and quite credible.

Back to reality; wouldn't it be nice if you could speak to a search engine, and get a concise answer? It's more than 40 years since the HAL9000's dialog with his crewmates, and search technology still isn't there.

But think about the implied assumption behind HAL9000 — that, given enough time, even a human researcher could always find an answer for your question 100% of the time — and that you'd get the same answer if you asked two, three or a dozen other people for an answer. It doesn't seem feasible that you and I would always agree on which documents are most relevant. And yet we expect a computer to do that!

There are some other flawed assumptions in the HAL9000 model. In the movie, the human operators ask well-thought-out questions, and those questions do have "correct" answers. And yet, when we have a query for today's search technology, we usually enter fewer than three terms, almost never a well-thought-out question. And even the correctness of answers is suspect; imagine the debate that would ensue when grading the results of the lengthier query "effectiveness of tax cuts to stimulate the economy." Regardless of your personal stance on this issue, you can imagine the wide differences of opinion on the matter.

So if this HAL9000 usage model is not in our immediate future, then what is?

Enterprise Search 2.0

Before we look at where we are today, let's look back for a moment. John Battelle, in his book *The Search*, makes a great analogy between search result lists and a textual list of files you might see from a `dir` command in MS-DOS. We call this the capabilities we dub *search dial tone*: you can search, but don't expect many advanced capabilities.

Search was often provided by IT to meet a check-box requirement: something that the organization needed but wasn't able to put any resources into making successful. Heck, just having search was better than before!

But now, Enterprise Search technologies like Microsoft's FAST are starting to give us the tools to implement better search, using things like facets which Microsoft calls refiners; best bets and content suggestions that can override default relevance algorithms for specific queries; the beginnings of social relevance that delivers results for 'people like you'. These capabilities improve usability and findability, and provide what we've called Enterprise Search 2.0 (ES2.0). The industry is still in the early stages of incorporating social and collaborative capabilities into commercial products, but most people understand the benefits; soon, all search technologies, both commercial and open source, will include these ES2.0 features.

What are some things that make Enterprise Search 2.0 better than earlier implementations? The primary characteristics of ES2.0 include search that is:

➤ Business-driven

➤ Conversational

➤ Socially aware

➤ Integrated with other content sources

Let's take a look into each of these in greater depth.

Business-Driven Search

At the beginning of the century, clever organizations realized that search as a back-end technology just wasn't cutting it. Tuning relevance required developer support and sometimes weeks of effort, and the web business model favored organizations that could adapt quickly. When a supplier offered price incentives to eCommerce companies, relevancy models had to shift quickly. Early Enterprise Search 2.0 companies created a business console that shifted responsibility for the search experience from IT to the business owner, who could not only observe search activity, but could change relevance in response to business needs.

Conversational Search

When you're on a trip to a new destination and want to find a nice place to eat, you may ask the hotel's concierge for a recommendation. Usually, the concierge will ask you a few questions before making a recommendation: what kind of food do you like? What price range are you looking for? What kind of atmosphere do you want?

In the past, typing a single term or two into a search form would produce answers, but the results were often ambiguous or imprecise. ES2.0 delivers a full result list with useful titles, dynamic summaries, and sometimes thumbnail images of the pages, but it also provides a number of options, such as facets and suggestions. These engage the search user in a conversation leading to more relevant results. This kind of iterative give and take is how human beings interact, and generally users will engage with the search platform if they think they are progressing toward a successful outcome.

Socially Aware

Saying a search platform uses social awareness in determining results may be one of the most ambiguous capabilities because it can mean different things to different people. For the purposes of this discussion, the term applies to search that considers proximity, similarity, and interests in determining relevance.

In the enterprise, employees can benefit from the knowledge that others in their department or location have: if you need something, you can ask the person at the next desk. But with telecommuting and remote employees, the next desk may be hundreds of miles distant. A search platform that can deliver results with a slight relevancy bias to documents your co-workers have authored or viewed can help offset that lack of personal contact.

Companies also have geographically distributed divisions or subsidiaries that may use similar technologies, so two people with similar jobs may not even be aware of each other. ES2.0 not only shows documents authored or viewed by distant employees with similar jobs; it can actually include information about these other people as well, facilitating personal contact.

Finally, regardless of job function or location, employees come with their own interests. Perhaps a biology researcher has an interest in a related technology and wants to stay current with that field. Based on search activity, an ES2.0 platform is aware of these searches, and can include documents that others who have similar interests have found and viewed in their search activity.

The important thing to remember is that a good ES2.0 platform doesn't remove documents from a result list because of social similarity; rather it provides a slight bias in relevancy to boost documents that others have found helpful.

Integrated with Other Content Sources

Too many disparate sources of organizational knowledge end up as silos of information that are not easily shared. By combing, or federating, results from a number of different repositories, search platforms deliver more relevant information.

And not all content that employees and customers need is located in a single repository or site. Some content just can't be indexed due to organizational structure or content ownership. For example: sales or inventory information may be in a database; other divisions may have their own search application; and some content may be provided by subscriptions from an external organization.

A good ES2.0 platform delivers results from these other repositories, both internal and external to the organization. The search user may see content from other repositories on different parts of the result screen suggesting content from LexisNexis, Wikipedia, or other document stores or databases in the organization that are relevant to the query.

Emerging Trends in Enterprise Search

The previous section covered the kinds of capabilities that define Enterprise Search 2.0, and the major vendors have started implementing many, if not most, of them. So the question at hand, then, is what will Enterprise Search look like in the future? Are we doomed to have organizational content continue its exponential growth and will the ability to find relevant content continue to be difficult for IT, business and content owners, and users? In this section, we'll take a look at some future trends — technologies and methodologies — that will help improve enterprise findability.

In some ways, the future is already here. Many of the technologies we'll discuss already exist in commercial products and open-source projects, and the features that are successful will find their way into more products throughout the industry.

Much of the innovation in search is happening on the public Internet: after all, that's where established Enterprise Search 2.0 features first appeared, including best bets, spelling suggestions, and document tagging. We can predict some of the future capabilities of Enterprise Search by observing new and innovative technology on the web today.

Another way to predict upcoming Enterprise Search capabilities is to study the problems enterprises and individuals have with search today, on the assumption that the most annoying problems will be addressed. Some of the biggest challenges may be solved using methodology rather than pure technology.

Let's break these technologies down into logical groups:

➤ **Business-based goals** — Solving organizational issues

➤ **User Experience** — How people will use and own search

➤ **Technology** — The basic components

➤ **Operations** — How changes in search will impact IT

Business-Based Goals

Enterprise Search has become a critical platform for large and small organizations, and will be even more so in the future as content volume grows. And well-implemented search will provide a competitive differentiation between excellent and mediocre companies. What changes will we see in how search is implemented in organizations?

Search Becomes More Vertical

Organizations have realized that a single, large search repository that includes all content from all internal data sources may not be the most effective use of resources. The ability to find content no matter where it resides is important; but increasingly, employees spend more of their time searching one or two specific sets of content. The ability to search across the enterprise remains critical; but the wisdom of using one single mega-index of all corporate content may be on its way out. Generalized search is helpful in many areas, including the following:

➤ Collaboration

➤ Office productivity

➤ Portal search

➤ Social tools

➤ Analytics

On the other hand, many tasks are best performed by search-based applications (SBA), programs that utilize search in solving a business problem. Consider specialized applications where search, and the ability to find content, is business-critical:

➤ Media search (audio/video/images)

➤ eCommerce

➤ eDiscovery

➤ Data cleansing

➤ Business intelligence

Search-Based Applications

As search becomes more targeted, vendors will create search-based applications, or SBAs. These applications, based on search, will address specific verticals: business intelligence, risk assessment, portfolio analysis, and others. Rather than create specific applications in-house, companies may be able to acquire off-the-shelf applications, based on Enterprise Search content, to solve specific business needs.

User Experience

Over the last 10 years, control and ownership of Enterprise Search has moved from the IT department to business and content owners. Back then, the content owner might have specified the requirement to have search, but the purchase decision and the implementation were totally in the realm of corporate IT. These good folks, almost universally overworked and understaffed, would buy a search engine based on minimal requirements, often interpreted loosely by vendors in their proposals. As a result, the content owner didn't get everything they hoped for, and users were unhappy that they couldn't find anything.

User Roles

How the user interacts with the search technology — or more precisely how the search technology interacts with the user — is another area rich in opportunity for the near future

Right now, search treats all users pretty much the same. Some, including Microsoft FAST products, consider social attributes like location and job function when determining relevancy; but today that generally applies only to people search. Where your office is located, and to a lesser extent what business unit you work in, can impact the documents you see, but these remain static over all of your searches unless you change jobs.

As we've said, not too long ago search results were relatively plain. There was an input box near the top of a web page, and you could enter a search. Usually the input box was very short, and sometimes it had options for where you wanted to search, but it provided basic functionality. The user would type in a word or two and press Search.

With luck, the user got a list of titles and descriptions, and maybe some metadata about the result — a date or an author. Maybe the user even saw a decimal fraction indicating the calculated relevance to five decimal places. Besides the fact that showing a score is bad user interface design, the whole result list left users wanting more.

Now, a number of products provide a wide search box, and result lists are presented with contextual summaries, external links, and facets to help refine your search. Better, yes, but there are even more ways to interact with search, and we think some of these will be more prevalent in the future.

Another element of role-based search is the default search form initially displayed to the user. Most users like the wide search form used by Bing or Google. And longer search fields encourage longer queries, which help.

Some users, however, are quite skilled in search, and their job requires detailed field-specific search. Researchers or corporate librarians are just a couple of the specialized search roles that may prefer a form-based advanced search.

Like the search form, the search result may be different according to the user's role. It may not show up for the initial search, but when advanced searchers search, the result page and subsequent searches could include the advanced form based on the search.

Contextual Search

Role-based search uses known attributes of the search user in determining relevance. Contextual search has more to do with how the user got to the search form, and may include data sources relevant to the user role; previous search and viewing behavior; and even the language of the query. The results displayed will vary with context, and two users may see different results list for the same query.

Yet, within your organization, people play different roles. Many of the searches you do might be related to your primary job function. Sometimes, however, you search in a different role: you want to find the company lunch menu or vacation policy, or you're helping a remote employee find content they need. Most technologies that use context now don't do a very good job of handling this very human characteristic; hopefully, search vendors will find better ways to solve the problem in the future.

Psychic search

One thing that makes the most popular Internet search provides like Google and Bing look so good is they seem psychic: they just know what the user is asking.

Some of this is based on pure statistical analysis: Google's popular page rank that boosts content based on how relevant the site and the page are for a given query. But even more of the psychic behavior is based on a context that few enterprise search technologies utilize yet: the query itself. If the query looks like a phone number, the internet search companies display maps of the area, and often (paid) links to services that provide directory assistance. If the query is a 12 digit number of a certain format, the services recognize it as a FedEx tracking number and link to FedEx to track that package. Note the engines rarely omit other results, but they recognize the query and make educated guesses.

Enterprise Search platforms, on the other hand, don't generally include this capability out of the box. New search technologies, including the new SharePoint search products from Microsoft, do provide some social integration. But Enterprise Search can recognize entity names at index time: there is no reason these shouldn't be valid for queries as well. Type a division name and see the division manger's name and email; enter a customer name and see a link to their purchasing history — all within the scope of security policy, of course.

One-Click Search

For many searches, the user is looking for a specific document: for example, the query "current annual report" is likely a search for a single document. Making it a suggestion is a good step; simply returning the current annual report might be better. The same is true for "lunch menu" and "holiday schedule." Google does this when a user clicks I'm Feeling Lucky in place of the standard Google Search button.

This one-click search can actually enable search as navigation: hyperlinks that perform a search that links to a result list or even directly to the appropriate page. Imagine an Open Tickets link on a customer-facing support site that when clicked, performs a search of all open support tickets for the (logged in) user.

You may not need that specific application on your sites, but I suspect your organization has similar reports that can be handled as a single web page. Be creative!

There is a specific sub-set of one-clock search known as zero-click search — search that happens automatically when a browser navigates to the page. The next section, on visualization, includes a link to such a page.

Visualization

Some people want textual information when they search, and standard results lists are fine for them. Others can obtain a better understanding of the results when they are presented with related graphics representations; and some types of queries also call for graphic and perhaps interactive results lists. For these people, and these cases, visualization is the answer.

SharePoint already provides a number of visualization capabilities, including document preview using Silverlight, tag clouds, graphic best bets. Others include timelines and interactive maps that display locations on a map as part of a result list.

Visualization is usually applied to graphic representations on a search result list. There are actually more complex requests that you may not think of as a search result but which in reality are. "What did the stock market do today including up and down price spreads ordered by sectors and by companies with the most volume?" is a query. *Smart Money* magazine has that search result answered with a single page, illustrated in Figure 12-1. You can find it yourself at http://www.smartmoney.com/map-of-the-market.

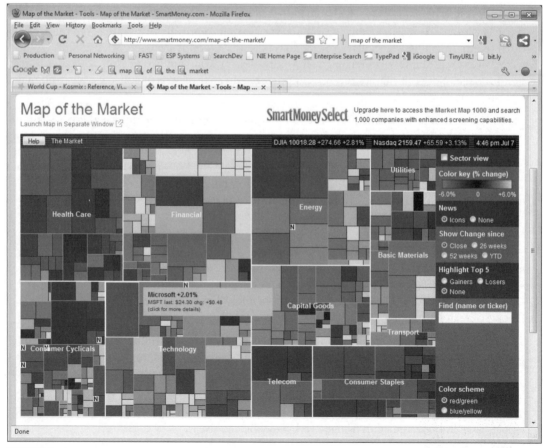

FIGURE 12-1

A final search visualization that is just starting to be available is the ability for users to customize the result lists. In the same way that Google supports extreme customization in its iGoogle pages, and to a lesser extent Bing performs some customization when logged in, Enterprise Search is beginning to provide individual users the capability to customize the search result page. The user decides to include or remove selected widgets (or web parts), and customize the look-and-feel of the result list. SharePoint search includes the ability to expose this capacity to users, and we'd expect to see more Enterprise Search platforms supporting this My Results capability.

Non-Web Clients

Some existing applications can benefit from embedded search, using smart phone operating systems such as Windows Mobile, Android, and iPhone, all of which have become increasingly popular as a portal into corporate and web content. Speaking of phones, voice recognition is also a prime area for search input and result browsing. Right now, it's not tough to write an application to serve these non-web clients via built-in browsers. Nonetheless, without special effort, conventional web result pages look off on smart phones and other mobile devices; but there is no reason why the search interface can't support these clients in native mode.

Creative Output Formats

Some queries are really done to generate a report. For example, a financial planner may want an update on portfolio stocks each Monday. A conventional result list might work well for interactive search, but a search result page delivered like a wiki page with articles, graphics, related company data and more would be a much richer experience, and one the planner could print and read on the train first thing every Monday morning. Which of the two search results in Figure 12-2 provide the best summary?

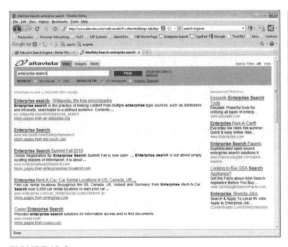 

FIGURE 12-2

We expect to see more users demanding document-style result lists, and the search platforms will be the right place to generate them.

Search Technology

The basic technology behind most search engines hasn't really changed much in years; the platform indexing utilities generate a list of all the words in all the documents, and provide some way to link the words to the documents that contain them. Oh, different platforms associate metadata, taxonomies, and synonyms differently, but the index is quite similar no matter which search platform does the work.

What's been happening over the last several years is adding smarts — lots of smarts — to the indexing side, the back-end of search; and to retrieval, the front-end of search. It is in these areas where the real difference exists among the various Enterprise Search platforms.

These enhancements are making search a bit better, and when combined with an attentive business owner monitoring search activity, can make search much better than it has been. Some of the search technologies discussed here are clearly front-end, but some apply to the back-end. Most, however, are related and interconnected, and innovations will impact both. We've always said that great search is a result of great indexing, and that applies to front end and back end: if you don't get the right content indexed, you'll have a tough time finding it in results.

Entity, Sentiment, and Fact Extraction

This one sounds like rocket science, but in reality commercial technologies are available today that can not only identify entities — people, places, and things — but they are also starting to understand sentiment and soon will be able to recognize facts.

Entity extraction is available today, and is typically a tool used to drive the facets or refiners you see in all of the SharePoint search technologies. In fact, one of the big differences between SharePoint Search Server and SharePoint ESP Search is the ability to use content extracted from documents as refiners, not simply the pre-existing meta-data and attributes. In SharePoint Search, you can have refiners like file size and date, title, and author; but you only see the values that are actually maintained as document metadata. In ESP, you can use any entity without document metadata.

ESP refiners generally come in two forms today: unsupervised and supervised. Unsupervised refiners are those that the engine can identify out of the box by using general language-specific dictionaries. Supervised clustering lets you have much finer control, to the point that you can provide your own dictionaries, which lets you use your product or division names, or even staff names within refiners.

This entity extraction provides the framework for the next, related technology: sentiment extraction. This lets you understand value judgments, and is generally pretty good, even given the tendency we human beings have to use irony and sarcasm. Sentiment extraction is around today; but we'd expect it to be part of any search technology you'll use in the future.

Finally, once you can extract entities and to a lesser extent sentiment, you're at the point where, given enough content and repetition, a search technology can start to identify facts. Entity extraction and semantic analysis will be able to answer the question "which folks worked on the Contoso account" without any need to have pre-defined synonyms and metadata.

The Internet search engines mimic this pretty well today based largely on high-value words and phrases, and on the actual content; give the technology a few years.

Automatic Indexing

When you think of it, why should indexing be some distinct process that has to be run to discover new documents? There are certainly sections of operating system code or database code that know where content has changed, and we'd expect in the future that search technologies will communicate with the repositories, so when new or updated content is available it will be indexed. The concept of crawling will become obsolete when updates are push driven rather than fetch driven, and documents will be indexed in near real time.

Open Pipelines/Open Search

We'll go out on a limb here and predict that an increasing number of vendors will update their technology to utilize the pipeline architecture common to many technologies, including those created by Microsoft.

The Open Search project (`www.opensearch.com`) has made great strides in improving the interoperability of search platforms. The SharePoint search platforms support this already, and ESP can support it with some customization on the query side. Open Search makes life easier for those who need to federate search as well, although as with most federation applications, implementing security can be harder to implement.

On the indexing side, the pipeline makes any customization easy to create, and easy to plug in; and the Open Pipeline (`www.openpipeline.org`) is a standards organization that would make it easy to mix and match different pipeline components from various sources. As more vendors and platforms adopt a pipeline approach for indexing, Open Pipeline should see higher adoption rates. We'd like to see Microsoft or one of the Open Pipeline partners write the necessary tools to integrate open Pipeline stages into Microsoft search.

Enterprise Capabilities

Some of the capabilities we would expect to see included in pretty much every Enterprise Search platform or application include features to solve problems, both those unique to Enterprise Search and those shared with Internet search. Let's look at a few such features that come to mind.

Near Duplicate Detection

While there is certainly duplication of content on the Internet, the problem really hits home in the enterprise. As we discussed in Chapter 2, duplicate and near duplicate documents are very common throughout the intranet because different versions of the same file have very similar file names, directory locations, metadata, and content. This sort of thing is even hard for humans to resolve — short of looking at the file creation date, and even then it can be tough to know which document is the latest, greatest version. Nearly everyone who works with documents has started a new proposal, PowerPoint stack, or spreadsheet by copying an existing document and simply editing the contents. But as we pointed out in Chapter 2, how many times does the new document metadata get updated properly — the new project, client name, and description? And yet people hope that the search technology is smart enough to understand what they meant, not what they actually did.

During the indexing process, we expect future search technologies to tag documents that are similar automatically, and thereby provide some guidance on where inside of multiple documents the contents are "just about the same." Most likely, this will happen at the sentence or paragraph level, and the search platform will not only recognize the content has changed, but using entity extraction and fact extraction, it will also understand what has changed.

Operations

So far we've talked about user-facing and technology changes in search. No doubt there will be significant changes in the operations and IT as well. Some of these changes are happening today, but there is even more opportunity for great leaps forward in the not-too-distant future.

Cloud Computing

We're already seeing a push to cloud computing and the capabilities it offers for expanding or decreasing a footprint dynamically on demand. It wasn't too long ago that organizations had to purchase huge server farms in anticipation of peak demand, when in fact the servers were often underutilized much of the time.

Seasonal organizations like eCommerce companies currently need to build technology infrastructure — including systems for search platforms — to meet the peak anticipated demand. Moving search, along with the full computing infrastructure, to the cloud lets these companies scale up and only pay for the needed technology.

Other organizations can benefit from cloud technology as well. Building a search index is a time consuming process for very large data sets. Yet some applications where data changes are rare don't have as demanding a need for updating indices. Using cloud-based servers provides a way to use the big horsepower when it's needed; and save money once the content is fully indexed.

We can imagine a not-too-distant time when Enterprise Search will enable indexing or search servers dynamically as needed, and just as quickly de-allocate resources when they are no longer needed.

Cores, Processors, and Virtualization

Most search platforms treat indexing and searching as linear tasks. While the processes can be distributed across multiple servers, not much has been done yet to enable use of multiple cores and processors working in conjunction. As operating system and compiler technology gets better at utilizing multiple cores and CPUs, search may not see much benefit; but once the base technology is there, search will need to follow. If different pipeline stages or query processes could be performed by different cores and CPUs, organizations would be able to tune search platforms for their unique needs.

As companies strive to be more energy efficient, may are turning to virtual systems using VMWare or Microsoft's HyperV. Both allow multiple virtual servers to exist within the same physical hardware. There may be some degradation in raw performance, but in limited tests some companies have found the performance hit not a big factor. Of course, sites serving petabytes of content or thousands of queries per second — as some ESP customers do today — need to approach virtual systems with care.

Search technology performance has always been tightly related to the performance of processors and especially disk throughput. Face it: indexing, especially during times of peak search activity, will place heavy demands on your infrastructure. ESP hits disk drives often, and FAST used to encourage its customers to locate indices only on high-speed SCSI drives attached to the indexing systems.

Shifting Control

As we've explained earlier, there is a trend going on in Enterprise Search whereby control over the search relevancy is moving from IT toward the business line manager or content owner. Rather than require programming, relevance is form driven and can be changed minute by minute during the day by administrative users in the business and content management parts of the organization. This trend will continue to accelerate, and successful Enterprise Search of the future will assume that the search business owner is the one in charge. This is one area where an organization's search center of excellence will play a major role.

Search as a Service

Related to this shift from IT to the business owner is search as a service. Today, chances are that centralized IT is responsible for operating search, as well as for rolling out any changes, including changes to relevancy algorithms and search-enabling remote sites.

Currently, when a site owner wants to add search to a web site, perhaps for a small division, central IT needs to be involved: programmers and project managers need to create and deploy code, and it's a long, costly process. Conceptually, there is no reason why a site owner cannot "claim" a starting URL, add a snippet of HTML or a widget to the site, and have search, driven by the central Enterprise Search technology. The site owner could even provide synonyms, specialized vocabulary, and best bets for the site without involving resources of centralized IT.

ESP and the Search Business Console offers some of this technology today, with minor tuning and limited control; but most Enterprise Search applications still require intervention from the group that runs the platform. When you add the power to view search activity reports and control best bets and boosts, you really have a good step toward true Search as a Service.

Smart Indexing

Indexing is not one of the most intelligent parts of the search preparation process. Any special mark-up or customization during indexing usually requires at least a bit of coding, but even script coding can be a challenge for business line managers.

Part of Smart Search is the ability to track and understand everything that happens in the organization. This area is often part of eDiscovery, and is often provided specifically for legal and regulatory reasons. However, there is little regulatory control or policy imposed on the indexing side.

If we were to never index inappropriate content, we wouldn't never have to worry about finding it for a deposition. If we have a records retention policy, why can't the search engine know that policy and help enforce it by deleting content that has passed its retention period? This is the start of smart indexing in conjunction with business rules, and we're pretty sure the future will feature indexing that understands and assists in managing policy.

Hardware Searching

When you think about it, most of our organizational content passes through our routers at times that can be critical for search: when a document is added, viewed, displayed, or removed. Wouldn't it be nice if we could tie our search technology to our routers, so that at every time a document is touched, the search technology understands and verifies that the latest version is indexed properly?

We're starting to see this now: Barracuda Networks has released a network appliance that automatically search-enables email from Exchange and Lotus Notes. Expand this to all corporate content, and you've really got something there. The problem right now is that the companies that include search in their products — content management systems, routers, or applications — tend to include barebones search functionality. Once they begin to realize how critical great search is to originations today, we hope we will see more and more really advanced search appliances throughout the network, making latency a thing of the past.

Enterprise Search 3.0 — and Beyond

So we've looked at things past, present, and in our near future. What about the future? How will search be different ten or more years from now?

Search is everywhere — ubiquitous — mobile; proactive; a knowledge navigator.

The future doesn't arrive all at once. Some of the capabilities we talked about earlier in the chapter are already available and will be integrated, improved, and enhanced. Google wasn't a quantum breakthrough in search when it first began operations; it improved as the content got better, popularity became more defined, and users did more searches and document views.

Agents and Smart Agents

Sometimes called stored queries or alerts, agents are queries that users need to do repeatedly. Maybe every week a user wants to see updates from support, or new content about corporate policy.

Some current search products let users create these agents, and even schedule them to execute on schedule at a specific time. But few let you use agents in a way that make them really helpful, including:

➤   Share agents with co-workers

➤   Modify another person's agent and save it as your own

➤   Update your copy of an agent when the original creator updates it

Perhaps most importantly, agent systems don't yet seem to know when a document is new, versus as opposed to when it's indexed for the first time. Relying on a file-or web server–provided date usually means that the date a search platform indexes with a document is incorrect much of the time. A really good agent system will recognizes not only a "first seen on" date, but it will attempt to extract a data from the document to identify when it was really created. And the agent needs to track which documents have already been delivered so the user doesn't see documents again unless they have changed.

Finally, an agent should be able to recognize when something has changed — a new employee, a new directory, a new product. Like interactive search, agent technology should interact with fact extraction, discussed earlier in this chapter.

Smart agents are similar to automated personas, except that the user doesn't need to take any specific action: the smart agent learns by observing. Think of a smart agent as the Did you mean..? prompt that you see when you've misspelled a search term in today's platforms.

A really helpful agent should help you do your job. Depending on your job, you may find that you get requests for the same basic information from a number of people — and that information is probably available through search. A smart agent can also watch monitor your incoming email; and, if you authorize it, can respond automatically to the user with the top likely answers to the question. That may be a policy or a product plan, but as long as the agent understands the security associated with the document and the requester, it can do some of your repetitive tasks for you — and, of course, report what it's done.

Behavioral Tagging

Another element that many search technologies use today is the ability to use tagged content to determine relevancy. The trick is, most of these technologies use only explicit tagging — tags that have been either specifically associated with a document by a user or associated with a document by means of a taxonomy.

The problem is that there is a different type of tagging that makes much at least as much sense: implicit tagging. That is, the search engine identifies a user's interests based not only on an explicit profile, but also on the searches performed and documents viewed. It helps search to know you are a support rep; but it's more helpful to know that you often search for, and view, documents about operating system parameters.

The trick is that this implicit tagging has to be used in conjunction with your current role, or the search engine might end up treating you as an HR staffer because of your recent searches for holiday and vacation policies. As the technology advances, the search platform should be able to identify the intent of your search based on a number of parameters including what you were doing just prior to the search; what documents you were viewing; and even content extracted from your calendar and location.

An important aspect to unsupervised behavioral tagging is that the user should have an opportunity to provide feedback: When users find what they are looking for, they won't bother with feedback that the search platform did well; users are busy. But they are happy to tell you when they don't get the right document; and then, you, as the person responsible for search, have an opportunity. Provide the user with the ability to cast a thumbs down vote. Really good systems will ask, like the old animals game that kids play, how the system might have determined that the result presented was not what they were looking for. Make it quick — a pop-up window with a few options — but ask them. If users think someone will act on their input, they'll likely provide input.

Language Support

In this book, we haven't covered the issues around language support. Just indexing some languages is hard enough, especially multi-byte Asian languages that use Unicode character sets; when it comes to searching, it can be even more difficult to get right.

There are also issues in multinational organizations which have documents in many languages. Business line owners need to determine whether user queries should return documents that are relevant regardless of the language the document, or whether it is sufficient to return only documents in the same language as the query.

Hopefully, these issues will become less important as systems gain the ability to translate not only queries effectively, but also to search against documents regardless of the query and document language. The leading Internet sites are beginning to do this; but thus far it doesn't seem to have penetrated the enterprise market.

WHAT YOU CAN DO TODAY

So the future of search will be great. But what do you do if you have to manage organizational search today?

The good news is there really are a number of small, easy-to-manage steps you can take with today's search technology. Making search better is easy: once you install it, observe, tune, and repeat. Success in search remains an interactive process and users will always come up with ways to ask questions that no one has anticipated — slow and steady does it.

➤ **Know what you want** — Work with people in your organization who user search — or who it would be if you had search up and running. What content do they need to search, based on their job function? Talk to people in other companies that use search. Consider bringing in a consultant from one of the major consulting firms, or a firm that specializes in Enterprise Search. If you don't know where you need to go, just about any road is as good as any other.

➤ **Search best practices** — Great search is as much an art as it is a science. Read about search, attend the best trade shows, and connect with other users. Understand what features you can expect in Enterprise Search today. We've listed a few of these resources in the back of the book; use them.

➤ **Document your current state** — Are you using search already? What feedback can you gather from your users? Meet with search stakeholders — who will hopefully become part of your search center of excellence. Find out what users really need — in detail. Encourage feedback, and communicate. No matter where you want to go, if you don't know where you are starting from, it's hard to get there.

If you don't have search now, talk to potential users anyway. See what they need to find; see what they like and don't like in Internet search.

➤ **Prioritized features** — As you meet with users, document what features they want. Make sure they understand they may not get what they want but listen closely: sometimes people ask for a capability using a buzzword they've heard, when in fact that's not what they want.

Make up a list of required, desired, and optional capabilities.

➤ **Plan for staged rollout of capabilities** — As you prioritize features and capabilities, plan to implement them in stages. Roll out new capabilities, gather feedback, and re-evaluate your plan. And see the section "Roll Out Slowly" later in this chapter.

➤ **Define your metrics** — Part of knowing where you want to go is measuring how well you're doing. Before you begin to roll out capabilities, know what criteria you will use to determine whether each state is a success.

➤ **Examine your search logs** — This applies not only once you're up and running; do it with the search activity logs from your current search system. Even if your current search is old and doesn't include search activity reporting, you may be able to extract it from your web server logs. This will help you set up synonyms and best bets.

➤ **Implement psychic search** — As you've read, Enterprise Search still takes some extra work to emulate the features people expect from Internet search engines. If you have search already, examine your search activity reports to see if part numbers, division names, and employee names are common queries; implement code to respond to the queries accordingly.

➤ **Iterate and improve** — Remember that search is not fire and forget. Making search really good is an iterative process, and will never be good enough. Content changes and user needs change. Make sure your search engine is keeping up.

➤ **Track user search behavior** — Search activity can warn you of problems with your products, new business opportunities for your company, or even content that may need to be improved. Your users are telling you what's on their minds. Are you listening?

➤ **Define suggestions and synonyms** — When a user enters a term you have never seen on your site, make sure to update the synonym list so that the users who use that term can find the content they are looking for. Few things are more frustrating than a No Hits page.

➤ **Identify missing content** — When you get No Hits, it may not be the user's fault: your users may be telling you about content you need, whether products or services, or plain old enterprise content. Think of it as the way your users tell you what they want to find. Consider adding new content, not just adding synonyms.

➤ **Gather feedback** — Good and bad. Remember, people will certainly tell you when it's not working; encourage them to tell you when you got something right

➤ **Roll out slowly** — One of the worst things you can do is feature a major new roll-out of your "improved new search engine." Far better to roll it out quietly, get a few hard-core search users to try it out, and expand on your successes. When users hear that search is better, then they'll tell you how great it is!

SUMMARY

We've had a look at the technologies and capabilities that are likely to be common in Enterprise Search in the future, and hopefully we will have a few of our projections come to pass. Going back to our HAL analogy, remember that in the movie 2010, HAL's sister, SAL, was asked about the significance of "Phoenix," the folder that Dr. Chandra was going to use to file content about his attempts to repair HAL in deep space. Dr. Chandra is clearly thinking of the mythical bird rising from its ashes, but SAL's first guess is "Tutor of Achilles." At least SAL got the right answer on her second guess.

Let's hope we can do that well!

Resources

Enterprise Search is becoming a popular topic in books and in electronic media including newsletters and blogs. Rather than close the book without adding some of the resources we consider valuable in our work with Enterprise Search, we thought we'd include a list of the books, blogs, and sites that we find most useful.

BOOKS

➤ *Professional Microsoft Search: SharePoint 2007 and Search Server 2008* by Tom Rizzo, Richard Riley, Shane Young (ISBN: 978-0470279335). Our book is meant as a sequel to this 2008 Wrox book, but with a different bent. We focus on more advanced, business-impacting technologies rather than the entry-level products, since they are the ones that bring complexity and attract customization. We also have more business-impact and best practice tips throughout the book, making it useful to marketing professionals and to readers interested in Enterprise Search in general.

➤ *Inside the Index and Search Engines: Microsoft Office SharePoint Server 2007* by Patrick Tisseghem and Lars Fastrup (ISBN 978-0735625358). This 2007 Microsoft Press book covers some similar topics but is much closer to the information in the product documentation, and covers less advanced technology. Our book should be much more generally useful, as we will provide information about why and when to use search technology and how to apply it, not just how it works.

➤ *Making Search Work: Implementing Web, Intranet, and Enterprise Search* by Martin White (ISBN: 978-1573873055). This is a general business book about search technology and vendors.

➤ *Successful Enterprise Search Management* by Arnold & White (an eBook from Galatea Online available through Amazon.com) (ISBN: 978-0954307127). This book is a survey of Enterprise Search vendors and not primarily for IT Pros or Developers.

➤ *Lucene in Action — 2nd Edition* by Otis Gospodnetic and Erik Hatcher (ISBN: 978-1933988177). This is a programming reference book covering the low-level Lucene programming API with sample code.

➤ *Search User Interfaces* by Marti Hearst (ISBN 978-0-521-11379-3). This book provides an in-depth look at search usability from one of the pioneers in the field.

➤ *Faceted Search* by Daniel Tunkelang (ISBN 978-1598299991). This is a accessible, interesting discussion of faceted search in a technical, academically-oriented short volume. Part of the Morgan Claypool Synthesis Lectures on Information Concepts, Retrieval, and Services.

➤ *Exploratory Search: Beyond the Query-Response Paradigm* by Ryen White and Resa A. Roth (ISBN 978-1598297836). This book provides a great overview of how search works in information exploration. Part of the Morgan Claypool Synthesis Lectures on Information Concepts, Retrieval, and Services.

MICROSOFT ENTERPRISE SEARCH SITES

Microsoft maintains two enterprise search information centers.

➤ www.microsoft.com/enterprisesearch is part of the SharePoint 2010 marketing site. It contains information about product capabilities, resources, case studies, a partner finder, and other links.

➤ technet.microsoft.com/enterprisesearch is part of Microsoft TechNet. It includes documentation, downloads, training material, and technical information about all enterprise search products.

USER FORUMS

➤ Microsoft's Enterprise Search forums at http://social.technet.microsoft.com/Forums/en-US/category/enterprisesearch are the primary place for discussion and community Q&A around Microsoft Enterprise Search products. There are separate forums for different products. Some of the forums are shared between the Enterprise Search Category and the SharePoint categories.

➤ **SearchDev** at http://www.searchdev.org is a vendor-independent developer's forum covering the business and technology of search. SearchDev also has two technical forums for detailed vendor-specific questions dealing with everything from coding and scripting to problem resolution, with more in the works:

> ➤ http://fast.searchdev.org

> ➤ http://autononmy.searchdev.org

➤ **Enterprise Search Engine Professionals Group** is a LinkedIn group for people involved with Enterprise Search in corporate environments worldwide. Search for it under the Groups menu at www.linkedin.com.

➤ **Enterprise Search Summit Group** is a group run by Michelle Manafy from *Information Today,* which provides industry news and information as well as details and podcasts about upcoming events.

NEWSLETTERS

➤ *Enterprise Search Newsletter* at http://www.ideaeng.com/newsletter is produced by New Idea Engineering. This newsletter covers business and technical issues of search, generally at a detailed, technical level. It covers all vendors, provides advice for improving your search, and includes Ask Dr Search, who answers technical questions from subscribers.

BLOGS

➤ **Enterprise Search Blog** at `http://enterprisesearchblog.com` is written by Mark Bennett, Miles Kehoe, and the other search experts at New Idea Engineering. Its focus is the business and technology of Enterprise Search.

➤ **The Noisy Channel** at `http://thenoiseychannel.com` comes from former Endeca and current Google employee Daniel Tunkelang, who provides a perspective on the technology of Enterprise Search from someone who knows search from the ground up.

➤ **Beyond Search** at `http://beyondsearch.com` is written by search guru Steve Arnold. The site delivers industry analysis, and insight into vendors and events in Steve's unique and whimsical format.

➤ **CMS Watch,** part of the Real Story Group, writes an interesting blog with a focus on search and content management at `http://www.cmswatch.com/Blog`. CMS Watch is one of the few truly independent analyst firms who don't count on the vendors they evaluate for revenue.

➤ **SearchTools,** at `http://searchtools.com`, is run by Avi Rappoport, who provides news, information, and a history of nearly every search technology known to humankind from her blog.

VENDOR BLOGS

➤ **Microsoft's Enterprise Search Blog** at `http://blogs.msdn.com/b/enterprisesearch` covers Microsoft search in general, with a real SharePoint spin. The blog is a good source of Microsoft news and information.

➤ **FASTforward Blog** is sponsored by Microsoft and billed as a discussion on Enterprise 2.0. Authors are independent bloggers who write about search and IT issues at `http://www.fastforwardblog.com/`.

➤ **Unified Information Access** blog is offered by Attivio. The search vendor has a useful blog that contains had good general information as well as Attivio-specific material at `http://www.attivio.com/blog`.

➤ **Endeca's Search Facets** at `http://facets.endeca.com` is a relatively new blog that provides good information as well as Endeca-specific information.

➤ **The Exalead Blog,** at `http://blog.exalead.com`, comes from this European vendor with growing presence in the United States. Topics range from web to Enterprise Search topics, and most recently, their acquisition by PLM leader Dessault Systemes.

➤ **Gilbane Group,** written by Lynda Moulton, tells sbout their search practice blog at `http://gilbane.com/search_blog`. Gilbane, now part of Outsell, focuses on content management and runs two trade shows each year that feature a search track.

➤ The **Official Google Enterprise Blog** at `http://googleenterprise.blogspot.com/` covers not only the Google Search Appliance but all of the Google Enterprise products. A useful look at Google's view of the enterprise.

➤ **Lemur Consulting** in the UK, written by the creators of Flax open-source search technology, offer more than just Flax, with good coverage of issues relevant to Enterprise Search in general at `http://www.flax.co.uk/blog`.

➤ **Kellblog,** written by MarkLogic CEO Dave Kellogg, covers Enterprise Search, next gen database, and content management. An interesting read that covers industry trends with unique senior management perspective at `http://www.kellblog.com`.

➤ **Sematext Blog at** `http://blog.sematext.com` is offered by Lucene and Solr. Otis Gospodnetic is one of the bloggers who provides in-depth technical news and information on open-source Enterprise Search projects.

➤ **Search Done Right** is the official blog of Vivisimo, an early leader in federation and clustering technology. The blog, at `http://searchdoneright.com`, provides great background information that anyone can benefit from reading.

➤ **SLI Systems,** a hosted search service, provides a newsletter at `http://www.sli-systems.com/blog` that addresses the problems they see in working with their customers, generally eCommerce site owners who like search and SEO combined into a single, hoisted service.

OTHER BLOGS

➤ Andrew McAfee of MIT and Harvard writes a blog at `http://andrewmcafee.org/blog` that covers the business impact of IT in a very entertaining, informative, and readable fashion. He is credited with coining the term "Enterprise 2.0" in 2006, and always posts interesting material.

➤ John Battelle, an author and speaker, writes SearchBlog at `http://battellemedia.com`. John approaches search from a business point of view and has more of a web-search point of view, but his book *The Search: How Google and its Rivals Rewrote the Rules of Business* is among our favorites, and his blog is quite informative.

TRADE SHOWS

In Enterprise Search, there are two organizations that run some pretty darned informative industry events each year. And both run two shows each.

➤ *Information Today* runs a number of shows throughout the year including the Enterprise Search Summit (`http://www.enterprisesearchsummit.com`) held in New York each Spring; starting in 2010, the show in Washington DC replaces the West Coast Fall event. Good event, great speakers, and exhibits from many of the major vendors in the industry.

➤ **The Gilbane Group** (`http://gilbane.com`) holds a web and enterprise content management conference each year: Boston in the fall and San Francisco in the spring. While CMS is the primary focus, Gilbane include a search track in each conference with a good mix of vendor and independent speakers.

INDEX

INDEX